Get the eBook FREE!

(PDF, ePub, Kindle, and liveBook all included)

We believe that once you buy a book from us, you should be able to read it in any format we have available. To get electronic versions of this book at no additional cost to you, purchase and then register this book at the Manning website.

Go to https://www.manning.com/freebook and follow the instructions to complete your pBook registration.

That's it!
Thanks from Manning!

Phoenix in Action

Phoenix in Action

GEOFFREY LESSEL
FOREWORD BY SAŠA JURIĆ

MANNING
SHELTER ISLAND

For online information and ordering of this and other Manning books, please visit www.manning.com. The publisher offers discounts on this book when ordered in quantity. For more information, please contact

Special Sales Department
Manning Publications Co.
20 Baldwin Road
PO Box 761
Shelter Island, NY 11964
Email: orders@manning.com

Manning Publications Co.
20 Baldwin Road
PO Box 761
Shelter Island, NY 11964

Development editor: Kristen Watterson
Technical development editor: Marius Butuc
Review editor: Ivan Martinović
Production editor: Deirdre Hiam
Copy editor: Andy Carroll
Proofreader: Katie Tennant
Technical proofreader: Kumar Unnikrishnan
Typesetter and cover designer: Marija Tudor

ISBN 9781617295041
Printed in the United States of America

contents

foreword

As you're holding this book, starting your journey into the world of Elixir and Phoenix, I'm very excited for you! You're about to discover a technology stack that can help you start your projects very quickly and move forward at a steady pace. At the same time, the technology will help you deal with highly complex challenges at a large scale. With Elixir and Phoenix, you'll get a combination of a simple-start technology and a long-run one, a perfect combination that was out of reach just a few years ago.

In the summer of 2010, I started using Erlang, the technology that's the foundation of Elixir and Phoenix. Back then, Erlang was one of the few available languages suitable for the challenge we were facing. Erlang made it simple for us to implement a real-time push server, requiring a surprisingly small amount of code. The initial prototype, which could manage tens of thousands of simultaneous users, required about 200 lines of code!

Over the next few years, I developed a love-hate relationship with Erlang. I was blown away by its first-class support for massive concurrency, scalability, and fault-tolerance. Writing highly concurrent code never felt so easy and natural. Our system scaled beautifully, and it kept the impact of errors to a minimum, preserving most of the service at any point in time, self-healing as soon as possible. But at the same time, working with Erlang felt tedious in many ways, with basic tasks, such as creating a new project or deploying to production, requiring a lot of manual steps. The code itself seemed burdened with a lot of boilerplate, and the language made it difficult to flush that boilerplate out. Finally, the ecosystem was much smaller than it is today, which required reinventing a lot of wheels.

I remember having mixed feelings about Erlang back then. I really felt (and I still do!) that it is the soundest foundation for building any sort of a backend side system (which includes any kind of a web server). However, the lack of tooling and libraries made the task of building such systems with Erlang harder than it should be. People used to joke that Erlang made hard things easy, but at the same time it made easy things hard.

Things started improving with the arrival of Elixir, which, compared to Erlang, seemed more focused on developer productivity, shipping with simple-to-use tools, and promoting first-class documentation. In addition, as a more complex language, bringing to the table additional features such as metaprogramming and pluggable polymorphism via protocols, Elixir allowed me to be more expressive, better organize my code, and reduce boilerplate. And at the same time, targeting the same runtime and being semantically close to Erlang, Elixir could reap all the great benefits of Erlang, and seamlessly use everything from its ecosystem (standard library, OTP, third-party libraries, and tools).

As the adoption of Elixir increased, its ecosystem expanded. The introduction of Plug and Ecto paved the way for the Phoenix framework, which finally got us to the point where we could quickly start building a typical web-facing CRUD, without needing to reinvent a bunch of wheels in the process. Phoenix quickly gained traction, and people started using it in production. As a result, the core team developers gathered a lot of feedback, which helped them evolve the tool further. Some original ideas were abandoned and some new ideas introduced, and currently Phoenix seems quite different from it's early days, or even from the 1.0 release. But at this point, it feels that we're past the initial development stages. The amount of deprecations and disrupting changes seems to decrease with each new version. It's always hard to predict the future, but I don't expect significant deprecations in future versions.

Therefore, I feel that the time to start learning Phoenix has never been better. The framework is mature and stable, the community is large and helpful, the technology has been used in various systems, and many good patterns and practices have been established. And on top of all that, there are many learning resources available, such as this book.

Back in early 2013, when I first started using Elixir, there were no books about it. Instead, I'd read the reference documentation and post questions to the mailing list, where most of the answers would be given by José Valim, who was pretty much the only qualified person to answer any Elixir-related question at the time. When Chris McCord first announced Phoenix, there wasn't even a reference document available. Learning to work with Phoenix required a combination of trial and error, reading the Phoenix code, and asking around on mailing lists or IRC. This learning process had a certain charm, but it was definitely far from perfect. As a result, a lot of the early code written with Elixir and Phoenix was ridden with weird approaches and techniques. It took some time and a lot of strayed paths before the early adopters became familiar with these tools and understood how to use them properly.

But you don't have to go through the same trials and tribulations. By starting your Phoenix journey now, you can avoid the mistakes made by the early adopters, and immediately start learning about proper ways to use the tools. This is where I see the biggest value of *Phoenix in Action*. This book will teach you the mechanics of the technology, but more importantly, it will explain how to think in Phoenix, by discussing established patterns, practices, and approaches. In addition, by cleverly avoiding the trap of writing a big reference book of epic proportions and carefully choosing which topics to discuss, Geoffrey makes your bootstrap experience smooth and easy. You won't learn everything there is to know about Elixir and Phoenix, but no book can do that for you anyway. What you will learn, though, are the most important pieces you'll need in pretty much any web-facing Elixir system, regardless of its shape and size.

This is why I'm really excited for you. For many of us, the learning road was long and winding, but you've arrived at the party at the perfect time. Having this great book to bring you into the exciting world of Elixir and Phoenix, you're off to a good start, and your journey is about to become much more exciting. I wish you a lot of fun on that journey!

— Saša Jurić, author of *Elixir in Action*

preface

I remember when I created my first true website—it was called *The U2 Shack*, and, as the name suggests, it was a site dedicated to the band U2. This was back in 1998, and it was handwritten with Windows Notepad in straight HTML. The site was hosted on GeoCities and was part of a link ring. It took forever to update because it was all hard-coded HTML, but it was mine and I was proud of it.

Fast forward about three years, and I was introduced to Perl and then PHP. I was amazed that the server could process variables given to it by the web browser and spit out custom-built HTML based on the user's request. For example, one fun site I made in those early days was a word-search generator. The user could input a list of words they wanted to be in a puzzle, as well as the width and height and whether to allow some words to be hidden backwards. The server would take all this information, brute-force a custom word-search puzzle, and output it in HTML for the user to print.

I happily developed sites with PHP for years, and then Ruby on Rails dropped. Like many developers of the time, I was amazed at a video of the Rails author creating a fully functional blog engine in 10 minutes. I was sold. Almost instantly, I switched over to learning Ruby and developing websites with Ruby on Rails. I had tolerated Perl and PHP but fell in love with Ruby in 2005. For over a decade, Ruby and Ruby on Rails were my tools of choice, and I still use them every day.

However, in 2014, I heard rumblings of a new language called Elixir, by José Valim. José was a major contributor to Ruby on Rails (and is still listed as number five on the all-time contributor list), but he was feeling some of the shortcomings of the Ruby language (like memory usage and the difficulty of developing for parallel and distributed programs). I bought a book about Elixir that year and fell in love all over again.

Also in 2014, Chris McCord began building the web framework known as Phoenix on top of Elixir. Phoenix version 1.0 was ultimately released in August of 2015, and its major features were real-time communications, productive tooling, and blazingly fast responses. It's been quite a journey since the days of developing in straight HTML, but ever since I discovered Phoenix, every web project I start begins with `mix phx.new`.

I've had the pleasure of speaking at multiple Elixir conferences over the years and blogging about Elixir, Phoenix, and Ecto at geoffreylessel.com. I now have the great pleasure of introducing you to Phoenix in this book. I sincerely hope that the topics presented in this book allow you to build amazing applications of your own. If you do, I'd love to hear about it at geo@phoenixinaction.com.

Happy reading!

acknowledgments

As with any creative endeavor, there were many ups and downs during the creation of this book. But regardless of my feelings during the process, there were a number of people rooting for me, without whom this project would have been doomed.

First and foremost, I'd like to thank my family. Kelly, my work on this book meant more work for you as well. Without your help and support, I'd never have been able to reach the finish line. Although none of the words in this book are yours, you are my coauthor. I love you. Special acknowledgments go to Olivia, Max, and Calvin. You were very patient with me throughout the process, and a father couldn't ask for better children. I love you and am proud of you. I also thank my parents, John and Carolyn, who let me mess around and test my curiosity on the family computer, growing up.

Next, I'd like to thank Kevin Harreld and Kristen Watterson at Manning. You both made major editorial contributions during the project, and this book would be much harder to read if it weren't for you. Your dedication to excellence has made *Phoenix in Action* a hundred times better than it would have been without your involvement. Beyond Kevin and Kristen, my thanks go to the whole team at Manning for development, marketing, and production support. Deirdre Hiam, Andy Carroll, Katie Tennant, and Nichole Beard, I see and feel the results of your efforts. When I started on this project, I didn't realize how much support I would truly receive from the Manning team. Thank you.

I would also like to thank the following people who all took the time to review and comment on the book: Alessandro Campeis, Amit Lamba, Andrew Courter, Arun Kumar, Fillipe Massuda, Grzegorz Bernas, Gustavo Filipe Ramos Gomes, Jay Kelkar, Jeff Smith, Joel Kotarski, Johan Mattisson, John Kasiewicz, Lane LaRue, Luis Miguel Cabezas Granado, Massimiliano Bertinetti, Noel Martin Llevares, Olaoluwa Oluro, Peter Sellars, Piotr Kopszak, Ryan Huber, Samuel Bosch, Victor Durán, and Vincent Theron.

Thank you, Jeff Berg, Daniel Murphy, Jesse Anderson, Michael Chan, and all my coworkers at Planning Center, who continually asked how the book was coming along. Thank you, all the MEAP readers and reviewers who submitted comments, suggestions, critiques, and praise for the book as it was being written.

Thank you, Chris McCord, José Valim, and all the Elixir and Phoenix contributors. You have created tools that are a joy to use and excellent documentation that sometimes made me feel like my words were superfluous.

Finally, thank you, my readers! I hope you enjoy this book.

about this book

Who should read this book

Phoenix in Action was written to help you learn the Phoenix framework from ground zero. We'll start as if you have no knowledge of how the framework functions, and by the final chapter, you'll have written a functioning auction site (in the spirit of eBay). The web application you'll create isn't going to be feature-complete, and it won't win any awards for design, but what you'll learn in this book will give you the tools to expand on the application and continue to build it. Or, if you'd rather, you can finally create that web application that's been bouncing around in your head for months.

Both beginner and experienced developers will find a home in this book. But if you've *never* written code before, this book won't serve as an introduction to general programming. For those who've never written any Elixir, chapter 2 will give you an overview of the language and teach you just enough to get you going. As you progress through the book, I'll introduce new techniques and ideas as you need them, and I'll point out best practices when I can. Beyond that, I'll remind you of things we've covered in previous chapters in order to solidify that knowledge.

How this book is organized: a roadmap

Phoenix in Action is divided into 3 parts that consist of 14 chapters.

Part 1 covers the basics of Phoenix and Elixir and introduces the broad topics of programming in each:

- Chapter 1 introduces Phoenix and Elixir and discusses the benefits that each provides to today's developer. There's even a section that describes some of Elixir's downsides and the reasons why it and Phoenix may not be the best choice for a particular project.

- Chapter 2 goes deeper into the basics of the Elixir programming language. Even if you've never seen a line of Elixir code, this chapter will provide you with enough of an overview that you can start developing with it. If you're already well versed in Elixir, feel free to skip to chapter 3.
- Chapter 3 delves into the Phoenix framework. By following a web request all the way from the user typing a URL into a browser through the various parts of a Phoenix application, you'll understand how Phoenix is organized and what each file is responsible for.

In part 2, you'll start developing a Phoenix application—an auction site in the spirit of eBay. This part will provide you with what you *need* to know to create interactive websites in Phoenix:

- Chapter 4 is where you'll dust off the text editor and start writing some code. You'll begin by creating a public interface for the data portion of your eventual website. You'll learn why it's important to keep the business logic of your application separate from the presentation of that data through Phoenix, and you'll learn how to do so. By the end of this chapter, you'll be able to send Elixir commands to your application and list and find auction items.
- Chapter 5 introduces the Mix tool and will teach you how to organize an Elixir application. You'll move from the everything-in-a-single-file approach in chapter 4 to a legitimate Elixir umbrella application (don't worry—we'll cover what an umbrella is too). You'll also bring external dependencies into the application to give it extra functionality.
- Chapter 6 brings Phoenix into the application. Previous chapters did the backend work of the business logic, but here you'll use Phoenix to display auction items in a web browser.
- Chapter 7 introduces Ecto, an Elixir package that allows you to interact with databases. In previous chapters, all the data in your application was read-only and hardcoded. In this chapter, you'll move on to actually storing and retrieving data to and from a real database.
- Chapter 8 takes the topic of database interactions to the next level by teaching you how to edit and update information in the database. Using Ecto changesets, we'll also discuss how to validate and restrict what data gets to the database, to ensure that no junk gets through.
- Chapter 9 brings all the things you learned in previous chapters back into Phoenix. You'll use forms in Phoenix to allow the user to create and update an auction item in their browser.
- Chapter 10 discusses using plugs to deal with a user's session data. We'll go over user registration, authenticating those users, allowing them to log in and out, and restricting users from areas where they shouldn't be allowed.

- Chapter 11 is all about data relationships. In particular, an item belongs to a user, and a user can bid on an item. You'll learn how to keep all those relationships in order, and you'll create an interface allowing users to bid on items.

Part 3 has chapters designed to take your application to the next level:

- Chapter 12 dives into real-time communication via Phoenix channels. This will allow real-time push updates to all users on an item's detail page. You'll enable the application to update the list of bids in real time for every logged-in user when a new bid is created.
- Chapter 13 demonstrates how to create a simple API boundary for your Phoenix application. You'll respond to user requests with JSON that you'll build in Phoenix.
- Chapter 14 provides an overview of testing and documentation. Both are very important in the Elixir world, and Elixir and Phoenix provide amazing tools out of the box, not only for testing your functions, but also for testing your documentation!

About the code

Every chapter in this book has code listings (though the code in chapter 1 is very rudimentary). All the code in the book, organized by chapter, can be found on GitHub at https://github.com/PhoenixInAction/phoenix-in-action. Each chapter directory contains a reference for how the code should look at the end of that chapter. For example, if you follow through all the code listings in chapter 10, your code will roughly match the ch10 directory in the GitHub repo.

During the course of writing this book, Elixir went from version 1.6 to 1.8.0-rc.1, and Phoenix went from version 1.3 to 1.4. The Elixir code should work in any version from 1.5 through 1.8 (and beyond), but the listings were written in version 1.7. If you have a different version, your output may look a bit different than what's shown in the book, but that shouldn't affect the results in any way. All the code in the book is meant to be run with Phoenix version 1.4, and although the future beyond 1.4 is mostly unknown to me, it should run just fine with little modification for many versions.

This book contains many examples of source code both in numbered listings and in-line with normal text. In both cases, code is formatted in a `fixed-width font like this` to distinguish it from ordinary text.

In many cases, the original source code has been reformatted; I've added line breaks and reworked indentation to accommodate the available page space in the book. In rare cases, even this was not enough, and listings include line-continuation markers (➥). Additionally, comments in the source code have often been removed from the listings when the code is described in the text. Code annotations accompany many of the listings to highlight important concepts.

liveBook discussion forum

Purchase of *Phoenix in Action* includes free access to a private web forum run by Manning Publications where you can make comments about the book, ask technical questions, and receive help from the author and from other users. To access the forum, go to https://livebook.manning.com/#!/book/phoenix-in-action/discussion. You can also learn more about Manning's forums and the rules of conduct at https://livebook.manning.com/#!/discussion.

Manning's commitment to our readers is to provide a venue where a meaningful dialogue between individual readers and between readers and the author can take place. It is not a commitment to any specific amount of participation on the part of the author, whose contribution to the forum remains voluntary (and unpaid). We suggest you try asking him some challenging questions lest his interest stray! The forum and the archives of previous discussions will be accessible from the publisher's website as long as the book is in print.

about the author

Geoffrey Lessel is a developer with 20 years of experience. He's seen the world of open source web development move from Perl scripts to PHP, to Ruby on Rails, to Elixir and Phoenix, and he has developed in each along the way. He loves to teach what he learns and has spoken at multiple Elixir conferences over the years. He blogs about Elixir and Phoenix at http://geoffreylessel.com.

about the cover illustration

The figure on the cover of *Phoenix in Action* is captioned "A man from Ostrov, Dalmatia, Croatia." The illustration is taken from a reproduction of an album of Croatian traditional costumes from the mid-nineteenth century by Nikola Arsenović, published by the Ethnographic Museum in Split, Croatia, in 2003. The illustrations were obtained from a helpful librarian at the Ethnographic Museum in Split, itself situated in the Roman core of the medieval center of the town: the ruins of Emperor Diocletian's retirement palace from around AD 304. The book includes finely colored illustrations of figures from different regions of Croatia, accompanied by descriptions of the costumes and of everyday life.

Dress codes and lifestyles have changed over the last 200 years, and the diversity by region, so rich at the time, has faded away. It's now hard to tell apart the inhabitants of different continents, let alone of different hamlets or towns separated by only a few miles. Perhaps we have traded cultural diversity for a more varied personal life—certainly for a more varied and fast-paced technological life. Manning celebrates the inventiveness and initiative of the computer business with book covers based on the rich diversity of regional life of two centuries ago, brought back to life by illustrations from old books and collections like this one.

Part 1

Getting started

Phoenix is a web framework that's built on top of the Elixir programming language. It describes itself in three words:

- Productive
- Reliable
- Fast

Although those words certainly describe Phoenix, there's so much more to be excited about.

In chapter 1 of *Phoenix in Action*, you'll be introduced to Phoenix at a broad level—what it is and what it's good (and not so good) at doing. In case you don't know Elixir, the language that Phoenix is built on, you'll be introduced to this amazing functional language in chapter 2. In chapter 3, we'll take a closer look at how Phoenix is organized by tracing a web request from the user's browser all the way to the response provided by Phoenix.

1 Ride the Phoenix

This chapter covers

- What Phoenix is and its benefits
- The power of the Elixir programming language
- The differences between object-oriented and functional programming
- Some potential drawbacks to using Phoenix and Elixir

Phoenix is a web framework built on top of the Elixir programming language. Every day, Phoenix and Elixir applications

- Provide real-time communications between thousands and thousands of users on limited hardware
- Process data on highly distributed systems
- Respond gracefully to errors by having supervisors restart workers when they crash
- Provide simple or complex websites to users all over the world

In this chapter, you'll be introduced to the Elixir programming language and the Phoenix web framework. We'll take a look at the main advantages and disadvantages a language like Elixir and a framework like Phoenix provide. By the end of the chapter, you'll have a good overview of these technologies and why they exist, and you'll be ready to jump into learning the details and creating your own web applications.

1.1 What is Phoenix?

Phoenix is a web framework that aids in the creation and maintenance of dynamic websites, but it doesn't attempt to copy the big players in this space, such as Ruby on Rails. Phoenix is built on top of the Elixir programming language, which is a functional language. Although Phoenix has best practices and suggestions for structuring and maintaining your applications, it isn't as dogmatic about these suggestions as Ruby on Rails and other frameworks are, giving you the flexibility to write your applications as you see fit.

Figure 1.1 Phoenix is written in Elixir, which compiles down to run on the Erlang VM.

As shown in figure 1.1, the Phoenix framework is written in the Elixir language, which in turn runs on the Erlang VM (virtual machine).

Over the years, some high-profile companies have embraced Phoenix and Elixir. They have done so in varying degrees—some started with just API servers, some used them for internal tooling, and some have gone all-in and moved everything over. Companies such as Pinterest, Slack, Discord, Lonely Planet, Bleacher Report, Undead Labs (the company behind the hit video game *State of Decay*), and Opendoor are on this ever-growing list. The ability to dip a toe into the world of Phoenix or fully dive in is one of the great things about Elixir and Phoenix. They can handle any size of project you throw at them, and do so very cost-effectively.

Phoenix goes beyond many web frameworks as well. For example, Phoenix has the concept of *channels* built in. Channels allow for "soft-realtime" features to be easily added to applications. We'll cover the topic of channels in depth in later chapters, but they allow you to have chat applications, instantly push updates to thousands of simultaneous users, and update pages without a full-page refresh. These kinds of features can be difficult to add in other languages and frameworks, but it borders on trivial for Phoenix applications—you'll learn how to add them to your applications in a single chapter.

1.2 Elixir and Phoenix vs. the alternatives

Let's look at a few of the exciting things Phoenix offers. The following sections certainly don't provide an exhaustive list of Phoenix's benefits, but they will give you an idea of some areas in which the framework shines. We'll cover a number of these in more detail in this book.

1.2.1 Real-time communication

What can you do with real-time communication? Well, any time you want to push information to many users simultaneously, you'll need some solution for that. For example, in a chat application where users can send chat messages to thousands of other users and receive them in return, you need to keep each client up to date when another user submits a new message. A more complex example would be an auction site that wants to provide users visiting the auction item's page with up-to-the-second information regarding the state of the bids. You might have a workplace collaboration site where users are sharing files and even working on the same file simultaneously. Or perhaps you want to build a real-time multiplayer game server, and you need to ensure that all players have the same information at the same time. Real-time communication is necessary in many different situations and beneficial in many more.

Figure 1.2 illustrates a typical "pull" request, in which the user has to request new information from the server.

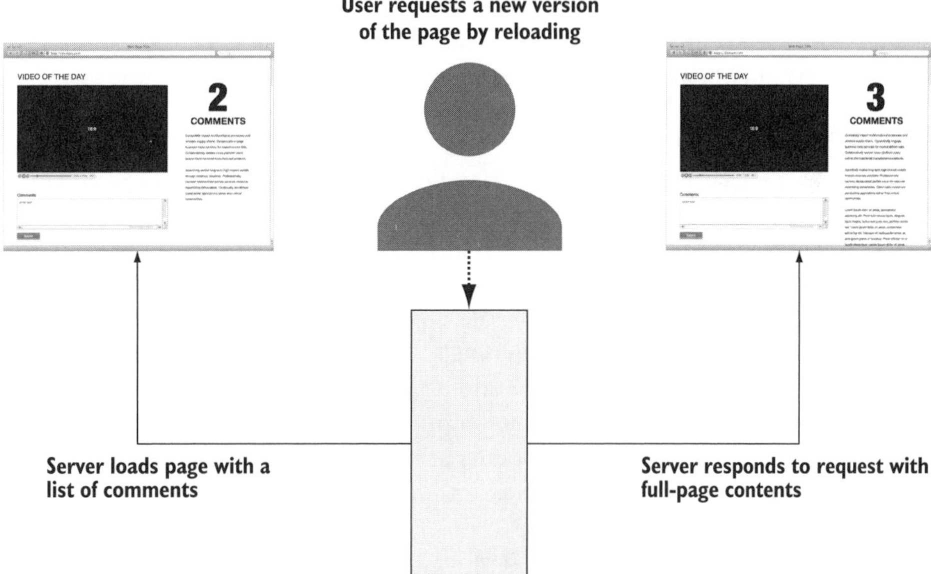

Figure 1.2 Traditional "pull" refreshes require the user to initiate the request and the server to return the entire web page.

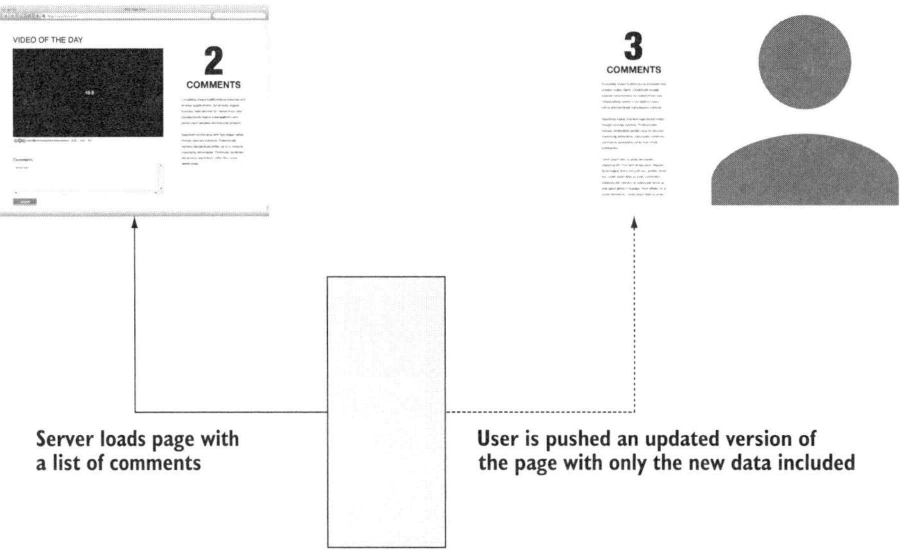
VIDEO OF THE DAY
2
COMMENTS
3
COMMENTS
Server loads page with a list of comments
User is pushed an updated version of the page with only the new data included

Figure 1.3 A "push" request originates from the server and pushes new information (typically only changed information) to the user, greatly reducing the payload and speeding up page rendering.

Figure 1.3 illustrates a simple situation in which bandwidth can be saved and the user experience improved by pushing data to the user instead of requiring the user to pull the data from the server.

As the world moves more and more toward mobile communication, the real-time aspects of Phoenix can be hugely beneficial.

1.2.2 *Efficient, small processes*

Elixir can spawn and efficiently handle hundreds of thousands of processes without blinking an eye (we'll go into a bit more detail later in this chapter). When creating channels for real-time communication, Phoenix spawns each channel in its own process, so that no single process can damage or take down any of the others—they're isolated.

Using these processes and channels, Phoenix can handle hundreds of thousands of connections on a single server. Kudos to you if your web application ever has hundreds of thousands of simultaneous users wanting to communicate in real time, but that gives you an idea of the power of Phoenix and channels running within processes.

You'll add channels in the application you'll build over the course of this book.

1.2.3 *Background computation*

There will be times during development when you'll want to execute a long-running computation or process but won't want to keep the user from interacting with your application. For example, a user of an e-commerce site may want to purchase a product

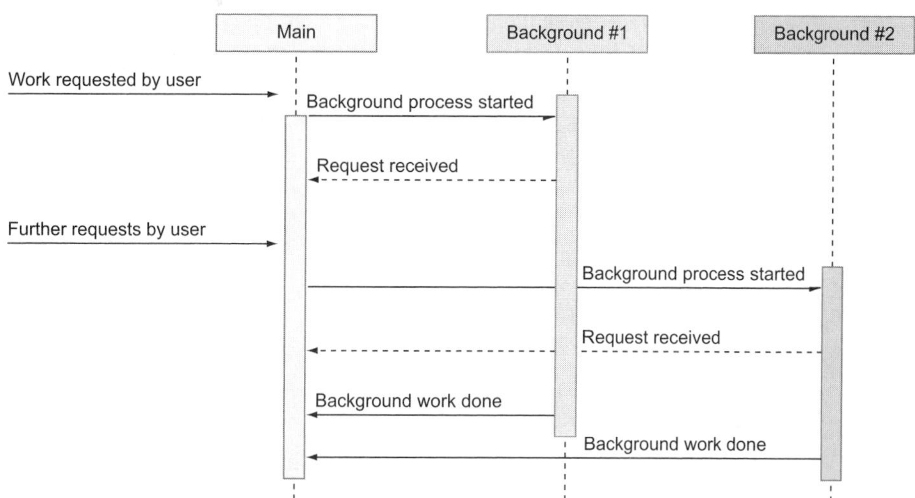

Figure 1.4 Background processes can do complex work without holding up the main responses to the user.

that's first customized and then downloaded. When the user finalizes the purchase, you don't want to require them to wait on that page until the personalization process is complete. Instead, you'd like them to continue to browse your store or set up their profile. This is a simple scenario in which background computation can play a role. Figure 1.4 shows how a similar asynchronous request may progress.

If your application needs to do more than a small amount of computation in the background (normally asynchronously), it's a perfect fit for a framework built on top of Elixir, like Phoenix. It's trivial to kick off asynchronous background processes with Elixir.

1.2.4 Minimal hardware requirements, low-cost scaling

If you look at any hosting provider's offerings, you'll notice that adding more CPU power or cores usually costs less than adding more RAM. This fits perfectly with the way Elixir works. Elixir automatically utilizes all the CPU cores available to it and uses a relatively small amount of RAM in order to run. Compare this to a web framework and language like Ruby on Rails, which is RAM-hungry.

Other web frameworks built on different programming languages can scale, but if you're looking for a low-cost way to scale quickly, Elixir and Phoenix might be a good choice. Pinterest explains in a blog post that they moved one of their systems from Java to Elixir (http://mng.bz/6jMA):

> *So, we like Elixir and have seen some pretty big wins with it. The system that manages rate limits for both the Pinterest API and Ads API is built in Elixir. Its 50 percent response time is around 500 microseconds with a 90 percent response time of 800 microseconds. Yes, microseconds.*

We've also seen an improvement in code clarity. We're converting our notifications system from Java to Elixir. The Java version used an Actor system and weighed in at around 10,000 lines of code. The new Elixir system has shrunk this to around 1000 lines. The Elixir based system is also faster and more consistent than the Java one and runs on half the number of servers.

1.2.5 It's not all roses

Although the Elixir language and the Phoenix framework are awesome and are usually what I reach for when starting new projects, they're not always the best choice for the job. Some areas in which Elixir doesn't do as good a job as the alternatives include the following:

- *Time to productivity*—If you're already productive in a different web framework using a different programming language, it may be hard to justify the cost of getting up to speed in something new like Elixir. If you're just getting started in development, one consideration is how long it will take you to become productive in your new chosen language. Some people I've spoken to believe it's harder to learn functional programming (FP) than object-oriented programming (OOP), and others swear it's the other way around—functional programming just clicks with them. Either way, I believe that Elixir and Phoenix offer enough reasons for you to take the plunge and learn the language, regardless of your past experience levels.
- *Numbers*—Elixir isn't a number-crunching powerhouse. It will never match the pure computational speed of something lower-level like C or C++. I'd even go so far as to say that if you're primarily looking to crunch large numbers, even Python would be a better choice. Elixir can do it and do it well, but it will rarely win in a head-to-head competition in this area.
- *Community*—Although the community behind Elixir, Phoenix, and Erlang is very helpful and enthusiastic, it's not as large or established as the communities for Ruby, Python, Java, or even PHP. Those languages have a deeper and longer history in the web application world, and it might be easier to find help with your project in one of those communities. But more and more meetups, conferences, blogs, and jobs are arriving all the time for Elixir, and I believe the future holds great things for the Elixir community.
- *Packages*—In keeping with Elixir's smaller and younger community, the number of open source packages available for use in your project is smaller. As I write this, there are currently just under 8,000 packages available on hex.pm, the package manager source for Elixir. Contrast that with rubygems.org, which has over 9,800 packages, and PyPI (the Python Package Index), which has over 165,000. But although it may be harder to find something that exactly matches what you had in another programming language, more packages are being built all the time. This also means there's space for *you* to create a helpful new package and help grow the community.

- *Deploying*—I originally considered including a chapter on deploying applications in this book, but this is an area that's still in need of a single, "best" solution. Deploying an Elixir application (including ones that use the Phoenix web framework) is pretty tricky and involves multiple steps—steps that are still not clearly defined and that don't have mature tools to help with the process. However, many smart people are putting tremendous resources toward a solution, and I believe one is just around the corner (it may be available by the time this book is released).

Phoenix provides a lot of things that help you add normally complex features to your web applications, but it won't be the foundation of your application. It may be strange to read that in a book specifically about Phoenix, but the truth is that Phoenix derives its powers from the amazing Elixir programming language.

1.3 The power of Elixir

Phoenix is a framework built on top of Elixir—so what is Elixir? Here's a quote from the Elixir homepage (http://elixir-lang.org):

> *Elixir is a dynamic, functional language designed for building scalable and maintainable applications.*
>
> *Elixir leverages the Erlang VM, known for running low-latency, distributed and fault-tolerant systems, while also being successfully used in web development and the embedded software domain.*

Erlang has a long and interesting history. It was developed at Ericsson (the telecommunications company) and first appeared in the world around 1986. Ericsson used it internally for years to handle telecommunication jobs (such as powering telephone exchanges) around the world, but it became open source in 1998. Erlang is known to be a good fit for applications that must be fault-tolerant, distributable, highly available, and performant. One of the exciting things about Elixir is that it's built on top of this 30-year old VM, and it utilizes those decades of knowledge and experience and marries them with nice syntax and metaprogramming support (among other things).

Let's look at some more things that make Elixir an exciting language to work with.

1.3.1 Scalability

One of the amazing things about Elixir is its scalability. Elixir has the idea of processes running on your machine. These aren't processes as you may have thought of them in the past—they aren't threads. Elixir processes are extremely lightweight (the default initial size is 233 words or 0.5 KB) and are independent of all other running processes. You'll build a Phoenix application through the course of this book, and you shouldn't find it surprising that a nontrivial number of concurrent processes will be running on your machine to allow the application to run. These processes are *fast*, are independent of each other, have unshared memory, and can easily send messages to and receive them from other processes on distributed nodes (different machines potentially in different parts of the world).

1.3.2 Supervision trees

Elixir applications (including Phoenix apps) have *supervisors* and *workers*. Supervisors monitor the workers and ensure that if they go down for one reason or another, they're started right back up. This provides an amazing backbone of fault-tolerance without much work on your part. You can configure how you'd like your supervisors to handle their workers if something *does* happen to them, including shutting down and restarting any sibling workers. Beyond that, supervisors can supervise other supervisors! The supervision tree can get pretty large and complex, but this complexity doesn't necessarily mean your application will be harder to comprehend.

Figure 1.5 shows a scenario in which a supervisor is in charge of rooms for scheduling purposes. Among those rooms, there's another supervisor that's in charge of a subset of rooms. The top-level supervisor can certainly supervise the supervisor.

Figure 1.6 illustrates a real-life application developed by a friend of mine. Each dot is either a supervisor, a process being supervised, or both, which should give you an idea of how many processes can be spawned during the running of a moderately complex application. This application is constantly running in the background to find scheduling conflicts for an organization's physical assets, such as rooms, buildings,

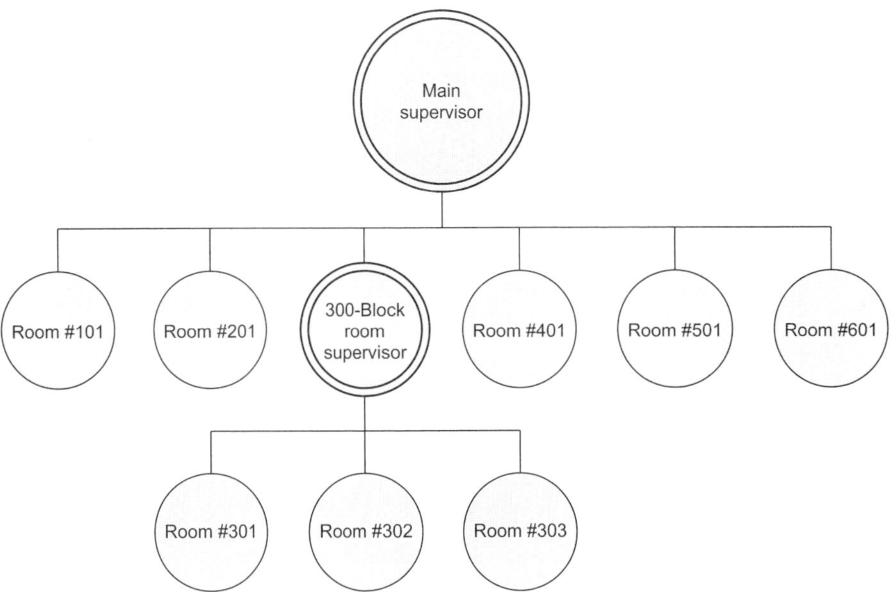

Figure 1.5 Supervisors and workers

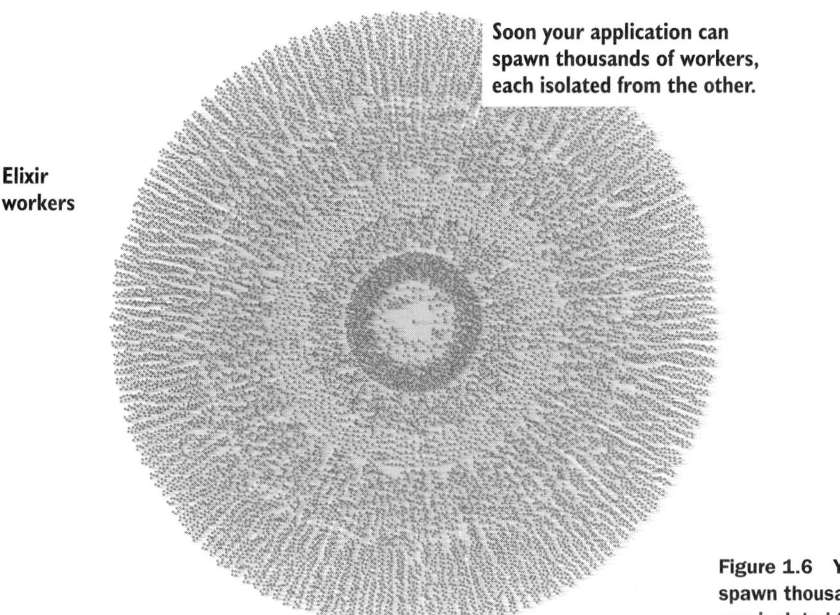
Soon your application can spawn thousands of workers, each isolated from the other.
Elixir workers

Figure 1.6 Your application can spawn thousands of workers, each one isolated from the others.

projectors, chairs, and the like. Each supervisor handles a group of rooms. When a request comes in, each supervisor gets a request to ask each of the rooms it supervises whether there are any scheduling conflicts. If any of the child processes has any trouble and crashes, the supervisor notices and starts it right back up.

The benefits of these processes and supervisors are many. One, in particular, is that creating distributed systems is much easier than is possible in other languages. You can deploy your code to multiple servers in multiple locations around the world (or in the same room) and have them communicate with each other. Need more power? You can bring up another server node, and your previous nodes can communicate with the new node with minimal configuration, passing off some of the required work as they see fit.

1.3.3 Erlang VM

The preceding features are available to us because the backbone of Elixir is Erlang. Erlang has been around for decades now, silently and dependently providing services to many of the things you use on a daily basis. Erlang was created with the telecommunications industry in mind, and what does a telecommunication service require? High fault-tolerance, distributability, live-updating of software—things that a modern-day web application should also be able to rely on. Elixir runs on top of the Erlang VM, which is rock-solid and has been for decades. You can even run Erlang functions and use Erlang modules directly in your Elixir applications! This book won't go into the details of Erlang and its VM, but there are plenty of resources available that cover Erlang.

> **Erlang and WhatsApp**
>
> There's a great story about Erlang and the popular messaging app WhatsApp, which was acquired by Facebook for $19 billion in 2014. When it was acquired, it had 450 million users sending over 70 million Erlang messages per second. If WhatsApp had been built on a programming language other than Erlang, it likely would have had a huge engineering staff. But because the application was written in Erlang, and Erlang provides so many benefits for real-time messaging applications, the engineering team at the time of acquisition consisted of only 35 people. Your application may not ever have 450 million users sending 70 million messages per second, but why not utilize technology that would allow you to easily do so if required?

1.3.4 *Macro and metaprogramming support*

Although Elixir runs on the Erlang VM, it is itself written in Elixir. How is that possible? This is another of the great things about the Elixir language—macros. Elixir is extensible via built-in support for macros, which allow anyone to define their own language features. You can build your own little language or DSL within Elixir itself. As figure 1.7 illustrates, 90% of the Elixir codebase is itself Elixir—the rest is made up of Erlang and various shell files.

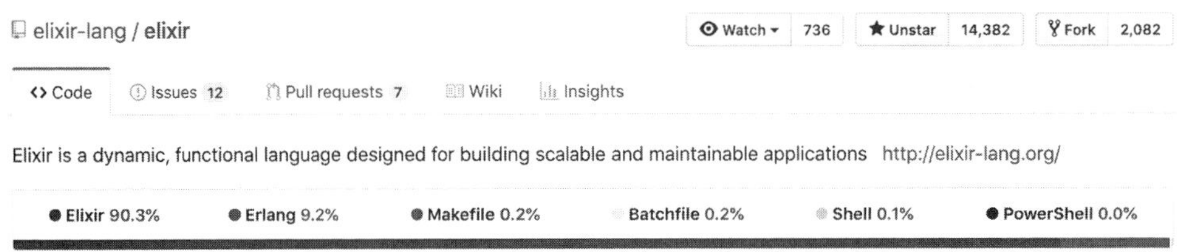

Figure 1.7 Breakdown of language types in Elixir's source code (as of December 2018)

1.3.5 *OTP*

One feature of Elixir that can't go unmentioned is its ability to utilize OTP. *OTP* stands for *Open Telecom Platform*, but that name isn't very relevant anymore, so you'll almost always just see OTP.

OTP is a set of functions, modules, and standards that make using things such as supervisors and workers—and the fault-tolerance that goes along with them—possible. OTP includes concepts such as servers, concurrency, distributed computation, load balancing, and worker pools, to name just a few. It's been lightheartedly said that any complex problem you're attempting to solve has likely already been solved in OTP.

> *If half of Erlang's greatness comes from its concurrency and distribution and the other half comes from its error handling capabilities, then the OTP framework is the third half of it.*
>
> —Frederic Trottier-Hebert, "What is OTP?"
> in the tutorial *Learn You Some Erlang for Great Good!*

With all that greatness backing Phoenix, what if you don't know Elixir? That's OK. Elixir is a relative newcomer in the world of programming languages. Chapter 2 will take you through the basics of the Elixir language, and you can refer to appendix B for some extra resources you can check out. As a teaser, the next section is a very brief tour of what Elixir looks like and how it functions.

1.4 Functional vs. object-oriented programming

First and foremost, Elixir is a functional programming language. A few of the biggest bullet points of the benefits of FP include

- Data is treated as immutable (unchangeable).
- When given the same input, a function will always return the same output.
- The code produces no side effects.

As a result, applications developed in functional languages are relatively easy to reason about, predict, and test.

Ruby, Python, Java, and C# are all OO languages and are widely used in web application development. In recent releases, even historically procedural languages like PHP and Perl have been gaining OO features. And although the number of developers productively using these languages remains high, there seems to be a recent shift away from the notion that OOP is the best way forward, and toward more FP languages (such as Elixir, Haskell, Lisp, Clojure, and so on). Even though most OOP languages can be applied in a functional way, having a language that's strictly functional from the beginning has its advantages.

1.4.1 Overview of functional programming

Functional programming is all about data transformation. Mutable (changeable) data and changing state are avoided (and in some cases are impossible). A function that's called with the same parameters any number of times will return the same answer every time. In purely functional code, no data outside of that function will be considered when the return value is computed. One of the results of this is that the return values of functions need to be captured in order to be used again—there's no object involved that encapsulates its own state.

Let's suppose you want to do some calculations regarding a race car and keep track of things like what kind of tires it has, its speed, its acceleration, and so on. You could group that information into an Elixir module that would not only define the structure of the data but also be a central place to hold all the race car functions.

Let's take a look at what a race car module might look like in Elixir. Don't worry too much about the syntax—we'll cover that later. The following listing should give you an idea of the code syntax and structure.

Listing 1.1 An example RaceCar module in Elixir

```
defmodule RaceCar do
  defstruct [:tires, :power, :acceleration, :speed]   # Defines a struct and the attributes it will have

  def accelerate(%RaceCar{speed: speed, acceleration: acceleration} =
➥ racecar) do
    Map.put(racecar, :speed, speed + acceleration)   # Map.put doesn't modify the original variable's data but instead returns a new representation with the updated data.
  end
end

ferrari_tires = [
  %Tire{location: :front_right, kind: :racing},
  %Tire{location: :front_left, kind: :racing},
  %Tire{location: :back_right, kind: :racing},
  %Tire{location: :back_left, kind: :racing}
]   # Tires are defined as four Tire structs. The Tire definition isn't in this listing.
ferrari = %RaceCar{tires: ferrari_tires,   # Creates the RaceCar
                   power: %Engine{model: "FR223"},
                   acceleration: 60,
                   speed: 0}
ferrari.speed
# => 0
RaceCar.accelerate(ferrari)   # Tells the RaceCar module to accelerate the ferrari
# => 60
ferrari.speed   # The underlying data doesn't change.
# => 0
new_ferrari = RaceCar.accelerate(ferrari)   # You need to capture the output if you want to use the data after acceleration.
new_ferrari.speed
# => 60
ferrari.speed
# => 0
```

Look carefully—the `ferrari` variable isn't changed when you pass it to the `RaceCar.accelerate/1` function.[1] You could run that line 1,000 times and you'd get the same return value every time: an updated structure of the `ferrari` with a new speed. But remember, the *original* `ferrari` doesn't change in memory. You have to capture that return value in order to use it later.

What this kind of programming offers is the elimination of side effects. You can run your function at any time and be confident that it will always return the same value for the same input—regardless of the time of day, global state, what order the functions were called in, and so on.

> *Eliminating side effects, i.e., changes in state that do not depend on the function inputs, can make it much easier to understand and predict the behavior of a program, which is one of the key motivations for the development of functional programming.*
>
> —Wikipedia "Functional programming"

[1] The `RaceCar.accelerate/1` syntax means the `accelerate` function inside the `RaceCar` module that has argument arity (the number of function arguments) of 1.

In simple terms, OOP involves objects holding onto their own state (data) and providing methods that allow the outside world to access, modify, or even delete that data. In contrast, Elixir modules don't store state (data) on their own—they simply provide functions that operate on the data passed to them and return the resulting data to the caller.

Figure 1.8 illustrates how objects handle data in OOP, and figure 1.9 illustrates how FP paradigms handle data. In the latter case, the data does *not* belong to the module.

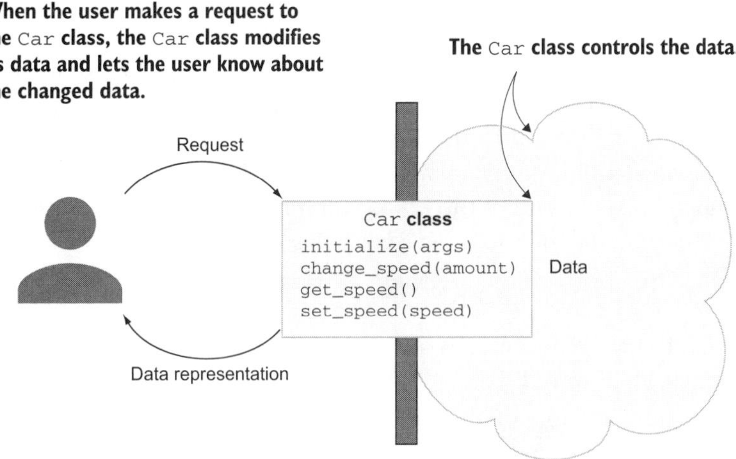
When the user makes a request to the Car class, the Car class modifies its data and lets the user know about the changed data.
The Car class controls the data.
Request
Car class
initialize(args)
change_speed(amount)
get_speed()
set_speed(speed)
Data
Data representation

Figure 1.8 Object-oriented programming generally involves an object that keeps track of its own data (state). Methods are used to manipulate that internal state and retrieve it for other uses.

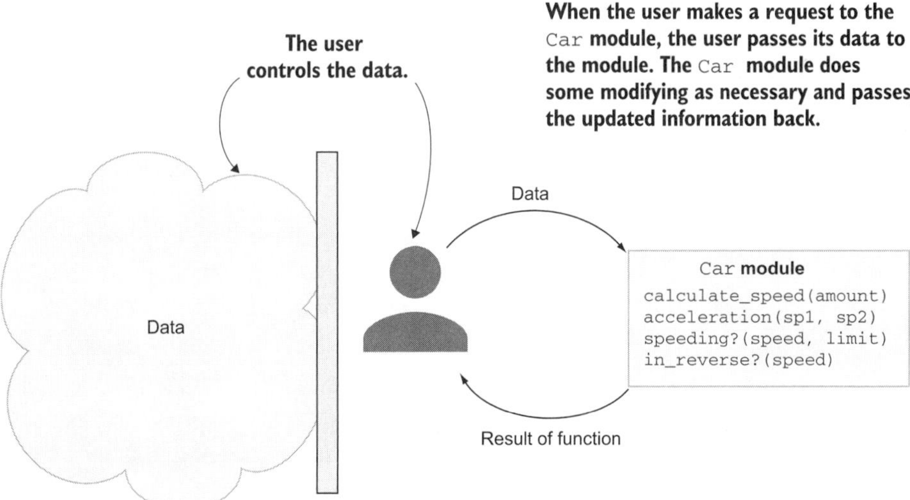
The user controls the data.
When the user makes a request to the Car module, the user passes its data to the module. The Car module does some modifying as necessary and passes the updated information back.
Data
Car module
calculate_speed(amount)
acceleration(sp1, sp2)
speeding?(speed, limit)
in_reverse?(speed)
Data
Result of function

Figure 1.9 Functional programming generally involves a module that contains functions that act together for a purpose. The module holds no data (state) but returns the result of the function acting on data the caller gives it.

In the world of OOP, an object's internal data or state can be mutated by many things during an operation. Because of the often dynamic nature of OO languages, a third-party package could hook into your codebase and modify your data without you even knowing. In contrast, when working with Phoenix, the data flows in a single line from the user making the request to the requested page being displayed. And for each step the data takes, you specify how that data is passed along. The side effects are therefore minimal (and usually are eliminated entirely).

1.5 Keep reading

This chapter has provided a brief overview of what Phoenix and Elixir are and some of the benefits they provide to developers. Hopefully, it has also piqued your interest in the language and framework. In the next chapter, you'll be introduced to the Elixir language, in case you're not already familiar with it. Then, starting in chapter 3, we'll dive into Phoenix. By the end of the book, you'll have written a very basic auction site (like eBay) with real-time bidding. Let's get going!

Summary

- Phoenix has many advantages over similar web frameworks, and much of that is because it's built with Elixir.
- Elixir is built on top of Erlang, which is accompanied by decades of work, knowledge, and best practices.
- Functional languages provide a different style of thinking than object-oriented languages. Although there are benefits to each, a purely functional style is gaining favor among web developers.
- Some companies have utilized Elixir and Phoenix in just a few key areas of their applications, and others have embraced them in every aspect of their business.

2 Intro to Elixir

This chapter covers

- The basics of the Elixir programming language
- Creating a module
- Using built-in tools to help you work smarter

Now that you've learned a bit about the benefits Phoenix can bring to your web application development, you'll need to know Elixir. Phoenix is a web framework that's built on top of the Elixir language (which is built on the Erlang VM, known as BEAM). So what if you don't know Elixir?

This chapter will get you up to speed on Elixir. If you already know Elixir, you can probably skip this chapter entirely. If you don't know Elixir or need a refresher, this chapter will cover just enough Elixir to get you going. Some concepts won't be covered in this chapter—I'll teach you about them later in the book when you need to know them. I'll also point you to more resources at the end of the chapter, in case you'd like to dive deeper into the language and all its features.

2.1 The basics

Before we begin writing Elixir, I'll show you a quick example of what a module might look like (a module can be thought of as a collection of functions). Have you heard of the "fizz buzz" programming exercise? This is the basic idea:

1. Take any series of numbers, one at a time.
2. If the number is divisible by 3, print "fizz."
3. If the number is divisible by 5, print "buzz."
4. If the number is divisible by 3 *and* 5, print "fizzbuzz."
5. Otherwise, print the number.

Listings 2.1, 2.2, and 2.3 show different variations of how you could implement this in Elixir. If you don't know Elixir, don't worry—just take a look at the syntax and see if you can recognize some features that are available in any other languages you know.

Listing 2.1 is an example of *function overloading* (defining multiple functions with the same name). Elixir will run the first function definition that matches what it's given in terms of argument count and situation (such as `when rem(num, 5) == 0`, which means "when the remainder of `num` divided by `5` equals `0`").

Listing 2.1 FizzBuzz implementation 1

```
defmodule FizzBuzz do
  def go(min, max) do
    min..max
    |> Enum.each(fn(num) -> go(num) end)
  end
  def go(num) when rem(num, 15) == 0, do: IO.puts "fizzbuzz"
  def go(num) when rem(num, 3)  == 0, do: IO.puts "fizz"
  def go(num) when rem(num, 5)  == 0, do: IO.puts "buzz"
  def go(num), do: IO.puts num
end

FizzBuzz.go(1, 100)
```

There are five functions named "go" in this example: one expects two arguments, and four expect one argument

Elixir knows which function to run based on which definition first matches the situation.

Listing 2.2 illustrates the basic use of `cond`. Inside the `cond` block, Elixir will execute the first condition that is `true`.

Listing 2.2 FizzBuzz implementation 2

Enum.each/2 enumerates over the collection of integers from min to max and runs the go function for each.

```
defmodule FizzBuzz do
  def go(min, max), do: Enum.each(min..max, &(go(&1)))
  def go(num) do
    cond do
      rem(num, 3) == 0 && rem(num, 5) == 0 -> IO.puts "fizzbuzz"
      rem(num, 3) == 0 -> IO.puts "fizz"
      rem(num, 5) == 0 -> IO.puts "buzz"
```

```
      true -> IO.puts num
    end
  end
end

FizzBuzz.go(1, 100)
```

If no preceding condition matches, this line is executed because true will always be true.

Finally, listing 2.3 uses the case statement and pattern matching to implement the exercise requirements.

Listing 2.3 FizzBuzz implementation 3

```
defmodule FizzBuzz do
  def go(min, max), do: Enum.each(min..max, &go/1)
  def go(num) do
    case {rem(num, 3), rem(num, 5)} do
      {0, 0} -> IO.puts "fizzbuzz"
      {0, _} -> IO.puts "fizz"
      {_, 0} -> IO.puts "buzz"
      _ -> IO.puts num
    end
  end
end

FizzBuzz.go(1, 100)
```

Ensures two numbers are in a tuple (such as {0, 4})

Pattern-matches on those numbers. The underscore (_) means you don't care what is in this spot.

Uses the underscore (_) to match any situation that hasn't already been matched

Each of these listings showcases some neat things you can do with Elixir:

- Module declaration (`defmodule`)
- Named function declaration (`def`)
- Anonymous function declaration (`fn(x) -> ... end`)
- Function overloading (multiple `go` functions defined)
- Guard clauses (`when ...`)
- Pattern matching (`{0, _}` for example)
- `cond` and `case` statements
- Using functions from other modules (like the `each` function from the `Enum` module)
- Various Elixir data types (`Range`, `Tuple`, `Integer`, Boolean)
- The pipe operator (`|>`)

Again, if all this is foreign to you, don't worry. You'll understand them after you've digested this chapter.

If you haven't yet installed Elixir, now is the time to do so (appendix A will guide you through the installation process).

2.1.1 IEx

Once Elixir is installed, you'll have some new executables available, including IEx. In this chapter (and a few beyond), you'll use an `iex` session. *IEx* stands for *Interactive Elixir*, and it's a REPL (read-eval-print loop) for Elixir. A REPL takes user input, evaluates it,

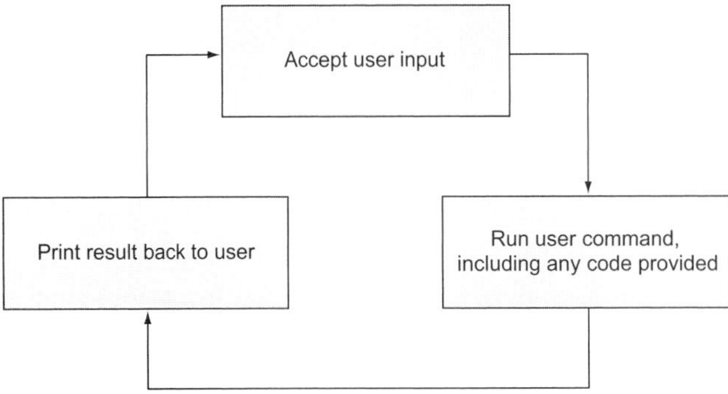

Figure 2.1 A REPL takes user input, evaluates it, prints it out to the user, and loops back around to take user input again.

prints the result out to the user, and loops back around to take user input again. Figure 2.1 illustrates this loop.

IEx will act as our Elixir playground as we get started. But don't let that fool you—it's a pretty powerful tool even for the most advanced Elixir users. Let's fire it up and see what we get.

To start a new session, open your terminal program and type `iex` (or `iex.bat` in Windows). You'll see something like this:

```
Erlang/OTP 21 [erts-10.1.3] [source] [64-bit] [smp:8:8] [async-threads:1]
     [hipe] [dtrace]

Interactive Elixir (1.7.4) - press Ctrl+C to exit (type h() ENTER for help)
iex(1)>
```

There's a lot of debugging information displayed here, and most of those numbers and terms won't matter in our use of IEx. In fact, some of it may look a little bit different on your computer. Don't worry about it too much. The two most important things to look at are the Erlang/OTP version (21 in this example) and the Elixir version (1.7.4 here) that you're running. If you're ever in need of assistance in online discussions, those two version numbers will likely be important to those who are assisting you.

Another thing to notice is that the output provides you with two hints:

- `press Ctrl+C to exit`
- `type h() ENTER for help`

When the time comes to close your `iex` session, press Ctrl-C on your keyboard. Once you do, you'll see this:

```
BREAK: (a)bort (c)ontinue (p)roc info (i)nfo (l)oaded
       (v)ersion (k)ill (D)b-tables (d)istribution
```

For now, don't worry about those options other than `(c)ontinue`. If you pressed Ctrl-C by accident or now regret your decision, you can press `c` to continue your `iex` session. If you indeed want to quit and move on to other things, press Ctrl-C a second time or `a`. Those will dump you back into your terminal.

The `h()` is for help. You can follow along by typing `h()` in your IEx session now.

Listing 2.4 Getting help from an IEx session

```
iex(1)> h()
                                  IEx.Helpers

Welcome to Interactive Elixir. You are currently seeing the documentation for
the module IEx.Helpers which provides many helpers to make Elixir's shell more
joyful to work with.

This message was triggered by invoking the helper h(), usually referred to as
h/0 (since it expects 0 arguments).

You can use the h/1 function to invoke the documentation for any Elixir
     module
or function:

    iex> h Enum
    iex> h Enum.map
    iex> h Enum.reverse/1

You can also use the i/1 function to introspect any value you have in the
shell:

    iex> i "hello"

There are many other helpers available, here are some examples:

# --- snip ---
```

The documentation gives you pointers on how to use the documentation.

I've truncated this output, but the rest of these helpers are good to use. Experiment in your IEx session.

Whoa, that's quite a bit of text! But don't get overwhelmed—all of it is very helpful. One of the great things about Elixir is its idea of documentation being a first-class citizen along with your code. We'll get into code documentation in later chapters, but as a quick example, if you type `h(clear/0)`, it will give you documentation on the `clear/0` function.

That documentation is written just above the function declaration in the Elixir source code. Figure 2.2 is a screenshot of the source code for `clear/0`. You can see that the number of lines dedicated to documentation closely matches the number of lines of code for the function.

```
@doc """
Clears the console screen.

This function only works if ANSI escape codes are enabled
on the shell, which means this function is by default
unavailable on Windows machines.
"""
def clear() do
  if IO.ANSI.enabled? do
    IO.write [IO.ANSI.home, IO.ANSI.clear]
  else
    IO.puts "Cannot clear the screen because ANSI escape codes are not enabled on this shell"
  end
  dont_display_result()
end
```

Figure 2.2 The source code and in-line documentation for `clear/0`

This is an example of a function with light documentation. The documentation can be extensive, sometimes running to dozens of lines with multiple examples. This makes reading Elixir source code files easy. It also makes discovering how to use new modules and functions easy!

2.1.2 *Basic types*

Now that you know how to get help and how to exit an IEx session, let's play around with some of the basic building blocks of the Elixir language. There are several basic types in Elixir that you'll need to know. Table 2.1 lists the type names and provides an example of each type. We'll go into detail on each of these types later in this chapter.

Table 2.1 Basic Elixir types

Type	Examples
Integer	`34`
Float	`387.936`
Boolean	`true/false`
String	`"Phoenix in Action"`
Charlist	`'Phoenix in Action'`
Atom	`:phoenix_in_action`
List	`[34, 387.936, false]`
Tuple	`{34, 387.936, false}`
Map	`%{name: "Geoffrey", location: "Oceanside, CA"}`
Range	`1..100`

These are basic types in Elixir. If you enter these in IEx and don't do any manipulation of the data in them, IEx will just echo back the result (which is the data itself). You can follow along with the following listing by typing the same things in your IEx session.

Listing 2.5 Using different data types

```
iex(3)> 34                                                    <-- Each line is executed.
34                  <-- The result is printed. In all of these examples, the results are the inputs themselves.
iex(4)> 387.936
387.936
iex(5)> true
true
iex(6)> "Phoenix in Action"
"Phoenix in Action"
iex(7)> 'Phoenix in Action'
'Phoenix in Action'
iex(8)> :phoenix_in_action
:phoenix_in_action
iex(9)> [34, 387.936, false]
[34, 387.936, false]
iex(10)> {34, 387.936, false}
{34, 387.936, false}
```

We'll cover each of these types in more depth in this chapter, so there's no need to memorize them now.

2.1.3 A small detour into functions

Before we go into the details of the basic types, let's take a quick tour of functions in Elixir. Why the detour? Well, some of the things you'll do while exploring the basic types will use functions, so you'll need to know about them first.

There are two main types of functions in Elixir: *named functions* and *anonymous functions*. Most of the time, you'll write and use named functions, but anonymous functions are still very helpful.

NAMED FUNCTIONS

Named functions in Elixir are *always* within the context or scope of a module. A named function can't exist outside of a module.

You can think of a module as a collection of functions that are grouped together for a purpose. For example, you could group functions dealing with the manufacturing of shirts in a `Factory.Shirt` module. There's nothing special about the name of a module—the functions inside it could be defined in any module in your application and they would work the same way.

To recall the structure of a function call, you can remember *MFA—module-function-arguments.* The first thing you write in a function call is the module name, followed by the function name, and finally the arguments for that function. Figure 2.3 illustrates the different pieces that make up a function call in Elixir.

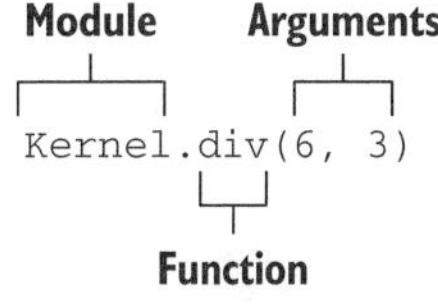

Figure 2.3 The module-function-arguments structure

A named function is called by its name, and you can provide it with the arguments it expects. This code calls the `is_integer` function inside the `Kernel` module:

```
iex(1)> Kernel.is_integer(3)
true
```

This example calls the `length` function inside the `Kernel` module:

```
iex(1)> Kernel.length([1, 2, 3])
3
```

One thing to note is that `Kernel` functions are available in most situations without explicitly typing `Kernel`. This makes these functions available almost everywhere (and we'll discuss how you can make your module functions act similarly later in the book). For example, these two calls are exactly the same as the previous two:

```
iex(1)> is_integer(3)
true

iex(2)> length([1, 2, 3])
3
```

Some special forms are also available. These include `+`, `-`, `*`, `/`, `==`, `!=`, and so on. There are quite a few of them. These special forms can be used everywhere and are actually function calls, but you can call them a bit differently, thanks to some syntactic sugar:[1]

```
iex(1)> 1 + 3
4

iex(2)> Kernel.+(1, 3)
4
```

Both of the preceding forms call directly to Erlang's implementation of `+`. You can also use Erlang's functions directly at any time:

```
iex(3)> :erlang.+(1, 3)
4
```

The `:erlang` syntax is special for Erlang, and you won't be using it much. If you'd like to explore the different `Kernel` functions available, take a look at the source code for the `Kernel` module. It's not as scary as it sounds. In fact, the vast majority of the file consists of documentation and examples.

ANONYMOUS FUNCTIONS

Anonymous functions are functions that aren't called by a name. They can exist outside of a module, unlike named functions. You can bind them to variable names that

---

[1] This is a good example of *prefix notation versus infix notation.* `Kernel.+(1,3)` is the normal prefix notation, but Elixir provides `1 + 3` with infix notation. Simply put, infix notation places the function call between the two arguments. Not very many functions have infix notation in Elixir, and you'll rarely write one of your own. But sometimes it's nice to know the correct terms for things.

you can use to call the functions later (with a slightly different syntax). You can think of an anonymous function as a simple (or complex) piece of data transformation that you may or may not need to repeat.

For example, suppose you're making sandwiches at a deli and you need to repeat the same process over and over again. If you had to write the sequence in code, you could write out each step every time an order came in. Or you could store the standard steps in a function and use that function every time an order came in. Then it wouldn't matter how many orders you received—your code could handle the extra business. In pseudocode, it might look like the following listing.

Listing 2.6 Pseudocode for making a sandwich

```
for each order received:
  on a plate:
    add bread
    add mustard
    add turkey
    add cheese
    add tomato
    add lettuce
    add bread
  return plate to customer
```

Explicitly adding every ingredient creates a lot of repetition. Let's slowly build an Elixir implementation of these steps using anonymous functions. Figure 2.4 illustrates the pieces required to define an anonymous function.

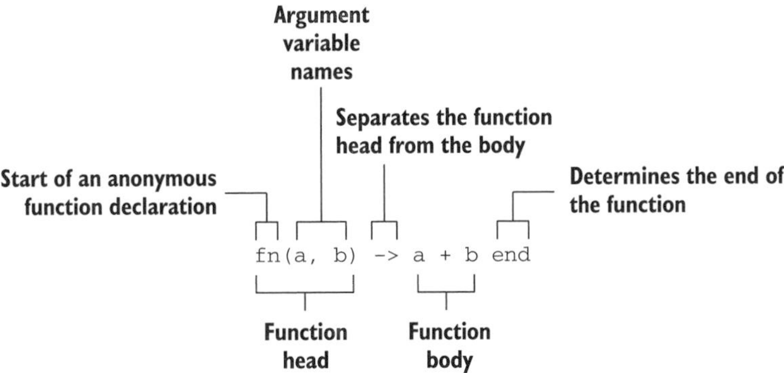

Figure 2.4 Pieces of an anonymous function

The standard procedure inside `on a plate:` could be contained in a function. To define an anonymous function, you start with `fn` and add any variable names you'd like to accept in your function enclosed in parentheses and separated by a comma. In the `add_ingredient` function in listing 2.7, you accept two variables and name them plate and ingredient. The function body is then indicated by a "stabby arrow" (->) and is contained between it and an end declaration. The function body in listing 2.7 adds the new ingredient to the plate. Note that Elixir functions implicitly return the last computed result of the function body.

Listing 2.7 Creating an anonymous function and binding it to add_ingredient

```
iex(1)> add_ingredient = fn(plate, ingredient) -> Enum.concat(plate,
      [ingredient]) end
#Function<12.52032458/2 in :erl_eval.expr/5>
```

Uses a List for the ingredient list

Let's now take our knowledge of anonymous functions and expand the previous pseudocode so it's a little more functional.

Listing 2.8 Using an anonymous function

```
for each order received:
  plate = []
  plate = add_ingredient.(plate, :bread)
  plate = add_ingredient.(plate, :mustard)
  plate = add_ingredient.(plate, :turkey)
  plate = add_ingredient.(plate, :cheese)
  plate = add_ingredient.(plate, :lettuce)
  plate = add_ingredient.(plate, :tomato)
  plate = add_ingredient.(plate, :bread)
  return plate to customer
end
```

The plate starts out as an empty List of ingredients.

Calling anonymous functions is slightly different than calling named functions that are contained within a module. You must use the variable name you bound your function to (add_ingredient in the preceding example) followed by a dot and opening and closing parentheses. Inside the parentheses you put the values to pass to the function.

```
add_ingredient.(plate, ingredient)
```

Most of the time, your functions will require multiple lines and can be written as such. Whitespace, such as newlines, are generally not strictly enforced in Elixir.

```
iex(1)> add_ingredient = fn(plate, ingredient) ->
...(1)> Enum.concat(plate, [ingredient])
...(1)> end
```

You won't be using many anonymous functions in this book. There are times when you *will* be writing them, such as using them to perform actions over a set of data, but you won't be binding them to a variable very often. The following example shows an anonymous function that isn't saved for later. Don't worry too much about the syntax or what it's doing—just try to recognize the anonymous function being used.

```
iex(1)> Enum.filter([1, 3, 5, 7, 9], fn(x) -> x < 6 end)
[1, 3, 5]
```

2.1.4 Data type details

I introduced the basic data types in Elixir, but we haven't really dug into them very much. Let's look at the types in some detail, along with some example usage.

INTEGERS AND FLOATS

Numbers in Elixir are pretty straightforward, but there are a few things you'll need to know before we dive into the other data types.

When writing a float that's between -1 and 1, it must be preceded by the 0 (for example, `0.125`, `-0.87`).

The division operator (/) always returns a float value, even when dividing two integers. Alternatively, `div/2` does integer division, and `rem/2` returns the remainder of a division. These functions (and many more in this section) are part of the `Kernel` module (`Kernel.//2`, `Kernel.div/2`, `Kernel.rem/2`). As you'll recall, `Kernel` module functions are always available without explicitly preceding the function call with the module name.

```
iex(1)> 8 / 4
2.0
iex(2)> 8.0 / 5
1.6
iex(3)> div(8, 5)
1
iex(4)> rem(8, 5)
3
```

You can round a value by using the `round/1` function. `trunc/1` returns just the integer portion of a float value.

```
iex(1)> round(1.6)
2
iex(2)> trunc(1.6)
1
```

BOOLEANS

Booleans simply represent a `true` or `false` value.

```
iex(1)> 1 == 5
false
iex(2)> is_integer(5)
true
```

The double-equals (==) tests for equality.

STRINGS

As you've seen in the preceding examples, strings are enclosed in double quotes (`"a string"`). They're *not* in single quotes (`'not a string'`), which are charlists (explained a bit later in this chapter).

Because Elixir supports UTF-8/Unicode by default, strings are stored as UTF-8 encoded binaries, where each character is stored as its Unicode bytes. As a result, Elixir considers strings a binary type.

Here are a couple of examples of working with strings:

```
iex(1)> is_binary("Phoenix in Action")
true

iex(2)> "Phoenix" <> " in " <> "Action"          <-- Uses the <> operator to concatenate (join) strings
"Phoenix in Action"
```

For longer, multiline strings (like documentation), it may be easier to define them with three double-quotes (`"""`), known as a *heredoc*. Everything inside the opening and closing `"""` will be retained, including spacing and line feeds.

```
iex(3)> haiku = """
...(3)> Build web apps for fun, profit
...(3)> Phoenix in Action
...(3)> Learn the things you need to know
...(3)> """
"Build web apps for fun, profit\nPhoenix in Action\nLearn the things you need
     to know\n"                                   <-- \n is the ASCII character for a newline.
```

Strings can also be interpolated with `#{ }`. Interpolation prints the string value of the code or variable contained within the curly braces.

```
iex(4)> subject = "Phoenix"
"Phoenix"

iex(5)> "#{subject} in Action"
"Phoenix in Action"
```

Further information can be found in Elixir's `String` documentation: https://hexdocs.pm/elixir/String.html.

CHARLISTS

The charlist is one type you need to pay special attention to because it has a gotcha. In Elixir, strings must be denoted using double quotes (`"`), whereas charlists are denoted using single quotes (`'`). A charlist is actually a special kind of list—it's a list of ASCII number values that represent the characters, rather than being a list of the characters themselves. This may sound like a minute distinction, but as you'll see in the following listing, this can lead to some funky and unexpected results.

Listing 2.9 Discovering charlist gotchas

```
iex(1)> 'Geo'
'Geo'

iex(2)> i('Geo')          <-- Uses the i/1 function to inspect information about the passed value ('Geo')
Term
  'Geo'
Data type
  List                    <-- Elixir sees the 'Geo' term as a list data type because of the single quotes.
Description
  This is a list of integers that is printed as a sequence of characters
  delimited by single quotes because all the integers in it represent valid
  ASCII characters. Conventionally, such lists of integers are referred to as
```

```
  "charlists" (more precisely, a charlist is a list of Unicode codepoints,
  and ASCII is a subset of Unicode).
Raw representation
  [71, 101, 111]
Reference modules
  List
Implemented protocols
  IEx.Info, Collectable, Enumerable, Inspect, List.Chars, String.Chars
```

Elixir informs you that, internally, 'Geo' is represented by the list [71, 101, 111].

```
iex(3)> [71, 101, 111]
'Geo'
```

What happens if you use that raw data? What will Elixir echo back to you?

```
iex(4)> {71, 101, 111}
{71, 101, 111}
```

Surrounding these numbers in curly brackets {} gives you a tuple rather than a list. Tuples don't have the same issue as lists or charlists.

If you look at the end of the preceding listing, you can potentially imagine a confusing scenario. Suppose you have a function that returns a list containing the results of three calculations that return three integers (perhaps X, Y, Z coordinates). You run the function, and your `iex` session reports that the result is `'Geo'`—it doesn't look like a list at all, especially not one filled with three integers. But it is: 71, 101, and 111. In these cases, IEx is trying to be smart and helpful about displaying the data it received, but it turns out to be confusing, especially to beginners. Your data is still there as you'd expect it to be (those three integers representing your X, Y, Z coordinates), but IEx displays it in this way.

You won't be using charlists much at all in this book. In fact, as an Elixir developer, I've rarely found the need for a charlist as opposed to a string. They're mostly a hold-over from Erlang. But you need to be aware that this particular gotcha exists.

ATOMS

Atoms in Elixir are like symbols in other languages. Atoms start with a colon (`:`), they're constants, and they are their own value. For example, `:foo` can never mean or be more than `:foo`—it can't be rebound, its value (`:foo`) can't change, and what you see is what you get. When I initially came across atoms, it seemed like there should be more to them ... but there isn't. They really are that simple.

Atoms are used regularly in Elixir, especially in situations in which a function returns a status along with a value. Let's take, for example, the `Enum.fetch/2` function. Its documentation states this:

> *Finds the element at the given index (zero-based). Returns {:ok, element} if found, otherwise :error.*

You can demonstrate this by using `Enum.fetch/2` in an IEx session. First, you look for a value for a position that does exist in the list (the 2nd item in this list). Next, you try to fetch the value for a position that doesn't exist in the list (the 15th item in the list). Notice that the return values contain atoms.

```
iex(1)> Enum.fetch([1, 2, 3, 4], 1)
{:ok, 2}
```

Fetches index 1 of the list, which is 2.

```
iex(2)> Enum.fetch([1, 2, 3, 4], 14)     <-- There is no index
:error                                       14 in the list.
```

This pattern of using atoms to indicate success or error will be repeated in Elixir. You'll see it often, so it's a good idea to start writing a lot of your functions with the same pattern.

One caveat to atoms is that they're the only Elixir data type that's not garbage-collected. This means that if you create enough atoms, you *can* crash your system when it runs out of memory trying to allocate them. It's a good idea to avoid using atoms for user-entered data, as an overload of them can be used as an attack vector against your server.

LISTS

You can think of a list in Elixir as similar to an array in other languages, or as simply a list of items that may or may not be similar types. Depending on the language you're most familiar with, it may even have similar syntax.

An Elixir list is a list of items contained in a single type (you'll see in a moment that they're more than that, though). Lists can contain any other Elixir types (even mixed types) and can even contain references to other lists.

```
iex(1)> list = [1, 2]
[1, 2]
iex(2)> [:numbers, "for example", list]
[:numbers, "for example", [1, 2]]
```

The interesting thing about lists in Elixir is that they're *linked* lists. Each item in a list has an internal pointer to the next item in the list (see figure 2.5). You'll never interact, see, or really know anything about that internal pointer—just trust that it's there. Practically, this means that a number of typical operations are fast and memory-kind. It's efficient to add items to the beginning of a list, but adding items to the end of a list can get slower as the list grows in size.

The advantages and disadvantages of linked lists are a deep computer science topic that we won't dive into, but if you're interested in some additional reading on the topic, Wikipedia has a nice summary in its "Linked list" article: https://en.wikipedia.org/wiki/Linked_list.

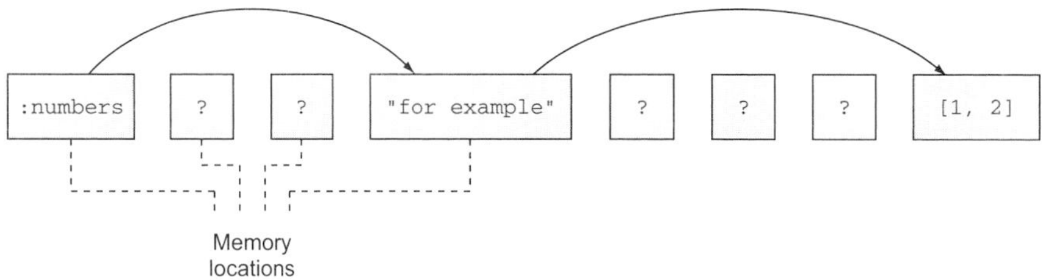

Figure 2.5 Lists are linked, meaning that each entry contains a pointer to the next item's memory location.

Lists can be concatenated and subtracted from using ++ and --.

```
iex(1)> [1, 2] ++ ["three", :four]
[1, 2, "three", :four]
iex(2)> [1, 2, 3] -- [1, 3]
[2]
```

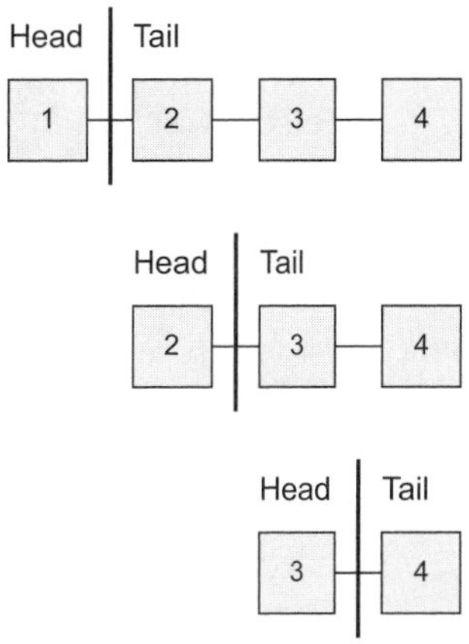

Figure 2.6 Each list has a head and a tail. You can use | to separate the head from the tail.

You'll do a number of things with lists in this book, and you'll often hear about the "head" and "tail" of a list—so much so that there are built-in functions and patterns you'll use for both. The *head* of a list is, as you've probably guessed by now, the first item in the list. The *tail* is everything in the list that isn't the head (in other words, the rest of the list). Figure 2.6 illustrates that each list has a head and a tail.

The | character is used to denote the break between the head and tail. I affectionately call it the "guillotine," as it separates the head from the rest of the list.

```
iex(1)> [head | tail] = ["Phoenix", "in", "Action"]
["Phoenix", "in", "Action"]
iex(2)> head
"Phoenix"
iex(3)> tail
["in", "Action"]
```

The | character denotes the break between the head and tail.

The hd function returns the head of a list (but, as in all of Elixir, it doesn't modify the value sent to it).

```
iex(4)> hd(tail)
"in"
iex(5)> tail
["in", "Action"]
```

Internally, because Elixir uses linked lists, you can actually write out how Elixir "sees" them (a value acting as the head, followed by another list as the tail). The head of the following list is 1. The tail is itself a list consisting of 2 as its head and an empty list as its tail:

```
iex(1)> [1 | [2 | []]]
[1, 2]
```

You can use this pattern to easily prepend items to a list.

```
iex(1)> trees = ["Oak", "Pine"]
["Oak", "Pine"]
iex(2)> more_trees = ["Maple" | trees]
["Maple", "Oak", "Pine"]
```

There are lots of powerful list functions and great documentation online. If you want to dive further into lists, check out Elixir's documentation: https://hexdocs.pm/elixir/List.html.

TUPLES

Tuples are stylistically similar to lists, but instead of being surrounded by square brackets ([and]), tuples in Elixir are surrounded by curly braces ({ and }). They can also store an undetermined number of elements of differing types, like lists can. Under the hood, however, tuples are different. They are ordered and store their data contiguously in memory. Therefore, accessing any element in a tuple is a constant-time operation (unlike lists).

The Elixir documentation is a great resource for information on tuples. Here's what it has to say:

> *Tuples are not meant to be used as a "collection" type (which is also suggested by the absence of an implementation of the Enumerable protocol for tuples): they're mostly meant to be used as a fixed-size container for multiple elements. For example, tuples are often used to have functions return "enriched" values: a common pattern is for functions to return {:ok, value} for successful cases and {:error, reason} for unsuccessful cases.*

As discussed in the section on functions, you'll see the `{:ok, value}`/`{:error, reason}` pattern all through Elixir and Phoenix. Get used to it and learn to love it.

You can use the `Kernel.elem/2` function to access a zero-based index of a tuple.

```
iex(1)> tuple = {:ok, 5, ["Phoenix", "in", "Action"]}
{:ok, 5, ["Phoenix", "in", "Action"]}
iex(2)> elem(tuple, 1)
5
```

For more information about tuples, check out Elixir's documentation: https://hexdocs.pm/elixir/Tuple.html.

MAPS

Maps are key/value stores in which each value can be bound to a unique key. In other languages, similar structures are called hashes or dictionaries. The key can be any data type, as can the values it's related to. Ordering within a map is not deterministic, so you can't rely on a map to return its pairs in the same order in which you wrote them. Maps are defined by enclosing their contents in `%{}`. The key of the entry is entered first, and its corresponding value is separated from the key with =>.

Here are some examples of using maps in an IEx session.

Listing 2.10 Playing with maps in IEx

```
iex(1)> map = %{:status => 200, "content" => "Hello world!"}
%{"content" => "Hello world!", :status => 200}

iex(2)> Map.fetch(map, "content")
{:ok, "Hello world!"}
```

Uses the Map.fetch/2 function to access a map's value for a given key (annotation to `iex(2)`)

When you're using atoms in a map as either the only keys or the last-passed keys, you can use a shorthand syntax: the atom name followed by a colon (`:`) and the value for that atom's key. For example, `%{a: 1}` is functionally the same as `%{:a => 1}`, but it's shorter to write and, in my humble opinion, nicer to look at. But you can't use this syntax if you follow it with keys of a different type—Elixir will complain about this syntax, as you can see in the following listing. Elixir doesn't know what to do with this syntax mixing, but if the shorthand is used in the last-passed keys, the syntax works.

Listing 2.11 Using the alternate atom key syntax for maps

```
iex(4)> %{a: 1, b: 2, c: 3}
{:b => 2, :a => 1, :c => 3}

iex(5)> %{a: 1, "hello" => :world}
** (SyntaxError) iex:5: syntax error before: "hello"

iex(6)> %{"hello" => :world, a: 1}
%{:a => 1, "hello" => :world}
```

The order of the keys in the returned value may not be the same as the order you specified. The order doesn't matter.

Fails because a: 1 is before "hello" => :world

Works because the special a: 1 syntax is last

Apart from the `Map.fetch/2` function used in listing 2.10, there are other, potentially more common ways to access a key's value in a map. For example, you can use the `map_name[key]` shorthand to access a map's value for the specified key. This works with any of the key types in Elixir.

Another way to access atom-based keys is by separating the variable name and the key to be retrieved with a period (`.`). But unlike the `[key]` style of access, this style of access *only* works with atom-based keys, as you can see in the error provided in the following snippet. Elixir specifically looked for the key `:hello` in the map.

Here are examples of both of those methods:

```
iex(1)> map = %{"hello" => :world, a: 1}
iex(2)> map[:a]
1

iex(3)> map["hello"]
:world

iex(4)> map.a
1

iex(5)> map.hello
** (KeyError) key :hello not found in: %{:a => 1, "hello" => :world}
```

You can't use this type of getter with keys that are not atoms.

You'll be using maps *a lot* in this book, so take some time to play with them in your IEx session. Also, read up on the power of maps and some of the included functions in the map documentation: https://hexdocs.pm/elixir/Map.html.

2.1.5 Back to modules and named functions

Most of your code won't be simple anonymous functions. You'll be organizing and reusing large portions of your codebase. To keep things organized, you can group functions that have things in common into modules. For example, if you had a group of functions that did mathematical calculations, you might group them together in a Math module. Let's look at a few interesting aspects of modules.

All module definitions start with `defmodule` followed by the name of the module and `do`. Module names are InitCase, and you can also namespace modules with dot notation (`.`). For example, if you had a subset of math functions that dealt with mortgages, you could create a Math.Financial.Mortgage module. For now though, let's keep the Math module simple:

```
defmodule Math do
  # ...
end
```

A function inside a module is defined with `def`, followed by the function name and any arguments it accepts. For an `add` function, you accept two arguments and assign them the variable names of `a` and `b`. Because Elixir implicitly returns the result of the last executed line of a function, you don't have to explicitly return the value of adding `a` and `b`.

```
def add(a, b) do
  a + b
end
```

A shorthand version of the function definition can be helpful when your function does one thing or is a one-liner. The differences between the multiline and one-line function definitions are small: there's an additional comma (`,`) after the argument collection and a colon (`:`) after `do`. Also note the lack of `end`:

```
def subtract(a, b), do: a - b
```

Functions can take any number of arguments, and if they take none, the parentheses can be omitted entirely.

```
def one, do: 1
```

Elixir allows you to define multiple functions with the same name, so how does it know which one to execute? It does pattern matching on the function signatures and uses the first one that matches. We'll go deeper into pattern matching later in this chapter, but for now, think of it as looking for the function signature. A function signature is its name and the number of arguments it accepts (or it's *arity*).

In the following listing, you have one `even_numbers` function that expects two arguments and another that accepts zero or one arguments—functions can have default argument values, specified by the `\\` characters. You can call `even_numbers` with a single number and have it find even numbers from 0 to the provided number, or you can call it with no arguments and have it default to returning even numbers from 0 to 10. Stylistically, functions with the same name are grouped together.

Listing 2.12 Demonstrating function overloading

```
defmodule Math do
  def even_numbers(min, max) do
    Enum.filter(min..max, fn(x) -> rem(x, 2) == 0 end)
  end
  def even_numbers(max \\ 10) do
    even_numbers(0, max)
  end
end
```

min..max creates a range of integers from min to max. rem/2 returns the remainder of dividing the first argument by the second.

You can call even_numbers/2 inside the module it was defined in without using the module name.

Functions inside a module can call other functions inside the same module without using the module prefix. If there's ever a cause for confusion over function names, you can use the full name of the function (`Math.even_numbers`) instead.

Functions that you need to call internally but that you don't want exposed to the outside world, can be defined as *private*. You do this by using `defp` instead of `def` when defining the function.

```
defp internal_calculation(x), do: 42 + x
```

The following listing shows what our group of functions that deal with simple calculations might look like now.

Listing 2.13 Example Math module

```
defmodule Math do
  def add(a, b) do
    a + b
  end

  def subtract(a, b), do: a - b

  def one, do: 1

  def even_numbers(min, max) do
    Enum.filter(min..max, fn(x) -> rem(x, 2) == 0 end)
  end
  def even_numbers(max \\ 10) do
    even_numbers(0, max)
  end

  defp internal_calculation(x), do: 42 + x
end
```

Multiline function definition

Single-line function definition

Function overloading

Private function definition

Let's look at a few more points about modules before we move on.

2.1.6 alias

If you have a module name that's deeply namespaced and you don't want to type its long name every time, you can *alias* it, and then use only the last portion of the module name.

```
defmodule MyMortgage do
  alias Math.Financial.Mortgage

  def amount(args), do: Mortgage.calculate_amount(args)
end
```

Figure 2.7 illustrates what `alias` and `import` (covered next) do inside your module.

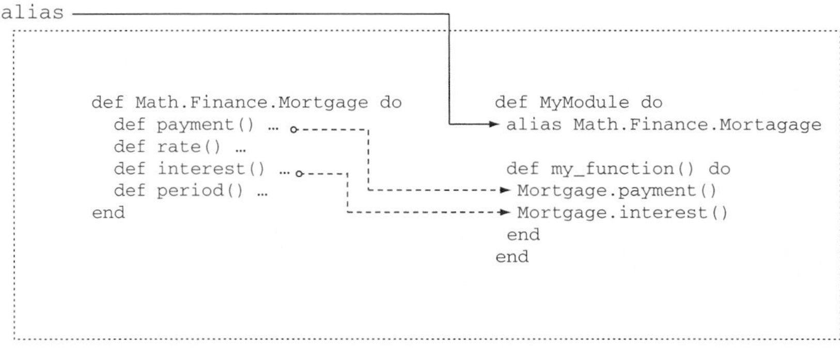

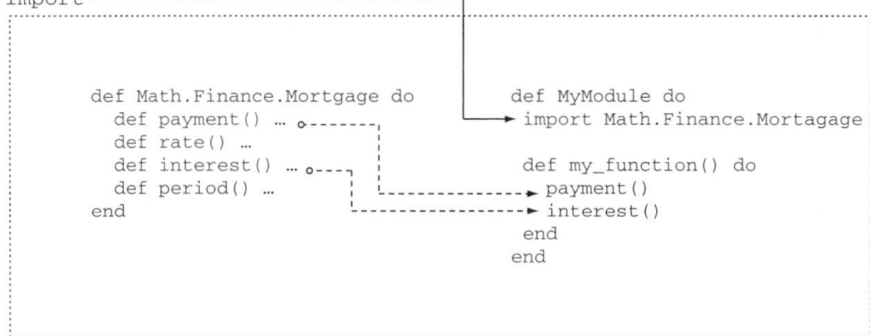

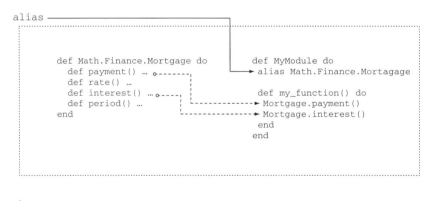

Figure 2.7 `alias` **allows you to shorten the module name, whereas** `import` **allows you to forego it entirely.**

2.1.7 import

You can further reduce typing and *import* the functions of a module into your module (as shown in listing 2.14). That will allow them to be called without prepending the module name. If you `import` a module without any arguments, *all* the public functions will be available. Alternatively, you can limit which functions are brought in by providing an `only` argument and a list of functions and their arity that you'd like to import. The following listing imports a fictional `Math.Financial.Interest.rate/1` function. Once the functions are imported, you can call them without using their full module names.

Listing 2.14 Importing functions from external modules

```
defmodule MyMortgage do
  import Math.Financial.Mortgage # contains calculate_amount/1
  import Math.Financial.Interest, only: [rate: 1]

  def amount(args), do: calculate_amount(args)

  def interest_rate(args), do: rate(args)
end
```

2.2 Other idiomatic Elixir language features

Some of the discussion so far has been somewhat dry, but it has set the stage for your use of Elixir in the context of Phoenix. We've covered most of the basics, but there are some other cool, idiomatic, and useful Elixir features that you'll be using extensively. Let's take a look at those.

2.2.1 The pipe operator

One of my favorite things about the Elixir language syntax is the pipe operator (`|>`) and how it can clarify the flow of data from one function to another. When used correctly, it will make you wish every other language could and would implement it (and some are working on that).

The pipe operator looks benign and unassuming, but it's very powerful. It allows you to pass one value into a function call as the first argument of that function call. With the pipe operator, the following two calls do the same thing:

```
Module.function(first_argument, second_argument)

first_argument |> Module.function(second_argument)
```

Why is that helpful? Why not just pass the value in directly as the first argument? Let's look back at the deli from earlier in the chapter.

Listing 2.15 Deli pseudocode

```
for each order received:
  plate = []
  plate = add_ingredient.(plate, :bread)
  plate = add_ingredient.(plate, :mustard)
  plate = add_ingredient.(plate, :turkey)
  plate = add_ingredient.(plate, :cheese)
  plate = add_ingredient.(plate, :lettuce)
  plate = add_ingredient.(plate, :tomato)
  plate = add_ingredient.(plate, :bread)
  return plate
end
```

Look at all that rebinding of plate. Pretty ugly and repetitive, isn't it? But notice how you wrote the add_ingredient/2 function: the first argument is expecting the current state of plate. Not only that, the function returns the *new* state of plate after adding ingredient. You can use the pipe operator to clean up this code greatly.

Listing 2.16 Deli pseudocode with the pipe operator

```
for each order received:
  new_plate()                          <-- new_plate sets up and
  |> add_ingredient.(:bread)               returns a new, empty plate.
  |> add_ingredient.(:mustard)
  |> add_ingredient.(:turkey)
  |> add_ingredient.(:cheese)
  |> add_ingredient.(:lettuce)
  |> add_ingredient.(:tomato)
  |> add_ingredient.(:bread)
end
```

The plate variable is now gone! You bound no variables in the process of creating the sandwich. Instead, you take the result of one function and let the next function use it, passing the state of the plate down through the assembly instructions for the sandwich. Finally, because add_ingredient/2 returns the state of the new plate, that means you implicitly return the plate to the customer.

When writing functions, it's normally worth the extra time to consider exactly how you want the data in your application to flow. With that in mind, you can arrange the functions as you've done here so that your Elixir code can read just like assembly instructions.

Get to know and love the pipe operator, because you'll see it all over the place in Elixir, and you'll be using it a lot. And believe me, you *will* love it.

2.2.2 Pattern matching

Think back on your personal experience with sandwiches. How do you recognize a sandwich? By the way it smells? Perhaps. By the way it sounds? Probably not. By the way it looks? Most likely, yes. Typically, sandwiches are made up of smaller building blocks, such as bread and meat, as in the deli examples. But you won't typically recognize a sandwich by individually identifying all the smaller parts—normally you'll recognize the *pattern* of those smaller objects that create a sandwich. That's because your brain is wired to recognize patterns. Elixir is also wired to recognize patterns.

Suppose I want to verify that an object I've been given is a cheese sandwich. Someone hands it to me and says, "Here's a cheese sandwich," but I'm not sure if I can trust them. I'd use what I know about cheese sandwiches and use pattern recognition. Is it bread, cheese, and then bread again? If so, I've verified the pattern.

The same can be done with Elixir:

```
iex> cheese_sandwich = [:bread, :cheese, :bread]
[:bread, :cheese, :bread]
```

```
iex> [:bread, :cheese, :bread] = cheese_sandwich
[:bread, :cheese, :bread]
```

The first call in the preceding example sets up the variable with a list of atoms. The second call does the pattern check. The fact that I don't receive an error on the second IEx call verifies that the pattern I told it to expect on the left side of the = sign is indeed the pattern on the right.

What would have happened if the patterns were different?

```
iex> [:bread, :cheese, :tomato, :bread] = cheese_sandwich
** (MatchError) no match of right hand side value: [:bread, :cheese, :bread]
```

I'd get a `MatchError`, which tells me that the pattern I told it to expect (with `:tomato`) is not what's on the right side. This works for any Elixir type. Figure 2.8 illustrates how pattern matching works with this sandwich example.

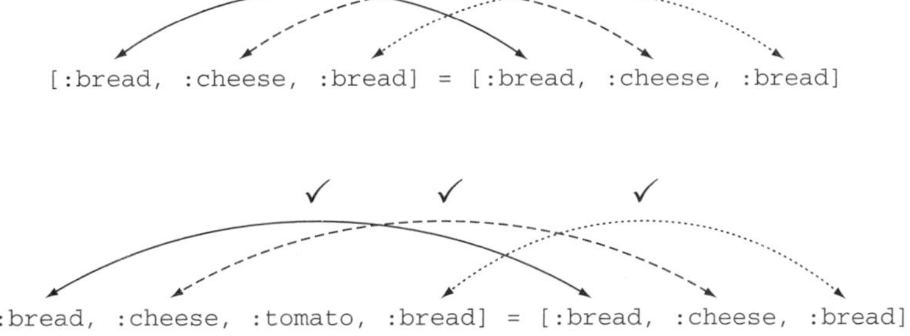

Figure 2.8 Pattern matching compares the two sides of a call. If everything matches on both sides of the equal sign (=), it's a successful match. If one side is different from the other, as in the bottom example, an error will be returned.

Beyond simple pattern verification with explicit values, you can give it a pattern with variable placeholders, and bind the unknown values to those placeholders. Suppose I knew this strange sandwich-giver gave me *something* between two pieces of bread, but I wasn't sure what it was. I can verify what I know about the pattern and bind the unknown to a variable to learn what's in between those slices of bread.

```
iex> unknown_sandwich = [:bread, :olive_loaf, :bread]
iex> [:bread, mystery_meat, :bread] = unknown_sandwich
[:bread, :olive_loaf, :bread]
iex> mystery_meat
:olive_loaf
```

I can use that `mystery_meat` variable later in my code (perhaps to decide whether or not to actually eat the strange sandwich).

As previously mentioned, one pattern you'll see a lot in Elixir is `{:ok, value}` or `{:error, reason}`. This is an idiomatic pattern, because it's easy to match on in your code, to decide whether to continue the operation or present an error to the user. Take, for example, the `Map.fetch/2` function. It takes a map and a key and, if it finds that key in the given map, it will return that key's value as `{:ok, value}`. If the given map doesn't have the provided key, it will return `:error`.

I can use that knowledge to search my memory to see if the mystery meat is something I'll eat. But first, let's check to make sure things are working as expected. I love turkey sandwiches, so let's verify that `:turkey` is `true` in the `edible_meats` map:

```
iex> edible_meats = %{turkey: true, chicken: true, ham: false, olive_loaf:
     false}
iex> {:ok, edible} = Map.fetch(edible_meats, :turkey)
{:ok, true}
iex> edible
true
```

I'll eat the turkey! Now let's use `mystery_meat`, which has the value of `:olive_loaf`, to see if I'll eat that:

```
iex> {:ok, edible} = Map.fetch(edible_meats, mystery_meat)
{:ok, false}
iex> edible
false
```

Checking the edible_meats map for the :olive_loaf key

So I'll pass on the olive loaf sandwich. But what happens when I'm given a meat I've never encountered—one for which I have no listing in my map? I'd expect to get an error, right?

```
iex> {:ok, edible} = Map.fetch(edible_meats, :head_cheese)
** (MatchError) no match of right hand side value: :error
```

My pattern match failed because I expected `{:ok, value}` but instead got `:error`. Awesome! Elixir can tell you when an unexpected pattern is used.

Let's write a little function using pattern matching that will help me decide whether I'll eat a mystery sandwich. Here's how I'll make my decision (also illustrated in figure 2.9). When I receive a sandwich, I'll do the following:

1. Set up a map of acceptable meats.
2. Use pattern matching to pull the mystery meat out of the list. (Yes, this means that this function only works if there's exactly one thing between two slices of bread. You can expand on this if you'd like, but we'll keep it simple for now.)
3. See if that meat is in my list of known meats.
4. If it is, and it's edible, I'll return "Yes, please!"
5. If it's in my list of known meats and I don't like that particular meat, I'll return "No thanks."

6 If I get an `:error`, which means the meat isn't in my list of known meats, I'll return "I don't know what this is!"

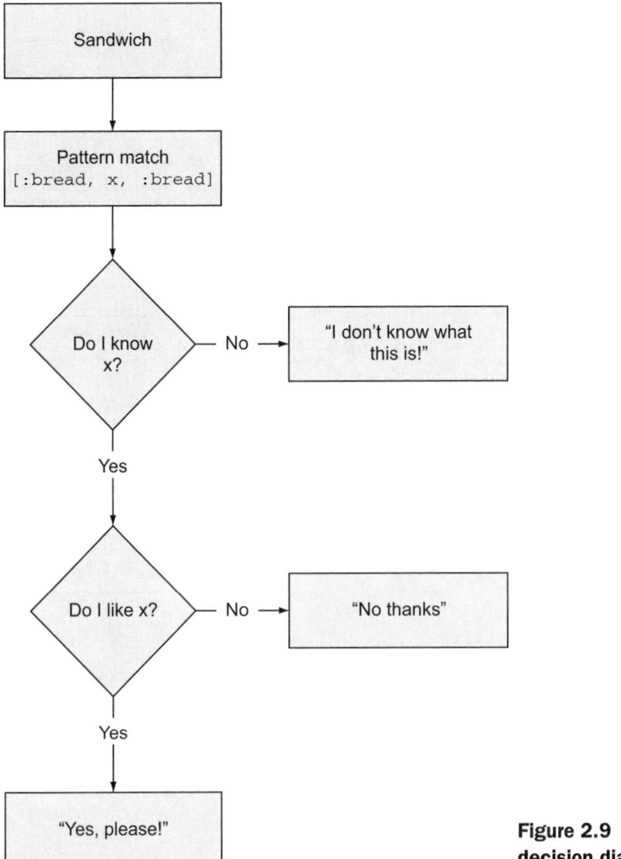

Figure 2.9 `Sandwich.accept?/1` **decision diagram**

The following listing shows the function.

Listing 2.17 Should you eat the mystery sandwich?

```
defmodule Sandwich do
  def accept?(sandwich) do
    edible_meats = %{turkey: true, ham: false, chicken: true, olive_loaf:
     false}
    [:bread, mystery_meat, :bread] = sandwich

    case Map.fetch(edible_meats, mystery_meat) do
      {:ok, edible} ->
        if edible, do: "Yes, please!", else: "No thanks."
      :error ->
        "I don't know what this is!"
```

```
    end
  end
end
```

Let's use the new function:

```
iex> Sandwich.accept?( [:bread, :turkey, :bread] )
"Yes, please!"
iex> Sandwich.accept?( [:bread, :olive_loaf, :bread] )
"No thanks."
iex> Sandwich.accept?( [:bread, :head_cheese, :bread] )
"I don't know what this is!"
```

You'll often reach for the case statement to match a variety of expected results in order to correctly respond to the result of a function.

There will be times when you won't know what value will be in a given pattern, and you want to bind it but then use the value of that variable in a future binding. In the pattern matching we've looked at so far, that won't quite work:

```
iex(1)> [:bread, mystery_meat, :bread] = [:bread, :turkey, :bread]
iex(2)> mystery_meat
:turkey

iex(3)> [:bread, mystery_meat, :bread] = [:bread, :ham, :bread]
iex(4)> mystery_meat
:ham
```

You might have expected an error in call 3 because you wanted to ensure you got the same sandwich twice, no matter what the mystery_meat was. Instead, you rebound mystery_meat to :ham. How can you pin the value of a variable in pattern matching like this?

You can use the pin operator (^)! With it, you can pin the value in a pattern match so that you can match on that variable's value instead of rebinding it with the right-side value.

```
iex(1)> [:bread, mystery_meat, :bread] = [:bread, :turkey, :bread]
iex(2)> mystery_meat
:turkey

iex(3)> [:bread, ^mystery_meat, :bread] = [:bread, :ham, :bread]
** (MatchError) no match of right hand side value: [:bread, :ham, :bread]
iex(4)> mystery_meat
:turkey
```

This time, because you pinned the variable ^mystery_meat, you didn't rebind it but instead attempted to match on its value. Because the right side of the pattern match didn't match the left, you got a MatchError. Finally, you verify that your mystery_meat variable wasn't rebound to a value of :ham and instead retains its original :turkey value.

Pattern-matching maps can be fun and very code-efficient. In the following example, you pattern-match the key of :bass from the band variable, which contains a map of band member names. If you find a :bass key, you ask Elixir to bind the value of that key to the variable of `name`. Finally, you verify that you indeed now have `"Adam"` as the value of `name` straight from the `band` map.

```
iex(7)> band = %{vocals: "Paul", guitar: "Dave", bass: "Adam", drums: "Larry"}
iex(8)> %{bass: name} = band
iex(9)> name
"Adam"
```

Sometimes you'll want to make sure a pattern is matched, but you don't really care about storing a value for later use, nor do you care even which value is in a particular position. For example, you've used the `Map.fetch/2` function often in this chapter, and you'll remember that it returns `{:ok, value}` on a successful match. For the times when you don't want to store that value, you can use the underscore (_) character to let Elixir know you expect something in that position, but you don't really care what.

```
iex(1)> {:ok, _} = Map.fetch(%{b: 2}, :b)
{:ok, 2}
iex(2)> {_, _} = Map.fetch(%{c: 3}, :c)
{:ok, 3}
```

You can also prepend variable names with an underscore (_) to give the value an identifier but also let Elixir know that you don't expect to use that variable's value anywhere in your code.

```
iex(1)> {:ok, _name} = Map.fetch(%{vocals: "Paul"}, :vocals)
```

Pattern matching is not only incredibly useful and fun, it's used quite often in Elixir code. You'll also write a number of functions that use pattern matching in Phoenix. Take some time to play with pattern matching in Elixir.

2.2.3 Using IEx.Helpers.v/1

Even though I've used IEx for quite a while now, I have times when I've forgotten to capture the output of a long command, or I want to go back in my history to a different function's result. IEx provides a nice helper function named `v` to help you out. You may have noticed the number following the `iex` in your IEx sessions (for example, `iex(3)>`). This is when those numbers will change from being visual noise to being potentially very helpful.

When it's called without an argument, (`v()`), `v/1` will return the last result again. When passed an argument, (`v(3)`), `v/1` will return the result of the numbered past IEx expression (in this example's case, `3`; modify your call accordingly). Let's take a look at some examples:

```
iex(1)> 1 + 5
6

iex(2)> six = v()        <-- Uses v() to return the value of the previous result
6
```

```
iex(3)> six + 3000
3006

iex(4)> (0.0056283568467 * 100_000) |> round()
563

iex(5)> v() + v(3)
3569
```

Uses v(3) to return the result of a specific previous expression

You won't be using this helper function at all in your modules, but it can be incredibly useful as you're learning or experimenting with Elixir in an IEx session, or even when you're debugging your code, trying to figure out exactly how things work.

If you'd like to dive deeper into learning Elixir, several great resources are listed in appendix B.

Summary

- You can use IEx to practice, experiment, and learn Elixir in an interactive REPL. This is an easy way to get to know the basics of the language.
- Ask for help from Elixir itself by using the `h/1` IEx helper function.
- Create named functions inside a module. Anonymous functions can be bound to a variable outside of a module for later use.
- Use modules to keep your code together in sensible groupings of functions.
- Take advantage of Elixir's pipe operator (`|>`). It's incredibly useful and can make your code read more like a sentence describing how your data will be transformed from one function through the next.
- Utilize pattern matching in your code to quickly verify that a return value is in a pattern you expect, and to grab desired data directly from the structure of the return value. Pattern matching is also used by Elixir to determine which function to execute when multiple function definitions have the same name. The first one to match gets executed.

3 A little Phoenix overview

This chapter covers

- What Phoenix is and how it relates to Elixir
- The flow of a web request through Phoenix's structure
- An overview of the different modules you'll create in this book
- The transformation of data as it flows from one place to the next
- The basic structure of a blogging application built on top of Phoenix

In the last chapter, you learned some of the basics of the Elixir programming language. If it was your first experience with the language, I hope you spent some time in an IEx session to play with different concepts and see how things work. We'll be looking at and writing a lot of Elixir from this point on.

In this chapter, we'll look at an example Phoenix application—one that isn't too complex and, to be honest, doesn't really *do* all that much. But we'll look at it from a bird's-eye view, so we don't want complexity. We just want to look at the basics of how a Phoenix application is pieced together. In later chapters, you'll build a much more complex web application from the ground up, and we'll dive deeper into the topics introduced here.

The application is a simple blog engine—one that doesn't look pretty but allows the owner to create and edit blog posts, and enables a visitor to read those posts and add comments on those posts. Figure 3.1 shows what the blog looks like and provides a small breakdown of its parts. You won't be able to jump in and build your own Phoenix application after reading this chapter, but you'll have a better understanding of what you'll build in future chapters.

If you don't understand all the code in this chapter, that's fine. What I hope you get out of this chapter is a basic understanding of the different pieces of a Phoenix application and how they all fit together to take a visitor's web request from an initial server request to a rendered page. Later chapters will go into each area in more detail as you build a more useful application.

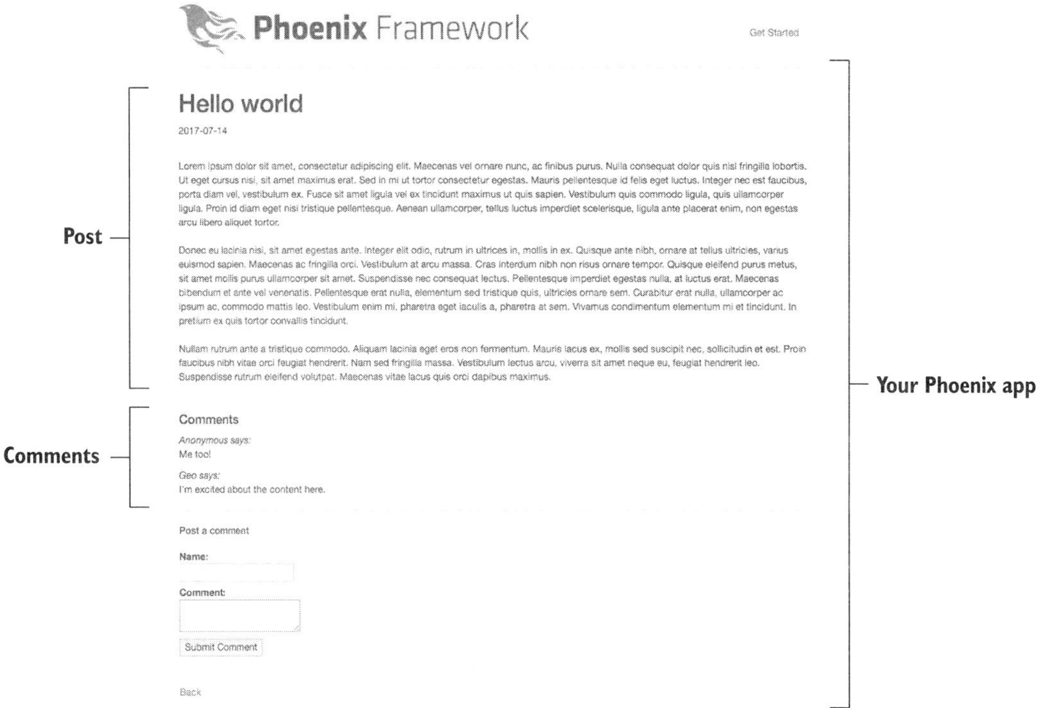

Figure 3.1 The example in this chapter is a simple blogging application.

The name of your application will be "Blog." Really creative, huh? It's important that you know the name of the application, because almost every module defined in the application will have `Blog` prepended to the name, which makes it very easy to namespace. Namespacing not only helps you keep track of your code, but it provides an easy way to merge two applications in the future or call one application from another. It also allows for nice mental and physical code organization.

3.1 Follow the data

For our dive into Phoenix, you'll follow the flow of a web request. As you'll see in the coming sections, you'll take information (data) from a user request and pipe it from one function to another until you have what you need to form and deliver a response. In view of this, following the flow of data makes for a good starting point for discovering Phoenix's various parts.

3.1.1 The basics of a web request

Before we get into the specifics of how Phoenix handles a web request, let's take a quick, shallow dive into the details of a web request. Let's look at an example web request from a web browser such as Chrome, Firefox, or Safari.

When you type in the URL of a website (such as www.phoenixinaction.com), the request first goes to a DNS server to translate the human-readable URL to a computer-readable IP address, which is the ultimate location of the website. It's like looking in an old telephone book to translate the name *Geoffrey Lessel* into my phone number. You need to do the same with www.phoenixinaction.com.

Once you have the IP address (which looks like xxx.xxx.xxx.xxx, where "x" is an integer from 0 to 9), the browser then formats your request into an HTTP request message with details about how it would like to receive data back and what kind of data it will accept. That request message ends up on a server somewhere in the world, and it interprets the message. It then either responds with its own message stating it can't or won't respond to that request, or it returns a specific file (such as a JPG or PDF file) or the result of running a program on the server.

In the case of Phoenix, the server will run a program and forward the information about the original request. Phoenix will then execute its code and will respond to the request appropriately.

NOTE Phoenix runs on an Erlang web server known as Cowboy. In our interactions with Phoenix, that fact won't really ever come into play, so don't worry about remembering it or noting it as important. But it's nice to know.

Figure 3.2 shows how your Phoenix application will handle a web request to your blog. Right now, the figure just shows an empty box where Phoenix comes into play. In each section of this chapter, you'll uncover an additional step in the Phoenix process, taking

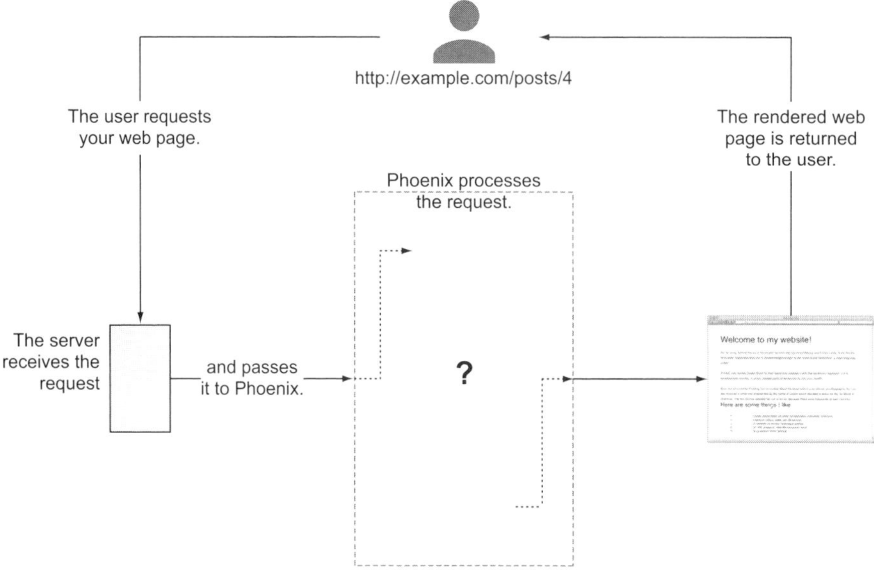
http://example.com/posts/4
The user requests your web page.
The rendered web page is returned to the user.
Phoenix processes the request.
The server receives the request
and passes it to Phoenix.
?
Welcome to my website!

Figure 3.2 The steps a request takes from the user, through your Phoenix application, back to the user

the request from the previous step. You'll slowly reveal what's inside that Phoenix-shaped box between the point when a user request hits your server and when you send the user back the HTML required to render a web page.

The code we'll be reviewing is from an already-built application. A surprising amount of it is unchanged from the code that Phoenix automatically supplies when you generate a new application, but I added some to create the blog-like features you need. All of the code for this simple blog application can be found at www.phoenixin-action.com/code/blog.

3.1.2 Endpoint

When a request comes in to the website, Cowboy is the server that handles it. You don't need to know anything about Cowboy except that it's what hands the request to Phoenix. After the Cowboy server does its thing, your journey in Phoenix begins.

The first piece of Phoenix code that handles this request is the `Endpoint` module. Take a look at figure 3.3 to see an illustration of this step.

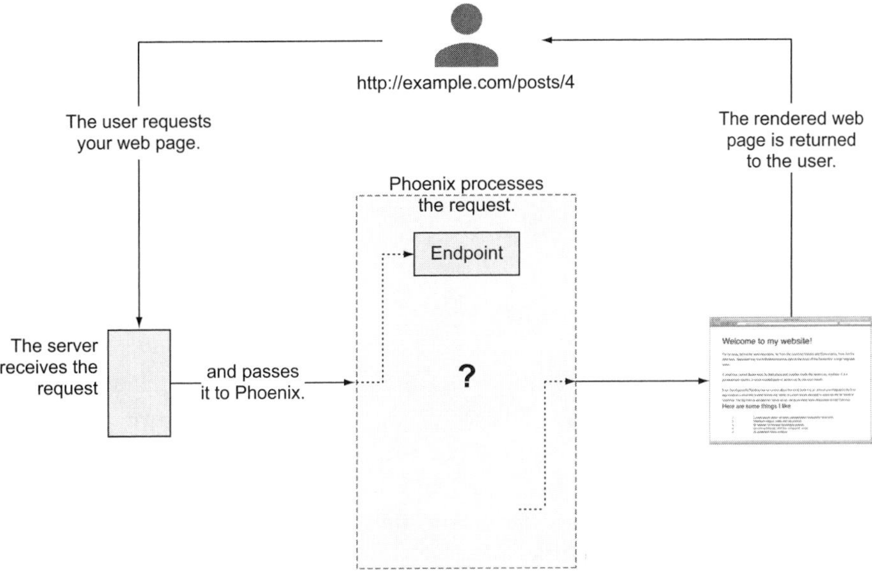
http://example.com/posts/4
The user requests your web page.
The rendered web page is returned to the user.
Phoenix processes the request.
Endpoint
The server receives the request
and passes it to Phoenix.
?
Welcome to my website!
Here are some things I like

Figure 3.3 The endpoint is where your Phoenix journey begins.

All the code in the `BlogWeb.Endpoint` module in the following listing was automatically generated when I first created the Phoenix application.

Listing 3.1 The `Blog.Web` module (lib/blog_web/endpoint.ex), comments removed

```
defmodule BlogWeb.Endpoint do
  use Phoenix.Endpoint, otp_app: :blog

  socket "/socket", BlogWeb.UserSocket, websocket: true, longpoll: false

  plug Plug.Static,
    at: "/", from: :blog, gzip: false,
    only: ~w(css fonts images js favicon.ico robots.txt)

  if code_reloading? do
    socket "/phoenix/live_reload/socket", Phoenix.LiveReloader.Socket
    plug Phoenix.LiveReloader
    plug Phoenix.CodeReloader
  end

  plug Plug.RequestId
  plug Plug.Logger

  plug Plug.Parsers,
    parsers: [:urlencoded, :multipart, :json],
```

Sets up the endpoint with shareable code from Phoenix.Endpoint

The majority of the endpoint is made up of plugs.

```
    pass: ["*/*"],
    json_decoder: Phoenix.json_library()

  plug Plug.MethodOverride
  plug Plug.Head

  plug Plug.Session,
    store: :cookie,
    key: "_blog_key",
    signing_salt: "JN+IDg+a"

  plug BlogWeb.Router
end
```

Almost everything you see in the preceding listing begins with `plug`. `plug` is a macro that sets up a `Plug`, which simply receives a connection and returns a connection (see the documentation at https://hexdocs.pm/plug/readme.html). Although we didn't cover it in chapter 2, a macro is essentially a way to write code that writes code. In this example, each `plug ...` line adds a specified `Plug` to the pipeline that the data from a request flows through. The flow goes from the top to the bottom of the file, and even without knowing what each of these plugs do, you can take a reasonable guess from their module names. You'll eventually write your own Plug module, so don't worry too much about the details of `Plug` for now.

The first plug you encounter is `Plug.Static`:

```
plug Plug.Static,
  at: "/", from: :blog, gzip: false,
  only: ~w(css fonts images js favicon.ico robots.txt)
```

Its job is to serve up static files in your application. It specifies that you'd like to serve them at /, not compress them, and serve only files in the css, fonts, images, and js directories, as well as the specific files favicon.ico and robots.txt.

Even though no pipe operator (|>) is explicitly shown in the `Blog.Web` module (listing 3.1), one of the cool things about `Plug` is that it basically pipes one result into the next, just like the pipe operator does.

```
if code_reloading? do
  socket "/phoenix/live_reload/socket", Phoenix.LiveReloader.Socket
  plug Phoenix.LiveReloader
  plug Phoenix.CodeReloader
end
```

Figure 3.4 illustrates the fact that each plug has the opportunity to affect the request data as it passes through.

After you have the static file-serving set up, you check to see if code reloading is enabled (which it is by default in development). If it is, you set up some live-code-reloading plugs. Live-code reloading listens for changes in your code and automatically reloads the current page in your browser to display the updated results. In my experience, it's not uncommon for the system to notice the change, send a reload request to

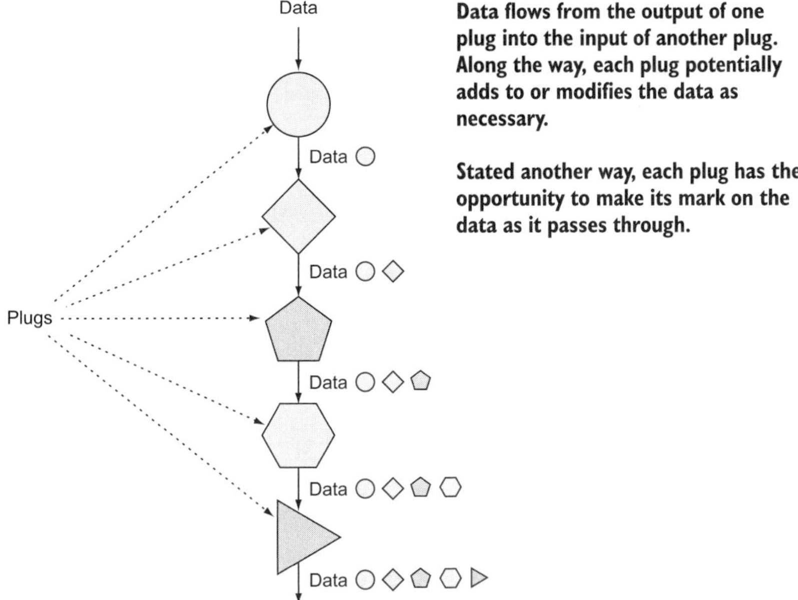
Data
Data
Data
Data
Data
Data
Plugs
Data flows from the output of one plug into the input of another plug. Along the way, each plug potentially adds to or modifies the data as necessary.
Stated another way, each plug has the opportunity to make its mark on the data as it passes through.

Figure 3.4 Every plug has an opportunity to make its mark on the data as it passes through.

the browser, reload all the data, and render it before I can even bring the browser window back into the foreground of my monitor. It's blazing fast.

Next, `Plug.RequestId` generates a unique ID for each request (https://hexdocs.pm/plug/Plug.RequestId.html).

The data transformation continues into `Plug.Logger`, which sets up logging for your application. The logger automatically logs information for each request made to the server, and you can explicitly log your own information as well.

From there, you move into `Plug.Parsers`, which sets up different file handlers. In listing 3.1 you tell Phoenix you'd like to decode your JSON data with the default library.

The next two plugs are mostly for Phoenix's benefit under the hood, and you don't need to concern yourself with them too much. The request data is sent into `Plug.MethodOverride`, which overrides some browser requests so that Phoenix can better handle them (https://hexdocs.pm/plug/Plug.MethodOverride.html) That's then fed into the `Plug.Head` plug, which simply converts `HEAD` requests to `GET` requests (https://hexdocs.pm/plug/Plug.Head.html).

Next, `Plug.Session` sets up a session, which will handle your session data, such as cookies, used for serving up dynamic web pages that are customized for each user. Finally, your data is transferred to the `BlogWeb.Router` plug, which ultimately routes the request to the correct handler within the application (we'll look at that next).

One thing you'll notice about each of these plugs is that they're small, and they're focused on relatively small tasks. There's a whole plug dedicated to generating a unique ID—that's pretty focused, and it's a good pattern to follow. When you write a plug, you'll attempt to do the same: keep the scope small and focused.

3.1.3 Router

The last plug the `Endpoint` module sends the request data through is `BlogWeb.Router`. This reveals the next step inside your Phoenix box (figure 3.5).

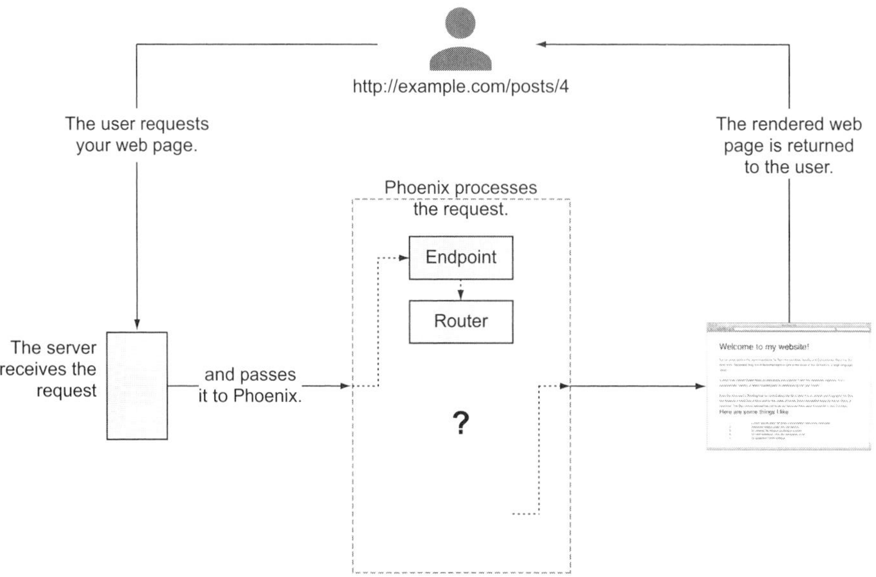
http://example.com/posts/4
The user requests your web page.
The rendered web page is returned to the user.
Phoenix processes the request.
Endpoint
Router
The server receives the request
and passes it to Phoenix.
?
Welcome to my website!
Here are some things I like

Figure 3.5 After the `Endpoint` module finishes setting up the request, it passes the request to the `Router` module.

The `Router`'s job is to examine the user request, along with any additional data the `Endpoint` added along the way, and decide which part of the application should respond next. It does that by examining the path the user requested (in this particular case, you assume the user requested the URL http://example.com/posts/4), piping that request through appropriate pipelines, and then sending it on to the appropriate handler.

Figure 3.6 breaks down how the router might decide where to send a request, and the following listing shows the code in the `Router` module.

Listing 3.2 The `BlogWeb.Router` module (lib/blog_web/router.ex)

```
defmodule BlogWeb.Router do
  use BlogWeb, :router

  pipeline :browser do
    plug :accepts, ["html"]
    plug :fetch_session
```

Each pipeline sets up plugs that define functions for different kinds of requests.

```
    plug :fetch_flash
    plug :protect_from_forgery
    plug :put_secure_browser_headers
  end

  pipeline :api do
    plug :accepts, ["json"]
  end

  scope "/", BlogWeb do
    pipe_through :browser

    get "/", PageController, :index
    resources "/posts", PostController do
      resources "/comments", CommentController, only: [:create]
    end
  end

  scope "/api", BlogWeb.API do
    pipe_through :api

    resources "/posts", PostController, only: [:index, :show]
  end
end
```

Scopes group-related request paths and allows namespacing

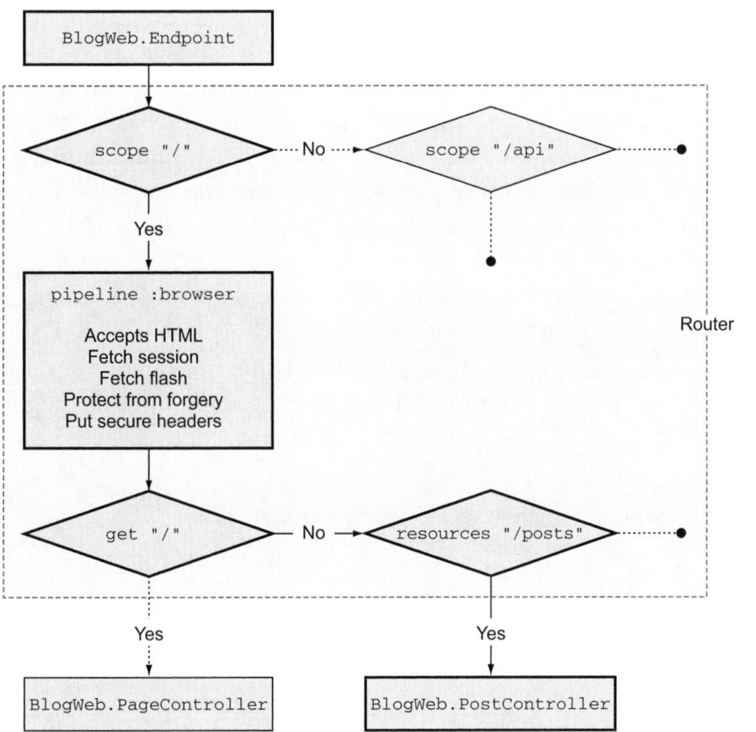

Figure 3.6 The `Router` module decides which controller to send the request to.

We'll take a closer look at each section next. Within the `Router` module, you can see that you again have a lot of `plug` statements. But these are different in one major aspect: these are being sent an atom of a function name as their argument, rather than a module name like in `Endpoint`. We'll go into more detail about the differences when you create your own plugs later in the book. For now, you can surmise from the names of the functions what each does:

```
pipeline :browser do
  plug :accepts, ["html"]
  plug :fetch_session
  plug :fetch_flash
  plug :protect_from_forgery
  plug :put_secure_browser_headers
end
```

This pipeline groups plugs for a typical browser request.

```
pipeline :api do
  plug :accepts, ["json"]
end
```

This pipeline groups plugs for a typical API request.

The plugs themselves are grouped together into what's known as a *pipeline*. A pipeline is just a group of plugs that are used for a particular purpose. In this router, you have two different pipelines: one for a typical browser request, and one for a typical API request.

In the `browser` pipeline, you accept `"html"` requests, getting the session and the flash (which stores temporary messages for the user, such as success, info, or warning messages); you set up forgery protection for your forms; and you put secure browser headers into the data. In the `api` pipeline, you only accept `"json"` requests. This makes sense—why get the flash and set up form forgery protection when a typical API request doesn't utilize either of those features? Note that these pipelines are set up by default when you create a new Phoenix application—these pipelines haven't changed at all from the defaults.

This is a good example of the explicitness of Elixir and Phoenix. You can see in these pipelines exactly what's included or excluded from each type of request. Why waste the processing power and potential database calls where those results are never used?

You now have the pipelines set up, but you don't use them until you get into the `scope` blocks.

```
scope "/", BlogWeb do
  pipe_through :browser # Use the default browser stack

  get "/", PageController, :index
  resources "/posts", PostController do
    resources "/comments", CommentController, only: [:create]
  end
end
```

The first scope, `scope "/"`, listens for requests that are at the root level of the web page (`"/"`). Everything in its `do`/`end` block can be thought of as children of that root path, so the top-level request of http://example.com/ would be in this block. You first tell Phoenix that you want to pipe these requests through the `:browser` pipeline you set up previously. From there, if it's a `GET` request to `/`, you send it to `BlogWeb.PageController` and the `index` function within that module.

> **NOTE** You'll notice that the preceding `get` line only contains a reference to `PageController`. Because this is nested under the `scope "/", BlogWeb` call, Phoenix knows to namespace the calls within it to be under `BlogWeb`—it will prepend that name before any module name.

Next, we'll move on to the `resources` call. That single call creates handlers for a full complement of RESTful actions (`index`, `new`, `create`, `show`, `edit`, `update`, and `delete`) at the `/posts` location. In other words, if a user visits http://example.com/posts, it will forward the request to the `BlogWeb.PostController`'s `index` function. All seven functions are forwarded to the `BlogWeb.PostController`.

Because this `resources` call has a `do`/`end` block, you can add more routes within it, so you'll add another resource for `/comments`, handled by the `BlogWeb.CommentController`. For this resource, you limit the RESTful actions to `create`.[1]

You could have written the following to achieve the same thing:

```
resources "/posts", PostController do
  post "/comments", CommentController, :create
end
```

If a user `POST`ed a form or other data to http://example.com/posts/1/comments, where `1` is the ID of the blog post they were commenting on, the `BlogWeb.CommentController` module would handle that request with the `BlogWeb.CommentController.create/2` function.

Besides `GET` and `POST` requests, Phoenix also has function definitions for setting up individual `PUT`, `PATCH`, and `DELETE` requests (among others—https://hexdocs.pm/phoenix/1.3.0/Phoenix.Router.html) with `put`, `patch`, and `delete` functions.

Finally, you've set up a scope for `/api`, which is handled under the `BlogWeb.API` namespace:

```
scope "/api", BlogWeb.API do
  pipe_through :api

  resources "/posts", PostController, only: [:index, :show]
end
```

Instead of piping the requests to `/api` through the `browser` pipeline, as you did for the / scope, you pipe this one through the `api` pipeline set up at the top of the file. Within your API, you have one resource, `posts`, and it's handled by `BlogWeb.API.PostController`. You've limited access to only the `index` and `show` functions.

---

[1] It's usually a good idea to limit the endpoints of your web application to the ones you're currently using. Leaving other ones open could lead to security concerns.

Notice how in both scopes you have a PostController. This might cause name collisions in other frameworks, but remember that the scopes prepend controller modules with their own names. In this case, you have a BlogWeb.PostController and a BlogWeb.API.PostController—two different controller modules for different types of requests for blog posts.

As with the other sections of this chapter, don't sweat the details. We'll look at the details of routes and resource in chapter 9.

If at any time you'd like to see what routes your router is creating, you can run mix phx.routes in the terminal from the root directory of your application. The following listing shows the output of your currently set-up routes.

Listing 3.3 mix phx.routes output

```
        page_path  GET     /                 BlogWeb.PageController :index
        post_path  GET     /posts            BlogWeb.PostController :index
        post_path  GET     /posts/:id/edit   BlogWeb.PostController :edit
        post_path  GET     /posts/new        BlogWeb.PostController :new
        post_path  GET     /posts/:id        BlogWeb.PostController :show
        post_path  POST    /posts            BlogWeb.PostController :create
        post_path  PATCH   /posts/:id        BlogWeb.PostController :update
                   PUT     /posts/:id        BlogWeb.PostController :update
        post_path  DELETE  /posts/:id        BlogWeb.PostController :delete
post_comment_path  POST    /posts/:post_id/comments
➥ BlogWeb.CommentController :create
        post_path  GET     /api/posts     BlogWeb.API.PostController :index
        post_path  GET     /api/posts/:id BlogWeb.API.PostController :show
```

You can see the route name (post_path, which we'll look at later), the method the browser uses to access the route (GET), the path of the route in the user request (/posts), and the names of the module and function that handle the request (BlogWeb.PostController; :index).

For our purposes in this chapter, we'll follow a GET request to /posts/:id. In a RESTful application, that will typically be a request to see the page for a blog post with the specified ID. You can see from listing 3.3 that this type of request is forwarded to the BlogWeb.PostController.show/2 function. Let's head into the controller next.

3.1.4 Controller

After the router handles the initial part of the request, it's passed on to the controller. This unveils the next step in your Phoenix black box (figure 3.7).

Guess what a Phoenix controller is? If you guessed another Plug, you win the grand prize! The entire purpose of a controller is to gather and set up all the data that the next steps will require, so that they can return an appropriate response to the requesting user. That may or may not include getting data from a database, an external API endpoint, or some sort of static file.

A controller's functions are also called actions. Because you're following a request to /posts/:id, you'll look specifically at the BlogWeb.PostController.show/2 function (the show action), which handles the request.

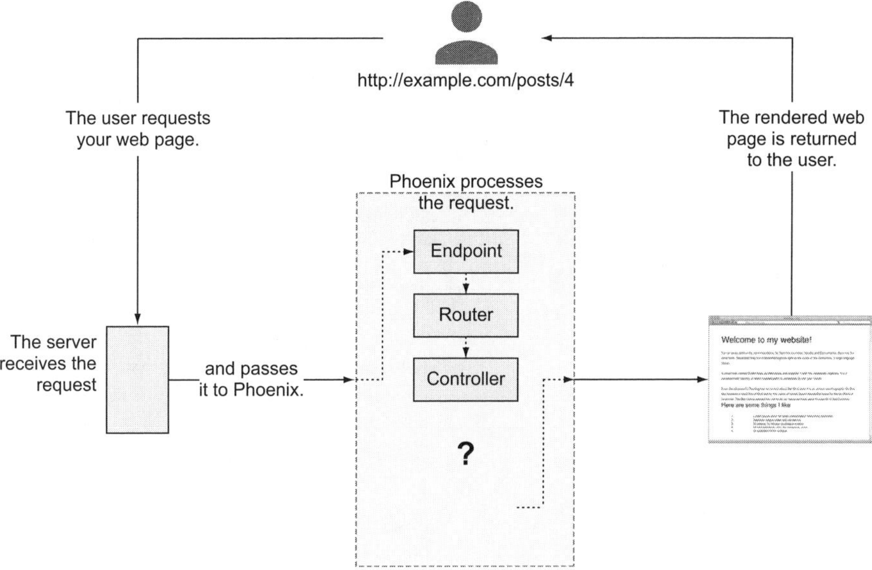

Figure 3.7 The router passes the request in to a controller.

As figure 3.8 shows, you want your function to gather specific information that will be passed on to the next step in the process. First, you want to get the post that was requested from the database, along with any associated comments. Next, you want to

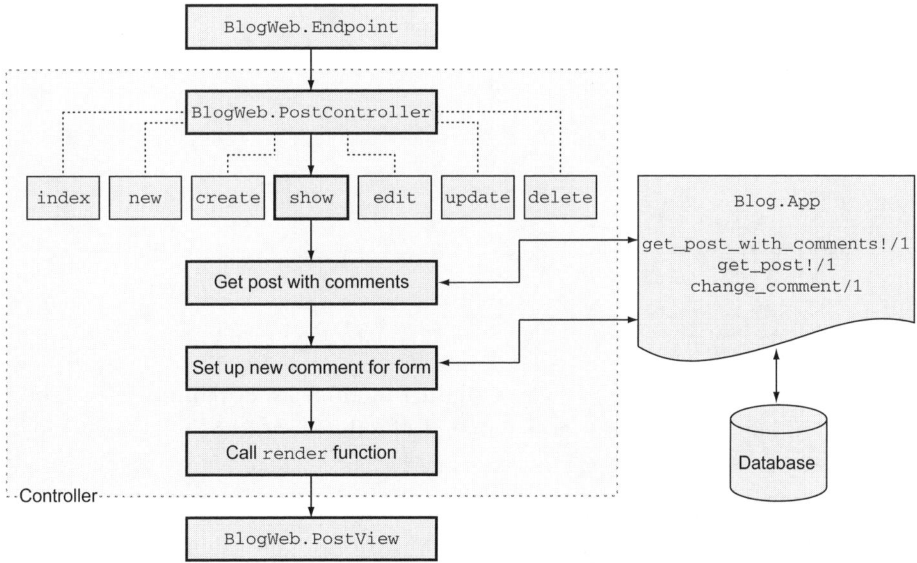

Figure 3.8 The controller makes sure everything is available for rendering the response.

set up the basic structure of a new comment to seed the comment form with, so you can track any changes the user makes in the form when submitting a comment. Then, you want to render the requested page and make sure you send the post and new comment along with it.

The following listing offers a truncated look at the controller code.

Listing 3.4 `BlogWeb.PostController` (lib/blog_web/controllers/post_controller.ex)

```
defmodule BlogWeb.PostController do
  use BlogWeb, :controller

  alias Blog.App          <-- Aliases Blog.App, so, for the rest of the
                              file, any call to App will go to Blog.App
  def index(conn, _params) do
    # ...
  end

  def new(conn, _params) do
    # ...
  end

  def create(conn, %{"post" => post_params}) do
    # ...
  end

  def show(conn, %{"id" => id}) do
    post = App.get_post_with_comments!(id)
    new_comment = App.change_comment(%App.Comment{})
    render(conn, "show.html", post: post, new_comment: new_comment)
  end

  def edit(conn, %{"id" => id}) do
    # ...
  end

  def update(conn, %{"id" => id, "post" => post_params}) do
    # ...
  end

  def delete(conn, %{"id" => id}) do
    # ...
  end
end
```

I've commented out the details of all the functions except for `show/2` so you can focus on that one function. But notice that all the different RESTful actions are accounted for: `index`, `new`, `create`, `show`, `edit`, `update`, and `delete`.

SHOW/2 FUNCTION DEFINITION DETAILS

The first detail we'll look at in `show/2` is the function definition: `def show(conn, %{"id" => id}) do`. You can see that two parameters, `conn` and a map, will be passed to `show`—every function in the controller expects the same by default. The map is a map of the request parameters from the user.

A large number of parameters could get passed into the request by the site visitor, but the only one you care about in `show` is the `id` param, so you'll use pattern matching to pull out the `id` from the parameter map. If you remember from our list of routes, /posts/:id is the path that gets you to this function. The ":id" portion of that route specifies that whatever you put into that position will be passed as the `id` in the params map.

Here are a few more examples of pattern matching the parameter map in the other functions:

- For `index/2` and `new/2`, the params passed in with the request have no bearing on the response, so you ignore the params map. You signify the fact that you're ignoring that data by prepending the variable name with an underscore (`_params`).
- For `create/2`, you want to capture all the data that's sent to you in the web form when an author creates a `Post` for your blog. You expect all that data to come in via a param named `post`, so you capture it in a `post_params` variable for later use (which you won't see here because I've commented it out).
- `edit/2` and `delete/2` are like `show/2` in that the only request parameters you care about are the `id` of the `Post` to work with.
- `update/2` requires both the `id` of the `Post` as well as the form data in the post portion of the params map. The `id` is required, so you know which `Post` to update with the rest of the data passed in.

SHOW/2 FUNCTION BODY DETAILS

The first line inside the show/2 function is

```
post = App.get_post_with_comments!(id)
```

The `App.get_post_with_comments!/1` function expects the `id` of a `Post` to retrieve. When you defined the `show/2` function, you pattern-matched the params and captured that `id`. You can now use that `id` to look up the specific `Post` associated with it. If the user requested `/posts/392`, then `392` would be passed to the function. If the user requested `/posts/my-best-day-ever`, then `my-best-day-ever` would be passed.

Because you aliased `App` near the top of the file, the full module name is `Blog.App`, and that's where you'll find the `get_post_with_comments!/1` function defined. The following listing offers a truncated look at that module.

Listing 3.5 The `Blog.App` module (lib/blog/app/app.ex)

```
defmodule Blog.App do
  import Ecto.Query, warn: false
  alias Blog.Repo

  alias Blog.App.{Post, Comment}
```

```
  # ...

  def get_post_with_comments!(id) do
    get_post!(id)
    |> Repo.preload(:comments)
  end

  def get_post!(id), do: Repo.get!(Post, id)

  # ...
end
```

You can define functions that provide you with exactly what you need in the controller in order to set up the view.

Short, one-line functions can be well suited to this function definition shorthand.

In the first few lines of the file, you set up the environment for the rest of the file by importing and aliasing as needed. Don't worry about the details of these lines for now. Just know that `Ecto` is the package Phoenix uses by default as a database adapter. It provides functions that make working with a database easier. `Repo` is your repository, and it uses `Ecto` to make those database calls. Again, we'll go deeper later.

In short, `get_post_with_comments!/1` fetches the `Post` from the database by looking it up using the `id` you passed it. It then preloads all the comments associated with it. If you want to display relevant comments, you need to let the database know ahead of time. Not only is this more explicit, but it reduces unneeded database calls further down the stack.

Let's move back up to the controller, shown earlier in listing 3.4:

```
def show(conn, %{"id" => id}) do
  post = App.get_post_with_comments!(id)
  new_comment = App.change_comment(%App.Comment{})
  render(conn, "show.html", post: post, new_comment: new_comment)
end
```

You take the `Post` fetched from the database, along with any associated comments, and store that in the `post` variable. On the next line, you set up a new `App.Comment`. This may look a bit confusing because you're using the function named `App.change_comment/1` to do so, but you're passing it a freshly initialized struct, so it's basically setting up what's known as a *changeset* for the new comment. You bind that fresh comment into the variable `new_comment`. A changeset allows you and the database to easily track changes and any validations needed on the comment. We'll go much deeper into changesets later in the book and use them extensively.

Once you have the `post` and `new_comment` variables set up, you head to the last line: `render(conn, "show.html", post: post, new_comment: new_comment)`. This calls the `render/3` function.

The first parameter you pass it is `conn`, which every function definition has and uses—it's the connection you've been passing from `Plug` to `Plug` up to now. It contains all the information about the request and connection that you've captured and set up to this point—through the endpoint and the router to here. It's officially a `Plug.Conn` struct, and the `render/3` function requires it.

The second parameter you pass `render/3` is the template you want rendered. In this case, you want to render the show.html template. (We'll look at templates shortly.)

Finally, you pass `render/3` a keyword list or map of the variables you'd like the show.html template to have access to. You want to pass in the `post` and `new_comment` data that you captured in the first two lines of your function. In your template, those will be accessible by the name of the key prepended with `@` (for example, `@post` for your `post` data).

Now that the `render/3` function has been called, you're finished with the controller. So what did the controller ultimately do? It took the request, captured any request parameters that it needed, set up variables, and forwarded the request and variables to the appropriate view.

3.1.5 Views

The next reveal in the Phoenix black box is the view (figure 3.9). The view is responsible for rendering templates and for setting up helper functions that you can use in those templates. The functions defined here are similar to decorators or presenters in other frameworks.

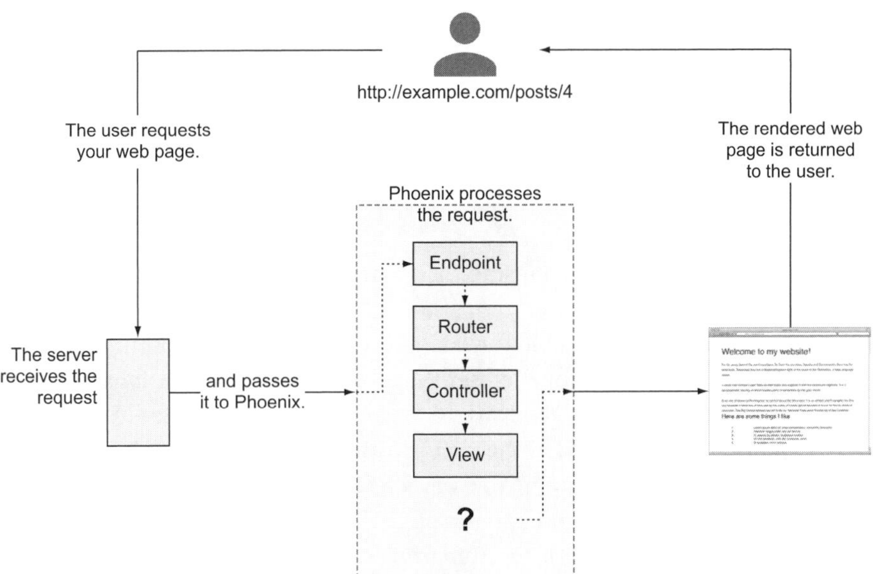
http://example.com/posts/4
The user requests your web page.
The rendered web page is returned to the user.
Phoenix processes the request.
Endpoint
Router
The server receives the request
and passes it to Phoenix.
Controller
View
?
Welcome to my website!

Figure 3.9 The controller calls functions defined in the view.

By default, the view module with the name corresponding to the controller module name is the one that's called. In your application, `BlogWeb.PostController` will render the show.html template specified in `BlogWeb.PostView`. Let's peek into your `BlogWeb.PostView` module.

Listing 3.6 `BlogWeb.PostView` (lib/blog_web/views/post_view.ex)

```
defmodule BlogWeb.PostView do
  use BlogWeb, :view

  def date(date_to_display), do: Date.to_string(date_to_display)
end
```

Most of the functions the template needs are brought in automatically.

Not a lot in there, is there? Most of the functionality is handled on the second line: `use BlogWeb, :view`. This brings a number of functions into the view, including `render/3`, which ultimately handles the request. You'll notice that you don't define your own `render` function—it's defined in that `use` call.

This is one of the strengths of Elixir—metaprogramming is still possible, even though it's a compiled language. The details of what actually happens when you `use` a module is beyond the scope of this book, but everything you need in order to render your templates is set up in that call.

You've also defined a lone function: `date/1`. This is used in the templates. You'll see its use in the next section. All it does is convert a passed-in Elixir date to a string representation of it. Any function you define in this view will be available to the templates rendered by it.

Because your controller passed in show.html as the template name in the `render/3` call, show.html is what the view will attempt to render. Let's look at the template.

3.1.6 Templates

We've come to the final step inside the Phoenix black box: the template. Figure 3.10 shows you the full picture.

The template is responsible for taking the data you've been building up and using that to render something for the user that requested it. It doesn't have to be HTML—it could just as easily be JSON, XML, CSV, and so on. In this case, you want to render good, old-fashioned HTML in the user's browser, as in figure 3.11.

Something very neat about the way Phoenix handles template files is that when Phoenix compiles, it turns every template file into a `render/2` function inside the view module. The return value of the function is the resulting HTML from the template. This means that rendering is just another function and just another way to transform data. No HTML is stored on disk or in memory, and it's *fast*.

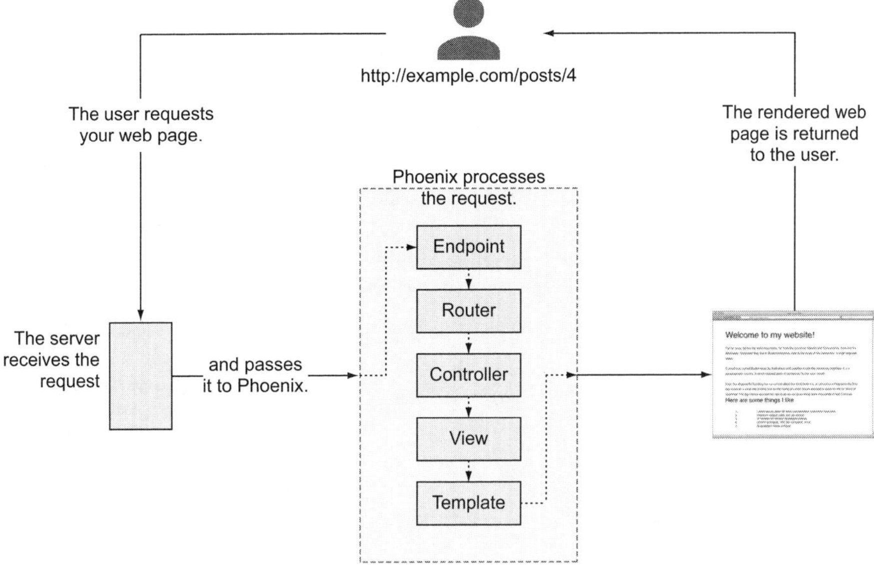

Figure 3.10 The final step: the template

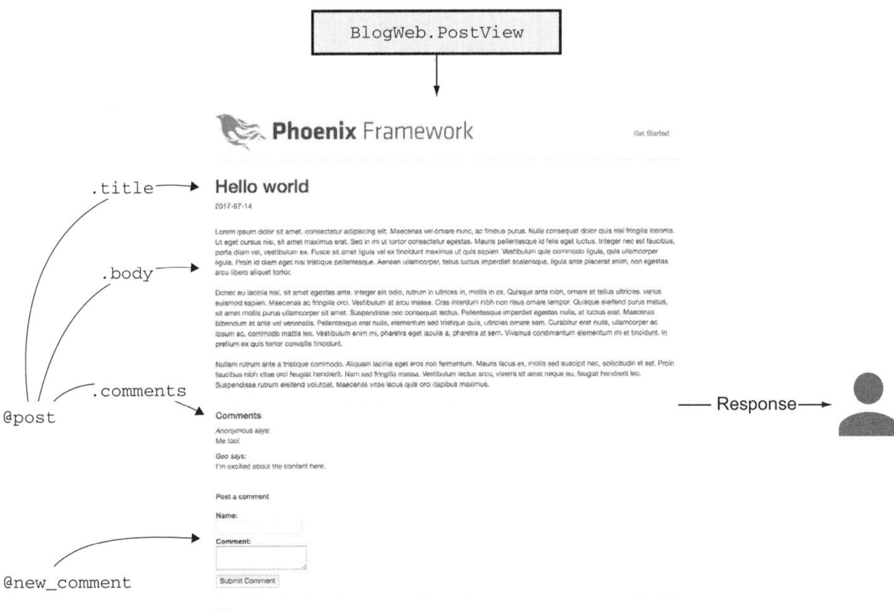

Figure 3.11 The template is what's rendered as a response to the user.

As you look at the template code in listings 3.7 and 3.8, take note of a few things:

- It's a mix of HTML and Elixir code. You'll notice that the file extension is .eex—it's an Embedded Elixir file (or EEx).
- The template doesn't contain all the HTML that's ultimately rendered. For example, where's the `<html>` opener?
- This won't render the prettiest web page in the world, but it's a start.

Listing 3.7 show.html.eex (lib/blog_web/templates/post/show.html.eex)

```
<h1><%= @post.title %></h1>

<div>
  <p><%= date(@post.inserted_at) %></p>
  <%= text_to_html(@post.body) %>
</div>

<hr />

<h4>Comments</h4>
<div>
  <%= for comment <- @post.comments do %>
    <div>
      <em><%= comment.name %> says:</em>
      <%= text_to_html(comment.body) %>
    </div>
  <% end %>
</div>

<hr />

<h5>Post a comment</h5>
<%= form_for @new_comment, post_comment_path(@conn, :create, @post),
➥ fn f -> %>
  <div>
    <label>
      Name:<br />
      <%= text_input f, :name %>
    </label>
  </div>
  <div>
    <label>
      Comment:<br />
      <%= textarea f, :body %>
    </label>
  </div>
  <%= submit "Submit Comment" %>
<% end %>

<hr />

<div>
  <span><%= link "Back", to: post_path(@conn, :index) %></span>
</div>
```

Renders the result of Elixir code by enclosing it in a <%= %> block. Because you passed the Post data into the view/template with the post key, it's available in this template as @post.

Uses the date/1 function defined in the PostView module

text_to_html/1 is a helper method provided by the Phoenix.HTML.Format module.

Phoenix.HTML.Form provides the form_for/3 function that allows you to easily set up a form.

Phoenix.HTML.Form also provides helper methods to add all the form elements you need.

link/2 renders a link to a specific path—in this case, the post_path named path in your routes list (shown earlier in the chapter).

As with most things in this chapter, don't worry about understanding all that's going on. We'll dive into the details in later chapters. This chapter is just intended to give you an overview of what's in these files. The output of this EEx template is shown in figure 3.12.

What about the rest of the HTML you'd expect, like the `<html>`, `<head>`, and `<body>` tags? Those are all provided in a file known as a *layout*. An app can have multiple layouts, though typically only a small number are used. The layout defines the HTML that's the same from one page to another, like CSS and JavaScript includes, analytics embeds, or page navigation. By default, app.html is the layout that's called by Phoenix.

Figure 3.12 The part of the page inside the box is what was rendered from the template.

3.2 Putting it all together

We've just walked through the typical path a web request takes from its initial handling by the endpoint, through the router, and into a controller, which then uses a view to render a template. Along the way, data is transformed into exactly what's needed, as determined by the initial request. That's done through plugs in the initial stages, and then more explicitly in the controller, where you set up the data that both the view and template will ultimately need.

One thing I'd challenge you to do is to look through more of the source code for the blog app.[2] Try these:

- Trace a `POST` request to /posts where you create a new post for the blog. Can you figure out what's going on there, based on the code?
- Trace a `GET` request to /api/posts/:id. How is that handled differently than a request to /posts/:id?
- Open the lib/blog_web.ex file. Here you can see all the modules that are made available to the controllers, views, router, and channels (which is a more advanced topic).

Here's a hint: take the requests through each step as you did in this chapter. You can skip the endpoint though, as each of the preceding requests will be passed through the endpoint in the same way. That means the router should be your first stop.

In the next chapter, you'll start building your own web application from the ground up.

Summary

- You can think of a web request as a chunk of data that's built and modified as it passes through your application and is formed into a response to the user.
- The endpoint sets up the initial portions of the environment by using plugs.
- The router takes the request from the endpoint and acts as a director of sorts, deciding where to send it next.
- The appropriate controller is called by the router, taking the request and readying all the data that will need to be returned to the user.
- The controller calls the `render/3` function of a view. The view can define helper methods to be used in a template and also does the work of actually rendering the appropriate template.
- The template renders the HTML response (for an HTML request) to the user based on their request. In our example, this included the details of the blog post along with a list of comments and a form to allow the user to submit their own comment.

[2] See https://github.com/PhoenixInAction/phoenix-in-action/tree/master/ch03/blog.

Part 2

Diving in deep

Now that you know the basics of Elixir and how Phoenix is organized, you'll get started writing an application—an auction site in the spirit of eBay. You'll allow users to sign up, log in and out, and create items to bid on, manage their items, and bid on items.

You'll start by working out and developing the foundation of your application's business logic. You'll then methodically build on that and add functionality and a UI to the application with Phoenix. By the end of this part, you'll know what you *need* to know to create interactive websites in Phoenix.

You'll learn how to

- Organize your Elixir/Phoenix application
- Use the command-line tools provided by Elixir
- Declare and use external dependencies
- Securely deal with user information such as passwords
- Maintain a clean database by strategically filtering out extraneous data

There's also plenty more that part 2 covers. Let's jump in and get coding!

4 Phoenix is not your application

This chapter covers

- How Phoenix interacts with the business logic of an application
- Creating an Elixir module
- The role of a repo and its usage

Part 1 of this book covered the basics of Elixir and Phoenix and got you up to speed regarding basic syntax, as well as the flow of a web request from the user, through the Phoenix framework, and back to the user. In part 2, you'll create a full-featured web application from the ground up. This application will be a simple live auction site, something like eBay. Your feature list won't be nearly as long as eBay's, but there will be plenty of opportunities for you to add your own features as we go along.

Your simple auction site will allow users to view items that are up for auction. These items will be owned and created by registered users of the site. A visitor will be able to create an account and, once they're logged in, create new items for bid and bid on other users' items. Some areas of the site will be restricted, by authorization

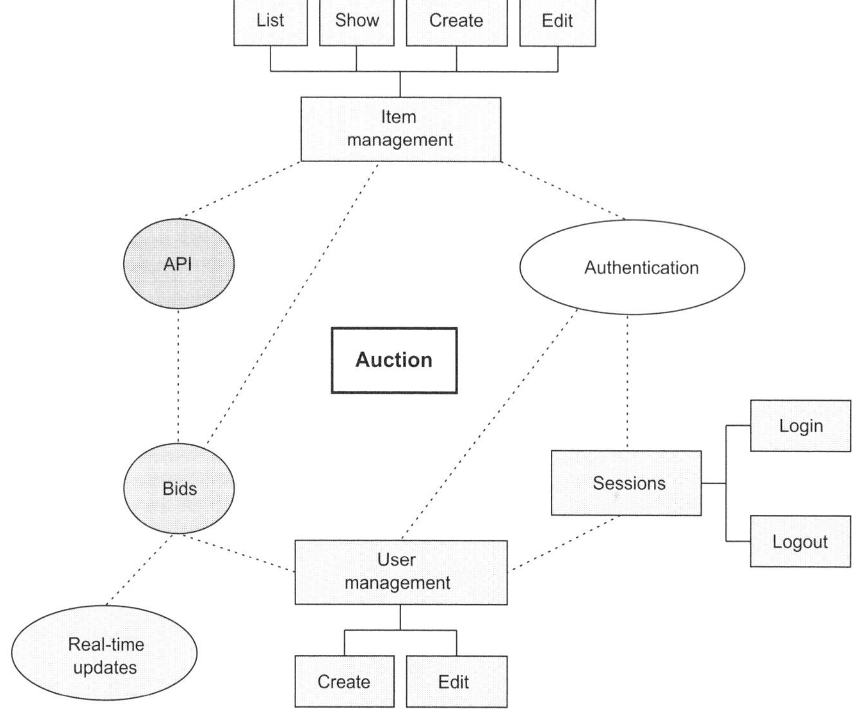

Figure 4.1 The major parts of your auction application

logic you'll write, to logged-in users or specific users. Figure 4.1 illustrates the major parts of the application.

Ready to dive in? Let's get going.

4.1 I thought this book was about Phoenix

Phoenix, possibly more than most web frameworks, tries to stay out of the way of your real application. What does that mean in practice? Phoenix should be thought of not as your web application itself, but as a border surrounding your application that allows your application to easily "speak web." Your application should be able to be separated from the Phoenix framework and still be usable to some extent. Decoupling your business logic code from the Phoenix framework code may seem strange at first, but it will allow you greater flexibility as your application grows and more use cases arise.

This is what Phoenix developers mean when they say that "Phoenix is not your application."[1] It should be a part of making your application web accessible, but don't

[1] Special acknowledgements to Lance Halvorsen who gave a talk entitled "Phoenix is Not Your Application" at ElixirConf EU 2016. In fact, the phrase "X is not your application" goes back many, many years and has been applied to multiple programming domains.

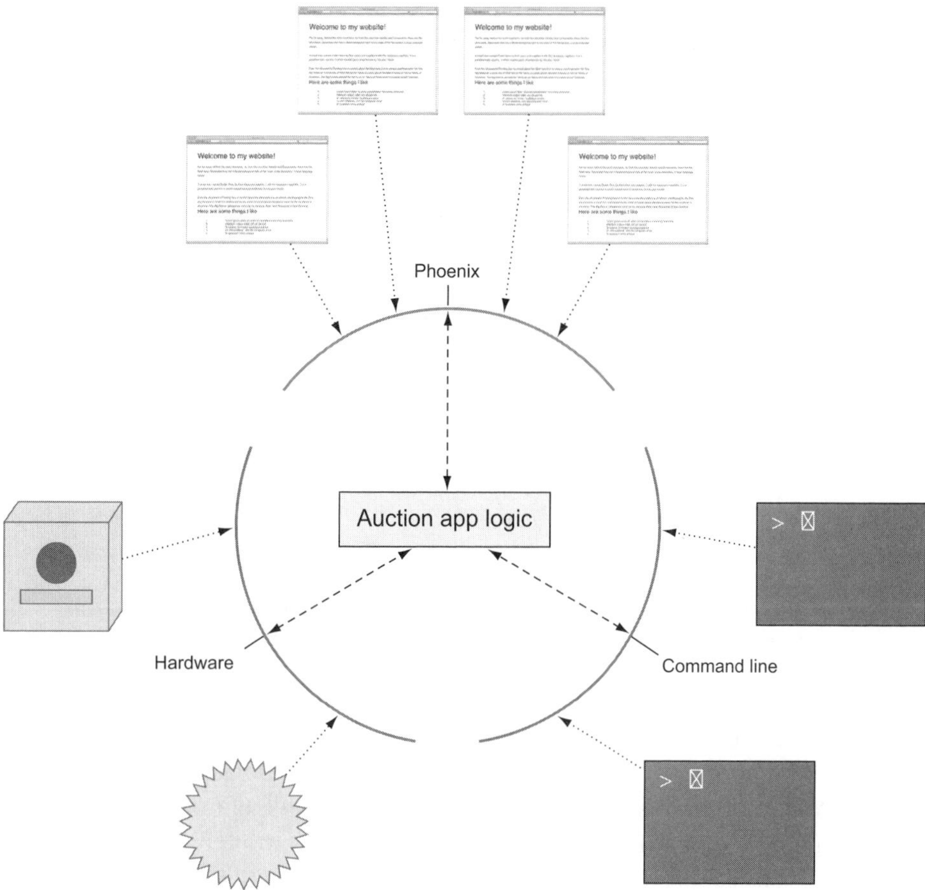

Figure 4.2 Phoenix is just a border around your application.

mistake that with the business logic of your application. Your underlying application could be used through the command line or perhaps through embedded hardware, as illustrated in figure 4.2.

For example, what if your live-auction application needed to be integrated with RFID-enabled bidding devices that enabled real-time, in-person bidding on items, with just a tap? You could have many entry points to the business logic of your application, and in this case, Phoenix is the main one. But assuming from the beginning that your app might be used in multiple ways in the future is always a good way to go.

Because of this, you'll build your application from the inside out. You'll start by creating the basic building blocks of the business logic in Elixir, and then you'll focus on the web portion with Phoenix. You'll also keep the database concerns separate from your business logic. (You won't be using a real database yet—you'll be using

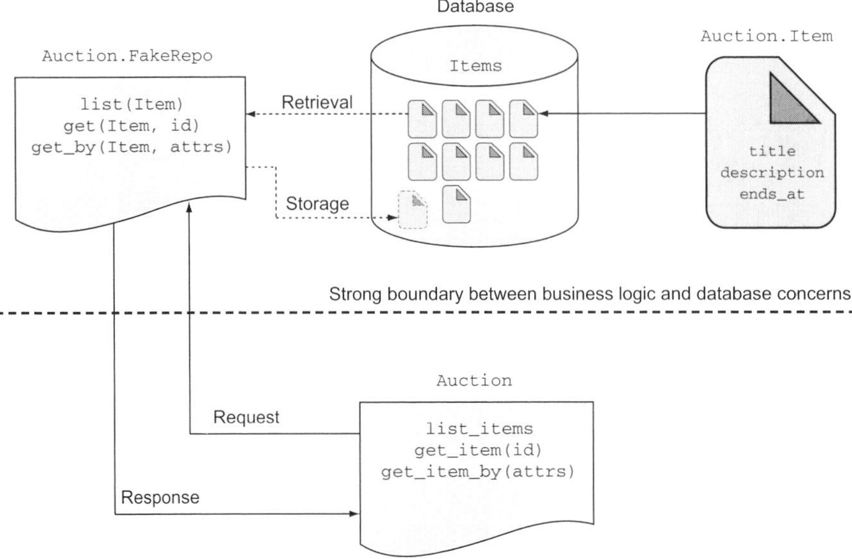

Figure 4.3 The first building blocks of your auction application. You want to keep the database and public interface separate.

something that will act like a database while you get up to speed.) Figure 4.3 shows the different parts of the application you'll develop in this chapter.

You won't have a usable web interface for a while, but your initial application will be usable through IEx. You'll build it step by step, starting by defining what an auction item looks like in your database; then defining the set of items to be stored in an in-memory, "fake" database; and finally interacting with those items and your "database." By the end of this chapter, you'll be able to do the following:

- List all the items in the database
- Get a specific item based on its ID in the database
- Get a specific item based on other defining attributes

4.2 The first steps in building your application

Now that you know the plan for this chapter (and others to come), let's get started. There will be four initial pieces to your application:

- An `Auction.Item` module will define the data structure for your auction items.
- An in-memory (fake) database will store a list of items for you to interact with.
- An `Auction.FakeRepo` module will directly interact with the database.
- An `Auction` module will provide a public interface to get the data you need.

4.2.1 Defining an item

You'll start by creating the first building block of your auction site: an auction *item*. The purpose of this item will be to represent the data for the different things to be auctioned. Eventually, it will also house some other functions that will help you maintain the items. The highlighted portion of figure 4.4 is what you'll focus on.

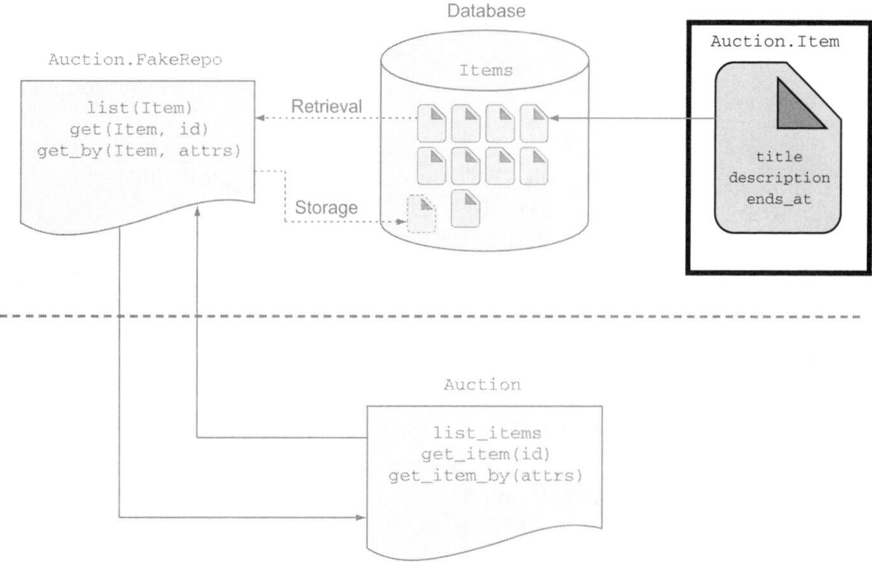

Figure 4.4 Your first step is defining what an item is.

For now, you'll create a struct that will contain the structure of an item in your auction's marketplace. Make a directory somewhere in your development environment—you'll use this directory as a playground of sorts while you start development.

For your auction application, you need to define what attributes an item should expect to possess. You can define data structures in Elixir inside your modules using `defstruct`. For the auction item, you'll initially keep track of the ID, a title, a description, and when the auction should end. In your preferred text editor, create a file named auction.ex and key in the following.

Listing 4.1 Creating the Item module

```
defmodule Auction.Item do
  defstruct [:id, :title, :description, :ends_at]
end
```

Structs in Elixir can be thought of as special maps. When you define the `Item` module (namespaced inside `Auction`), you also define the structure of the data you'd like it to contain with `defstruct`. If you wanted those particular attributes to contain default values, you could have defined those as well, as follows.

Listing 4.2 Creating defaults for a data structure

```
defmodule Auction.Item do
  defstruct id: 0,
            title: "default title",
            description: "default description",
            ends_at: ~N[2020-12-31 23:59:59]
end
```

The ~N sigil creates a NaiveDateTime.

For your implementation, you don't want to include default values for your data, so you go with the first implementation.

NOTE The `~N` in the preceding listing is what's known as a sigil. Sigils start with a "~" and a letter. They represent different things in Elixir, but this one is an easy way to create a `NaiveDateTime`. It's considered "naive" because it doesn't know about the concept of time zones.

Let's try out your new struct. In your preferred terminal, navigate to your development directory and start up an IEx session, passing `iex` the `-r` flag and the filename. This will cause IEx to compile that file and make it available in the session.

```
> iex -r auction.ex
Erlang/OTP 21 [erts-10.1.3] [source] [64-bit] [smp:8:8] [ds:8:8:10]
     [async-threads:1] [hipe] [dtrace]

Interactive Elixir (1.7.4) - press Ctrl+C to exit (type h() ENTER for help)
iex(1)> %Auction.Item{}
%Auction.Item{description: nil, ends_at: nil, id: nil, title: nil}
```

You can see the available flags for IEx by entering iex --help.

You now have the first building block of an auction item for your application. Now you can try using some data in your new struct:

```
iex(2)> alias Auction.Item
Auction.Item

iex(3)> book = %Item{
...(3)> id: 1,
...(3)> title: "Phoenix in Action",
...(3)> description: "Learn Phoenix with Manning's 'in Action' series",
...(3)> ends_at: ~N[2018-07-01 12:30:03]}
%Auction.Item{description: "Learn Phoenix with Manning's 'in Action' series",
 ends_at: ~N[2018-07-01 12:30:03], id: 1, title: "Phoenix"}

iex(4)> book = %{book | title: "Book -- Phoenix in Action"}
```

Aliases Auction.Item so that you only have to type Item from now on

You can modify information by using the special map modifier of | as long as the key already exists in the map being modified.

```
%Auction.Item{description: "Learn Phoenix with Manning's 'in Action' series",
 ends_at: ~N[2018-07-01 12:30:03], id: 1, title: "Book -- Phoenix in Action"}
```

Congratulations! You've created your first module! Unfortunately, any data you create in IEx will be lost as soon as you exit. If only some data already existed for you to play with!

4.2.2 Adding a fake database

Eventually, all the item data for your auction application will live in a database. For now, though, you won't add the overhead and complication of a database. Instead, you'll use an in-memory "database" of your own creation. The difference between your implementation and a real database is that once you exit your application, none of the changes you make to your data will be persisted. While this obviously isn't a solution for the long term, it does allow you to create a simple public interface in order to play with data as if it were a real database. Figure 4.5 illustrates the portion of this chapter's process that we'll focus on in this section.

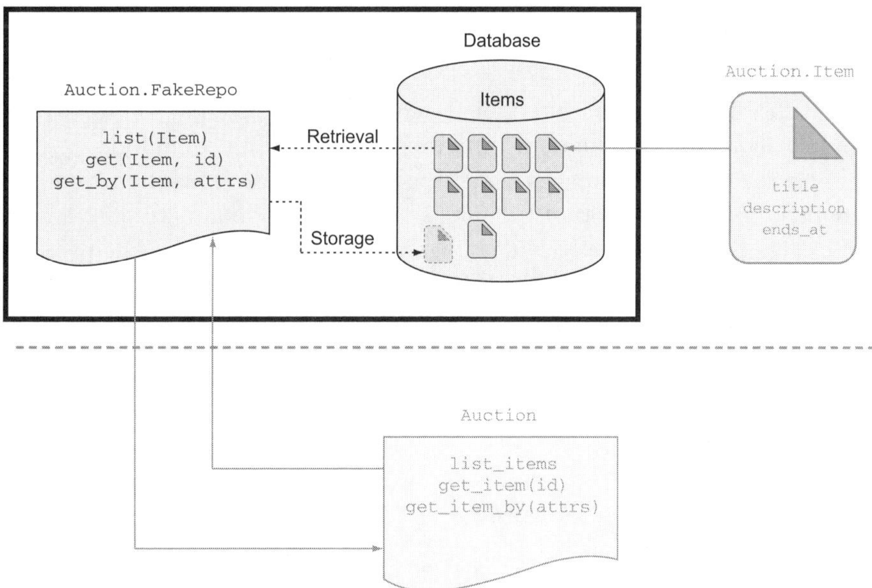

Figure 4.5 Your fake database will contain a static list of items.

As mentioned in this chapter's introduction, your initial database implementation needs to do a few things:

- List all the items in the database
- Get a specific item based on its ID in the database
- Get a specific item based on other defining attributes

Before you talk directly to your database, you'll create a public interface to keep the boundaries of application and database clear. In the same file as before (auction.ex), add the following module.

Listing 4.3 An `Auction` module to help retrieve data from the database

```
defmodule Auction do
  alias Auction.{FakeRepo, Item}

  @repo FakeRepo

  def list_items do
    @repo.all(Item)
  end

  def get_item(id) do
    @repo.get!(Item, id)
  end

  def get_item_by(attrs) do
    @repo.get_by(Item, attrs)
  end
end
```

This notation aliases several modules at once. This expands to alias both Auction.FakeRepo and Auction.Item.

You'll shortly define a module called `Auction.FakeRepo` that will hold your data for this particular implementation. Until then, this file won't compile.

Instead of calling `Auction.FakeRepo` directly in each function, you can set your preferred repo at the top of the file as a module attribute (`@repo FakeRepo`, in this case). This will make it easier to change the repo in the future when you move to an actual database implementation. When that happens, instead of changing every function call from `Auction.FakeRepo`, you'll only have to change this one line to point to the new repo.

Module attributes

Module attributes in Elixir can serve a few different functions, but here, `@repo` is used as a form of a constant value. When the module is compiled, the value of the module attribute is read and inserted into any code that references the attribute. Because it's compiled, it can't be set or changed at runtime.

Module attributes can also be used as file annotations, such as documentation, or as temporary storage. To read more about module attributes and their uses, check out the Elixir guides page on the topic: https://elixir-lang.org/getting-started/module-attributes.html.

One question you may have after looking through listing 4.3 is, "Why are we passing `Item` as the first argument to each function in `@repo`?" Although you currently only have items in your database, you'll soon have other things like bids or users that you'll

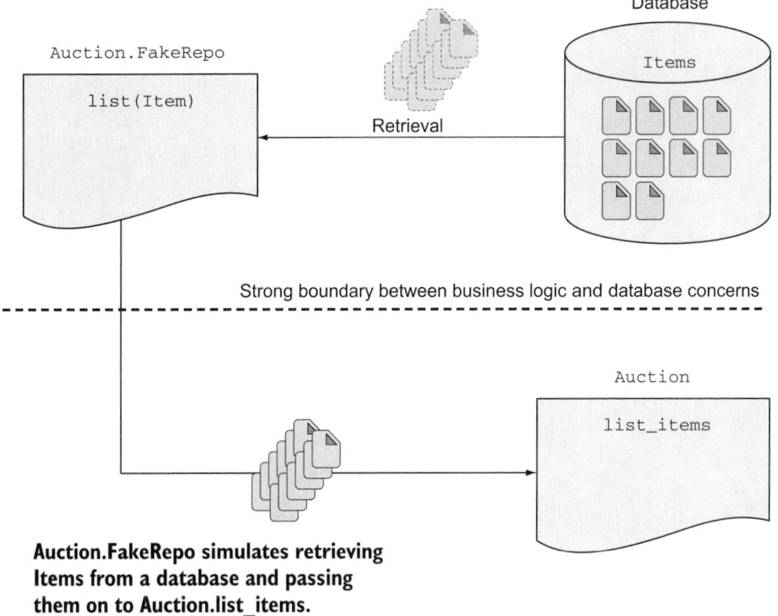

Figure 4.6 `Auction.FakeRepo.all/1` **and** `Auction.list_items/0` **will be used to retrieve all the** `Items`**.**

need to store and retrieve. When you pass `Item` in as the first argument, it lets the repo know which database table (set of data) you're requesting.

Listing 4.3 shows a good way to isolate your business logic from your database calls. You'll see modules and functions like this used as a kind of standard in Phoenix—a border between two different parts of your app that contain completely different domain knowledge. Figure 4.6 illustrates what you're attempting to do with these modules: create a way for data to be passed from the database/repo to the rest of your application.

Let's now continue on and add the `FakeRepo` module. This repo will act as an in-memory database, and it will contain a list of `Items` that are up for sale. Beyond that, you need a way to get to that data and manipulate it if necessary. First, you'll define the list of `Items` that exist in your database. Then, you'll create the functions necessary to handle the function calls you created in listing 4.3.

Add the following module into the auction.ex file. (In the next chapter, you'll break the modules out into separate files and we'll talk a bit about project file structure.)

Listing 4.4 Adding a fake repo

```
defmodule Auction.FakeRepo do
  alias Auction.Item

  @items [
      %Item{
```

@items is a list of Items. You'll use this as the data in your "database."

```
        id: 1,
        title: "My first item",
        description: "A tasty item sure to please",
        ends_at: ~N[2020-01-01 00:00:00]
      },
      %Item{
        id: 2,
        title: "WarGames Bluray",
        description: "The best computer movie of all time, now on Bluray!",
        ends_at: ~N[2018-10-15 13:39:35]
      },
      %Item{
        id: 3,
        title: "U2 - Achtung Baby on CD",
        description: "The sound of 4 men chopping down The Joshua Tree",
        ends_at: ~N[2018-11-05 03:12:29]
      }
    ]

  def all(Item), do: @items
end
```

The all/1 function is called to return all the Items in the database—it returns the @items module attribute.

As in listing 4.3, you use a module attribute (`@items`) to store the list of `Items` as a constant that will be evaluated at compile time. `Auction.FakeRepo.all/1` takes the list of items you provide in that attribute and returns it to the user.

Note that pattern matching is used in the function definition. This particular function will only be called if the first argument to `all` is `Item`. You can return other types of data in the future, perhaps adding `all(User)` and `all(Bid)` as the application grows.

What is a repo?

I've used the term *repo* enough now that if you're not familiar with it, you're likely wondering what it is. Very simply, the repo (or repository) is a mapping to a data store. In your case, the data store is your static `@items` module attribute, but normally the repo maps to an actual database (as you'll do in the next chapter).

The database is the component that actually stores the data; the repo is the application's gateway to the data inside the database. Your repo will translate what you'd like from the database into "database speak" through a defined public interface. This is really neat, because as long as an adapter for your database is available, the repo can talk many different database "languages," but the public interface your application uses to talk to the repo remains the same.

Now that you have a fake database with some data in it, you can try using it. You wrote a function in listing 4.3 to be a boundary between your application and the database (`Auction.list_items/0`), so let's use that. That way you can verify that your modules are working well with each other, and you can get used to calling your boundary functions instead of working directly with your repo.

You'll use this new fake database layer of your application in IEx. Whenever you modify a file and want to use those modifications inside an already-running session of IEx, you can run `c "filename.ex"` to recompile it and redefine the module (and yes, the quotes are required).

```
# ...continuing from our previous iex session
iex(5)> c "auction.ex"
warning: redefining module Auction.Item (current version defined in memory)
  auction.ex:1

[Auction.FakeRepo, Auction, Auction.Item]

iex(6)> Auction.list_items()
[%Auction.Item{description: "A tasty item sure to please",
  ends_at: ~N[2020-01-01 00:00:00], id: 1, title: "My first item"},
 %Auction.Item{description: "The best computer movie of all time, now on
     Bluray!",
  ends_at: ~N[2018-10-15 13:39:35], id: 2, title: "WarGames Bluray"},
 %Auction.Item{description: "The sound of 4 men chopping down The Joshua
     Tree",
  ends_at: ~N[2018-11-05 03:12:29], id: 3, title: "U2 - Achtung Baby on CD"}]
```

Remember to recompile the file you've changed.

These warnings are fine.

Receives all the auction items in the fake database

Ta-da! You can now list all the items in your database.

The next step is to make it just a little more useful. You definitely want to do at least two more things before moving on:

- Get a specific `Item` based on its `id`
- Get a specific `Item` based on other identifying information, such as its title or description

Let's build those out in `FakeRepo`.

4.2.3 *Getting an Item by id*

When you want to get a specific `Item`, you'll usually know the `id` of that `Item`. For example, a web page request might be something like http://myawesomeauction.com/items/8746, and `8746` would be the `id` of the `Item` loaded. What you need your finder to do is iterate through the list of `@items` and find the one with the `id` you're looking for. Figure 4.7 is a simple illustration of what you're trying to achieve.

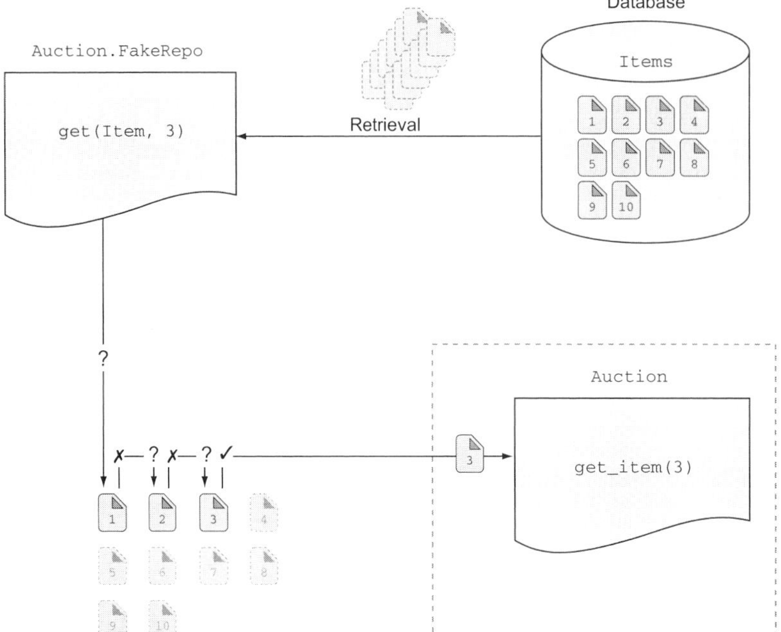

Figure 4.7 Checking each `Item`'s `id` to find the one you're looking for

Thankfully, you can use `Enum.find/2` for exactly this purpose. `Enum.find/2` expects two things to be passed in:

- A collection of things to iterate over.
- A function to call for each thing in the collection. The function should take one argument, which is the thing in the collection currently being examined.

In the `Auction` module, add the following function definition.

Listing 4.5 Defining `Auction.FakeRepo.get!/2`

```
def get!(Item, id) do
  Enum.find(@items, fn(item) -> item.id === id end)
end
```

`Auction.FakeRepo.get!/2` will get the first `Item` in the list of `@items` that has the `id` you're looking for. Figure 4.8 breaks down this function call into small pieces and describes what each piece is responsible for.

`Enum.find/2` will loop through each item in the collection until it finds one for which the passed function returns `true`. Your function simply compares the `id` of the item currently being examined with the `id` passed into the `get!/2 function` itself. Here it is in use (don't forget to recompile auction.ex with `c "auction.ex"` before

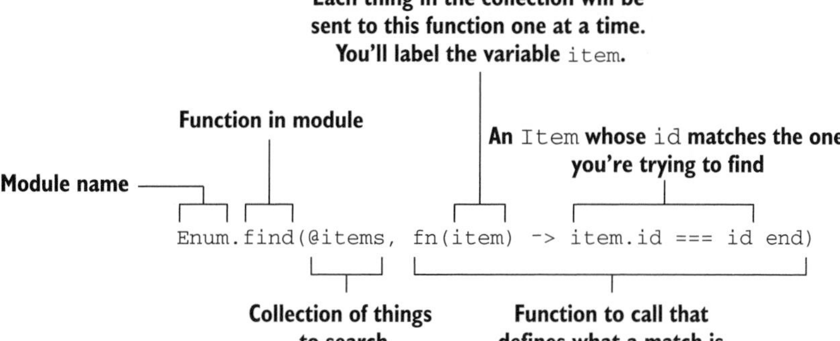

Figure 4.8 Breaking down `Enum.find/2`

trying to use this new function). You'll try using it directly with the `FakeRepo` and then again with your boundary `Auction` module:

```
iex> Auction.FakeRepo.get!(Auction.Item, 2)
%Auction.Item{description: "The best computer movie of all time, now on
     Bluray!",
 ends_at: ~N[2018-10-15 13:39:35], id: 2, title: "WarGames Bluray"}

iex> Auction.get_item(2)
%Auction.Item{description: "The best computer movie of all time, now on
     Bluray!",
 ends_at: ~N[2018-10-15 13:39:35], id: 2, title: "WarGames Bluray"}
```

As expected, `get_item/1` returns the `Item` with the `id` of `2`, which is what you asked it for.

4.2.4 Getting an Item based on other information

You'll often know the `id` of the `Item` to look up, but you still need to account for getting an `Item` by other identifying information. For example, what if a user searches for an `Item` by title? Handling user queries can be a complex subject, but you can account for exact matches with your function. You'll create `get_by/2` to handle finding an `Item` with a map of matching information.

Before you add any code, let's think about what it is you want to accomplish with this search:

1. Deal with each `Item` in the list, one by one.
2. One by one, compare the attributes of the `Item` to the attributes you're looking for.
3. If you've gone through all the attributes and they've all matched, you've found the `Item` you're looking for! Return that `Item` to the user.

4. If any attribute doesn't match, you haven't found the `Item` you're looking for and should move on to the next.
5. If there are no more `Items` to check, none of the `Items` in the list match all the attributes you were looking for. Return `nil` to indicate that nothing matched.

Figure 4.9 illustrates this strategy of searching.

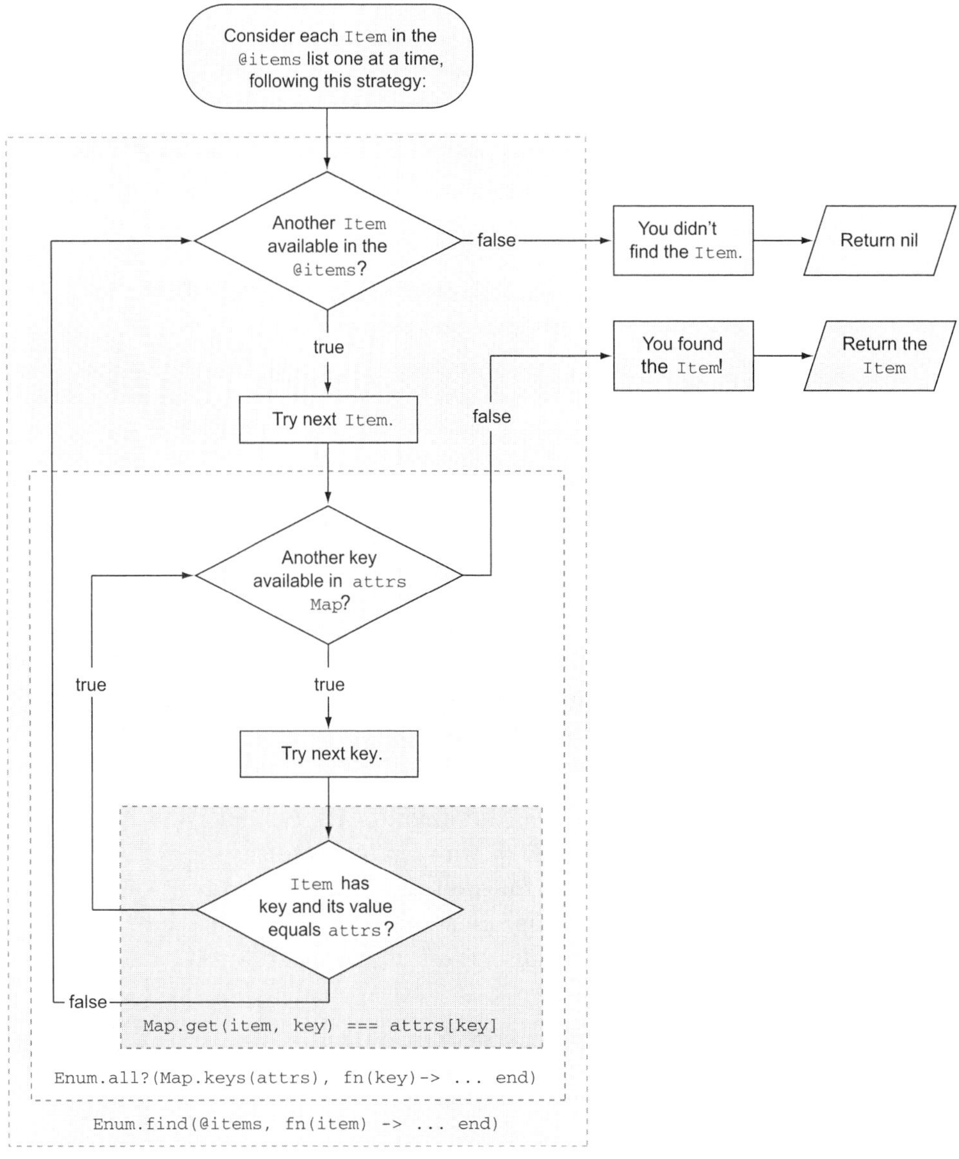

Figure 4.9 How `get_by/2` determines if it has found the `Item`

Now that you've decided on your search strategy, you can start adding some code. Add the following code to your `Auction.FakeRepo` module.

Listing 4.6 Adding `get_by/1` to `Auction.FakeRepo`

```
def get_by(Item, attrs) do
  Enum.find(@items, fn(item) ->
    Enum.all?(Map.keys(attrs), fn(key) ->
      Map.get(item, key) === attrs[key]
    end)
  end)
end
```

I understand what you might be thinking *What?* This is the most complex-looking function you've looked at yet, but don't let the nesting scare you off. If you peel the layers back one at a time, it's actually not that hard to grasp. Before reading further, try to understand on your own what this does. The names of the functions you haven't seen yet should give you some clues as to what's going on.

OK, got an idea? (Or just want to get on with it?) Let's take a look:

- You've already seen `Enum.find/2` in use in the `FakeRepo.get!/2` function: this time, the function that examines each item in the `@items` list is just a bit more complex.
- `Enum.all?/2` is a lot like `Enum.find/2` in that it takes a collection of things and a function to run on each of them. The difference is that instead of returning the first thing that returns `true`, it runs through the entire collection until either the passed anonymous function returns `false` or every run of the function has returned `true`. Put another way, `Enum.all?/2` returns `true` if, when passed everything in the collection, the provided function returned `true`. It returns `false` if even one thing examined returned `false`. It essentially asks if *all* of every run of the function provided can be evaluated to `true`.
- Into `Enum.all?/2` you pass all the keys of the `attrs` map passed in to `get_by/2`. This allows you to search for one thing (like `%{title: "WarGames Bluray"}`) or multiple things at the same time (like `%{title: "WarGames Bluray", id: 2}`).
- For each of the keys in `map`, you see if the examined `item` has that key, and, if it does, whether it matches the `map`'s value for the same key.

Let's use it now:

```
iex> Auction.get_item_by(%{id: 2})
%Auction.Item{description: "The best computer movie of all time, now on
     Bluray!",
 ends_at: ~N[2018-10-15 13:39:35], id: 2, title: "WarGames Bluray"}

iex> Auction.get_item_by(
...> %{description: "A tasty item sure to please", id: 1}
...> )
%Auction.Item{description: "A tasty item sure to please",
 ends_at: ~N[2020-01-01 00:00:00], id: 1, title: "My first item"}
```

Your current implementation of `Auction.FakeRepo` should match the following listing.

Listing 4.7 The full `Auction.FakeRepo` module

```
defmodule Auction.FakeRepo do
  alias Auction.Item

  @items [
      %Item{
        id: 1,
        title: "My first item",
        description: "A tasty item sure to please",
        ends_at: ~N[2020-01-01 00:00:00]
      },
      %Item{
        id: 2,
        title: "WarGames Bluray",
        description: "The best computer movie of all time, now on Bluray!",
        ends_at: ~N[2018-10-15 13:39:35]
      },
      %Item{
        id: 3,
        title: "U2 - Achtung Baby on CD",
        description: "The sound of 4 men chopping down The Joshua Tree",
        ends_at: ~N[2018-11-05 03:12:29]
      }
    ]

  def all(Item), do: @items

  def get!(Item, id) do
    Enum.find(@items, fn(item) -> item.id === id end)
  end

  def get_by(Item, map) do
    Enum.find(@items, fn(item) ->
      Enum.all?(Map.keys(map), fn(key) ->
        Map.get(item, key) === attrs[key]
      end)
    end)
  end
end
```

`Auction.FakeRepo` defines a list of `Items` to seed your database, a function to get all the `Items` from the database (`all/1`), a function to get an `Item` by its `id` (`get!/2`), and a function to get an `Item` by some other identifying information (`get_by/2`).

4.3 Next steps

So far, you've designed a way to retrieve `Items` from your database, but you've quickly come upon a limitation—you can't add `Items`, you can't update an `Item`, and you can't delete an `Item`. Those three things, along with the things you've implemented in this chapter (listing, getting by `id`, searching by attributes) are fundamental concepts for a database. You could implement more fake database functions to allow you to do those things (perhaps with an agent[2]), but that's beyond the scope of this chapter.

Instead, in the next chapter, you'll move from having all your code in one file to having an actual Elixir application. Plus, you'll learn how to bring in outside Elixir packages to help make your code even more useful.

Summary

- Phoenix is not your application, but just one entry point into it.
- Your application can have various entry points, such as the web, hardware, the command line, and others.
- Because there can be various entry points, it's a good idea (and standard practice) to keep your business logic isolated as much as possible. Don't let things like computation get mixed in with things like the workings of the database.
- Nested enumerators can look intimidating, but breaking them down into a flowchart can make them seem very approachable.

[2] Check agents out—they're amazing: https://hexdocs.pm/elixir/Agent.html.

5 Elixir application structure

This chapter covers

- Organizing Elixir code in a project
- Using the Mix utility to manage your Elixir projects
- Using hex.pm to make use of third-party tools and libraries

So far, you've been writing and using Elixir code in an IEx session or, in chapter 4, in a single file. The majority of your Elixir and Phoenix projects won't be organized like this, however. As your application grows in complexity, it's important to impose some sort of organizational structure to keep things manageable.

In this chapter, we'll cover the structure of a typical Elixir application. Along the way, you'll use the Mix utility to automate a lot of tasks that would take some effort if done manually. Finally, you'll use the Hex package manager to bring third-party tools and libraries into your application. All of this will help you get your application set up properly before you tackle using a real database in chapter 6.

5.1 Moving from a single file to an application

Your auction application in chapter 4 consisted of a fake repo, a public interface layer to access the data in the repo, and an `Item` struct that defined the data structure of your auction items. All that code—three modules—existed in a single file. Once you start adding more functionality, that kind of project structure will become unmaintainable.

You could break up the modules into separate files. This is a great idea on the surface, but as you increasingly need to use code from one file in a different file, you'll end up with a web of interconnected files that all depend on one another.

Fortunately, there's a standard directory structure for Elixir projects. As you can see in figure 5.1, there are usually three top-level directories for every Elixir application:

- Configuration code goes in the config subdirectory.
- The bulk of the modules and business logic go into the lib subdirectory.
- Tests go into the test subdirectory.

Along with the standard directories, you'll typically find a file named mix.exs. This file can be considered the brain or mother ship of your application. You'll look at this file in the next section.

Although simple applications are typically structured in this way, you'll be creating multiple applications—one for the business logic you've been working on and one for

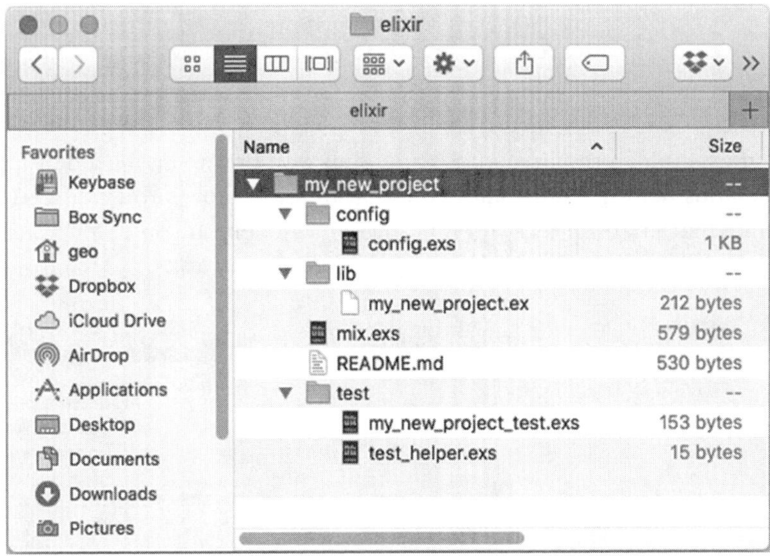

Figure 5.1 The standard directory and file structure of an Elixir project

your Phoenix application. But you'll also create another skeleton application to tie them together. This kind of pattern is called an *umbrella application*. The top-level umbrella application will contain the subapplications that contain the logic.

5.1.1 Using Mix to create a new application

You may be thinking, "Oh, great. Every time I want to start a new Elixir application, I have to remember this standard structure." If you are indeed thinking that, I've got some great news for you! You don't have to remember it at all! All you have to remember is `mix`. Like IEx, the Mix utility is installed when you install Elixir. And also like IEx, it has an excellent help system. If all you remember is the command `mix`, you can figure out how to get the rest.

The following listing jumps directly into using the Mix tool (in the terminal). It will tell you all the different things it can do.

Listing 5.1 Letting `mix` tell you what it can do

```
> mix
** (Mix) "mix" with no arguments must be executed in a directory with a
     mix.exs file

Usage: mix [task]

Examples:

    mix              - Invokes the default task (current: "mix run")
    mix new PATH     - Creates a new Elixir project at the given path
    mix help         - Lists all available tasks
    mix help TASK    - Prints documentation for a given task
```

Mix provides usage examples to help you figure out exactly what you want to do.

The second example in the preceding listing tells you how to create a new Elixir project. That sounds helpful. But what if you want to know more? You can see in the following listing that `mix` even tells you how to get more help. If you enter `mix help new` it will give you all the help documentation for that specific task.

Listing 5.2 Using `mix help new` to learn about creating a new Elixir project

```
> mix help new

                                                mix new

Creates a new Elixir project. It expects the path of the project as argument.

    mix new PATH [--sup] [--module MODULE] [--app APP] [--umbrella]

A project at the given PATH will be created. The application name and module
name will be retrieved from the path, unless --module or --app is given.

A --sup option can be given to generate an OTP application skeleton including a
supervision tree. Normally an app is generated without a supervisor and without
```

Arguments presented in brackets [like this] are considered optional.

```
the app callback.

An --umbrella option can be given to generate an umbrella project.

An --app option can be given in order to name the OTP application for the
project.

A --module option can be given in order to name the modules in the generated
code skeleton.

## Examples

    mix new hello_world                  <-- This is the simplest usage example for mix new.

Is equivalent to:

    mix new hello_world --module HelloWorld

To generate an app with a supervision tree and an application callback:

    mix new hello_world --sup

To generate an umbrella application with sub applications:

    mix new hello_world --umbrella
    cd hello_world/apps
    mix new child_app
```

You can see that there are a number of options you can specify when creating a new Elixir application. If you wanted to create a new Elixir application, you'd definitely want to use this tool as the first step. `mix new` will not only generate the standard Elixir application directory structure but also give you some files that are starting points for your application.

Before you create an application for your auction backend, let's use the tool on a throwaway project just to see how it works. Because the first option to `mix new` is the path of the project as well as the application name, you need to avoid most special characters. Like in variable names, you avoid using dashes, but you can use underscores. If you're like me and prefer dashes to underscores in your directory names, you can specify an alternative name for the application itself (with `--app`) that uses underscores instead.

Suppose you want to create a Facebook replacement named FriendFace.[1] In a temporary directory somewhere, run the following command.

Listing 5.3 Using `mix new`

```
> mix new friend-face --app friend_face
* creating README.md
* creating .formatter.exs
```

[1] Thanks to the show "The IT Crowd" for the name inspiration.

```
* creating .gitignore
* creating mix.exs
* creating config
* creating config/config.exs
* creating lib
* creating lib/friend_face.ex
* creating test
* creating test/test_helper.exs
* creating test/friend_face_test.exs

Your Mix project was created successfully.
You can use "mix" to compile it, test it, and more:

    cd friend-face
    mix test

Run "mix help" for more commands.
```

The generator creates a test file for you.

It even suggests you run it right away to make sure it's hooked up correctly.

You can see that not only did the `mix new` command create your directory structure, but it also gave you a README, a .gitignore file for ignoring files in your Git repo if you were to create one, a config file, a skeleton module for your `friend_face` application, and even a test file. You can peek into each of these files and see that they're not just empty files. They're files that have actual uses as they are, and they're very helpful as you're getting started. If you follow the instructions at the end of listing 5.3 and run `mix test` in your project directory, you'll even discover that it already has a passing test.

After you're done exploring this test application, feel free to delete the directory and all the files it generated for you. You won't need them.

5.1.2 Generating an auction umbrella application

Now that you've seen the basics of how `mix` works, let's create an application for your auction site. You'll use the `mix new` command like before, but this time you'll do it in a nontemporary directory that you use for your projects. The first thing you need to generate is the umbrella itself. You'll then create an auction application inside that umbrella.

Creating an umbrella application is very simple: pass the `--umbrella` flag to `mix new`. Let's call this umbrella structure `auction_umbrella` to make it recognizably an umbrella structure. I got the following output in my terminal when I ran that command.

Listing 5.4 Generating an umbrella application

```
> mix new --umbrella auction_umbrella
* creating README.md
* creating .formatter.exs
* creating .gitignore
* creating mix.exs
* creating apps
* creating config
* creating config/config.exs
```

```
Your umbrella project was created successfully.
Inside your project, you will find an apps/ directory
where you can create and host many apps:

    cd auction_umbrella
    cd apps
    mix new my_app

Commands like "mix compile" and "mix test" when executed
in the umbrella project root will automatically run
for each application in the apps/ directory.
```

Unlike running "mix new" without --umbrella, no tests are created (because you don't yet have an app).

It gives you instructions on how to create the first app inside the umbrella.

This kind of structure allows you to create sub-applications under the umbrella application. You don't really need to modify anything it generated at the moment, but the output does offer a good clue as to what you should do next. All the sub-applications of an umbrella application are stored in the apps directory (auction_umbrella/apps in this case). You can `cd` into that subdirectory and run `mix new app_name` to generate a sub-application.

You'll name your application *Auction*. Catchy, huh? `cd` into auction_umbrella/apps and type `mix new auction --sup` in your terminal. What does the `--sup` do? It creates an application skeleton along with the files to easily create a supervision tree. This won't make much difference now, but it will as you go on (you'll use that supervisor in chapter 7—it will do things like make sure the database connections are maintained). You should see output like the following.

Listing 5.5 Generating the Auction application

```
> mix new auction --sup
* creating README.md
* creating .formatter.exs
* creating .gitignore
* creating mix.exs
* creating config
* creating config/config.exs
* creating lib
* creating lib/auction.ex
* creating lib/auction/application.ex
* creating test
* creating test/test_helper.exs
* creating test/auction_test.exs

Your Mix project was created successfully.
You can use "mix" to compile it, test it, and more:

    cd auction
    mix test

Run "mix help" for more commands.
```

Make sure you run this inside the auction_umbrella/apps directory.

You may have realized that you now have two mix.exs files in your umbrella application—one at the top level of the umbrella, and one in the new Auction application.

That's perfectly fine—they'll live well with each other. But the rest of the work you'll do in this chapter will be strictly inside the auction_web/apps/auction directory.

5.1.3 The magic mix.exs file

For any Elixir application, the mix.exs file is pretty magical. In it, you define things like the current version of your application, your application's name, the version of Elixir it runs on, any outside dependencies that your application requires in order to run, and any additional applications or supervisors that also need to be started when your application is started.

If you take a peek inside the auction_umbrella/apps/auction/mix.exs file that the `mix new` task generated for you, you can begin to see just how helpful that Mix task is.

Listing 5.6 The auction_umbrella/apps/auction/mix.exs file (some comments removed)

```
defmodule Auction.MixProject do
  use Mix.Project

  def project do
    [
      app: :auction,
      version: "0.1.0",
      build_path: "../../_build",
      config_path: "../../config/config.exs",
      deps_path: "../../deps",
      lockfile: "../../mix.lock",
      elixir: "~> 1.7",
      start_permanent: Mix.env() == :prod,
      deps: deps()
    ]
  end

  # Run "mix help compile.app" to learn about applications.
  def application do
    [
      extra_applications: [:logger],
      mod: {Auction.Application, []}
    ]
  end

  # Run "mix help deps" to learn about dependencies.
  defp deps do
    [
      # {:dep_from_hexpm, "~> 0.3.0"},
      # {:dep_from_git, git: "https://github.com/elixir-lang/my_dep.git",
     tag: "0.1.0"},
      # {:sibling_app_in_umbrella, in_umbrella: true},
    ]
  end
end
```

To read up on the details of these sections, run these commands.

These lines are commented-out, but they provide examples of how you can declare the dependencies for your app.

Let's further break down each of these functions.

What's the difference between .exs and .ex files?

You may have noticed that some of the files you're working with have the extension .ex, and some have the extension .exs. What's the difference? When do you use each?

- .ex files are for compiled code. When you'd like to execute the code in an .ex file, Elixir first needs to compile the code.
- .exs files are script files and are interpreted when they're executed (meaning they don't have to be precompiled).

Most of the time, you'll be writing .ex files, as you want all the benefits of compiled code (compiler optimizations, speed, and so on). .exs files, because they're interpreted, are slower to run (they have to go through parsing, tokenization, and so on). They are, however, a flexible choice when you don't require compilation. For example, the mix.exs file in an Elixir project and all test code files are .exs files.

THE PROJECT FUNCTION

The `project` function defines the top-level details of your Elixir application:

- The app name as an atom (`auction`) and the current version of the application (`0.1.0`)
- The Elixir versions your app will run on (`~> 1.7`[2])
- Configuration for the application, so that if it goes down either by failure or successful shutdown, other applications that your application started as dependencies will also be shut down (this is set as `true` in the production environment by the return of the comparison of the current Mix environment to the `:prod` atom.)
- A list of dependencies. This is a list of tuples containing external package names and version numbers, but for simplicity's sake, it's set up by default to rely on a private function, defined later, named `deps`. We'll cover the `deps` function shortly.

The following listing shows the `project` function.

Listing 5.7 The `project` function

```
def project do
  [
    app: :auction,
    version: "0.1.0",
```

[2] The ~> means the following version number can be incremented by the last dot value in the version. In this case, you could run versions 1.7 through 1.?, but not versions before 1.7 or versions 2.0 and later.

```
    build_path: "../../_build",
    config_path: "../../config/config.exs",
    deps_path: "../../deps",
    lockfile: "../../mix.lock",
    elixir: "~> 1.7",
    start_permanent: Mix.env() == :prod,
    deps: deps()
  ]
end
```

Configures the project with relative paths back to the umbrella application root

These are only some of the options that can be set here for your application. Elixir itself has a few more (which you can read about in its excellent documentation for `Mix.Project`: https://hexdocs.pm/mix/Mix.Project.html). Other dependencies of your application may also have options that will need to be set here.

THE APPLICATION FUNCTION

The `application` function (see listing 5.8) is pretty simple in terms of what's generated, but the functionality it provides is big. In simple terms, it's what tells the compiler that you'd like to generate an .app file for your application. According to the documentation (which you can read by typing `# Run "mix help compile.app",` as in the comment about the function declaration in listing 5.6), "An .app file is a file containing Erlang terms that defines your application. Mix automatically generates this file based on your mix.exs configuration."

Listing 5.8 The `application` function

```
def application do
  [
    extra_applications: [:logger],
    mod: {Auction.Application, []}
  ]
end
```

You can specify lots of other options here, but they're unnecessary for your starter application.

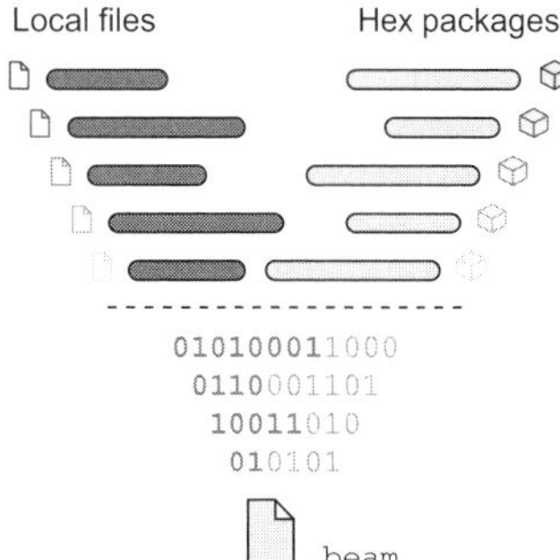

Figure 5.2 All of your files, plus all the dependencies, are compiled into files that can run on the BEAM VM.

An Elixir application compiles down to Erlang code (figure 5.2), which will run on the BEAM virtual machine, and the `application` function provides additional instructions to the compiler about how to compile Erlang code. The most-used options concern additional, external applications that need to be started along with your application. Any application name you provide to `extra_applications` (in `:atom` form) is guaranteed to start *before* your application, so that it will be ready to accept commands when your application needs it. By default, Elixir's built-in `Logger` application is started up to provide logging functionality.

Third-party applications and dependencies can tell the Elixir compiler that they need to be started along with your application. If they do, they'll be started automatically without you having to tell Elixir to do so. If an application needs to be included in `extra_applications`, the README for the library will let you know. If it doesn't mention the requirement, you can bet that it will either be started automatically or that it doesn't need to be started at all.

Finally, the `mod` key is an application callback. Any module you specify in this list (along with a list of arguments, which is currently empty) will be called when the main application starts. The callback expects `Auction.Application.start/2` to be defined. When you generated the application with the `--sup` flag, it created that module for you and placed the reference to it here in the `mod` key.

THE DEPS FUNCTION

The final function in your generated mix.exs file is `deps`. This is where you list all the external applications, packages, and libraries your application depends on. You can see in the following listing that you currently rely on no external packages.

Listing 5.9 The empty `deps` function

```
defp deps do
  [
    # {:dep_from_hexpm, "~> 0.3.0"},
    # {:dep_from_git, git: "https://github.com/elixir-lang/my_dep.git", tag:
     "0.1.0"},
    # {:sibling_app_in_umbrella, in_umbrella: true},
  ]
end
```

The in_umbrella: true option is for dependencies defined within the current umbrella app.

Dependencies are specified with the package name plus the version numbers accepted in a tuple (like `{:package_name, "~> 1.0"}`). For the version requirements, a few different options can be specified. For more details, check the `Version` documentation: https://hexdocs.pm/elixir/Version.html. You'll be using `deps` extensively in the coming sections.

OTHER OPTIONS

A handful of other options and functions you can use in your Mix file aren't generated in a skeleton application, and you won't use them in this book. For more information on these options, check out the `Mix.Project` documentation: https://hexdocs.pm/mix/Mix.Project.html.

5.2 Organizing, compiling, and running your new application

You've used `mix new auction` to generate a skeleton application structure and configuration for your Auction application, and now you need to move the code you created in chapter 4 from a single file containing multiple modules into separate files for each module.

NOTE I apologize for the little bit of busywork in this section—this is the only time in this book where you'll cut and paste code like this. In the last chapter, I wanted to make it clear that you could define as many modules as you wanted in a single file and that they would all compile. It was also the easiest way to use multiple modules without a full-on Mix application. But that means that you now need to break that file into three separate modules.

One of the cool things about Elixir is that you can name the files whatever you want in whatever structure you want. This allows you to structure your application as you see fit. The flip side is that unless you decide on some rules regarding how you're going to structure your application files, it can quickly get out of control.

5.2.1 Breaking apart the three modules

If you'll recall, you defined three modules in auction.ex in chapter 4:

- `Auction`
- `Auction.Item`
- `Auction.FakeRepo`

You'll therefore create three different files—one for each module. Usually the application and library code should go in the lib directory that `mix new` generated for you, so you'll start there.

The `mix new` task created an auction.ex file in the lib directory of your application. Paste all the code that made up the `Auction` module into that file. You'll notice that `mix new auction` generated a `hello` function in that file—it's safe to overwrite all the contents of the generated file. The following listing shows that module.

Listing 5.10 The new contents of lib/auction.ex is your `Auction` module

```
defmodule Auction do
  alias Auction.{FakeRepo, Item}

  @repo FakeRepo

  def list_items do
    @repo.all(Item)
  end

  def get_item(id) do
    @repo.get!(Item, id)
  end

  def get_item_by(attrs) do
    @repo.get_by(Item, attrs)
  end
end
```

This module is unchanged from chapter 4—it's just in a new location in your umbrella app.

For the `Auction.Item` module, you need to create a new file. You could create this file in the top level of the lib directory, but it's standard practice to match your directory structure to the namespacing of your module. `Item` is namespaced under `Auction` in your module name (`Auction.Item`), so a good rule of thumb is to create an auction subdirectory and have item.ex live in there. Figure 5.3 shows the file structure based on namespacing.

Paste the entirety of the `Auction.Item` module code into a file named lib/auction/item.ex (or whatever other name you may have chosen). The following listing shows the contents of that file.

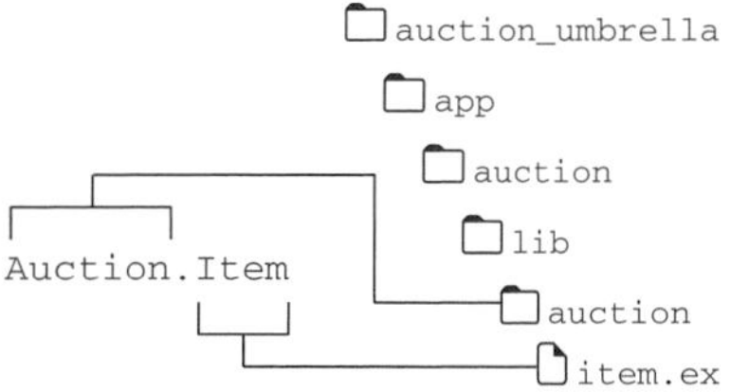

Figure 5.3 `Auction.Item` **file location**

Listing 5.11 Your `Auction.Item` module in the lib/auction/item.ex file

```
defmodule Auction.Item do
  defstruct [:id, :title, :description, :ends_at]    <-- Defines the data structure but doesn't provide default values
end
```

Finally, you have the `Auction.FakeRepo` code. Like `Auction.Item`, you match the module namespacing and your directory structure. Paste the `Auction.FakeRepo` module code a file named lib/auction/fake_repo.ex.

Listing 5.12 `Auction.FakeRepo` code in the lib/auction/fake_repo.ex file

```
defmodule Auction.FakeRepo do
  alias Auction.Item

  @items [                          <-- Feel free to customize the Items in your fake database to match your interests.
      %Item{
        id: 1,
        title: "My first item",
        description: "A tasty item sure to please",
        ends_at: ~N[2020-01-01 00:00:00]
      },
      %Item{
        id: 2,
        title: "WarGames Bluray",
        description: "The best computer movie of all time, now on Bluray!",
        ends_at: ~N[2018-10-15 13:39:35]
      },
      %Item{
        id: 3,
        title: "U2 - Achtung Baby on CD",
        description: "The sound of 4 men chopping down The Joshua Tree",
        ends_at: ~N[2018-11-05 03:12:29]
      }
    ]

  def all(Item), do: @items

  def get!(Item, id) do
```

```
      Enum.find(@items, fn(item) -> item.id === id end)
    end

  def get_by(Item, map) do
    Enum.find(@items, fn(item) ->
      Enum.all?(Map.keys(map), fn(key) ->
        Map.get(item, key) === map[key]
      end)
    end)
  end
end
```

All of these functions were written in chapter 4 and haven't been changed.

NOTE A good rule of thumb for filenames is to convert InitCase module names to lowercase and use an underscore before the previously capitalized letters. PhoenixInAction becomes phoenix_in_action, and "FakeRepo" becomes fake_repo.

5.2.2 Compile and run!

If you've followed along so far, you should have a directory structure similar to figure 5.4. But because Elixir is a compiled language, you need to compile your application before it can run. Thankfully, this is very easy.

Figure 5.4 The files in your Auction application

COMPILING

Now that you've got the code all organized, you may be wondering how to run it. In chapter 4, you compiled the file directly and brought it into an IEx session to play with. Now that you have a full-fledged application, you can use the `mix` utility. For example, to compile your application, you can issue the command `mix compile`.

```
> mix compile
Compiling 4 files (.ex)
Generated auction app
```

The first time you run this, it will go through your entire application looking for .ex files and compiling them into something that can run on the Erlang VM (using the mix.exs file). You'll notice in the preceding output that it compiled four files. Because there were no warnings during compilation, it tells you that it successfully generated the auction application.

If you run `mix compile` again right away, you'll get no output from the compiler. This is because Elixir's compiler is smart enough to recognize that no changes have been made since the last time you compiled, so nothing needs to be done. In fact, it's smart enough to know not only whether any files changed, but also *which* files have changed. If a file hasn't changed, it won't be recompiled (unless it's affected by a file that *did* change). This will save you lots of time as you build your app.

5.2.3 Running the Auction application for the first time

You now have a compiled application, so how do you run it? You haven't created a graphical interface for the application yet—only the code required to play with your fake data through a public interface. Because of that, the only way you can interact with the program at the moment is via IEx. But you'll start this IEx session a little differently than in the past.

In chapter 4, you started IEx while requiring a specific file (your application code, auction.ex). Now you no longer have a single file. Instead, you have an Elixir Mix application. To start up an IEx session and require an entire Mix application to be brought in, you can use the `iex -S mix` command inside the directory of a Mix application:

```
> iex -S mix
Erlang/OTP 21 [erts-10.1.3] [source] [64-bit] [smp:8:8] [ds:8:8:10] [async-
     threads:1] [hipe] [dtrace]

Interactive Elixir (1.7.4) - press Ctrl+C to exit (type h() ENTER for help)
iex(1)>
```

If you hadn't already compiled your application, it would compile here before starting IEx. But because you did compile it, it will start right up and include all the files of the Auction application. The following listing shows an example of testing the public interface you created.

Listing 5.13 Trying out the compiled Auction application

```
iex(1)> Auction.list_items |> Enum.map(fn(item) -> item.title end)
["My first item", "WarGames Bluray", "U2 - Achtung Baby on CD"]

iex(2)> Auction.get_item_by(%{title: "WarGames Bluray"})
%Auction.Item{description: "The best computer movie of all time, now on
     Bluray!",
 ends_at: ~N[2018-10-15 13:39:35], id: 2, title: "WarGames Bluray"}
```

You pipe the output of Auction.list_items/0 (with |>) into the first parameter for Enum.map/2.

It's all working! You didn't have to manually require any files or specify which files you were going to use—it all just worked! This is the magic of an Elixir application. I say *magic* because moving from using individual source code files outside of a Mix application (as in chapter 4, with a mess of file requires and effort needed to get everything working together) to having something that just *works* right off the bat (as in this chapter) is very refreshing.

5.3 Using Hex to get external dependencies

Now that you've gone through the configuration for the Auction application, you can move on to declaring the dependencies. Some very smart Elixir and Erlang developers have produced open source packages that can add functionality to your application, and one such package you'll eventually add to your application is Ecto. Ecto describes itself as "A database wrapper and language integrated query for Elixir."

You'll eventually need to move away from your `FakeRepo` and into a real repo so you can allow real functionality in your application. Ecto is currently *the* package to use when creating Elixir applications that need to talk to databases. In fact, you have to explicitly tell Phoenix *not* to bring in Ecto if you don't need it when creating a new Phoenix project.

As you'll recall from the discussion of the mix.exs file (section 5.1.3), your application keeps track of its required dependencies in the `deps` function. So far, you know you're going to require a package called Ecto and that it belongs in the mix.exs file.

Hex is Elixir's package manager. But Hex is more than that—it also comes with nice Mix tasks that make using the package manager easy. For example, there's a great search tool. Let's say you know you're going to need a package that makes rendering React.js components easier in your Phoenix application, but you don't know any package names. You can either go into a web browser and search the database through Hex's frontend (at https://hex.pm) or use the Mix task `mix hex.search PACKAGE`. The following listing shows the output from using the Mix task.

Listing 5.14 Searching Hex for a React.js package

There may be many more packages listed when you run this command.

```
> mix hex.search react
Package              Version              URL
reaxt                1.0.1                https://hex.pm/packages/reaxt
react_phoenix        0.5.0                https://hex.pm/packages/
     react_phoenix
lyn                  0.0.16               https://hex.pm/packages/lyn
phoenix_components   1.0.2                https://hex.pm/packages/
     phoenix_components
react_on_elixir      0.0.4                https://hex.pm/packages/
     react_on_elixir
phoenix_reactor      0.1.0                https://hex.pm/packages/
     phoenix_reactor
reactive             0.0.1                https://hex.pm/packages/reactive
reactivity           0.6.0                https://hex.pm/packages/reactivity
elixir_script_react  1.0.2-react.15.6.1   https://hex.pm/packages/
     elixir_script_react
Phoenix_react        0.1.0                https://hex.pm/packages/
     phoenix_react
```

NOTE If you get an error stating that "The task "hex.search" could not be found," run the command `mix local.hex` and try again.

The packages listed here have something to do with the word "react." It could be in the package name, in the description, or other places, and they're ordered loosely by popularity.

Sometimes you'll know what package you need, and you need to know the latest version number. In those cases, I've found the Mix task to be the fastest way to retrieve that information. For example, you know you'll need Ecto in your application, so the only further piece of information you require is the latest version number (unless you already know of a specific one you want to depend on). That means you can search for `ecto` with the Mix task, as shown in the following listing. Ecto is split into two distinct packages: `ecto` and `ecto_sql`. For now, you need the `ecto_sql` version in order to talk to your database.

Listing 5.15 Searching hex.pm for Ecto

```
> mix hex.search ecto                                    <-- There will be many more results when you run this command.
Package  Description                        Version  URL
ecto     A toolkit for data mapping...      3.0.3    https://hex.pm/packages/ecto
ecto_sql SQL-based adapters for Ecto...     3.0.3    https://hex.pm/packages/
     ecto_sql
# SNIP!
```

You can see that the latest version was 3.0.3 when I ran this command. Unless you have a compelling reason to use an older version of a package, it's generally a good idea to use the latest. You'll depend on at least version 3.0.3 in your application.

NOTE It's likely that by the time you read this, the version numbers will have advanced beyond 3.0.3. If that's the case, use the latest version available.

To specify the package name and version 3.0.3, your `deps` function would look like the following.

Listing 5.16 Specifying your first dependency

```
defp deps do
  [
    {:ecto_sql, "3.0.3"}        <-- Specifies that you want version 3.0.3
  ]
end
```

The preceding listing shows how to specify a dependency to a specific version requirement. But sometimes there are other ways you'd like to handle the dependency versions.

In general, Hex packages should use semantic versioning (`major.minor.patch`). In the case of Ecto, you're looking at the major 3, minor 0, patch 5 release. Major versions can have backward-incompatible changes in them—you'll normally require some migration in your usage of the package if you change major versions. Minor versions typically contain new functionality but don't break existing usage. Patch versions typically contain minor bug fixes and the like.

So what if you want to keep your Ecto package up to date but don't want to worry about manually editing the `deps` function every time there's a new release? There are a few options in the version specification syntax that you can use:

- `> 3.0.3`—This gives you any package as long as it's above version 3.0.3, including potentially breaking major releases. This does *not* include version 3.0.3 itself, so as I write this, Hex wouldn't be able to find a suitable version of Ecto for the package.
- `>= 3.0.3`—This gives you any package equal to or above 3.0.3. This includes any patch, minor, *and* potentially breaking major releases, so use this carefully.
- `< 4.0`—This uses any package found as long as it isn't version 4.0 or above. This could also mean that version 0.0.4 could be used just as well as version 3.0.3. Use this with caution as well.
- `>= 3.0.3 and < 3.1.0`—These gives you any package that's from the major 3 minor 0 releases, as long as it's equal to or above 3.0.3.
- `~> 3.0.3`—The preceding option is so common that a special symbol is used to denote this kind of requirement. `~> MAJOR.MINOR.PATCH` uses any version that's beyond the patch version but without incrementing the minor version. `~> MAJOR.MINOR` takes any minor or patch version up to the next major version.

Regardless of the version requirements, Hex will attempt to fetch the latest, most recent package version that meets the requirements specified. With that in mind, let's make sure you have Hex include any bug fixes in the 3.0 minor branch by using the `~> 3.0.3` format. The following listing shows what the `deps` function should look like.

Listing 5.17 Your newly specified dependency list

```
defp deps do
  [
    {:ecto_sql, "~> 3.0.3"}
  ]
end
```

Accepts any version from 3.0.3 to 3.0.x, as long as x is greater than or equal to 3

Ecto is an important part of your application, because it provides a wrapper around a database, but it doesn't speak to the database directly. Ecto requires an adapter specific to the database that you'd like to use. Why not use the adapter directly, without Ecto? Ecto provides a large range of utilities and functions that make working with a database *much* easier and without a lot of the boilerplate code that's usually necessary. And because you're writing code that Ecto then translates into database-speak, you can typically move from one database to another without having to change much (if any) of your code.

In this book, you'll be using the PostgreSQL database, so you'll use the PostgreSQL adapter. The vast majority of the code you'll write (if not all of it) will work as written with any of the other Ecto adapters. There may be small exceptions to this (mostly during the setup of the adapter itself), but the fact that databases are so easily interchangeable is one of the great things about using Ecto.

Because you're using PostgreSQL, you need to modify your `deps` function in mix.exs to include the dependency (`postgrex`), as in the following listing.

Listing 5.18 The newly specified dependency list

```
defp deps do
  [
    {:ecto_sql, "~> 3.0.3"},
    {:postgrex, "~> 0.14.1"}
  ]
end
```

postgrex is the Postgres Ecto adapter. Feel free to use the adapter you need for your preferred database.

If you'd rather use a different supported database for your application, be sure to use the correct adapter (see table 5.1).

Table 5.1 Ecto database adapters

Database	Ecto adapter	Dependency
PostgreSQL	`Ecto.Adapters.Postgres`	`postgrex`
MySQL	`Ecto.Adapters.MySQL`	`mariaex`
MSSQL	`MssqlEcto`	`mssql_ecto`
SQLite	`Sqlite.Ecto2`	`sqlite_ecto2`
Mnesia	`EctoMnesia.Adapter`	`ecto_mnesia`

5.3.1 Pulling in your dependencies

Now that you have the dependencies specified, you need to bring them into your application. You do that in the following listing by using a Mix task—`mix deps.get`. When you execute that task in your terminal, it will query hex.pm about the latest applicable versions of the dependencies you specified. It also does the job of fetching *their* dependencies, so you don't have to worry about manually ensuring that a long line of dependency requirements are met (see figure 5.5).

Listing 5.19 Getting dependencies with `mix deps.get`

```
> mix deps.get
Resolving Hex dependencies...
Dependency resolution completed:
```

```
New:
  connection 1.0.4
  db_connection 2.0.3
  decimal 1.6.0
  ecto 3.0.5
  ecto_sql 3.0.3
  postgrex 0.14.1
  telemetry 0.2.0
* Getting ecto_sql (Hex package)
* Getting postgrex (Hex package)
* Getting connection (Hex package)
* Getting db_connection (Hex package)
* Getting decimal (Hex package)
* Getting ecto (Hex package)
* Getting telemetry (Hex package)
```

You didn't request decimal—the packages you *did* request depend on them. (points to decimal 1.6.0)

ecto_sql relies on ecto, so it is brought in too. (points to ecto 3.0.5)

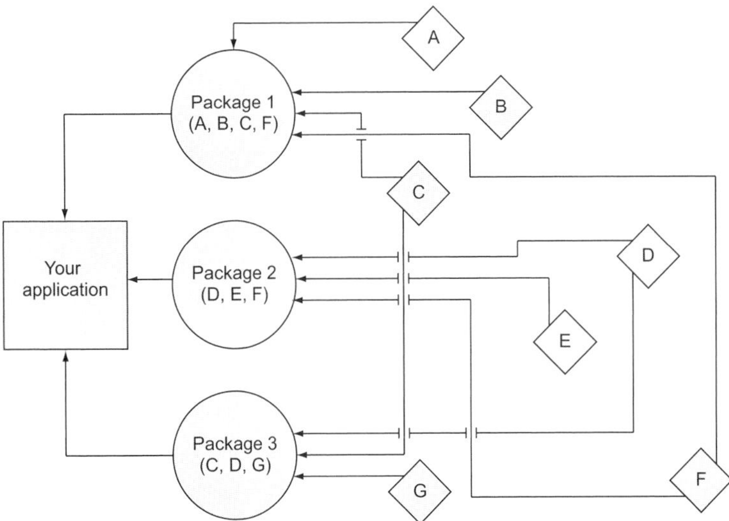

Figure 5.5 Hex manages the sometimes complex relationships between your app's dependencies.

The output you see is Hex fetching the required packages and putting them into the deps directory of your application. The next time you compile your application (whether explicitly via `mix compile` or by starting your application with `iex -S mix`), those dependencies will be compiled into your application for your application code to take advantage of.

We'll go deeper into using Ecto in the next chapter, but to demonstrate how you can use external dependencies with little fuss, let's temporarily add the UUID package to your application dependencies. Add the dependency requirement to your mix.exs file as follows.

Listing 5.20 Temporarily adding UUID to your dependencies

```
defp deps do
  [
    {:ecto_sql, "~> 3.0.3"},
    {:postgrex, "~> 0.14.1"},
    {:uuid, "~> 1.1.8"}
  ]
end
```

Your application can have as many dependencies as it requires.

Be sure to run `mix deps.get` again to fetch the newly added dependency.

Now, use it in your application's environment via an IEx session. UUID is a package that allows you to easily generate universally unique identifiers, so you'll test its ability to do so in the following listing by using its `uuid4/0` function to generate a version 4 UUID. You could even use it to generate auction titles.

Listing 5.21 Using the UUID package in your auction application

```
> iex -S mix
# ... likely lots of code compilation output

iex(1)> UUID.uuid4
"40a6eb21-4c85-46ac-a550-e18130187aee"

iex(2)> %Auction.Item{title: UUID.uuid4}
%Auction.Item{description: nil, ends_at: nil, id: nil,
 title: "592b2b0b-5f9e-4c74-91d9-478bd2ca1d9b"}
```

These ID strings will be different when you run this.

Because the purpose of UUIDs is to be "universally unique," your output will be different than mine was, but the formatting will be the same, and it will be a valid UUID string. It works!

You're now done with your little experiment, and you no longer need the UUID package. How can you get rid of once-required dependencies that are no longer needed? It's actually very easy. Simply remove it from the `deps/0` function in your mix.exs file.

Listing 5.22 Your `deps` function without UUID

```
defp deps do
  [
    {:ecto_sql, "~> 3.0.3"},
    {:postgrex, "~> 0.14.1"}
  ]
end
```

If you no longer need a dependency, just remove it from deps. UUID was previously here.

Once you've done that, you can again run `mix deps.get` and it will update your mix.lock file, which keeps track of all your dependencies. But if you look in your deps folder for your project, you'll still see a directory for UUID. If you'd like to get rid of that, you can manually delete it from the directory, or you can use the `mix` `deps.clean uuid` command in your terminal. It will determine that it's no longer needed and remove the package's code from your hard drive.

Summary

- When organizing Elixir projects, use multiple files instead of one large file.
- Use the `mix new` command to start a new Elixir project. That single task will generate the initial folder structure and files to get you started.
- Configuration of your application takes place in the mix.exs file.
- Hex.pm is the Elixir package manager, and it has many helpful third-party modules and applications to help you create your application.
- Your application's package dependencies are stated in the mix.exs file.

6 Bring in Phoenix

This chapter covers

- Configuring your environment to use Phoenix
- Creating a new Phoenix project inside your umbrella app
- Using the Auction business logic in a Phoenix project

So far, you've been running your Auction application in IEx. Although IEx does the job, is full-featured, and generally looks nice, the UI isn't going to raise millions of dollars in seed money for your auction startup. To get users on your site and bids on the items in your database, you need a web interface so users can interact with the data. It's time to bring in Phoenix.

The first thing you'll want to do with Phoenix is list the items in the database—that's what you'll do in this chapter. Creating, editing, and deleting the items and bidding on them will all come later. By the end of this chapter, you should have something like figure 6.1 in your web browser.

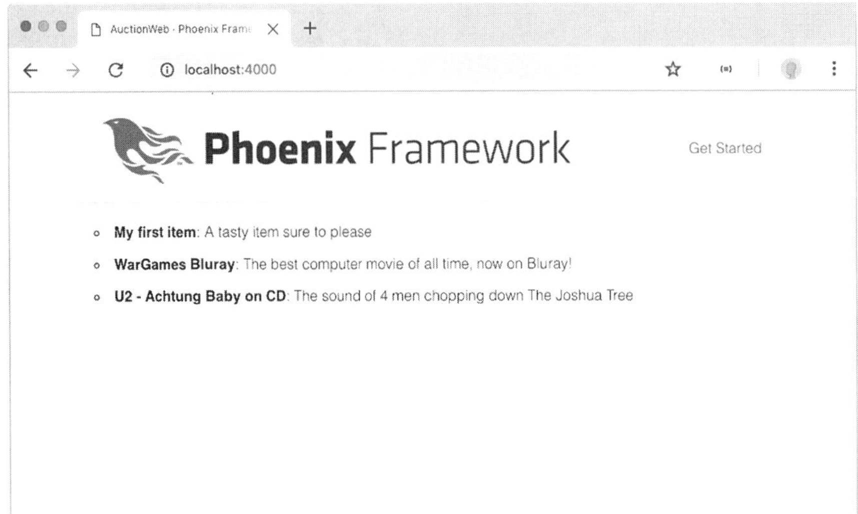

Figure 6.1 Listing items from your Auction's fake repo

6.1 Installing Phoenix on your system

The first thing you need to do to get your Phoenix application going is install Phoenix itself. If you've followed along so far, you should already have Elixir 1.5 or later installed on your system, as well as the Hex package manager tools.

The most up-to-date installation instructions are always found in Phoenix's documentation (https://hexdocs.pm/phoenix/installation.html#phoenix), and detailed instructions can be found in appendix A, but if you have all the prerequisites, you should be able to type the following line in your terminal to install the latest version of Phoenix:

```
mix archive.install hex phx_new 1.4.2
```

You also need Node.js (version 5.0.0 or greater), and you can find instructions for installing it on the Node.js download page (https://nodejs.org/en/download/) or in the Phoenix documentation (https://hexdocs.pm/phoenix/installation.html#node-js-5-0-0).

If you've installed Phoenix correctly, you should now see some entries for `mix phx` in the output of `mix help`

.

Listing 6.1 The new Phoenix Mix tasks

```
> mix help | grep phx

mix local.phx        # Updates the Phoenix project generator locally
mix phx.new          # Creates a new Phoenix v1.4.0 application
```

`| grep phx` takes the output of `mix help` and filters it to display only lines that contain `phx`.

```
mix phx.new.ecto        # Creates a new Ecto project within an umbrella project
mix phx.new.web         # Creates a new Phoenix web project within an umbrella
     project
```

These are some of the Mix tasks you'll use as you build your Phoenix application.

6.2 Creating a new Phoenix application

Once you've verified that Phoenix is installed on your system, you can ask it to create a new, blank Phoenix project. If you look at the output of listing 6.1, you'll see the `mix phx.new` task—that sounds like the one you want, but take a closer look at the last option. Because you've been building your application as an umbrella application, you can generate a new project *within* that application.

As discussed previously, you can ask Mix tasks for help to find out how to use them. In your terminal, type `mix help phx.new.web`.

Listing 6.2 The output of `mix help phx.new.web`

```
Creates a new Phoenix web project within an umbrella project.

It expects the name of the otp app as the first argument and for the command to
be run inside your umbrella application's apps directory:

    $ cd my_umbrella/apps
    $ mix phx.new.web APP [--module MODULE] [--app APP]

This task is intended to create a bare Phoenix project without database
integration, which interfaces with your greater umbrella application(s).
```

The Phoenix (web) portion of your application won't be using a database directly because you want to keep your domain logic separate from your web interface. All the database interactions will be handled in the Auction application you started in chapter 5. That means you won't need Ecto in this application, and you can pass the `--no-ecto` flag to `mix phx.new.web`.

Figure 6.2 shows what your current umbrella application directory looks like.

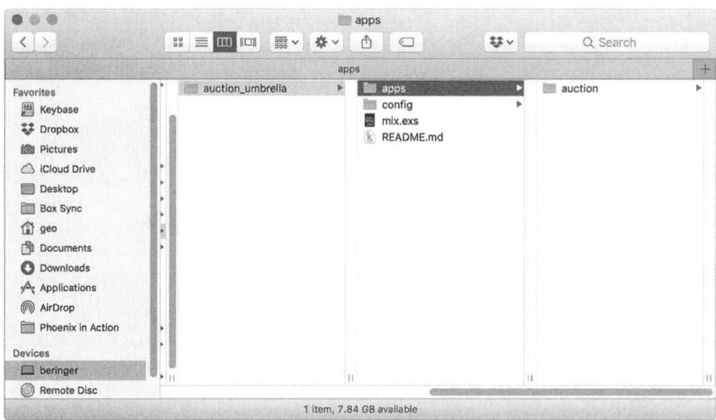

Figure 6.2 The umbrella app directories before you create a Phoenix app

To create the application, navigate to the apps directory of your `auction_umbrella` application (auction_umbrella/apps), and run this command:

```
> mix phx.new.web auction_web --no-ecto
```

You'll see a lot of output scroll by as the Mix task generates skeleton files for your application. Once those files are created, you'll be greeted by a prompt asking if you'd like to "Fetch and install dependencies? [Yn]." You can type `Y`(or just press Return), and it will fetch all the dependencies you'll need for your Phoenix application. Again, more text will scroll by as your dependencies are fetched from hex.pm.

You need to do one more thing before you can start up the server. Phoenix requires you to let it know which library you'd like it to use when processing data in JSON format. The default library that Phoenix uses is called Jason, and it's what you'll use as well. In the top level of your umbrella application, you need to configure the Phoenix dependency to use Jason. In auction_umbrella/config/config.exs, add the last line in the following listing.

Listing 6.3 Configuring Phoenix in auction_umbrella/config/config.exs

```
use Mix.Config

import_config "../apps/*/config/config.exs"    <-- Imports all the sub-application configurations

config :phoenix, :json_library, Jason    <-- Here is where you configure Phoenix to use Jason.
```

Now any app inside the umbrella application that relies on Phoenix will use the Jason package as its JSON processing library.

6.2.1 Running your server for the first time

Once your dependencies are fetched, you'll be greeted with some good news.

Listing 6.4 Your Phoenix application is ready!

```
We are all set! Go into your application by running:

    $ cd auction_web

Start your Phoenix app with:

    $ mix phx.server

You can also run your app inside IEx (Interactive Elixir) as:

    $ iex -S mix phx.server    <-- Allows you to enter commands for your application while also running the Phoenix server
```

You *do* want to start your application, so follow the suggestion and go into your new auction_web directory and run the Mix task to start your server (`mix phx.server`). As soon as you do so, you'll see *yet more* debug text scroll by, as your application is

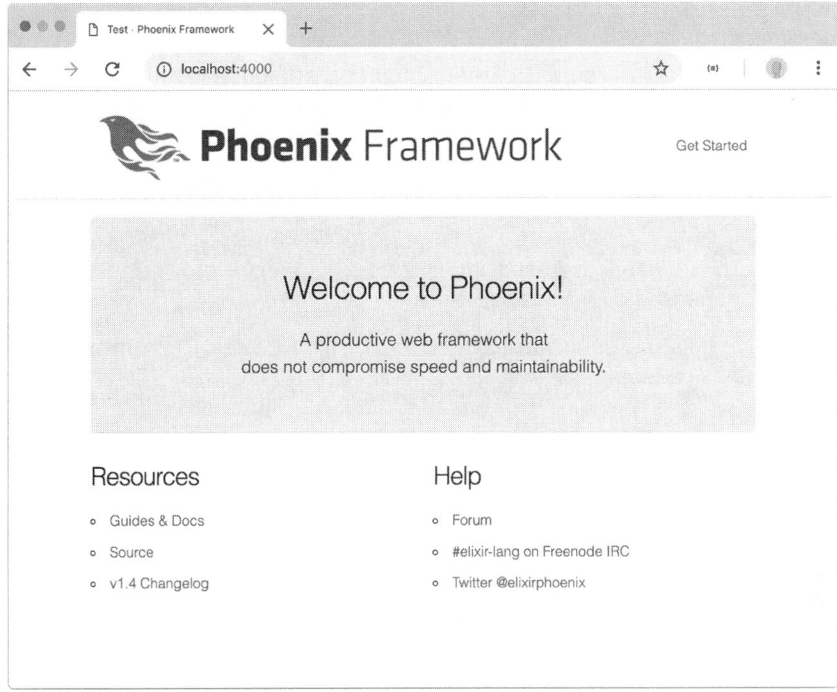

Figure 6.3 If everything has gone correctly, this is what you'll see—a web page served up from your local computer through Phoenix.

compiled and the server is started up. As soon as you see something like the following, you're serving web pages (like in figure 6.3)!

```
[info] Running AuctionWeb.Endpoint with Cowboy using http://localhost:4000
20:15:09 - info: compiled 6 files into 2 files, copied 3 in 970 ms
```

Now for the moment of truth. Fire up your favorite web browser and navigate to http://localhost:4000. You should see something similar to figure 6.1. You're now serving up web pages through Phoenix on your computer!

What is http://localhost:4000?

You may be used to entering domain names into your web browser—numbers and colons and unqualified domains may be foreign to you. So what does the localhost:4000 address mean?

The address can be broken down into two sections:

1 The IP address or domain
2 The port number

(continued)

The IP address is the address of the computer that's hosting the content. When you enter a domain name into your browser, that domain name is an alias for an IP address that your browser actually calls. `localhost` is simply the IP address of the local computer.

The port is like a tunnel that the connection uses when making requests. The Phoenix web server listens for connections on port 4000, so you're telling your browser go there explicitly. When you don't enter a port number, a browser uses port 80 by default for unsecured HTTP traffic.

Put the two together, and you have http://IP_ADDRESS:PORT, or http://localhost:4000, in this case.

To stop the server, you can press Ctrl-C twice in the terminal that's running the server.

6.3 Listing items from the fake repo

You now have a running Phoenix web application, but it's not going to take over the world. For starters, no auction items are listed. All you're seeing now is the placeholder stuff that the `mix phx.new.web` Mix task generated. Although it's exciting that you have a working web application, I, for one, want more. Let's list the items that you currently have up for auction.

If you've been following along in chapters 4 and 5, you've built an Auction application that contains all the business logic of your site. When you left it, it was using a fake repo to serve up hardcoded items. But the nice thing about *how* you created it is that you don't care what repo it uses, where it gets its items, or *anything* about its logic—you just want the items. This is where having strong boundaries between your interface (like a Phoenix web application) and your business logic has huge benefits. As long as your business logic provides a public interface you can use to get the information you're after, you can let *it* take care of where it keeps the data and how it gets it. You want your web interface to be as naive as possible about the inner workings of the business logic.

You *did* build a simple public interface to get the items from your database: `Auction.list_items/0`. You can bring in that application and use it in this application. How can you do that? Specify it as a dependency in your mix.exs file. The mix.exs file contains a function named `deps` where you can list dependencies for your application. Right now, it contains the default dependencies for a Phoenix application generated with the `phx.new.web` generator.

All you need to do is tell this web application about your Auction application. A dependency declaration typically contains the name of the application required, plus the version numbers that would satisfy the dependency. But there are other ways you can declare a dependency: via the `path` option to direct it to a directory machine, via the `github` option to specify a Git repo on GitHub, or via the `in_umbrella` option to tell it that the dependency is available as another app within the same umbrella. This last scenario is the one you have going on, so you'll use `in_umbrella`.

Add `{:auction, in_umbrella: true}` to the list of dependencies (don't forget the comma at the end of the line above it, if you're adding it to the end of the list). See the following listing as a guide.

Listing 6.5 The default list of dependencies

```
defp deps do
  [
    {:phoenix, "~> 1.4.0"},
    {:phoenix_pubsub, "~> 1.1"},
    {:phoenix_html, "~> 2.11"},
    {:phoenix_live_reload, "~> 1.2", only: :dev},
    {:gettext, "~> 0.11"},
    {:jason, "~> 1.0"},
    {:plug_cowboy, "~> 2.0"},
    {:auction, in_umbrella: true}          <-- Add this line.
  ]
end
```

Once you've added that dependency, you can use the `Auction` module in your new `AuctionWeb` Phoenix application inside the umbrella.

6.3.1 Modifying the controller and template

In order to see the list of items in your fake repo, you need to modify the controller and the view template. In the controller, you need to bind the result of the `Auction.get_items/0` function call to a variable, and then pass that to the view template. In the template, you need to iterate through that list of items and display information about each one.

THE CONTROLLER

If you're wondering which controller is being used to serve up the page you see when you navigate to http://localhost:4000, you can figure that out in a couple of different ways:

- Open auction_web/lib/auction_web/router.ex. In there, you can see that the root route (/) is handled by the `AuctionWeb.PageController` index.
- Inside the auction_web directory, run `mix phx.routes` in your terminal. The output of that is simply `page_path GET / AuctionWeb.PageController :index`, which indicates that the only route being handled right now is `GET /`, and it's being routed to the `AuctionWeb.PageController` index.

We aren't going to do anything super fancy in this chapter, so you'll reuse the controller that the Phoenix generator made for you: `AuctionWeb.PageController`. That controller was generated for you at auction_web/lib/auction_web/controllers/page _controller.ex. The contents of that file are shown in the following listing—it's a minimally defined controller.

Listing 6.6 `AuctionWeb.PageController`

```
defmodule AuctionWeb.PageController do
  use AuctionWeb, :controller

  def index(conn, _params) do
    render(conn, "index.html")
  end
end
```

Renders the index.html.eex template

You can see that the only function defined in the controller right now is the `index` function that the root route points to. In the `index` function, you need to do two things:

1. Get the list of `Items`, binding it to a variable.
2. Pass that list to the view template so you can render the `Items`.

A controller's functions are just like any other Elixir function definitions—you can call external modules' functions, bind the results of those to a variable, and transform data. Your `Auction` module's public interface was written so that you could easily get a list of `Items` with `Auction.list_items/0`. You'll use that function and capture the result. The following listing shows the modified `index` function.

Listing 6.7 Capturing the list of `Items`

```
def index(conn, _params) do
  items = Auction.list_items()
  render(conn, "index.html")
end
```

The new line, which grabs all the items up for auction

You now have the list of `Item` structs in the `items` variable, so step 1 is done. Step 2 is to pass the list to the view template. The second line of the `index` function is a call to `Phoenix.Controller.render/2`, and it takes two parameters: `conn`, which is the `Plug.Conn` struct that's passed through the application from the initial connection through rendering the view, and the name of the template Phoenix should render for this route (`"index.html"`).

If you're wondering why the generated code in the controller in listing 6.6 calls `render` instead of using the full name of `Phoenix.Controller.render`, take a look at the second line: `use AuctionWeb, :controller`. That line does a whole bunch of stuff behind the scenes, but the thing we're interested in here is that it calls `import Phoenix.Controller`. That allows you to use any `Phoenix.Controller` function in your module without having to type the full name.

Inside `Phoenix.Controller`, there's also a `render/3` that accepts a third parameter: assigns (variables) to be passed through to the view. All you need to do to use this other `render` function is add your `items` list to the render call.

Figure 6.4 gives an overview of how the group of `items` moves from a request from the controller, through the `Auction` module, to the `Auction.FakeRepo` module, and then back to the controller to be finally passed to the view and template.

Listing 6.8 Passing `items` to the view/template

```
def index(conn, _params) do
  items = Auction.list_items()
  render(conn, "index.html", items: items)    <-- Passes the list of items to the index.html.eex template
end
```

Now the view has access to your items through an `@items` variable.

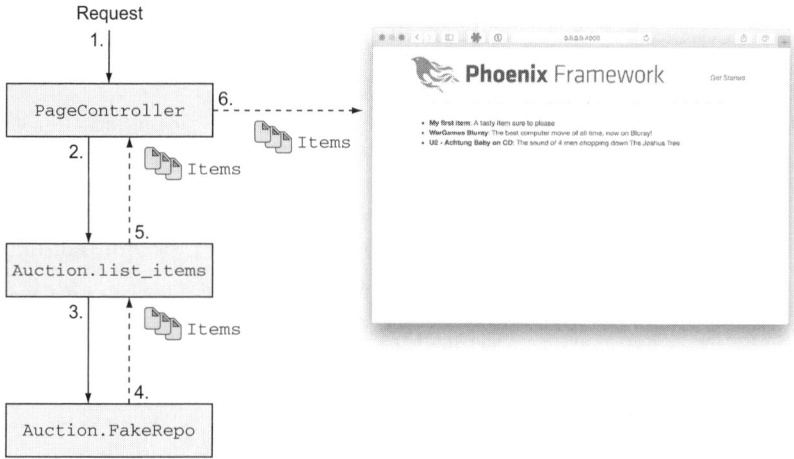

Figure 6.4 The flow of items from the fake repo to the view/template

THE TEMPLATE

The final step for rendering your list of items in the browser is to use the `@items` variable that you set up in the controller. As you'll recall, the second parameter of the `Phoenix.Controller.render/3` function on the last line of `index/2` is `"index.html"`. That defines the template Phoenix will use to render the web page. Phoenix will look for a file named index.html in the page subdirectory (short for `PageController`) of the templates directory. The full path of the template file is auction_umbrella/apps/auction_web/lib/auction_web/templates/page/index.html.eex.

This file is an .eex file, which means it will be preprocessed by Phoenix before the final HTML is output. This means you can use some Elixir inside the template file itself. Everything inside the `<%=` and `%>` tags will be processed by Elixir, and the result will be rendered in its place. You can also enclose Elixir code within `<%` and `%>` if you don't need to render the results.

If you open the index template file, you'll see some straight HTML that provides the "Welcome to Phoenix" banner and links to resources and help. You can safely delete all this HTML and replace it with your own. For your purposes, a simple unordered list (`<ul>`) will be enough to list your items. You can open the unordered list, but you still need to iterate through your list of items and output a list item (`<li>`) for each entry.

There's an idiomatic way to render each item in a list like this—using `for`. `for` is a *comprehension*, and according to the docs, "comprehensions allow you to quickly build a data structure from an enumerable." Figure 6.5 has a breakdown of the portions of the `for` comprehension as you'll use it.

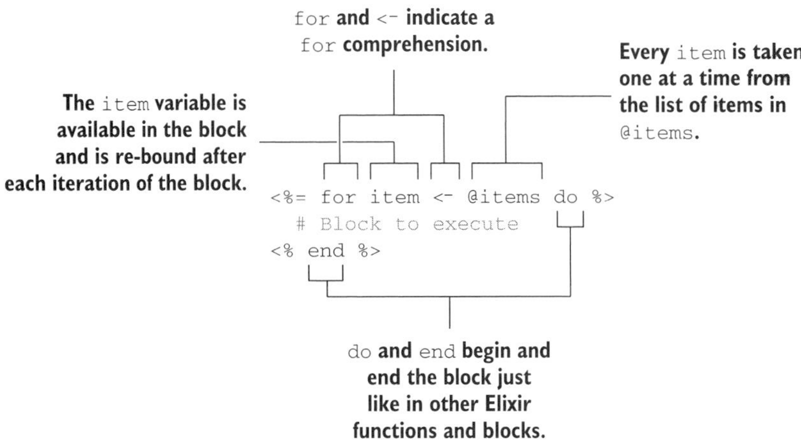

Figure 6.5 Breakdown of the `for` comprehension

The full documentation contains some pretty neat examples and shows how useful `for` can be (https://hexdocs.pm/elixir/Kernel.SpecialForms.html#for/1), but you'll use it pretty simply. The following listing shows how you can use `for` to iterate through the items in `@items` and output a `<li>` tag for each one.

Listing 6.9 Using the `for` comprehension in index.html.eex

```
<ul>
  <%= for item <- @items do %>
    <li>
      <strong><%= item.title %></strong>: <%= item.description %>
    </li>
  <% end %>
</ul>
```

Code contained inside <%= and %> will output into the view. (annotates `<%= for item <- @items do %>`)

Code contained inside <% and %> will not output anything. (annotates `<% end %>`)

Each `Item` struct from your list of `@items` is bound to the `item` inside the `do/end` block, one at a time. Inside that block, you render an opening `<li>` tag, render the title of your item with `<%= item.title %>` inside a `<strong>` HTML tag, and then render the description of the item with `<%= item.description %>`. Remember, anything inside the `<%=` and `%>` tags will be evaluated as Elixir code, and the result will be rendered. This allows you to get data from the database, transform the data in any way necessary, and then render what you need. Figure 6.6 breaks down how the listing is generated.

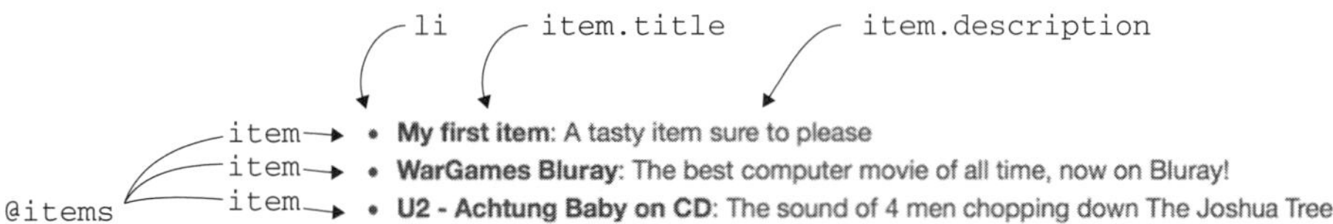

Figure 6.6 A breakdown of the list of items

Start your server up again (if you killed it earlier) with `mix phx.server` in the top level of your Auction umbrella application, and then point your browser to http://localhost:4000. You should see a list of your own like figure 6.7.

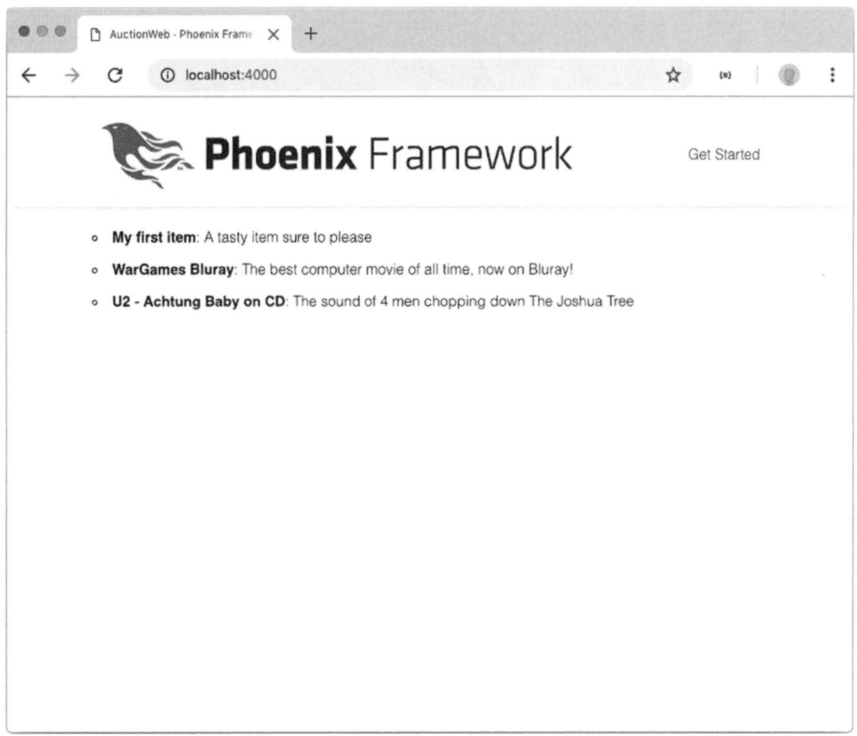

Figure 6.7 Listing items from your Auction's fake repo

You'll notice that there are some things on the web page that you didn't add. In particular, there's a large "Phoenix Framework" banner image and some baseline CSS and styles. Back in chapter 3, I briefly introduced the idea behind the layout and page templates. You edited the page template in this chapter, but the layout template wraps every page template. The banner and the rest of the wrapping HTML are contained in a layout template named app.html.eex. We won't cover it here, but if you'd like, go ahead and take a peek inside that file to see how it works.

In the next chapter, you'll bring in a real database and start persisting items into it

Summary

- Use `mix phx.new` to generate a brand new Phoenix application.
- Use the `mix phx.new.web` Mix task to generate a new Phoenix application *inside* an existing umbrella application.
- `mix phx.server` can be used to serve your Phoenix application locally at http://localhost:4000.
- Controllers are where you set up your application's state in order to correctly render what needs to be rendered to the user.
- Templates contain the HTML and Elixir code that's processed and sent back to the user to view in their browser.

7 Being persistent with a database

This chapter covers

- Configuring Ecto to use a real database
- Using Ecto to query the database for items
- Using Ecto to insert items into and delete them from the database

Your Auction application has a public interface where you can query for items, and you know how to bring external package dependencies into the application. In chapter 5, you readied the application for real database use by bringing in Ecto and `postgrex` (or a different database adapter based on your needs).

You originally set up your Auction application to use a "fake" repo so as not to introduce too much complexity while you built up a small public interface for querying items. It was relatively quick to set up, required no external dependencies, and was fast, but it only allowed you to read a static list of items. For a true data-driven web application, you need the ability to do complex queries as well as insert new items and update existing ones.

In this chapter, you'll get rid of the fake database and move to a real database. To achieve this, a few prerequisites need to be taken care of:

1. A database needs to be installed in your local dev environment. I'm using PostgreSQL, but other options are available in Ecto if you'd rather use them (such as MySQL or MSSQL). Because Ecto provides abstractions away from SQL-like language, there may be database-specific gotchas for your database of choice. Check the Ecto documentation to see if your database has any specific issues (https://github.com/elixir-ecto/ecto).
2. Once the database is installed, you need to know how to access it. This involves the database address (typically localhost or 127.0.0.1) as well as the port number.
3. You'll need a database user ID and password (either created specifically for the Auction application or one already available).

Once you have those things, you're ready to tackle the next section.

7.1 A quick intro to Ecto

Ecto does more than allow you to communicate with a particular database. It provides a unified language for talking to multiple kinds of databases—even simultaneously. It provides an easy way to specify module relationships, query databases, track changes throughout the lifecycle of a database request, and group multiple queries into a single transaction so that if one query fails, the rest of the queries can be rolled back.

It provides a way to describe how your structs will handle data and map them to specific database tables. It provides migrations so that you can track how a database's structure changes over time, and it allows you to migrate up or down any connected database to match the required structure. It provides module-side and database-side validations to ensure you don't have orphaned or bad data in your database.

There are many things that Ecto does well, and the best way to start learning about them is to dive in and get your hands dirty.

7.2 Configuring Ecto

If you haven't already specified Ecto as a dependency in your application (as in chapter 5), you need to do that first. The following listing shows what the `deps` function in your mix.exs file should look like.

Listing 7.1 Specifying Ecto and Postgrex as dependencies

```
defp deps do
  [
    {:ecto_sql, "3.0.3"},
    {:postgrex, "0.14.1"}
  ]
end
```

postgrex is the PostgreSQL adapter for ecto_sql. (annotation on the `{:postgrex, "0.14.1"}` line)

I'm using PostgreSQL in my version of Auction, so I've included `postgrex` as a dependency along with `ecto_sql`. Refer to table 7.1 if you're using a different database to make sure you've specified the correct adapter.

Table 7.1 Ecto database adapters

Database	Ecto adapter	Dependency
PostgreSQL	`Ecto.Adapters.Postgres`	`postgrex`
MySQL	`Ecto.Adapters.MySQL`	`mariaex`
MSSQL	`MssqlEcto`	`mssql_ecto`
SQLite	`Sqlite.Ecto2`	`sqlite_ecto2`
Mnesia	`EctoMnesia.Adapter`	`ecto_mnesia`

Your Phoenix application also needs to bring in some Ecto helpers. Even though you created your Phoenix app with the `--no-ecto` flag, there's a specific package that's nice to have when working with Ecto in Phoenix (which you'll be doing eventually). The `phoenix_ecto` package provides all you need to interact with Ecto within Phoenix.

To bring that dependency into your application, you need to edit the Phoenix app's mix.exs file, located at auction_umbrella/apps/auction_web/mix.exs. You can simply add `{:phoenix_ecto, "~> 4.0"}` to the list of dependencies inside `deps`. Once you have the correct dependencies listed, run `mix deps.get` in your terminal to fetch the packages from hex.pm.

In order for Ecto to work with the new database, you need to give it some information, such as the database name, the username and password it can access that database with, and the database adapter you'll be using. Application configuration like that is typically done in the config directory, more specifically, in the config.exs file.

You may (or may not) be surprised to learn that you already have an auction_umbrella/apps/auction/config/config.exs file in your Auction application. How did it get there? It was created along with the rest of the standard files and directories for the application when you used the `mix new` command line script. If you open that file, you'll notice that there's little in the file apart from comments. But these comments can be very helpful as you figure out what can be configured and how to read those configurations in your application.

For Ecto, the reading and using of the configuration are taken care of for you—you just need to tell Ecto about your local database environment. Specifically, there are three initial things you need to let Ecto know:

- What repos you have in your application
- How to access each of those repos
- The minimal setup for the repos

As described in the comments in config.exs, you do that with the `config` function. There are two different versions of `config`: `config/2` and `config/3`. You'll be using both. `config/2` requires the name of your application (`:auction`) and the key/value pairs you'd like to configure.

To start, you'll tell your application that the name of your repo is `Auction.Repo`. Ecto can handle multiple repos simultaneously, so it expects a list as the repo's value. Add the following line to your config.exs file.

Listing 7.2 Letting Ecto know which repos you have in your application

```
config :auction, ecto_repos: [Auction.Repo]
```

You'll use `config/3` to tell Ecto how your Auction.Repo repo will communicate with your database. `config/3` requires the name of your application (`:auction`), a key to store the configuration under, and key/value pairs for configuration. The following listing shows the basic values that Ecto requires in config.exs.

Listing 7.3 Configuring `Auction.Repo`

```
config :auction, Auction.Repo,
  database: "auction",
  username: "postgres",
  password: "postgres",
  hostname: "localhost",
  port: "5432"
```

Sets your username and password

These values should be pretty self-explanatory. Plug in the values that work for your local database. I'm using PostgreSQL, so the adapter for PostgreSQL is `Ecto.Adapters.Postgres`. If you require a different database adapter, refer to table 7.1.

Finally, you need to create a file that will house the code for your repo. This is super-simple as Ecto provides almost all the functionality you need. All you need in your module is `use Ecto.Repo`, the name of your application (`:auction`), and the adapter you're using. In a file named auction_umbrella/apps/auction/lib/auction/repo.ex, enter the code in the following listing. Naming the module `Auction.Repo` matches the Ecto configuration in listing 7.3.

Listing 7.4 Setting up the `Auction.Repo` file

```
defmodule Auction.Repo do
  use Ecto.Repo,
    otp_app: :auction,
    adapter: Ecto.Adapters.Postgres
end
```

Using Ecto.Repo to configure your application repo

By including `use Ecto.Repo, opt_app: :auction` in your module, you benefit from a number of functions that Ecto brings in and that you don't have to define yourself. This keeps boilerplate code to a minimum.

That's it on the Elixir side of things! You're now ready to use Ecto.

7.2.1 Using Ecto's Mix tools to set up your database

Believe it or not, you've already provided Ecto with the minimum amount of information it needs to start interacting with your application. The first thing you want Ecto to do is create the database you specified when you configured `Auction.Repo` in config.exs (`database: "auction"`). To make that happen, you'll use the Mix tasks that Ecto provides.

If you haven't yet installed your database and set up the user specified in your config file (`username: "postgres", password: "postgres"`), do that now, and make sure the user has the ability to create a database. Then you can run the `ecto.create` Mix task as follows:

```
> mix ecto.create
The database for Auction.Repo has been created
```

If you received the preceding response when you ran that command, you're in business! Your application can connect to the database and interact with it successfully.

7.3 Preparing Auction to use the database

Now that you've created the database, you need to create its structure. How will the information in the database be structured? What will it look like? What kind of data will you be storing? You need to provide this information to Ecto as a *schema*.

7.3.1 Defining the Auction.Item schema

A database is made up of tables that store information in rows, and each row has data that corresponds to the columns that the table defines. For example, if you needed to store data about a menu for a coffee shop, there could be a table named menu_items to store that data. The schema would define the kind of information you need to store in that database table. It could look something like table 7.2.

Table 7.2 A table storing menu items for a coffee shop

Column name	Data type	Example
`title`	String	Fancy Espresso
`description`	String	A little pick-me-up
`price`	Integer	295

NOTE In table 7.2, why store the price as an integer instead of a float (like 2.95)? Well, computers are notorious for rounding and precision errors. You can eliminate those by just multiplying your price by 100 and storing it as an integer.

If you open auction_umbrella/apps/auction/lib/auction/item.ex, you'll see something similar already defined—a `defstruct` defining what your data looks for an

Auction.Item. This was fine for your fake repo, but now you need to let Ecto know the details of how your data is structured. To do that, you delete the defstruct definition and instead use Ecto's Ecto.Schema.schema/2 function.

Ecto.Schema.schema/2 takes as arguments the table name that the data will live in, plus a list of field definitions (these will roughly match up with the columns in your table) defined by Ecto.Schema.field/2. It will have a familiar feel, but you'll provide Ecto with more information about your module's data structure, such as the data type and which table it can find all your information in.

The following listing shows the Auction.Item schema defined for Ecto.

Listing 7.5 Defining Auction.Item's schema for Ecto

```
defmodule Auction.Item do
  use Ecto.Schema

  schema "items" do
    field :title, :string
    field :description, :string
    field :ends_at, :utc_datetime
    timestamps()
  end
end
```

A convenience function that adds inserted_at and updated_at columns

Here are a few points to note about this schema:

- use Ecto.Schema allows you to type just the function names provided by the module (such as schema and field). Otherwise, you'd have to type Ecto .Schema.schema and Ecto.Schema.field. This line also provides other functions under the hood to allow Ecto to do what it needs to do.
- Ecto.Schema provides a pretty extensive list of types for your data (and even allows you to create custom ones). See table 7.3 for a list of possibilities.
- timestamps() is a simple way to let Ecto know that your data will have inserted_at and updated_at columns with timestamps of when the particular row was created and updated.
- You may have noticed that you aren't defining a field :id. Ecto realizes that most tables you create will have a corresponding id column, and it provides one by default. You can override that default if you'd like, but you want the id column, in this case.

Table 7.3 Some often-used Ecto data types

Ecto type	Elixir type	Example(s)
:id	Integer	1, 100, 1_000
:integer	Integer	1, 2, 3
:float	Float	3.14, 9.3976387565388

Table 7.3 Some often-used Ecto data types *(continued)*

Ecto type	Elixir type	Example(s)
`:boolean`	Boolean	true, false
`:string`	UTF-8 string	"Phoenix in Action"
`:date`	Date	2018-10-30
`:time`	Time	03:08:32.936199
`:naive_datetime`	NaiveDateTime	Date and time without time zone information
`:utc_datetime`	DateTime	Date and time with time zone information

7.3.2 Migrating the database

Now that you have your schema defined, Ecto knows how to interact with the database when dealing with `Items`. But the database itself doesn't know anything about `Items`. You've created the database itself, but you haven't created the table or columns that your `Auction.Item` schema is referencing. That's your next step—creating the table and columns in the database.

To do that, you can use another Ecto construct known as a *migration*. Migrations are pieces of code that allow you to build up and tear down your database programmatically. This allows you to commit your migrations into a version control system, share it with other developers, and recreate the database structure as needed. It also provides a good boundary separating code and database, allowing Ecto to do the hard work of interacting directly with the database.

Ecto provides a Mix task to easily create migrations: `mix ecto.gen.migration` will create the file (and any necessary directories) for a migration that's timestamped in order to maintain the order of migrations. Not only that, but like `mix new`, it will generate a small amount of boilerplate code that will help you get started on your migration. To use it, you simply type `mix ecto.gen.migration` along with the filename you'd like to use for your migration. It's typically a good idea to be descriptive about what you're doing to the database in your migration's filename so you can easily find it later if required.

Let's name your migration `create_items`, since you're creating the `items` table. The following code snippet shows the output when I ran the command on my development machine. Make sure you run this command in the auction_umbrella/apps/auction directory.

```
> mix ecto.gen.migration create_items
* creating priv/repo/migrations
* creating priv/repo/migrations/20181212023436_create_items.exs
```

If you peek into the file that was created (priv/repo/migrations/20181212023436_create_items.exs in my case; yours will be different depending on when you ran the command), you'll find that some boilerplate code was generated for you.

Listing 7.6 Boilerplate migration code

```
defmodule Auction.Repo.Migrations.CreateItems do
  use Ecto.Migration

  def change do
                        <-- Here's where you'd place the code detailing the change for the migration.
  end
end
```

An `Ecto.Migration` is made up of a single `change/0` function, or an `up/0` function accompanied by a `down/0` function. These tell Ecto how you'd like to change your database in this migration. If you provide both an `up/0` and a `down/0` function, Ecto will run the code in `up/0` as it's building your database, migration by migration, and it will run `down/0` as it's tearing your database down. If you only provide a `change/0` function, Ecto is smart enough to know how the database changes as it goes up and down. Typically, you'll only need to give Ecto a `change/0` migration, but there are times when you might need more control over how specific tables are torn down (such as removing specific data or notifying some external service). In your case, creating a table is simple enough that you'll stick with the provided `change/0` function.

Ecto provides a number of functions to define your table's structure. To create your table, you use the `create/1` function. `create` can create tables, indexes, and constraints, but you want to create a table, in this case. The argument you provide `create/1` is the directive to create a table, and you provide its name.

Then, you provide a list of actions (via functions) that should be performed on the table after creating it (adding columns, in this case). Each column is added by using the `add/3` function, which accepts the name of the column (provided as an atom), what type of data it'll contain, and any options you'd like to specify (such as default values). `add/3` will look a lot like the `field` function you used when defining the schema for `Auction.Item`. Also, like in your schema, you don't have to specify that you want an `:id` column (it creates one by default), and you can use the `timestamps()` function to automatically generate `inserted_at` and `updated_at` columns.

The following listing shows how you create the table in your migration.

Listing 7.7 Filling out the data for your table-creation migration

```
defmodule Auction.Repo.Migrations.CreateItems do
  use Ecto.Migration

  def change do
    create table("items") do          <-- "items" will be the name of the table. By convention, table names are plural nouns.
      add :title, :string
      add :description, :string
      add :ends_at, :utc_datetime
      timestamps()
    end
  end
end
```

Now that you have your migration filled out, describing to Ecto exactly what you'd like to do in the migration, you can use a Mix task to ask Ecto to run the migration. Ecto provides a Mix task that lists the application's migrations and their current status (whether they're "up" or "down"). Run `mix ecto.migrations` to see that list.

```
> mix ecto.migrations

Repo: Auction.Repo

  Status    Migration ID    Migration Name
--------------------------------------------------
  down      20181212023436  create_items
```

The down status shows that this migration hasn't yet been run.

You can see by the output that your new migration hasn't yet been run on the database. `mix ecto.migrate` will migrate any migrations that haven't yet been run. You've only got one so far, so that command will run it.

When you run it, you'll see some output from Ecto describing exactly what it's doing to your database. Here's the output I saw when I ran the command:

```
> mix ecto.migrate
18:36:48.180 [info]  == Running 20181212023436
     Auction.Repo.Migrations.CreateItems.change/0 forward
18:36:48.180 [info]  create table items
18:36:48.196 [info]  == Migrated 20181212023436 in 0.0s
```

Migrates the database in the up direction

You just created a database table! Really easy and fast, huh? You didn't need to know a lick of SQL or the small intricate differences between how one database does things versus another (like MySQL compared to PostgreSQL). It just works.

What if you made a mistake and weren't quite ready to migrate yet? Ecto provides a Mix task for that as well. You can run `mix ecto.rollback` to roll back just the last migration, either using its `down/0` function or by reversing the changes in the `change/0` function. Figure 7.1 illustrates the direction the database migrates when using up and down. You don't have any data in your database, so you can try out the feature without worrying about destroying any data.

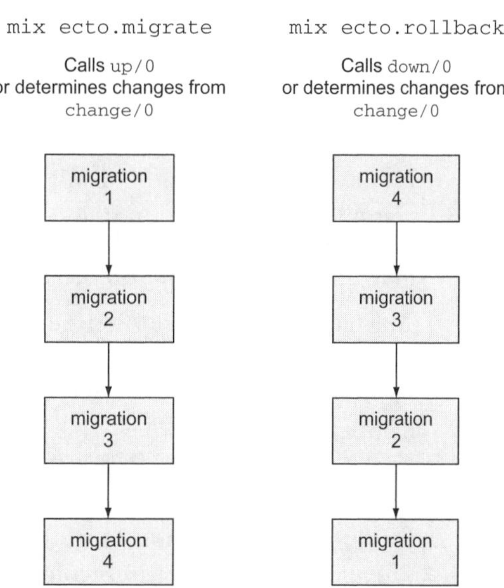

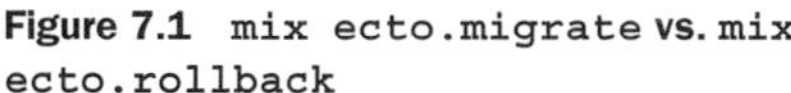
Figure 7.1 `mix ecto.migrate` **vs.** `mix ecto.rollback`

```
> mix ecto.rollback
18:37:23.710 [info]  == Running 20181212023436
     Auction.Repo.Migrations.CreateItems.change/0 backward
18:37:23.710 [info]  drop table items
18:37:23.714 [info]  == Migrated 20181212023436 in 0.0s
```

Migrates the database down, undoing the previous migration

You can see that Ecto is smart enough to know that you created an `items` table when you migrated forward (or *up*) and that the reverse is to drop (or destroy) the `items` table when you migrate backwards (or *down*). Note that `ecto.migrate` attempts to bring as many migrations up as possible, whereas `ecto.rollback` only rolls back one migration at a time.

Although `mix ecto.rollback` can be extremely helpful, it can be dangerous as well. If you had thousands of rows of customer data in that table, it would all be gone now! Use it with care.

To continue with your Auction application, you need that table to exist. Run `mix ecto.migrate` again to recreate the table before moving on.

7.3.3 Pointing the public interface to the new repo

When you initially created your Auction application, you also created a fake repo so you could develop your public interface. It's now time to point your public interface to use your *new* database. You made it really easy to do that by not referencing the repo directly, instead using a module context variable.

`lib/auction.ex` is the file that provides your public interface and does the work of talking with your repo. The only thing you need to change in that file now is which repo it points at. It currently reads

```
@repo FakeRepo
```

Change that line to point to your new repo:

```
@repo Auction.Repo
```

Because you're no longer using `FakeRepo` in that file, you can also remove it from the list of aliases. The compiler will spit out a warning (more like a *notice*) every time you compile your application unless you remove it.

7.3.4 Instructing the application to supervise the database connection

You have one final step before you can test your new database connection. You've defined your schema, created the table in the database, and pointed your public interface to the new repo, but you still haven't told your application to *connect to* the database.

The best way to do that is through a supervisor. We haven't discussed supervisors and workers much, but a supervisor can ensure that a worker is running. In this case, your worker will be the connection to the database server. Supervising the connection will allow it to attempt to reconnect to the database if the connection is ever severed (along with other benefits we won't discuss here). So you need to set up your first worker to be supervised.

The place to set up workers for supervision is in the auction_umbrella/apps/auction/lib/auction/application.ex file that was automatically generated when you used `mix new` with the `--sup` flag. Right now, it mostly contains comments that will help you configure your workers and supervisors.

All the options, and the great depth of functionality provided by supervisors and workers, can be a little overwhelming. Fortunately, Ecto makes it super easy. Do you remember how you put the line `use Ecto.Repo, otp_app: :auction` in the lib/auction/repo.ex module? That provided your module with all the information it needed to become a supervised Ecto worker. All you have to do now is specify that you'd like to have it supervised.

To do so, add `{Auction.Repo, []}` to the `children` list in lib/auction/application.ex. This provides your application with enough information to know that you want that worker (in the list of workers) to be supervised at startup. Right now it's the *only* worker, but you can add more to the list as needed.

The following listing shows what your lib/auction/application.ex module should look like after adding the worker.

Listing 7.8 Adding your repo to the list of workers to be supervised

```
defmodule Auction.Application do
  use Application

  def start(_type, _args) do
    # List all child processes to be supervised
    children = [
      # Starts a worker by calling: Auction.Worker.start_link(arg)
      # {Auction.Worker, arg},
      {Auction.Repo, []}                  <-- Tells Elixir you'd like
    ]                                         Auction.Repo to act as a worker

    opts = [strategy: :one_for_one, name: Auction.Supervisor]
    Supervisor.start_link(children, opts)
  end
end
```

With that simple addition, the `Auction.Repo` worker will be supervised at startup. This means that if it goes down for any reason, Elixir will do its best to bring it back up.

7.3.5 Testing it out

Finally, the exciting part—you get to test whether your database connection is running and you have set everything up correctly. Because you set up your database connection to start automatically with your application in listing 7.8, all you need to do is start the application. As in the past, you'll interact with your application through an IEx session for now (run `iex -S mix` now).

Once you're in IEx, you can use the public interface calls to interact with the database. To list all the items you currently have (which is none), you can run `Auction.list_items`, just like you did when you had your fake repo running. Right now, though, you get an empty list (as in the following example) because you haven't added any rows to the database (you'll do that soon). So why run the query? Running it will not only ensure that the database connection is up and running, but also that Ecto is talking to it correctly and without error.

```
iex(1)> Auction.list_items()

21:16:18.226 [debug] QUERY OK source="items" db=1.5ms
SELECT i0."id", i0."title", i0."description", i0."ends_at" FROM "items" AS i0 []
[]
```

[] is the return value. (You currently have no items.)

If you see something similar to the preceding output, congratulations! Your application is talking to your real database via Ecto. Ecto provides some debug output to show how it's interacting with the database. In this case, you can also see the SQL statement it generated for the PostgreSQL database to list the items (`SELECT i0."id", i0."title", i0."description", i0."ends_at" FROM "items" AS i0 []`). Finally, you can see the return of the function call (`[]`), which shows that you have no items yet.

You can also try running `Auction.get_item/1` and `Auction.get_item_by/1`. One will give you an error, and the other will return `nil`. Which do you think does what, and why? You'll fix both instances soon, but try experimenting a little with each of the three public interface calls you currently have in `Auction`, and examine Ecto's debug output. You'll soon get a good grasp on what it's trying to do.

7.4 Creating, retrieving, and deleting data in the database

You now have a working database connection and the beginnings of a public interface. If you were wondering how the public interface you built *just works* so easily, even after you moved from a fake, static repo to a live database, it's because you wrote functions for your fake repo that mirrored functions that Ecto provides. The sidebar "Some of Ecto.Repo's database functions" includes a truncated list of functions that Ecto.Repo provides (and that it gives your `Auction.Repo` through the `use Ecto.Repo` call at the top of the module). Many more functions are available, but these are the ones you'll likely use the most.

Some of Ecto.Repo's database functions

Ecto provides a number of functions through Ecto.Repo to interact with your database. Some often-used ones are listed in the following tables, but you can find them all in the full documentation, along with some great usage examples (https://hexdocs.pm/ecto/Ecto.Repo.html).

(continued)

Data retrieval

Function	Description	Returns
`all/2`	Retrieves every row in the database that matches the passed query	A list
`get_by/3`	Retrieves a single row from the database that matches the passed query	The row (if found) or nil if not found
`get/3`	Retrieves a single row referenced by the given primary key	The row (if found) or nil if not found
`one/2`	Retrieves a single row that matches the passed query	The row (if found) or nil if not found; if more than one row is found, an error is raised

`get_by/3` and `get/3` have sister functions that end with a bang (for example, `get!/3`). Those versions of the functions raise an error if a row can't be found based on the passed query (instead of just returning `nil`).

Data modification

Function	Description	Returns
`delete/2`	Deletes a row referenced by the given primary key	`{:ok, row}`
`insert/2`	Inserts a row into the database based on the given struct	`{:ok, row}` or `{:error, changeset}`
`update/2`	Updates a row with the data in the given struct referenced by the given primary key	`{:ok, row}` or `{:error, changeset}`

The preceding three functions have sister functions that end with a bang (for example, `insert!/2`). Those versions return the struct or row directly (instead of in a tuple with `:ok`) if found, or they raise an error if it's not found (instead of returning a tuple beginning with `:error`).

Each of the bang and nonbang versions have their uses, depending on how you want your application to react to data not found in the database.

7.4.1 *Inserting data*

The first thing you want to do with your new database setup is insert some data to play with. To do that, you use `insert/2` or `insert!/2`.

Because you typically want to keep your public interface separate from your database calls, you first create a function to insert an `Item` into the database in lib/auction.ex. `Ecto.Repo.insert/2` knows what table to insert the data into based on the struct that you give it. The only struct you currently have (`Auction.Item`) knows where it goes because of how you defined its `schema`. Can you start to see how the pieces are fitting together?

To make inserting `Item` data more explicit but also a little easier at the same time, you can design your public interface so that you only have to pass a map (`%{}`) instead of a full struct (`%Auction.Item{}`). Elixir provides a function named `Kernel.struct/2` that changes a map to a struct based on the arguments provided. You'll use that function to change a map and its data to the `Auction.Item` struct, and then pass that struct into the `Ecto.Repo.insert/2` function. The following listing shows this new function in the lib/auction.ex module.

Listing 7.9 Adding `insert_item/1` to `Auction`

```
def insert_item(attrs) do
  Auction.Item
  |> struct(attrs)
  |> @repo.insert()
end
```

insert/2 will return either {:ok, struct} or {:error, changeset}.

Because you're using the `insert/2` function instead of the bang version (`insert!/2`), you can expect to get either an `{:ok, struct}` or an `{:error, changeset}` as a return value. You won't worry about the second part of these return values for now, but you do want to know whether you're getting an `:ok` or an `:error` as the first value returned. You can use pattern matching to ensure the query took place as you intended.

> **NOTE** A changeset (in the second part of the return value) allows you to track changes to the data, as well as validations and any errors those validations may throw. We'll go into exactly what a changeset is in chapter 8.

Save lib/auction.ex with the new public interface function, and use it to insert your first `Item` into the real database. You'll pattern-match the return value with `{:ok, item}` to ensure there were no errors. You can attempt to do so on your own, in an IEx session, or follow along with the next listing.

Listing 7.10 Inserting the first `Item`

```
iex(1)> {:ok, item} =
iex...> Auction.insert_item(
iex...> %{title: "WarGames Bluray",
iex...> description: "Computer games and thermonuclear war",
iex...> ends_at: DateTime.from_naive!(~N[2019-02-22 11:43:39], "Etc/UTC")}
iex...> )

08:43:10.661 [debug] QUERY OK db=3.3ms
INSERT INTO "items"
     ("description","ends_at","title","inserted_at","updated_at") VALUES
     ($1,$2,$3,$4,$5) RETURNING "id" ["Computer games and thermonuclear war",
     #DateTime<2019-02-22 11:43:39Z>, "WarGames Bluray", ~N[2018-12-12
     02:54:15], ~N[2018-12-12 02:54:15]]

{:ok,
%Auction.Item{
  __meta__: #Ecto.Schema.Metadata<:loaded, "items">,
  description: "Computer games and thermonuclear war",
```

WarGames is my favorite movie. Feel free to input data about your favorite.

```
  ends_at: #DateTime<2019-02-22 11:43:39Z>,
  id: 1,
  inserted_at: ~N[2018-12-12 02:54:15],
  title: "WarGames Bluray",
  updated_at: ~N[2018-12-12 02:54:15]
}}
```

The preceding listing shows that Ecto provides debug output describing what it's doing with the database, including the SQL it generated and submitted to the database. It also shows the complete return value of `{:ok, ...}`, which you pattern-matched against with `{:ok, item}`.

You now have the database version of the data in the `item` variable, which you can use as you please.

7.4.2 Retrieving data

Now that you have some actual data to retrieve, you can use your data retrieval functions. You've created three functions in your public interface that allow you to retrieve items: `list_items/0`, `get_item/1`, and `get_item_by/1`. Because you now have an item in your database with an `id` of `1` and a `title` of `WarGames Bluray`, you can use those functions to practice retrieving data, as shown in the following listing. And guess what? Because you created your public interface to match Ecto's, no further changes are required in the `Auction` module.

Listing 7.11 Listing the items in your database

```
iex(3)> Auction.list_items

09:45:33.007 [debug] QUERY OK source="items" db=2.0ms
SELECT i0."id", i0."title", i0."description", i0."ends_at", i0."inserted_at",
     i0."updated_at" FROM "items" AS i0 []
[
  %Auction.Item{                                          <-- You received the WarGames item, which means that things are hooked up correctly.
    __meta__: #Ecto.Schema.Metadata<:loaded, "items">,
    description: "Computer games and thermonuclear war",
    ends_at: #DateTime<2019-02-22 11:43:39Z>,
    id: 1,
    inserted_at: ~N[2018-12-12 02:54:15],
    title: "WarGames Bluray",
    updated_at: ~N[2018-12-12 02:54:15]
  }
]
```

You can retrieve specific items as well, referencing them either with their `id` number or some other attribute.

Listing 7.12 Retrieving items from the database

```
iex(4)> Auction.get_item(1)                               <-- Auction.get_item/1 requests an item based on its id.

09:45:57.537 [debug] QUERY OK source="items" db=1.9ms
SELECT i0."id", i0."title", i0."description", i0."ends_at", i0."inserted_at",
     i0."updated_at" FROM "items" AS i0 WHERE (i0."id" = $1) [1]
```

```
%Auction.Item{
  __meta__: #Ecto.Schema.Metadata<:loaded, "items">,
  description: "Computer games and thermonuclear war",
  ends_at: #DateTime<2019-02-22 11:43:39Z>,
  id: 1,
  inserted_at: ~N[2018-12-12 02:54:15],
  title: "WarGames Bluray",
  updated_at: ~N[2018-12-12 02:54:15]
}

iex(5)> Auction.get_item_by(%{title: "WarGames Bluray"})

09:46:53.205 [debug] QUERY OK source="items" db=2.5ms
SELECT i0."id", i0."title", i0."description", i0."ends_at", i0."inserted_at",
     i0."updated_at" FROM "items" AS i0 WHERE (i0."title" = $1) ["WarGames
     Bluray"]
%Auction.Item{
  __meta__: #Ecto.Schema.Metadata<:loaded, "items">,
  description: "Computer games and thermonuclear war",
  ends_at: #DateTime<2019-02-22 11:43:39Z>,
  id: 1,
  inserted_at: ~N[2018-12-12 02:54:15],
  title: "WarGames Bluray",
  updated_at: ~N[2018-12-12 02:54:15]
}
```

Auction.get_item_by/1 requests an item based on specified attributes.

As you can see in the preceding listing, all of your `Auction` functions for retrieving items from the database appear to be working correctly.

7.4.3 Deleting data

There may come a time when you no longer need specific rows in the database, so you need a way to delete data. Ecto.Repo provides the `delete/2` and `delete!/2` functions for that purpose. They're simple functions that take a struct as their argument and delete the row that matches that struct's `id`.

By this point, you probably know the drill: you want to keep the database and public interface separate, so you'll create your own border in the `Auction` module instead of calling `Auction.Repo.delete/2` directly. Because Ecto's function is so simple, your border function will also be very simple—it will just pass the struct through to Ecto.

The following listing shows the function definition you need to add to lib/auction.ex.

Listing 7.13 Adding `delete_item/1` to Auction

```
def delete_item(%Auction.Item{} = item), do: @repo.delete(item)
```

Because the function body is so short, you use the inline version of the function definition.

Note how you pattern-match the first argument in that function definition to make sure that it receives an `Auction.Item` struct. You don't want to accidentally delete any non-items in `Auction.delete_item/1`.

7.4.4 Updating data

You've inserted, retrieved, and deleted data from your database. What about updating? In order to update data with Ecto, you need a changeset. At first glance, it can seem limiting that Ecto *requires* a changeset to simply update a row in the database, but you'll see that it's *very* powerful and can save you a lot of heartache when used correctly. In fact, this is such a deep and meaningful topic that the whole next chapter is devoted to changesets and to updating and verifying data as it goes into the database.

With that in mind, we'll wrap up this chapter. Before we move on, I encourage you to create, retrieve, and delete more items in your database. Doing so will get you used to interacting with your database and the public interface, and it'll provide more data for you to eventually work with.

7.4.5 What about the website?

One more thing: you know how I've been harping on keeping the database concerns and business logic separate from the website concerns? Let's look at one of the benefits of doing that.

Navigate to auction_umbrella/apps/auction_web and run `mix phx.server`. Load up http://localhost:4000 in your browser. What do you see? The auction site is now displaying data directly from your database instead of from the fake repo (see figure 7.2). You didn't have to change a single line of code on the web side of the umbrella app, because you kept the public interface of your business logic exactly the same.

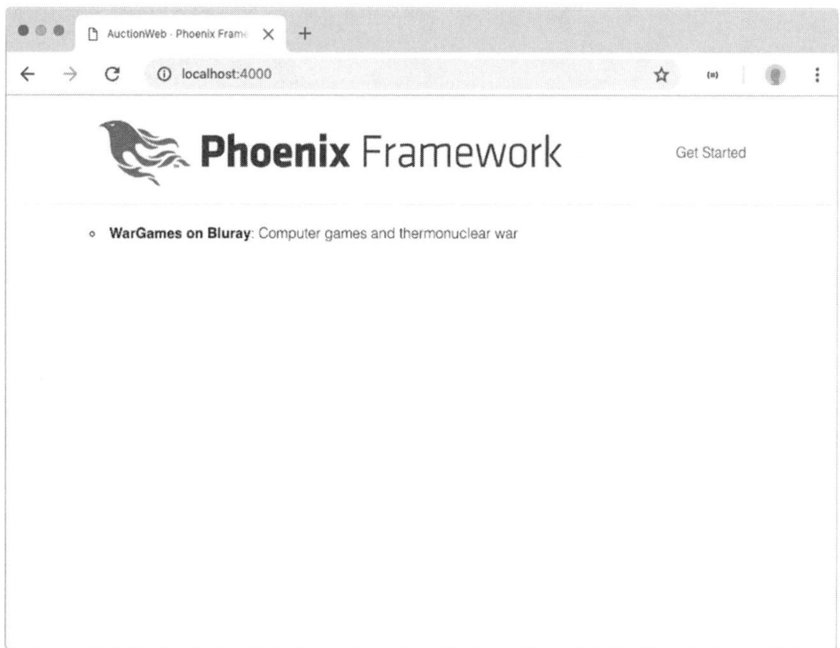

Figure 7.2 The web side of your application didn't require any changes to see the real database data.

Summary

- Ecto provides a number of Mix tasks to make interacting with your database setup simple, such as `mix ecto.create`, `mix ecto.migrate`, and `mix ecto.rollback`.
- Use Ecto's `Ecto.Schema.schema/2` function to let Ecto know how your data is structured in the database.
- Use Ecto's `Ecto.Migration` module and Mix task to create and run migrations that change the structure of your database programmatically.
- Ecto provides functions for inserting data into and retrieving and deleting data from the database, though it's a good idea to write your own functions that utilize Ecto's to provide a clean border between concerns.

8 Making changes with Ecto.Changeset

This chapter covers

- Discovering how Ecto deals with database updates
- Creating a changeset for `Auction.Item`
- Using changesets to update the database

So far, you've configured your Auction app to do a few nice things:

- Get `Auction.Items` from the database
- Save new `Auction.Items` to the database via IEx
- Display the `Auction.Items` in the database in a web page

It definitely needs to do a few more things before the investors come knocking on your door, begging to give you their money. In this chapter, we'll focus on updating data in the database. It sounds like it should be a simple thing to do, since you already know how to get and store records, but it's a bit more complex than that. Most times, added complexity is a bad thing. But with Ecto's changesets, I'd argue that the complexity is welcome and beneficial. By the end of this chapter, I think you'll agree.

8.1 Can't I just … update?

Nope. You can't.

Let me explain: Say you wanted to update your WarGames Bluray auction item. Using the code as it was at the end of chapter 7, you could attempt to use `Ecto.Repo.update/2`.

Listing 8.1 Attempting to use `Ecto.Repo.update/2` without a changeset

```
iex(1)> item = Auction.get_item(1)        <-- Retrieves the item from the database

15:18:45.223 [debug] QUERY OK source="items" db=2.2ms
SELECT i0."id", i0."title", i0."description", i0."ends_at", i0."inserted_at",
     i0."updated_at" FROM "items" AS i0 WHERE (i0."id" = $1) [1]

%Auction.Item{
  __meta__: #Ecto.Schema.Metadata<:loaded, "items">,
  description: "Computer games and thermonuclear war",
  ends_at: #DateTime<2019-02-22 11:43:39Z>,
  id: 1,
  inserted_at: ~N[2018-12-12 02:54:15],
  title: "WarGames Bluray",
  updated_at: ~N[2018-12-12 02:54:15]
}

iex(2)> item |>
...(2)> Map.put(:title, "A new title") |>      <-- Attempts to update the title to "A new title"
...(2)> Auction.Repo.update()

** (ArgumentError) giving a struct to Ecto.Repo.update/2 is not supported.
     Ecto is unable to properly track changes when a struct is given, an
     Ecto.Changeset must be given instead
    (ecto) lib/ecto/repo/schema.ex:296: Ecto.Repo.Schema.update/3
```

The error message states that Ecto requires a changeset.

When I first started playing with Ecto, I found it very easy to retrieve records with `Ecto.Repo.get/3`, store records to the database with `Ecto.Repo.insert/2`, and delete records from the database with `Ecto.Repo.delete/2`. I thought the story would be just as simple with `Ecto.Repo.update/2`. But although the former three functions only require the struct name (like `Auction.Item`) and some data (like the struct's attributes or the ID number of the record you'd like to retrieve), `Ecto.Repo.update/2` requires something called a *changeset*.

My first instinct was to say, "Can't I just pass in the record along with the changes and be done?" The answer was a surprising (to me) "no." The reason behind the "no" has saved my sanity and the information in my databases many times since then (see figure 8.1). `Ecto.Repo.update/2` requires a changeset to be passed in, which is something *you* have to generate. But the good news is that it's easy to do.

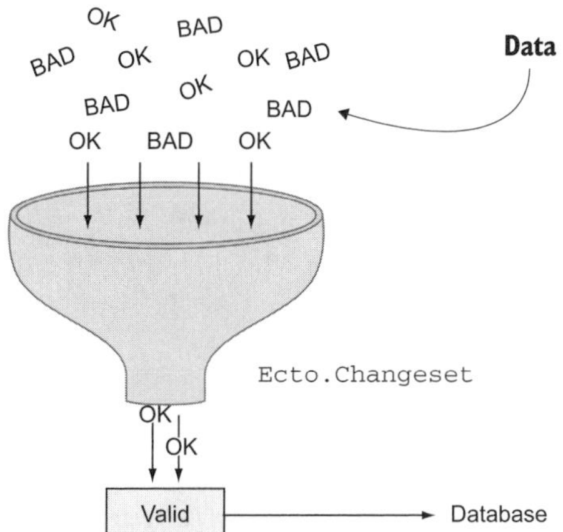

Figure 8.1 `Ecto.Changeset` **can help keep bad data out of your database.**

8.1.1 A brief intro to changesets

A changeset is actually an `Ecto.Changeset`. It allows you to track the changes made to a struct. Beyond that, it also allows

- Validating data inside the changes
- Casting values in the changes
- Defining constraints to the changes

And there's more!

A changeset allows you to verify that the data going into your database is valid. So far, you've allowed data to be inserted into your database without checking for anything—every attribute for `Auction.Item` could be blank, and you'd allow it. In a real application, you'll want to verify that the data in your database is trustworthy, and changesets are a perfect way to do that.

If something goes wrong during a database update, a changeset can also track the errors and give you information you can then either act on inside your application, or present to an end user so they can fix their submission. It will, at the same time, roll back any changes that would have happened during the failed update, keeping your database pristine.

8.1.2 Creating a changeset for Auction.Item

If you want to create a changeset for your `Auction.Item` (and you do), it's relatively simple. The idiomatic way to define a generic changeset is to define a `changeset/2` function inside your module.

For your first changeset, you'd like the following things to take place:

1. Only allow updates for the `title`, `description`, and `ends_at` fields. That leaves out the `id`, `inserted_at`, and `updated_at` fields.
2. Validate that `title` is present and that its length is greater than three characters (an arbitrary number, to be sure).

3. Validate that `description` is present and that its length is less than 200 characters (another arbitrary number).
4. Validate that `ends_at` is in the future.

Let's take each of those steps one at a time.

DEFINING AUCTION.ITEM.CHANGESET/2 AND LIMITING FIELDS FOR UPDATING

Before you can get to your constraints and validations, you first need to define the `Auction.Item.changeset/2` function. This function will accept two arguments:

- An `Auction.Item` struct that needs (or has) changes
- A map of attributes to update, with the default being an empty map

You can then define your function as in the following listing. This function will go in the `Auction.Item` module found in auction_umbrella/apps/auction/lib/auction/item.ex.

Listing 8.2 Defining `Auction.Item.changeset/2`

```
defmodule Auction.Item do
  # ...

  def changeset(item, params \\ %{}) do
  end
end
```

This is a typical changeset function pattern, but the empty function won't do anything in this state.

That function in itself won't do anything you need it to do—it's only the shell of what you'll add.

The first thing you want to do is to limit the fields that can be changed through this changeset. You can do that with the `Ecto.Changeset.cast/4` function. `Ecto.Changeset.cast/4` expects four parameters:

- The struct that you are starting from (including any corresponding data)
- A map of the parameters you're using for updating
- A list of fields that you'll allow to be changed
- An optional list of options to pass to `Ecto.Changeset`

With that knowledge, you can finish the first step of your changeset as in the following listing. You'll pass in the `item` and `params` from the parameters of your `changeset/2` function, and then pass a list of allowed fields (`:title`, `:description`, and `:ends_at`). Figure 8.2 illustrates how `cast/2` allows some keys, but disallows others.

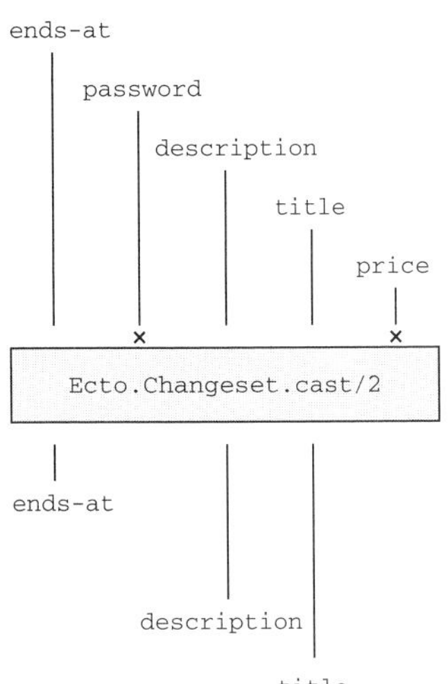

Figure 8.2 If someone attempts to submit attributes that you haven't included in `cast/2`, they will be filtered out.

Listing 8.3 Using `Ecto.Changeset.cast/4` to limit the fields you accept changes for

```
defmodule Auction.Item do
  # ...

  def changeset(item, params \\ %{}) do
    item
    |> Ecto.Changeset.cast(params, [:title, :description, :ends_at])
  end
end
```

Ecto.Changeset.cast/4 allows the provided keys to pass through (title, description, and ends_at)

You can try this out in IEx. You'll use IEx to see what's in this changeset that you're returning from your function. Follow along with listing 8.4 as you get a record from the database and use your new `Auction.Item.changeset/2` function to change some allowed fields.

As a reminder, you can start up IEx and have it include your application code by running `iex -S mix` from the root directory of the umbrella application (`auction_umbrella`).

Listing 8.4 Inspecting the return value of `Auction.Item.changeset/2` in IEx

```
iex(1)> item = Auction.list_items() |> Enum.at(0)
iex(2)> Auction.Item.changeset(item)
#Ecto.Changeset<action: nil, changes: %{}, errors: [], data: #Auction.Item<>,
     valid?: true>
```

Gets all the items from the database, but only takes the first one

The return value of the `Auction.Item.changeset/2` function is an `Ecto.Changeset` struct. Inside that struct, you can see some information regarding the changes that you're requesting and allowing. In this case, there are none, and Ecto reports that your changes are valid. If you then passed this on to `Auction.Repo.update/2`, it would consider it a valid change and implement the changes (though there are none, in this case).

What do you think it will return if you pass in a map with some changes as the second parameter to `Auction.Item.changeset/2`? If you attempt to change the `title` of your item, that will be shown in the `Ecto.Changeset` struct inside `changes`.

Listing 8.5 Attempting to change the `title` of your item

```
iex(3)> Auction.Item.changeset(item, %{title: "An updated title"})
#Ecto.Changeset<
  action: nil,
  changes: %{title: "An updated title"},
  errors: [],
  data: #Auction.Item<>,
  valid?: true
>
```

The changes are a new title here.

There are no errors in the changeset.

Because there are no errors and all validations passed, this change is marked as valid.

As expected, you can see the change listed in the data structure that's returned. You still have no errors, and the change is marked as valid. You'll recall that `title` is one of the fields that you allowed to be changed with `Ecto.Changeset.cast/4` in the `Auction.Item.changeset/2` function.

That begs the question: what will you get back if you attempt to change something that you don't allow to be changed, like `updated_at` or some arbitrary field like `hack_me`? Let's find out. Pass those as other attributes in the `changes` param to `Auction.Item.changeset/2`.

Listing 8.6 Attempting to change disallowed fields in an item

```
iex(4)> Auction.Item.changeset(
...(4)> item,
...(4)> %{title: "An updated title",
...(4)> updated_at: ~N[1980-01-01 00:00:00],       <-- Attempts to update updated_at and hack_me
...(4)> hack_me: true})
#Ecto.Changeset<
  action: nil,
  changes: %{title: "An updated title"},    <-- Because they weren't part of the Ecto.Changeset.cast/4 call in Auction.Item.changeset/2, they're dropped as unallowed changes.
  errors: [],
  data: #Auction.Item<>,
  valid?: true
>
```

Neither of the unallowed fields came through as changes. You didn't specify that including those fields would result in an error, so no errors have been added to the changeset, and it's still marked as valid. But neither did they make it through the `cast` filter, in which you specified which fields to allow. This keeps out data you don't want in your database, without fuss.

Note that you aren't actually changing anything in your database yet—you're just *preparing the changes* that will eventually be passed to `Auction.Repo.update/2`. If you're anxious to make the changes in the database, try passing the resulting changeset to `Auction.Repo.update/2` (note that the second parameter is optional, so you can just supply the changeset). You'll make changes in the database in section 8.2.

VALIDATING TITLE PRESENCE AND LENGTH

One thing you may have noticed is that the `Ecto.Changeset.cast/4` function returns an `Ecto.Changeset`. You may also be unsurprised to find out that most `Ecto.Changeset` functions accept either the module's struct or an `Ecto.Changeset` struct as their first parameter. What's the result of that? You can pipe the result of one into the next, creating a nice pipeline of validations and changes. You'll use this technique in this section, as you add validation for the presence and length of `title`.

There's a simple function in `Ecto.Changeset` named `validate_required/3`, which accepts a changeset or struct, a list of required fields, and an optional list of options. It then validates that the struct or changeset has a value set for the specified required fields. If it doesn't, it will return the changeset with errors, indicating that the fields are required. Note that `validate_required/3` doesn't mean that the fields are required in the changes of the changeset—they can be already present.

With this in mind, you can pipe the output of your `Ecto.Changeset.cast/4` function into the `Ecto.Changeset.validate_required/3` function and require that a `title` be set. Here's the updated function.

Listing 8.7 Updating `Auction.Item.changeset/2` to require `title`

```
defmodule Auction.Item do
  # ...

  def changeset(item, params \\ %{}) do
    item
    |> Ecto.Changeset.cast(params, [:title, :description, :ends_at])
    |> Ecto.Changeset.validate_required(:title)
  end
end
```

Tells Ecto that this changeset requires the title attribute to be set

Now if your item doesn't include a `title`, it will be considered invalid.

The following listing demonstrates the changeset being returned for a record that doesn't include a `title`. If you're following along and didn't exit and reenter IEx after making the change, be sure to recompile the `Auction.Item` module with `r Auction.Item` so your changes are picked up.

Listing 8.8 Not including a `title` in your `Changeset`

```
iex(1)> Auction.Item.changeset(
...(1)> %Auction.Item{},
...(1)> %{description: "I don't have a title!"})
#Ecto.Changeset<
  action: nil,
  changes: %{description: "I don't have a title!"},
  errors: [title: {"can't be blank", [validation: :required]}],
  data: #Auction.Item<>,
  valid?: false
>
```

Passes in an empty Auction.Item struct as the starting point of the changeset

Ecto complains because it doesn't have a title attribute.

You have errors! This is as expected. The errors contain information about which fields contained errors (`title`), an error description (`"can't be blank"`), and what validation they failed (`[validation: required]`). You can also see that the changeset has been marked as `valid?: false`. If you attempt to pass this invalid changeset into `Ecto.Repo.update/2`, it won't accept the changes and will return the error for you to handle.

NOTE The message returned from failed validations can be customized through the optional third parameter of `Ecto.Changeset.validate_required/3`. Take a look at the documentation for more information.

Hopefully, you're beginning to get a glimpse of the power of changesets in Ecto. With two function calls in listing 8.7, you've created an allow list of fields you'd accept for changes, and you've validated that all the records in your database should have a title.

Let's go a bit further in your validations. Surely no one would try to put a real item up for auction without a title of at least three characters (at least that's what you'll assume for the sake of example). You now need to require not only that the `title` field be set, but that it can't be less than three characters in length.

With `Ecto.Changeset.validate_length/3`, you can validate that a certain field is a required length—a minimum length, a maximum length, between minimum and maximum lengths, or an exact length. You'll use this function in your validation pipeline to keep out the unwelcome short titles.

Listing 8.9 Adding length validation to `title`

```
defmodule Auction.Item do
  # ...

  def changeset(item, params \\ %{}) do
    item
    |> Ecto.Changeset.cast(params, [:title, :description, :ends_at])
    |> Ecto.Changeset.validate_required(:title)
    |> Ecto.Changeset.validate_length(:title, min: 3)    <-- Specifies that the title must be at least 3 characters in length
  end
end
```

Now, try to get past your new validation.

Listing 8.10 Attempting to bypass the minimum-length restriction

```
iex(1)> Auction.Item.changeset(%Auction.Item{}, %{title: "!"})
#Ecto.Changeset<
  action: nil,
  changes: %{title: "!"},          <-- Attempts to make the title only 1 character
  errors: [
    title: {"should be at least %{count} character(s)",
      [count: 3, validation: :length, kind: :min]}      <-- Ecto knows it should be at least 3 characters.
  ],
  data: #Auction.Item<>,
  valid?: false                    <-- Ecto marks the change as invalid.
>
```

As expected, this change is considered invalid because the length of the title is less than three characters.

VALIDATING DESCRIPTION LENGTH

Now that you know how to validate the presence and length of a field, adding validation to the maximum length of `description` will be trivial. All you need to do is add that validation to the validation pipeline in `Auction.Item.changeset/2`. You want to

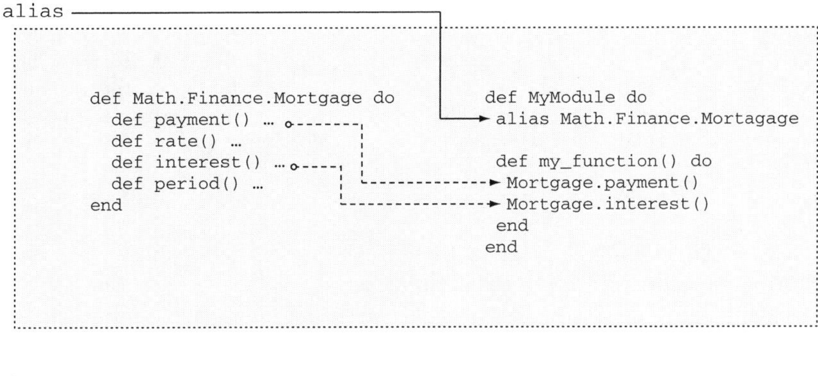


```
import

def Math.Finance.Mortgage do          def MyModule do
  def payment() …                       import Math.Finance.Mortagage
  def rate() …
  def interest() …                      def my_function() do
  def period() …                          payment()
end                                       interest()
                                        end
                                      end
```

Figure 8.3 Using `import` to cut down on repetition

allow users to not enter any description for their items, but if they do enter a description, you want to make sure it doesn't exceed 200 characters.

Before you do that, I'm sure you've noticed that you're typing "`Ecto.Changeset`" a lot—for each time you want to call a function in that module. You have a few more validations to go, and because you're a good, lazy programmer, you don't like repeating yourself if you don't have to. As you'll recall from chapter 2 (see figure 8.3), there's a great way to import the functions of one module into another module so that you can use them directly and don't have to type the full name with the module every time.

Here's a hint—it's in that last sentence. It's `import`. You can `import Ecto.Changeset` into `Auction.Item` to keep from having to type out that module name every time you want to use a function from it.

With that in mind, edit `Auction.Item.changeset/2` to utilize that benefit and add the `description` validation to your validation pipeline as follows.

Listing 8.11 Adding maximum-length validation to `description`

```
defmodule Auction.Item do
  import Ecto.Changeset      <-- Add this.
  # ...
```

```
  def changeset(item, params \\ %{}) do
    item
    |> cast(params, [:title, :description, :ends_at])
    |> validate_required(:title)
    |> validate_length(:title, min: 3)
    |> validate_length(:description, max: 200)
  end
end
```

Update these function calls to just the function name, because you imported Ecto.Changeset.

Add this.

Now you're requiring a title that's three characters at minimum, and the optional description can't be longer than 200 characters.

VALIDATING THAT ENDS_AT IS IN THE FUTURE

If you look at the documentation for `Ecto.Changeset`, you'll see a good number of built-in validations. Table 8.1 also lists a few of these validations.

Table 8.1 Built-in validation functions in `Ecto.Changeset`

Function	Description
`validate_confirmation/3`	Validates that two fields are identical (like `password` and `password_confirmation`)
`validate_exclusion/4`	Validates that a field's value isn't in the provided list
`validate_format/4`	Validates that a value matches a regular expression
`validate_inclusion/4`	Validates that a field's value is in the provided list; opposite of `validate_exclusion/4`
`validate_length/3`	Validates that a value is of a certain length
`validate_number/3`	Various validation options around numbers (less than, greater than, etc.)
`validate_required/3`	Validates that a field is present
`validate_subset/4`	Validates that a value, which is a list, is a subset of another list

These built-in validation functions are really handy and are used all the time. But some situations call for custom validations. In your case, you'd like to validate that the `ends_at` field isn't in the past. No built-in validators will provide that check for you.

For situations like these, `Ecto.Changeset` provides the `validate_change/3` and `validate_change/4` functions. The difference between the two is slightly complicated (the latter accepts metadata about the change; you can read more about them in the documentation), but you'll be using `validate_change/3` for your custom validation. `Ecto.Changeset.validate_change/3` accepts three parameters: a changeset, the field name you're validating, and a custom validator function.

Your custom validator function must return a list of errors to add to the changeset. If there are no errors, you return an empty list ([]). If there are errors, you return a list like `[field_name: "error message"]`.

For your custom validation, you need to do some comparing of dates. You could write your function in the `validate_change/3` function itself (which would make it an anonymous function), or you could create a new named function and pass a reference to it to `validate_change/3`. It's arguably more difficult to test anonymous functions in other functions, so you'll write a new named function in the `Auction.Item` module.

There are three things you'd like to accomplish with your function:

- You don't want to expose it to external modules.
- You want to return an empty list if `ends_at` is now or in the future.
- You want to return a list with an error present if `ends_at` is in the past.

To accomplish the first point, you just need to define a *private function* in your module. You can do that with the `defp` version of the function definition block.

To accomplish the second and third points, you can use the `DateTime.compare/2` function. It accepts two `DateTime` structs and returns an atom indicating whether the first `DateTime` is greater than (`:gt`), less than (`:lt`), or equal to (`:eq`) the second `DateTime`. If it's `:lt`, you need to return an error. Otherwise, `ends_at` is now or in the future.

`validate_change/3` provides the validation function with two parameters: the field name and the value of the field in the changeset. You can use the field name to pattern-match your function calls. This allows you to write many different functions with the name of `validate/2` that match based on which field you're actually validating. Write the function as follows.

Listing 8.12 Defining your custom validator for `ends_at`

```
defmodule Auction.Item do
  # ...

  defp validate(:ends_at, ends_at_date) do
    case DateTime.compare(ends_at_date, DateTime.utc_now()) do
      :lt -> [ends_at: "ends_at cannot be in the past"]
      _ -> []
    end
  end
end
```

case takes the result of the provided function and executes the first function that matches the result.

The special case (_) matches anything else.

NOTE In listing 8.12, you could explicitly match on `:gt` and `:eq`, but because those both return the same response, and they're the only other possible results, you can use the special case (_) to catch them both.

Now you can use that function in `Ecto.Changeset.validate_change/3` and add it to your validation pipeline. The following listing shows what that looks like.

Listing 8.13 Adding your custom validator to the validation pipeline

```
defmodule Auction.Item do
  # ...

  def changeset(item, params \\ %{}) do
    item
    |> cast(params, [:title, :description, :ends_at])
    |> validate_required(:title)
    |> validate_length(:title, min: 3)
    |> validate_length(:description, max: 200)
    |> validate_change(:ends_at, &validate/2)
  end

  defp validate(:ends_at, ends_at_date) do
    case DateTime.compare(ends_at_date, DateTime.utc_now()) do
      :lt -> [ends_at: "can't be in the past"]
      _ -> []
    end
  end
end
```

Add this. The &validate/2 call references your validate function with the arity of 2.

You can see your changes in practice in an IEx console. Make sure your new code is saved and recompiled, and then try creating an item with an `ends_at` value in the past.

Listing 8.14 Attempting to create an item with an `ends_at` in the past

```
iex(1)> Auction.Item.changeset(%Auction.Item{}, %{ends_at:
     DateTime.from_naive!(~N[2001-07-30 00:00:00], "Etc/UTC")})
#Ecto.Changeset<
  action: nil,
  changes: %{ends_at: #DateTime<2001-07-30 00:00:00Z>},
  errors: [
    ends_at: {"ends_at cannot be in the past", []},
    title: {"can't be blank", [validation: :required]}
  ],
  data: #Auction.Item<>,
  valid?: false
>
```

Attempts to make ends_at a DateTime in the past

Ecto knows that you don't allow a past DateTime.

As expected, Ecto doesn't allow you to make the `ends_at` attribute a `DateTime` in the past. The change is marked as invalid and will never make it to the database.

8.2 Now you can update!

All your work so far in this chapter has been to set up the changeset required to make changes to the database records. Now that you have that changeset pipeline set up, you can use it to start making changes.

As I mentioned early in this chapter, the `Ecto.Repo` module has `update/2` and `update!/2` functions that update the records in the database. The former returns a tuple containing its status (`:ok` or `:error`) and the changeset it attempted to use (on error) or the database record after it was updated (on success). The latter just contains the updated record. If there was an error in the `Ecto.Repo.update!/2` call, it would `raise` an error instead of just letting you know about it in the return tuple.

Let's do a bit of exploring in IEx. The first thing you'll try is to update a record with bad data. Then, you'll correct your errors and try updating the record with the corrected data. Follow along in your own IEx session if you like.

Listing 8.15 Updating a record using your changeset

```
iex(1)> item = Auction.list_items() |> Enum.at(0)
iex(2)> item |>
...(2)> Auction.Item.changeset(
...(2)> %{title: nil, ends_at: DateTime.from_naive!(~N[1980-01-01 00:00:00],
     "Etc/UTC")}) |>
...(2)> Auction.Repo.update()
{:error,
 #Ecto.Changeset<
   action: :update,
   changes: %{ends_at: #DateTime<1980-01-01 00:00:00Z>},
   errors: [
     ends_at: {"ends_at cannot be in the past", []},
     title: {"can't be blank", [validation: :required]}
   ],
   data: #Auction.Item<>,
   valid?: false
 >}

iex(3)> item |>
...(3)> Auction.Item.changeset(
...(3)> %{title: "My updated item", ends_at:
     DateTime.from_naive!(~N[2020-01-01 00:00:00], "Etc/UTC")}) |>
...(3)> Auction.Repo.update()
22:29:32.383 [debug] QUERY OK db=10.5ms
# ... Generated SQL removed
{:ok,
 %Auction.Item{
   __meta__: #Ecto.Schema.Metadata<:loaded, "items">,
   description: "Computer games and thermonuclear war",
   ends_at: #DateTime<2020-01-01 00:00:00Z>,
   id: 1,
   inserted_at: ~N[2018-12-12 02:54:15],
   title: "My updated item",
   updated_at: ~N[2018-12-12 03:39:55]
 }}
```

Remember that the pipe operator (|>) has to be at the end of the line in IEx.

Here's the error Tuple. It provides you with the invalid changeset.

You've now successfully updated a record in your database.

8.2.1 Adjusting the public interface for updating

As you've done in the past, you want to separate the business logic from the database concerns in your application with a clean boundary (see figure 8.4). You've been doing that in the apps/auction/lib/auction.ex file, and now you'll add an `Auction.update_item/2` function.

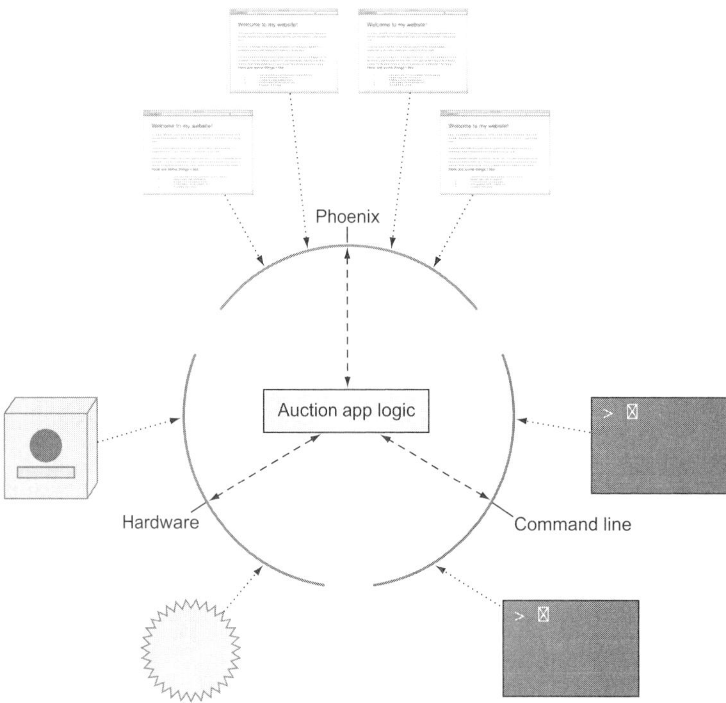

Figure 8.4 A reminder that Phoenix is just a boundary to your application

This `Auction.update_item/2` function will take the `Auction.Item` that needs updating as well as a map of changes that need to occur. It will then forward the item and params to your new `Auction.Item.changeset/2` function, which will do the heavy lifting for you. The following listing shows what this function will look like.

Listing 8.16 Adding `Auction.update_item/2` to your public interface

```
defmodule Auction do
  # ...

  def update_item(%Auction.Item{} = item, updates) do
    item
    |> Item.changeset(updates)
```

Pattern-matches on the first parameter to ensure that you're actually receiving an Auction.Item struct (annotation for the `def update_item` line)

```
    |> @repo.update()
  end
end
```

Recompile the Auction module (r Auction), or exit and restart IEx to make sure your changes are picked up. Then you can use your new function as follows.

Listing 8.17 Using `Auction.update_item/2`

```
iex(1)> item = Auction.get_item_by(%{title: "My updated item"})
iex(2)> item |>
...(2)> Auction.update_item(%{title: "WarGames on Bluray"})
13:54:21.530 [debug] QUERY OK db=4.9ms
UPDATE "items" SET "title" = $1, "updated_at" = $2 WHERE "id" = $3 ["WarGames
     on Bluray", {{2018, 4, 7}, {20, 54, 21, 524817}}, 2]

{:ok,
 %Auction.Item{
   __meta__: #Ecto.Schema.Metadata<:loaded, "items">,
   description: "Computer games and thermonuclear war",
   ends_at: #DateTime<2020-01-01 00:00:00Z>,
   id: 1,
   inserted_at: ~N[2018-12-12 02:54:15],
   title: "WarGames on Bluray",
   updated_at: ~N[2018-12-12 03:43:13]
 }}
```

Asks Ecto to make the changes you requested in the database

Ecto returns a tuple containing :ok and the resulting database change.

As you can see, the debug information shows that the database received the update and ran it, and the `Auction.update_item/2` function returned a tuple with `{:ok, updated_item}`.

As in previous chapters, you've taken steps to implement the business logic of your application *outside* of the context of Phoenix and the web. You can successfully update an `Auction.Item` via IEx, but that won't do anything for your users on the web.

In the next chapter, you'll create web forms in Phoenix that will allow you to create and edit the `Auction.Items` in your database.

Summary

- You can use tools provided by Ecto, such as changesets, to be proactive in making sure the information in your database is as clean as possible.
- Use an Ecto changeset to validate, require, filter, and constrain (and more) data before it gets into your database.
- If a changeset record is deemed to be invalid, Ecto will refuse to use the data in it to update your database. Beyond that, it provides meaningful error messages that you can either respond to yourself, or have your users do so.
- Ecto provides a number of built-in validates, and you can create your own data validations with `Ecto.Changeset.validate_change/3`.

9 Transforming data in your browser

This chapter covers

- Creating and editing items in the browser
- Creating new Phoenix routes, controllers, views, and templates
- Using Phoenix's form-builder helpers to create HTML forms

You can create, edit, and delete auction items and persist the changes in a real database, but you currently have no way to use those functions in the browser. What you need are HTML forms that enable users of your site to do those things—you certainly aren't giving them access to your IEx console.

In this chapter, you'll create those forms. As you do so, you'll touch almost every part of the route that data takes on its way through Phoenix—from the router to the template (we discussed that route in chapter 3).

Figure 9.1 shows how a user request travels through Phoenix. You can trace a user request through the server, endpoint, router, controller, view, and template, back to the user. With the exception of the endpoint, you'll touch on each of these areas in this chapter.

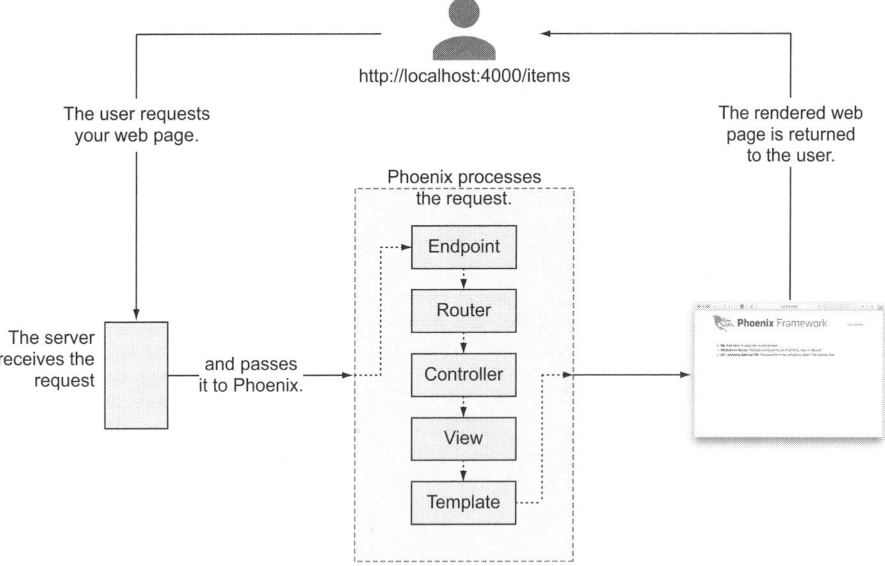
http://localhost:4000/items
The user requests your web page.
The rendered web page is returned to the user.
Phoenix processes the request.
Endpoint
Router
Controller
View
Template
The server receives the request
and passes it to Phoenix.
Phoenix Framework

Figure 9.1 A trace of a user request as it goes through Phoenix

9.1 Handling new routes in your application

You need a way for your users to *get* to the web page they'll interact with—you need a route that will respond to a request for a URL. The router module for your application can be found at auction_umbrella/apps/auction_web/lib/auction_web/router.ex.

9.1.1 Adding a new route

When you previously listed your database items on a web page, you used an already-existing route and controller (`get "/", PageController, :index`). These were the defaults set up by the Phoenix `mix phx.new.web` generator. It's time for you to branch out a bit and create your own controller, view, and templates to allow users to edit and update items.

The router.ex file contains the module that defines the routes for your website as well as the controllers and routes to route requests to. You need to define a new route (how about `/items`) that will be the base route for everything you eventually need to do for your items (create, read, update, delete). The `Phoenix.Router` module has functions that allow you to match on a specific type of request and route. You already have `get "/"` defined, and you can use the `delete/4`, `get/4`, `patch/4`, `post/4`, and `put/4` functions to define more.

Typically, for a RESTful application like the one you're building, each of the actions is defined for a resource. The routes in table 9.1 would typically be defined for an item.

Table 9.1 Typical RESTful routes

HTTP method	Handler CRUD action	Example route	Typical purpose
`GET`	`index`	`/items`	Provides a listing of `Items` or an overview of the `Item` resource
`GET`	`new`	`/items/new`	Displays a form to enable a user to provide attributes to create a new `Item`
`POST`	`create`	`/items`	Creates a new `Item` based on the attributes in the request payload; typically, this is hit from `GET /items/new`
`GET`	`show`	`/items/:id`	Views a single `Item` based on an identifier (like ID number)
`GET`	`edit`	`/items/:id/edit`	Displays a form so a user can provide attributes to edit a single `Item` identified by `:id`
`PATCH` or `PUT`	`update`	`/items/:id`	Updates an existing Item based on the attributes in the request payload; typically, this is hit from `GET /items/:id/edit`
`DELETE`	`delete`	`/items/:id`	Deletes an existing `Item` identified by `:id`

Imagine this, though: your number-one user comes to you requesting a special endpoint that only they know about, in order to display specific auction item listings. One of the nice things about Phoenix is that it doesn't limit you to specific actions or even to typical ideas about how the web works. If you want to allow a user to list items by requesting http://localhost:4000/cow/jumped/over.moon.html.js/forrealtho, you can certainly do that. Other users may scratch their heads, wondering what the web developer was thinking the day they made that route, but it's entirely possible.

But although that is technically possible, it's certainly not idiomatic or expected by your users. It would also probably confuse the future you or any developers you eventually bring on to your project. As a result, it's best to stick to convention. And more good news for the conventionalists among us—Phoenix makes that incredibly easy.

You could define a route for your application for each of the RESTful actions in table 9.1. If you did that, you could use the functions in `Phoenix.Router` to allow those. For example, `Phoenix.Router.get/4` takes the following parameters:

- The path to match from the URL (`/items`)
- The controller module that should handle the request

- The function in the module to call
- Any further options you'd like to specify (see the documentation for details)

If you defined all of those, your controller would look something like the following listing.

Listing 9.1 Defining a set of RESTful routes for items

```
defmodule AuctionWeb.Router do
  use AuctionWeb, :router

  pipeline :browser do
    # ...
  end

  scope "/", AuctionWeb do
    pipe_through :browser # Use the default browser stack

    get    "/items",          ItemController, :index
    get    "/items/new",      ItemController, :new
    post   "/items",          ItemController, :create
    get    "/items/:id",      ItemController, :show
    get    "/items/:id/edit", ItemController, :edit
    patch  "/items/:id",      ItemController, :update
    put    "/items/:id",      ItemController, :update
    delete "/items/:id",      ItemController, :delete
  end
end
```

Because this is nested inside the AuctionWeb scope, Phoenix will look for the function AuctionWeb.ItemController.index.

Those eight lines define the standard RESTful routes for the `Item` resource. This is so standard and is done so often that Phoenix has provided a function that makes it much easier—`Phoenix.Routes.resources/4`, which expects the following parameters:

- The base path to match the route on (`/items`, in this case)
- The controller module that should handle the request
- An optional list of options
- An optional block that allows you to define "nested" resources (which we'll cover in chapter 11)

Using this function reduces those eight lines to one, as follows.

Listing 9.2 Using `Phoenix.Routes.resources/4`

```
defmodule AuctionWeb.Router do
  use AuctionWeb, :router

  pipeline :browser do
    # ...
  end

  scope "/", AuctionWeb do
    pipe_through :browser # Use the default browser stack
```

```
    get "/", PageController, :index
    resources "/items", ItemController   <-- All the boilerplate from listing 9.1 is in this one line.
  end
end
```

The `resources "/items", ItemController` line creates the same eight routes that the eight lines in listing 9.1 created. This is obviously very nice and time-saving, allowing you to define a whole swath of routes with a single function call. You'll use this function extensively when you define routes in this book.

The first thing you want to do is list your items on a web page. You've done that previously at the `"/"` route, but let's also provide the list at `"/items"`, which is where it will live in the long term. (You'll free up `"/"` for some awesome marketing copy.)

For now, you only want that one route, but you know that you'll soon want to expand it to allow most of the RESTful interactions (if not all of them). For that reason, you'll define your route with the `Phoenix.Routes.resources/4` function. But because you currently only want to implement the `:index` action of that resource, you can pass an option to `Phoenix.Routes.resources/4` to direct it to only create that one route. You can do that with the `only: [:index]` option. Adding that to listing 9.2 will cause it to look like this.

Listing 9.3 Restricting the resource route creation

```
defmodule AuctionWeb.Router do
  use AuctionWeb, :router

  pipeline :browser do
    # ...
  end

  scope "/", AuctionWeb do
    pipe_through :browser # Use the default browser stack

    get "/", PageController, :index
    resources "/items", ItemController, only: [:index]   <-- Only the index action will be recognized by your Phoenix application.
  end
end
```

Why limit it to only create the `:index` action, especially when you know you'll very quickly implement more of the actions? I think it's good practice to only permit routes that you have already implemented or are currently implementing. Otherwise, you may get into the flow of implementing one route and forget that you also permitted other options.

`Phoenix.Routes.resources/4` also has an `except` option (which, if you used it, would make your resource declaration option look like `except: [:show, :new, :create, :edit, :update, :destroy]`). I personally add the actions I'd like to permit through an allow list (using `only`), rather than block the routes I want to prevent (using `except`).

9.1.2 Adding a new controller

Now that the route is defined, you need to implement the controller that you directed the route to: `AuctionWeb.ItemController`. Adding a new controller is relatively easy, especially after you've done it a couple of times.

Open a new file located at auction_umbrella/apps/auction_web/lib/auction_web/controllers/item_controller.ex. In that file, define a module as normal (named `AuctionWeb.ItemController`), and then bring in the code to handle requests for Phoenix (with `use AuctionWeb, :controller`). Once that's done, you can start adding functions for your actions. The following listing shows the barebones implementation of a Phoenix controller with no defined actions.

Listing 9.4 Barebones `AuctionWeb.ItemController` implementation

```
defmodule AuctionWeb.ItemController do
  use AuctionWeb, :controller          <-- Brings in a few helpers that Phoenix requires
end                                        (look in .../auction_web/lib/auction_web.ex)
```

This in itself won't handle any of the actions for the resource route. In the previous section, you told the router that `AuctionWeb.ItemController` would handle resource requests for `/items` (but only for the `:index` action). You need to implement an `index/2` function that will handle the request.

A Phoenix controller action is called with two parameters:

- The `Plug.Conn` struct that handles all the connection information for the request and response
- The parameters of the user request (such as an `id` or query)

In the case of a call to `index`, you need the `Plug.Conn` struct, so you can continue to build up a response to the user request, but you don't actually care about any parameters the user passed in with their request. This action is specifically built to list the items up for auction, so the user doesn't have any control over what's seen. You can thus ignore the params passed to your function.

Figure 9.2 illustrates how params are passed into the controller. In this case, you can safely ignore the `hack_me` and `report` keys, as you don't need them to successfully complete the request/response cycle.[1]

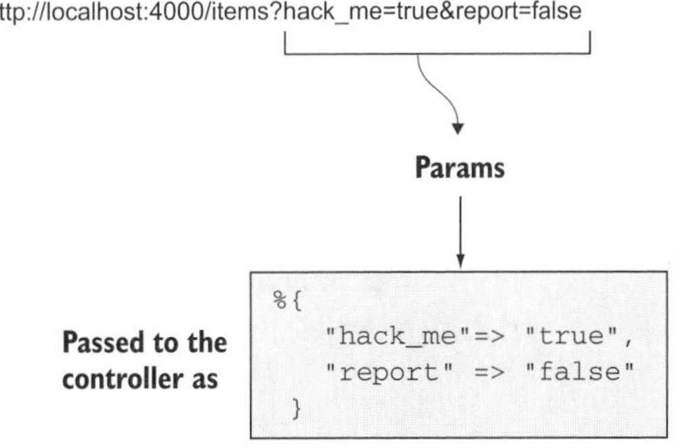

http://localhost:4000/items?hack_me=true&report=false
Params
Passed to the controller as
%{
"hack_me"=> "true",
"report" => "false"
}

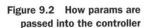

Figure 9.2 How params are passed into the controller

[1] If your mind was racing, thinking about controller function definitions and pattern matching on the params, nice job! That's a more advanced technique that can be very powerful when handling user requests.

You've actually already implemented this in the current AuctionWeb.PageController.index/2 function. You just need to copy the code from that function into your new function. The function will fetch the complete list of items in the database and render a view and template as a response. The following listing contains that code for AuctionWeb.ItemController.index/2.

Listing 9.5 Adding index/2 to AuctionWeb.ItemController

```
defmodule AuctionWeb.ItemController do
  use AuctionWeb, :controller

  def index(conn, _params) do
    items = Auction.list_items()
    render(conn, "index.html", items: items)
  end
end
```

Remember, preceding a variable name with an underscore (_) indicates you're acknowledging it but won't need it.

As you can see, render will pass conn, index.html, and items to AuctionWeb.ItemView, which you'll define next.

9.1.3 Adding a new view

As you'll recall from chapter 6, the Phoenix.Controller.render/3 function passes its parameters to a view module named, in this case, AuctionWeb.ItemView. Phoenix automatically infers the correct view module name based on the controller module name. Typically, the view module is very minimal. All the heavy lifting is done by Phoenix when you add use AuctionWeb, :view to the module definition. Create a new file at auction_umbrella/apps/auction_web/lib/auction_web/views/item_view.ex and add the following code to that view file.

Listing 9.6 Defining AuctionWeb.ItemView

```
defmodule AuctionWeb.ItemView do
  use AuctionWeb, :view
end
```

This one line will bring in all you need to get started with your view.

That's it! You can further use this module to add helper functions that you need or want to call in your EEx templates, but you don't need to add anything for now.

9.1.4 Adding a new template

As explained in chapter 6, the view passes on the Plug.Conn struct along with any other assigns you've declared (like @items) to the correct template. Figure 9.3 illustrates

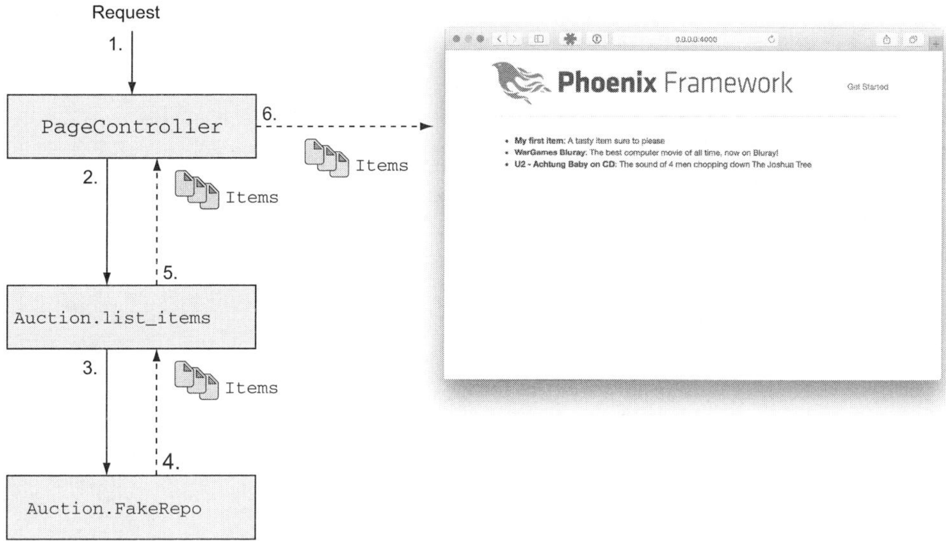

Figure 9.3 Reviewing how a controller and template relate

what we discussed in chapter 6. You declared the "correct" template when you called `render conn, "index.html", items: items` in `AuctionWeb.ItemController.index/2` —it will attempt to render index.html.

You're replicating (for now) the page you modified in chapter 6, so you can copy the EEx code from that file to this new one. This template will simply list the items for auction in your database. Create a new file at auction_umbrella/apps/auction_web/lib/auction_web/templates/item/index.html.eex and key in the following code.

Listing 9.7 Listing the items in the database

```
<ul>
  <%= for item <- @items do %>
    <li><strong><%= item.title %></strong>: <%= item.description %></li>
  <% end %>
</ul>
```

This for comprehension will loop through each item in @items.

If you start up the Phoenix server with `mix phx.server` and navigate to http://localhost:4000/items, you'll see your list of items, just like in chapter 6.

Figure 9.4 shows what I see when I load up the page in my browser.

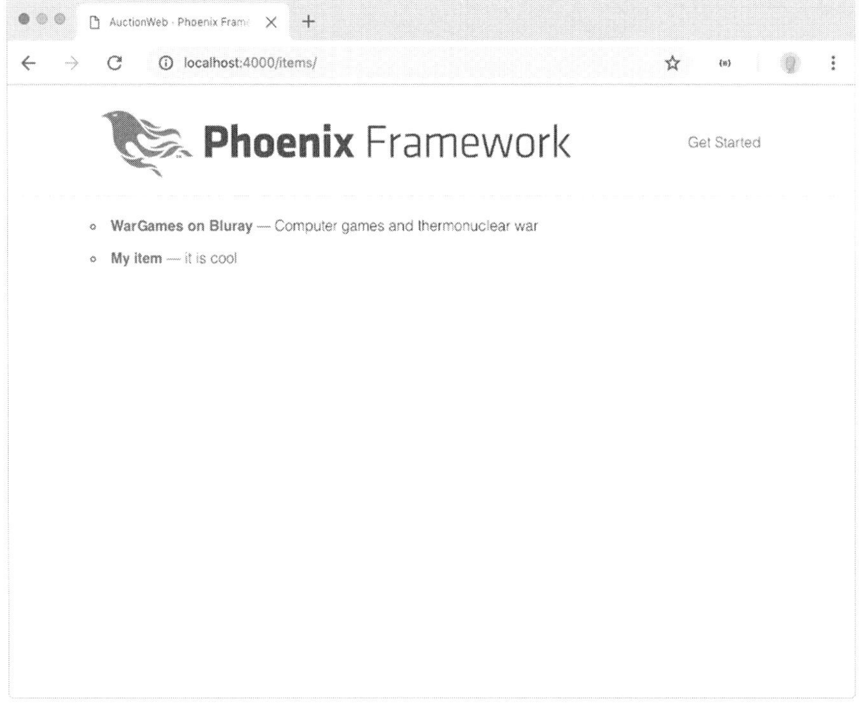

Figure 9.4 The list of items in your database—in the browser!

9.2 Viewing the details of a single item

A list of items is nice, but if a user wants to bid on an item, they'll probably want to view the details for that item. Beyond that, you need a page that allows users to bid on individual items. You'll combine those two pages into a single page based on the item ID. In a RESTful application, that sort of page is typically served by the `show` action and lives at a path like `/items/:id`, where `:id` is the unique identifier of the individual item.

Let's add that route and page to your application.

9.2.1 Defining the show route and function

In the router file, you've already specified that you want RESTful routes for items, but you've limited the action to `only: [:index]`. You need to add `:show` to that list and then define the `AuctionWeb.ItemController.show/2` function to handle the requests.

In the `AuctionWeb.Router` module, simply append `:show` to the list of allowed routes for the resource.

Listing 9.8 Adding the `:show` action to the allowed list

```
defmodule AuctionWeb.Router do
  use AuctionWeb, :router
```

```
  pipeline :browser do
    # ...
  end

  # ...

  scope "/", AuctionWeb do
    pipe_through :browser # Use the default browser stack

    get "/", PageController, :index
    resources "/items", ItemController, only: [:index, :show]
  end
end
```

Add the resources definition here.

Next, you need to modify `AuctionWeb.ItemController` to implement a `show/2` function. You want the function to do a few things:

- Accept a user request for a specific `Item`, specified by a unique identifier
- Retrieve that `Item` from the database using the unique identifier
- Render a web page that shows the details of the `Item`

Previously, the `AuctionWeb.ItemController.index/2` function didn't care what parameters the user passed in with their request because it made no difference in what was rendered. In the case of `show/2`, however, you need to know which `Item` the user requested. That identifier will be passed in a parameter map as the second argument to `show/2` (the first argument being the `Plug.Conn` struct).

As you'll recall, one of the great things about Elixir is that you can define functions with pattern matching built in. In this case, you'll define the `show/2` function to pattern-match on the params map to ensure that an `id` is indeed passed in with the request. If a user attempts to load a show page without an `id` or with some other param (`item_id`, maybe), the function won't match, and they'll receive an error. This will satisfy the first requirement in your list of three things the function should accomplish.

For the second requirement (retrieve the `Item` from the database), you'll use the public interface you wrote for dealing with your auction database. In this case, you use `Auction.get_item(id)` and bind the result to a variable. Finally, you pass that variable to the `render/3` function, which will use it to render the web page for the user.

Putting all this together, you can write `show/2` as follows.

Listing 9.9 Implementing `show/2`

```
defmodule AuctionWeb.ItemController do
  use AuctionWeb, :controller

  # def index...
  def show(conn, %{"id" => id}) do
    item = Auction.get_item(id)
    render(conn, "show.html", item: item)
  end
end
```

Ensures that an id is present in the params map of the request and binds it to the id variable for use in the function

How did you know the name of the id param?

When you defined your routes with the `resources/2` function in listing 9.8, the `:show` route defined a route like `get "/items/:id", ItemController, :show`. The `:id` in the route definition is a pattern-match holder. Anything matching the pattern of `/items/*` will forward the request to the controller, with whatever's in `*` as the `id` param.

9.2.2 Defining the show.html template

You don't need to change anything in `AuctionWeb.ItemView` for your template to be rendered, so you'll pass right over it and move on to the template itself. You can be as fancy with this template as you like, but for now I'll present a very simple implementation.

Your template will simply render each of the attributes of the item with an attribute title and value. Because you passed `item` into the `Phoenix.Controller.render/3` function in `AuctionWeb.ItemController.show/2`, it will be available in your template as `@item`.

Create a file at auction_umbrella/apps/auction_web/lib/auction_web/templates/item/show.html.eex and write the HTML you'd like. My implementation is in the following listing.

Listing 9.10 Showing the details of an item

```
<h1><%= @item.title %></h1>

<ul>
  <li><strong>Description:</strong> <%= @item.description %></li>
  <li><strong>Auction ends at:</strong> <%= @item.ends_at %></li>
</ul>
```

Remember that any code you put inside the <%= and %> tags will be output to the browser.

If you point your browser to a URL containing the `id` of an item in the database, you'll see something similar to figure 9.5. It's not the flashiest of pages, but it gets your data onto a web page, which is what you were aiming for.

Your next problem is that unless your users know the exact ID of the item they're interested in, they'll never be able to see these details. You need to *link* to the individual item pages from the `index` page.

9.2.3 Linking to individual items

To link to the individual items, you need to modify the index.html.eex file and use a new helper function that Phoenix provides: `Phoenix.HTML.Link.link/2`. Phoenix automatically imports `Phoenix.HTML.Link` into your templates, so you can simply call

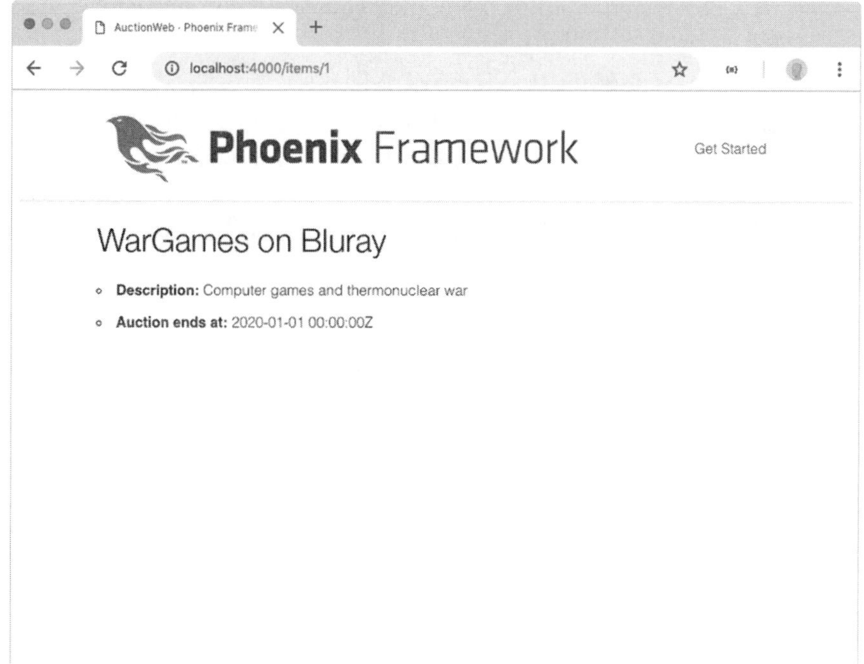

Figure 9.5 Showing the details of an item

link/2. link/2 requires two parameters: the text that you'd like the link to be linked from, and some options (importantly including the page to link to).

Something to keep in mind before you actually make the modifications to index.html.eex is that the Phoenix router generates named routes that you can use in your application. To see those routes, their names, and where they link to, you can run `mix phx.routes` from auction_umbrella/apps/auction_web. This is the output of that command from my local version:

```
> mix phx.routes
page_path  GET  /           AuctionWeb.PageController :index
item_path  GET  /items      AuctionWeb.ItemController :index
item_path  GET  /items/:id  AuctionWeb.ItemController :show
```

You'll only see the resource actions you put into your allow list.

You can see in the last two lines of output that you have a named route: `item_path`. You can use that named route when you specify the URL to link to in `link/2`.

Named routes require some parameters of their own:

- The `Plug.Conn` struct of the request (available in the templates as `@conn`).
- The action to link to and, if required, an `id` or a struct that has an `id` attribute (like an `Auction.Item`). Because you're looping through all the items, you can

simply pass each item into the named route function so that its own `id` can be inferred by the function.

With these things in mind, let's modify your index page so that the names of the auction items are the link's text. If a user clicks on the name, it will take them to the show page of that item. You can modify index.html.eex as follows.

Listing 9.11 Linking to each item's own page

```
<ul>
  <%= for item <- @items do %>
    <li>
      <strong><%= link(item.title, to: Routes.item_path(@conn, :show, item))
      ➥ %></strong> -
      <%= item.description %>
    </li>
  <% end %>
</ul>
```

Uses the item_path helper to generate a link to each item

When I load up http://localhost:4000 locally, I see the page in figure 9.6. It may be a bit hard to tell, with images printed in black and white, but each item name is a blue link that I can click to take me to the show page of that item.

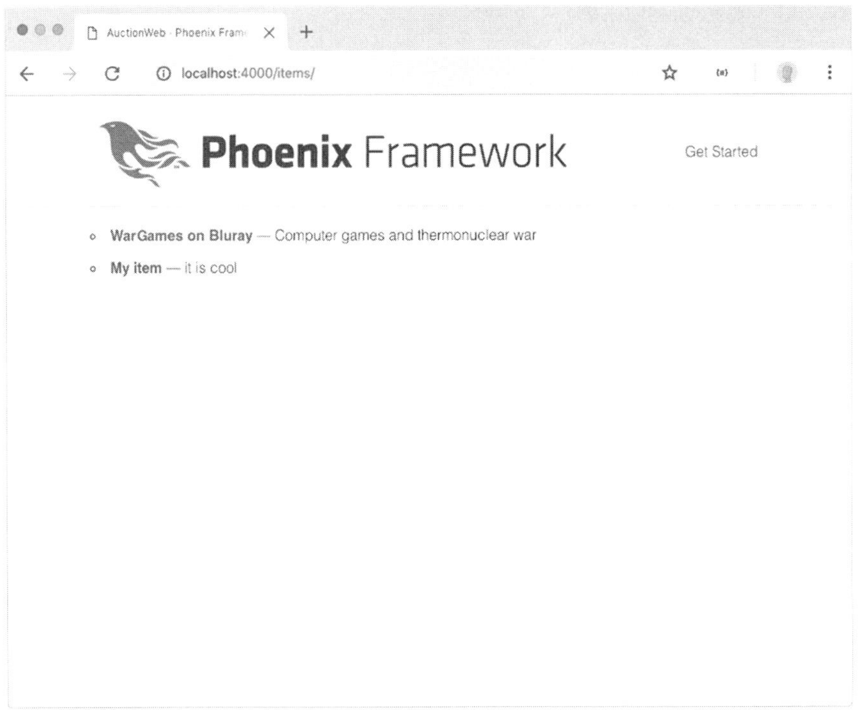

Figure 9.6 Items linked from the index page

9.3 Creating items through web forms

You can view your items in a browser, and you can create and modify items inside an IEx session. What you need now is a way to create and modify items in a browser. Most websites provide a way for users or admins to do that kind of thing through a web form. In this section, you'll create a web form that allows you to create an item.

The steps in this section will be similar to those for the `index` action, but they won't be quite as extensive, because most of the modules have been created already. You're just going to add to them.

9.3.1 Defining the new and create routes

It's time to expand the allowed list to include the `:new` and `:create` actions. This will increase the HTML methods available in your app to those in table 9.2.

Table 9.2 Implemented RESTful routes

HTTP method	Handler CRUD action	Example route	Typical purpose
`GET`	`index`	`/items`	Provides a listing of `Items` or an overview of the `Item` resource
`GET`	`new`	`/items/new`	Displays a form where a user can provide attributes to create a new `Item`
`POST`	`create`	`/items`	Creates a new `Item` based on the attributes in the request payload; typically, this is hit from `GET /items/new`
`GET`	`show`	`/items/:id`	Shows a single `Item` based on an identifier (such as an ID number)

As when you added the `:show` action, you need to add the `:new` and `:create` actions to the allowed list for the items resource. Edit the `AuctionWeb.Router` module as follows.

Listing 9.12 Adding `:new` and `:create` to your items resource

```
defmodule AuctionWeb.Router do
  use AuctionWeb, :router

  pipeline :browser do
    # ...
  end

  # ...

  scope "/", AuctionWeb do
    pipe_through :browser # Use the default browser stack

    get "/", PageController, :index
    resources "/items", ItemController, only: [:index, :show, :new, :create]
  end
end
```

Add the resources function call here.

This is largely unchanged, but you've added new and create to the allow list.

9.3.2 Defining the "new" controller function

With that done, you can move on to creating the controller actions required to handle the requests. You'll need to implement AuctionWeb.ItemController.new/2 and AuctionWeb.ItemController.create/2. Both of these functions will accept two parameters: the Plug.Conn struct that contains the request and response information, and the map of parameters from the user request.[2] For new/2, you don't care about the user request params, because you don't need them to display an empty form for creating a new item. But for create/2, you care a great deal about the user request params—they contain all the information about the item that the user would like to create.

You'll first implement the new/2 function, as it's the first step in the process of creating a new item. There are two things you need your controller to do:

- Set up a new Auction.Item changeset with no set attributes
- Pass that struct to the template for rendering a form for user input

Why do you want a blank changeset? Phoenix provides some form-builder helpers that allow you to easily track and display errors. When you eventually create an edit/update form, you'd like the form to be the same as the new/create form. For it to be a single implementation, you need a changeset to allow Phoenix's form-builder helpers to do their thing.

Setting up the changeset will also require some new implementation in your Auction public interface module. But before you head back into that module, you'll write the controller function with how you'd *like* the public interface to be used. Then, you'll implement the function.

All you really need to do in the controller is set up a blank changeset. The following listing calls a function, Auction.new_item/0, that will set up the empty changeset. The second step, passing the struct to the template, will be handled through the Phoenix.Controller.render/3 function. The following listing shows the new/2 function.

Listing 9.13 Implementing AuctionWeb.ItemController.new/2

```
defmodule AuctionWeb.ItemController do
  # ...
  def new(conn, _params) do
    item = Auction.new_item()                      <-- Sets up a new blank item for the form
    render(conn, "new.html", item: item)               that will be eventually rendered
  end
end
```

Note that Auction.new_item/0 doesn't yet exist—you need to implement that. All you need it to do is return an empty Auction.Item changeset, and the following listing

[2] You may be starting to see a pattern in these controller functions—they all have the same required parameters.

shows how simple that can be. This module is implemented in auction_umbrella/apps/auction/lib/auction.ex.

Listing 9.14 Implementing `Auction.new_item/0`

```
defmodule Auction do
  alias Auction.{Repo, Item}
  # ...
  def new_item, do: Item.changeset(%Item{})     <-- Returns an Auction.Item struct with no changes
end
```

If you'd like, fire up an IEx session and the Phoenix server with `iex -S mix phx.server` and look at what `Auction.new_item/0` returns:

```
iex(1)> Auction.new_item()          <-- Calls your newly created function, which returns an Ecto changeset
#Ecto.Changeset<
  action: nil,
  changes: %{},
  errors: [title: {"can't be blank", [validation: :required]}],
  data: #Auction.Item<>,
  valid?: false
>
```

You can see that you have errors in the changeset because you have no `title`. You can also see that no changes are being tracked, and the changeset is considered invalid.

There's also an attribute called `action`, which tracks what kind of action was attempted on the changeset—in this case `nil`, because you didn't attempt to create, update, or delete it. You can use this attribute to conditionally display errors to the user. When you create a brand new changeset with `Auction.new_item/0`, you have errors, but you don't want to display those errors to the user (displaying them would be confusing, since they haven't entered any information yet).

9.3.3 Defining the "new" template

Now that you've created the empty changeset and defined the controller function, you can move on to creating the form that will be displayed to the user and accept their input. The `Phoenix.HTML.Form` module contains a number of helper functions you'll use to build your form. The documentation has plenty of great examples and usage information,[3] but table 9.3 briefly outlines each of the functions you'll use.

Table 9.3 Some useful functions in `Phoenix.HTML.Form`

Function	Description
`form_for`	The main form-builder helper; generates the `form` tag and opens up a form block. Requires the changeset you're building the form for, the URL the form should `POST` to, and a form-builder function.

[3] See https://hexdocs.pm/phoenix_html/2.11.2/Phoenix.HTML.Form.html#form_for/4.

Table 9.3 Some useful functions in `Phoenix.HTML.Form` (continued)

Function	Description
`label`	Creates a label tag that corresponds to a specific form field.
`text_input`	Creates an `<input type='text'>` tag for text input. Requires the form-builder param and an atom matching the attribute that the field is for.
textarea	Creates a `<textarea>` tag for long-form text input. Requires the form-builder param and an atom matching the attribute that the field is for.
datetime_select	Creates a series of drop-down fields that allow a user to indicate a date and time. Requires the form-param and an atom matching the attribute that the field is for.

Create a new file at auction_umbrella/apps/auction_web/lib/auction_web/templates/item/new.html.eex and input the HTML in the following listing. Note that Phoenix brings in a minimal stylesheet to provide some default styling.

Listing 9.15 Creating a template at .../templates/item/new.html.eex

```
<h1>New Item</h1>

<%= form_for @item, Routes.item_path(@conn, :create), fn f -> %>
  <%= label f, :title %>
  <%= text_input f, :title %>

  <%= label f, :description %>
  <%= textarea f, :description %>

  <%= label f, :ends_at, "Auction ends at" %>
  <%= datetime_select f, :ends_at %>

  <div>
    <%= submit "Submit" %>
  </div>
<% end %>
```

label can automatically generate a human-readable label based on the column name (represented by an atom) provided here.

Sometimes you may need to provide the full string for the label as the third argument.

If you start up your Phoenix server (`mix phx.server`) and load up http://localhost:4000/items/new, you'll see something similar to figure 9.7.

9.3.4 Defining the create controller function

You've defined the form that enables users to submit the data required to create a new item, but if you try submitting that form, you'll get an error. Why? Well, the URL you pointed your form to (`item_path(@conn, :create)`, which is `POST /items`) doesn't yet handle requests. You need to define the `AuctionWeb.ItemController.create/2` controller function so it can handle those requests, accepting the same parameters as the other controller functions: the `Plug.Conn` struct and the user parameters submitted in the request.

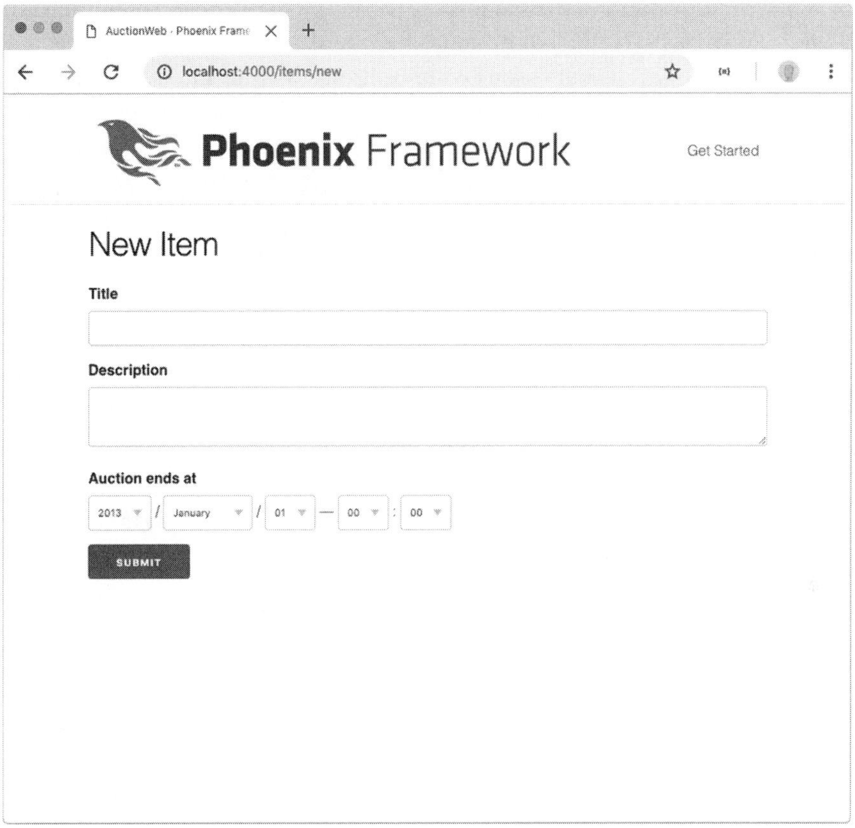

Figure 9.7 Loading http://localhost:4000/items/new after defining the `new` template

If you did try out your form before discovering that it would fail, you'd have seen something like the following in the Phoenix server logs:

```
14:38:29.152 [info] POST /items
14:38:29.167 [debug] Processing with AuctionWeb.ItemController.create/2
  Parameters: %{"_csrf_token" =>
    "ITxiPmdYCzgzJQpsCDZ0BUBSZzJDJgAAMr7L02MBun98IlDSy11J2Q==", "_utf8" =>
    "✓", "item" => %{"description" => "it is cool", "ends_at" => %{"day" =>
    "5", "hour" => "9", "minute" => "0", "month" => "4", "year" => "2021"},
    "title" => "My item"}}
  Pipelines: [:browser]
14:38:29.198 [info] Sent 500 in 46ms
```

Shows the request was received

Shows which module and function are handling the request

Shows that Phoenix sent a response along with the response code

For every request that Phoenix handles, you'll see log statements similar to these. In this case, you can see the parameters that were submitted along with the request. There's a `_csrf_token` that ensures the request was submitted from a form that you control (it's generated automatically by the `form_for` form-builder function), but the important thing here is the `item` map, which contains the data submitted with the form. You can see the `description`, `ends_at`, and `title` attributes.

The `AuctionWeb.ItemController.create/2` function will care about what's in the parameters (unlike `new/2` and `index/2`) because all of the user's submitted form data is in there. You'll pattern-match on that `item` map in your function definition, create the item, and redirect the user to the new item's page.

Listing 9.16 Implementing `AuctionWeb.ItemController.create/2`

```
defmodule AuctionWeb.ItemController do
  # ...
  def create(conn, %{"item" => item_params}) do
    {:ok, item} = Auction.insert_item(item_params)
    redirect(conn, to: Routes.item_path(conn, :show, item))
  end
end
```

Pattern-matches on {:ok, item} to successfully create an item in the database based on the params received

You're pattern-matching the return value of `Auction.insert_item/1` for the success case, and redirecting the connection to the individual item path on success.

What happens in the case of an error (if the `Auction.Item` was invalid, for example)? For now, you'll get an error at the controller level because it wouldn't match the pattern `{:ok, item}` successfully (it would return `{:error, item}` instead). You'll handle the error path momentarily. But first you need to make a small change in your `Auction` module.

`Auction.insert_item/1` was written before you implemented changesets. Now that we've discussed changesets, you can modify the function to pass the attributes through a changeset, which will do all the necessary things required of the changeset before the data is inserted into the database. The changes required are very minimal, as shown in the following listing.

Listing 9.17 The new `Auction.insert_item/1`

```
defmodule Auction do
  alias Auction.{Repo, Item}
  # ...
  def insert_item(attrs) do
    %Item{}
    |> Item.changeset(attrs)
    |> @repo.insert()
  end
end
```

Uses an Ecto changeset to track any errors that may have surfaced

This changeset will allow you to track the changes and errors you need in order to present them to the user.

With that change made, if you now submit your form with valid data, you should see it flow from the new form page (`new`) to the individual item page (`show`). For example, I entered some data into the form in figure 9.8, and I was taken to the page shown in figure 9.9. If you submit the form with bad data (such as an `ends_at` date in the past), you'll get an error from the controller.

This redirection not only indicates to the user that the item was created successfully, but it also gives them a chance to view the details.

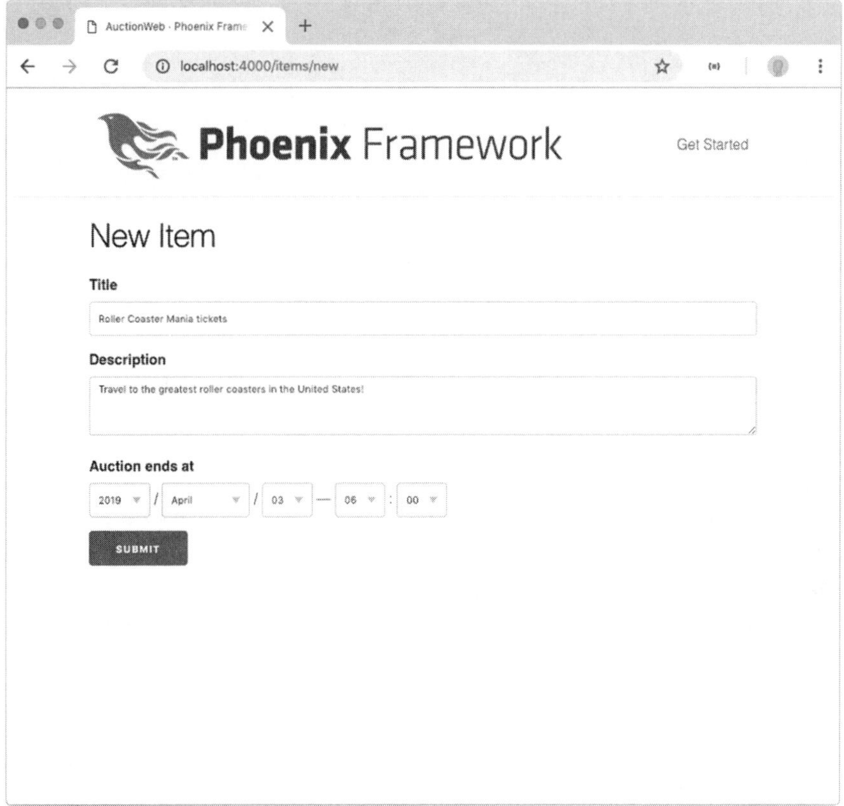

Figure 9.8 Your filled-out new item form

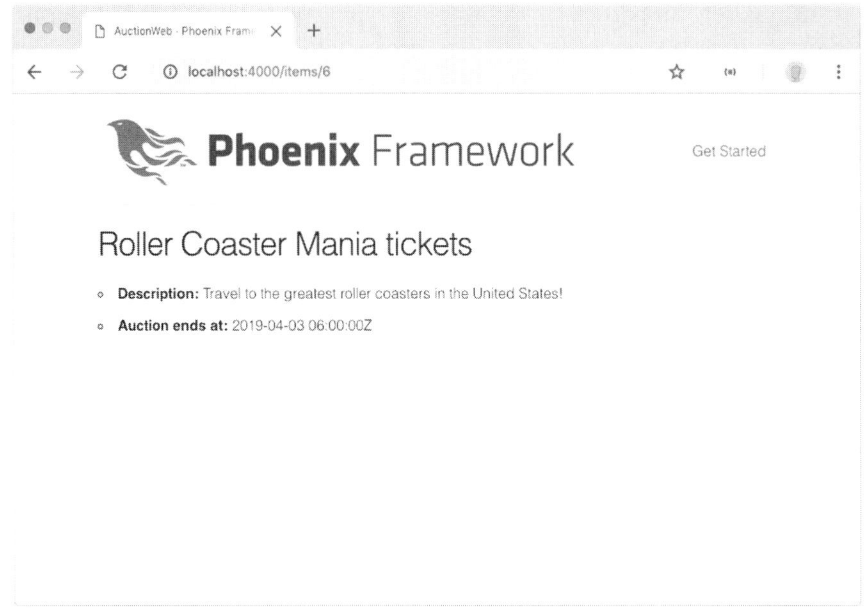

Figure 9.9 Redirected to the new item's detail page

HANDLING ERRORS IN THE CHANGESET

If the `Auction.Item.changeset/2` function determines that the changeset is invalid, `Auction.insert_item/1` will return `{:error, item}`, with `item` being the changeset with an `errors` attribute. In the case of an invalid item, you want to rerender the form and notify the user of any errors so they can fix them. You need to make changes in two places: `AuctionWeb.ItemController.create/2` and .../templates/item/new .html.eex. In the former, you need to handle the error case and render the form again. In the latter, you need to display any relevant errors.

In the controller, you'll modify the function to use a `case` statement, which takes the result of one function and matches that result to potential cases. The first match's function is executed.

Listing 9.18 Matching the return value of `Auction.insert_item/1`

```
defmodule AuctionWeb.ItemController do
  # ...
  def create(conn, %{"item" => item_params}) do
    case Auction.insert_item(item_params) do
      {:ok, item} -> redirect(conn, to: Routes.item_path(conn, :show, item))
      {:error, item} -> render(conn, "new.html", item: item)
    end
  end
end
```

Takes the argument provided (the return value of Auction.insert_item) and pattern-matches the result, running the first matched state

As stated in the requirements for this function, if the item is inserted correctly (`{:ok, item}`), you redirect the user to the item's show page. If the item isn't inserted correctly (`{:error, item}`), you render the `new` page again. This time, the `item` variable has a list of errors that need to be corrected to make the changeset valid. You can use that in the template to inform the user.

When you first issued the command `mix phx.new`, one of the files that was generated for you was `AuctionWeb.ErrorHelpers`. These helpers can be used in your templates to display errors—in particular `AuctionWeb.ErrorHelpers.error_tag/2`. `error_tag/2` is smart enough to not display the errors unless an action has been attempted on the changeset (an insert, update, or delete). It knows whether or not one has been attempted by looking at the `action` attribute in the changeset struct. You'll use `error_tag/2` much like you use `text_input/2`, because it accepts the same inputs: the form and the attribute to display an error for.

You can modify the new.html.eex template to display each field's errors below the field (see figure 9.10). You'll also see if there's an `action` set for your changeset, and if

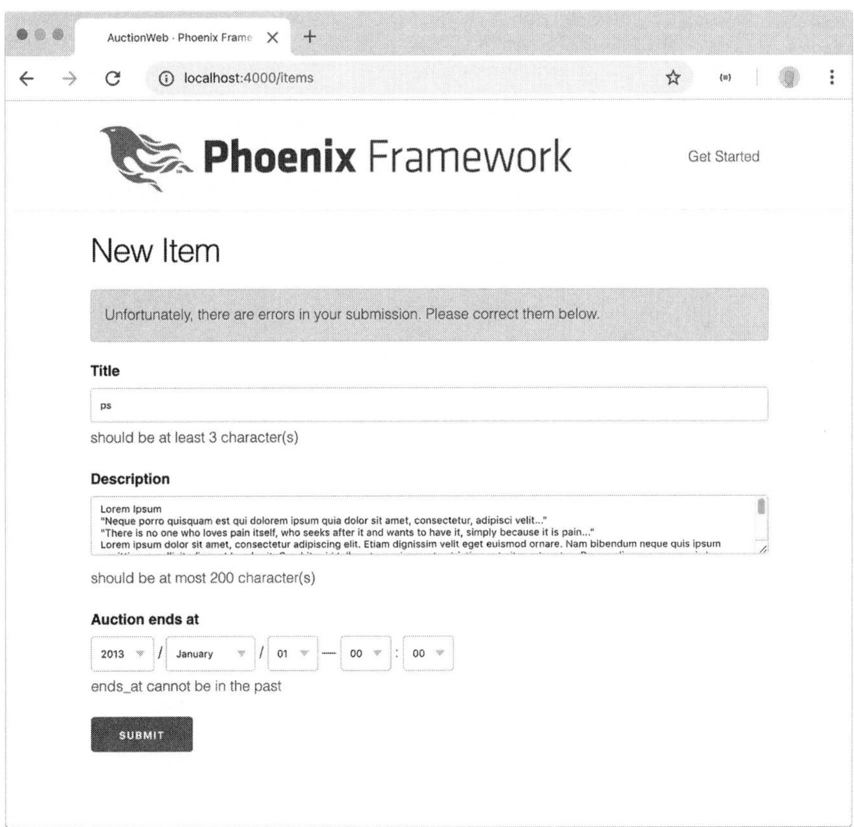

Figure 9.10 Errors showing up near the form fields

there is, display an error banner indicating that the form has errors needing correction. The following listing implements these changes.

Listing 9.19 Showing errors on your form

```
<h1>New Item</h1>

<%= form_for @item, Routes.item_path(@conn, :create), fn f -> %>
  <%= if @item.action do %>                                   <-- If @item.action is defined, you know you have errors, so display this banner.
    <div class="alert alert-danger">
      Unfortunately, there are errors in your
      submission. Please correct them below.
    </div>
  <% end %>

  <%= label f, :title %>
  <%= text_input f, :title %>
  <%= error_tag f, :title %>                                  <--

  <%= label f, :description %>
  <%= textarea f, :description %>
  <%= error_tag f, :description %>                            <-- These error_tags will display any errors that exist for the field.

  <%= label f, :ends_at, "Auction ends at" %>
  <%= datetime_select f, :ends_at %>
  <%= error_tag f, :ends_at %>                                <--

  <div>
    <%= submit "Submit" %>
  </div>
<% end %>
```

With these changes made, you can now see the errors below the fields that have them, when someone submits an invalid item.

9.4 Editing items through web forms

The last step you have to cover in this chapter is editing your items through web forms. We'll move a bit more quickly through this section, because many of the steps are similar to those covered in the previous sections, where you listed, viewed, and created items.

Briefly, these are the steps you'll take:

1. Add the `edit` and `update` actions to the list of allowed routes for the resource.
2. Define the `edit/2` and `update/2` controller functions.
3. Create an edit.html.eex template file.

9.4.1 Defining the edit and update routes

First, you need to add `:edit` and `:update` to the allowed list for the `Auction.Item` resource.

Listing 9.20 Adding `edit` and `update` to the routes

```
defmodule AuctionWeb.Router do
  # ...
  scope "/", AuctionWeb do
    pipe_through :browser # Use the default browser stack

    get "/", PageController, :index
    resources "/items", ItemController, only: [
      :index,
      :show,
      :new,
      :create,
      :edit,
      :update
    ]
  end
end
```

For the sake of line length, I broke the list into multiple lines.

At this point, the only action missing from your `only` allowed list is `:delete`. You may be tempted to change the list to `except: [:delete]` instead of the long list for `only`, and you can certainly do that. Personally, I rest easier knowing that I have an allowed list as opposed to a block-list protecting my routes.

9.4.2 Defining the "edit" controller function

You've got the route defined. Now you just need a controller function to handle the request. We'll focus first on `edit`, so that you can present the form to the user before you have to deal with processing it.

By now you probably know the drill: `AuctionWeb.ItemController.edit/2` accepts a `Plug.Conn` struct and a map of the request params. In this case, you need to know which item the user wants to edit, so you'll grab that information as you pattern-match in the function definition.

Listing 9.21 Defining `AuctionWeb.ItemController.edit/2`

```
defmodule AuctionWeb.ItemController do
  # ...
  def edit(conn, %{"id" => id}) do
    item = Auction.edit_item(id)
    render(conn, "edit.html", item: item)
  end
end
```

This is a new function that you'll define next.

The controller function is pretty straightforward, but you need to define another function in the `Auction` module that sets up a changeset for the item with the specified ID. That function is also very straightforward.

Listing 9.22 Defining Auction.edit_item/1

```
defmodule Auction do
  # ...
  def edit_item(id) do
    get_item(id)
    |> Item.changeset()       <-- Returns an Ecto changeset so the changes can be appropriately tracked
  end
end
```

Your function returns an Ecto changeset so the changes, errors, and validations can be passed through to each subsequent step.

9.4.3 Defining the edit.html.eex template

You'd ideally like your edit form to be exactly the same as your create form. You could just copy and paste the form code from new.html.eex into edit.html.eex, but then if you needed to make a change to the form in the future, you'd have to change it in both places. Thankfully, Phoenix provides a way to render HTML templates within other HTML templates. That means that you can create form.html.eex and include it in both new.html.eex and edit.html.eex. That way, if any changes are needed in the future, you just have to change one file.

With that in mind, you also need a different way to specify which route you need to point the form to, and even which HTML action is required! More specifically, you need the form to `POST` to `/items` when you're creating a new item, and to `PUT` or `PATCH` to `/items/:id` when you're updating an item. The function that renders the template can accept a list of assigns you'd like available in the rendered template, just like in a controller. Knowing that, you can pass the route and action that you need the form to point to through the render function and into the form template.

Let's first edit the new.html.eex template, so you can see what it looks like to render a template within it. You only need to provide the template name and the assigns you'd like available within the template. The following listing shows what your .../templates/item/new.html.eex template should look like.

Listing 9.23 Rendering one template inside another

```
<h1>New Item</h1>

<%= render("form.html", item: @item, action: Routes.item_path(@conn,
     :create)) %>       <-- Most of the heavy lifting is done inside form.html.eex.
```

That looks pretty simple, right? The heavy lifting of your form is now done in .../templates/item/form.html.eex. Apart from one small change, as indicated in the following listing, you can just cut and paste the form code from the old version of new.html.eex to form.html.eex.

Listing 9.24 Creating the form template

```
<%= form_for @item, @action, fn f -> %>
  <%= if @item.action do %>
    <div class="alert alert-danger">
      Unfortunately, there are errors in your
      submission. Please correct them below.
    </div>
  <% end %>

  <%= label f, :title %>
  <%= text_input f, :title %>
  <%= error_tag f, :title %>

  <%= label f, :description %>
  <%= textarea f, :description %>
  <%= error_tag f, :description %>

  <%= label f, :ends_at, "Auction ends at" %>
  <%= datetime_select f, :ends_at %>
  <%= error_tag f, :ends_at %>

  <div>
    <%= submit "Submit" %>
  </div>
<% end %>
```

Uses the @action assign to allow different routes to be taken, depending on where you render the form

The only change required is on the first line, where you tell `form_for/3` where to point the form it generates. Because you passed `item_path(@conn, :create)` into the template as the `@action` assign, you can tell `form_for/3` that `@action` contains the information it needs. That also frees you up to call this template from an edit.html.eex template.

The .../templates/item/edit.html.eex template will look as simple as new.html.eex does now.

Listing 9.25 Creating the edit.html.eex template

```
<h1>Edit <%= @item.data.title %></h1>

<%= render("form.html", item: @item,
                        action: Routes.item_path(@conn, :update, @item.data)) %>
```

Most of the heavy lifting for edit is done inside form.html.eex.

You may have noticed that the `edit` template is very similar to the `new` template, with a couple of important differences:

- You use the item's title in the `h1` tag of the page.
- You need to pass the item data to `item_path` so it knows how to build the `:update` path (remember that `update` requires the ID, which it will get from the item).

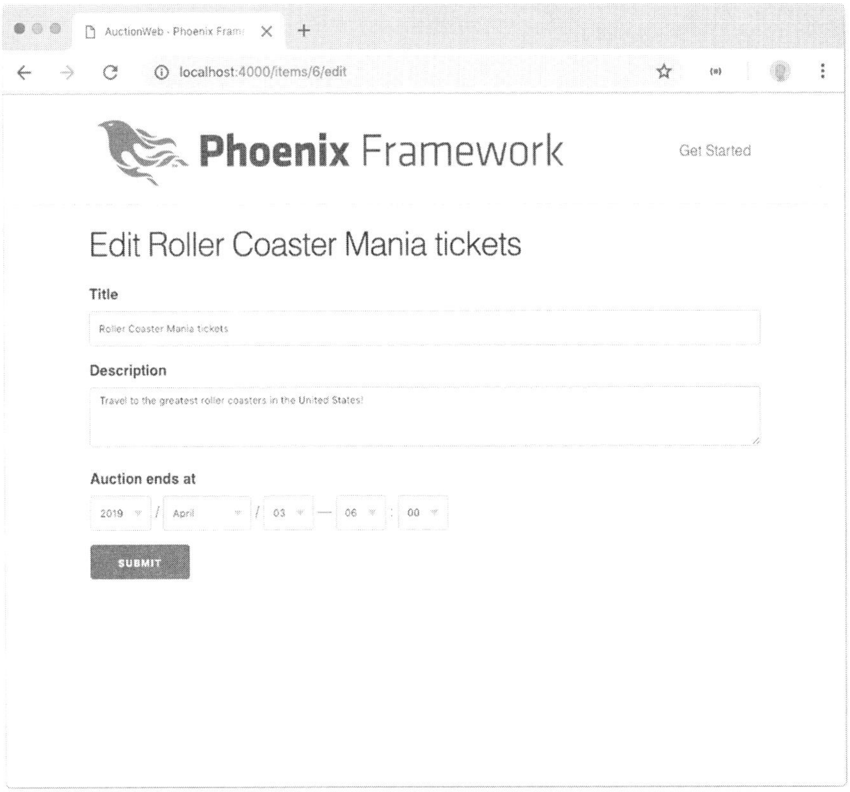

Figure 9.11 Editing the "Roller Coaster Mania tickets" item

In both of these cases, you access the attributes through `@item.data`. It's forgivable to think that you could just call `@item.title` to get to it, but remember, `@item` is a changeset, not an `Auction.Item` struct. The attributes of the underlying record of the changeset can be accessed through the `data` attribute of the changeset.

If you navigate to the detail page of an item in your database and tack on `/edit` in the URL (such as http://localhost:4000/items/4/edit), you'll see the form you created for `new` but prefilled with information from the item. Figure 9.11 shows what I see when I edit my "Roller Coaster Mania tickets" item.

I can edit any information I need to from here, and click Submit to submit the changes. But so far, that controller function hasn't been defined (`AuctionWeb.ItemController.update/2`). Let's define it now.

9.4.4 Defining AuctionWeb.ItemController.update/2

`update/2` will be remarkably similar to `create/2`—you need the params from the item's form, but this time you also need the ID of the item to update. You'll also pattern-match on the success or failure of the submission, so you know where to send your user next. Finally, you'll also use `Auction.update_item/2` instead of `Auction.create_item/1`.

Listing 9.26 Listing 9.26 Defining `update/2`

```
defmodule AuctionWeb.ItemController do
  # ...
  def update(conn, %{"id" => id, "item" => item_params}) do
    item = Auction.get_item(id)
    case Auction.update_item(item, item_params) do
      {:ok, item} -> redirect(conn, to: Routes.item_path(conn, :show, item))
      {:error, item} -> render(conn, "edit.html", item: item)
    end
  end
end
```

A case statement is used here, just as in create.

Looks very familiar, doesn't it (like a mix between `show/2` and `create/2`)? You'll find that once you catch on to the main concepts of Phoenix (and Elixir), making it do the things you need will become easier and easier, because a lot of the idioms are the same and patterns repeat themselves.

After implementing `update`, I edited my "Roller Coaster Mania tickets" to be "Whitewater Mania tickets" instead (see figure 9.12).

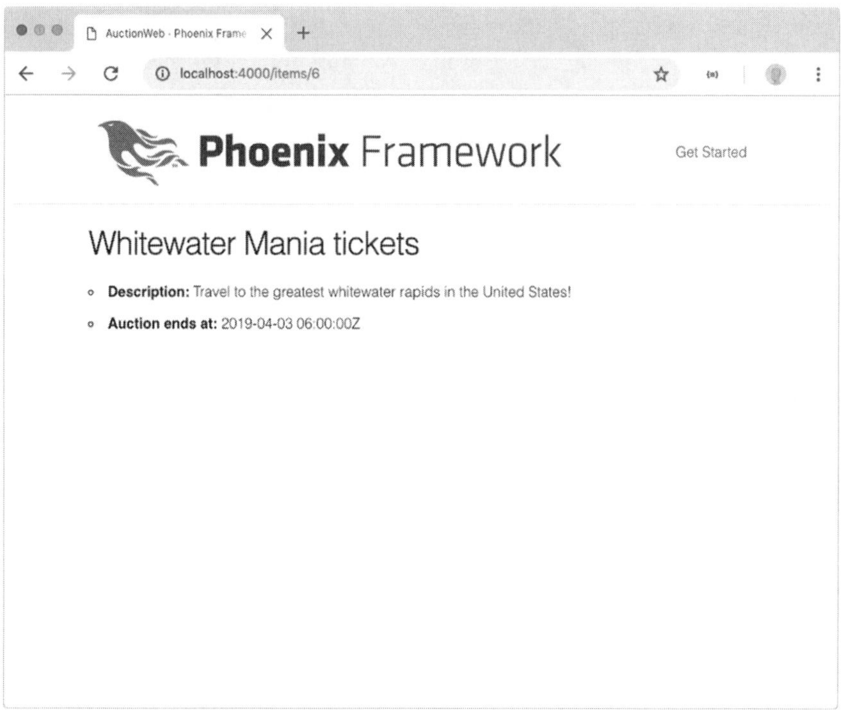

Figure 9.12 These are Whitewater Mania tickets now.

Wow, you made it! This was a pretty long and deep chapter, but it covered the essential actions that a user will take every day on your websites. There are some other things that would be nice to have on the site (like links to edit each item from their detail pages) but we've covered enough in this chapter that you should be able to tackle those things on your own.

Summary

- A good workflow when adding new functionality is to
  - Add the routes
  - Create the controller (if necessary)
  - Create the controller functions
  - Create the HTML template
- A RESTful resource contains actions for `index`, `show`, `new`, `create`, `edit`, `update`, and `delete`.
- Each controller function accepts two parameters: a `Plug.Conn` struct and the parameters from the user request.
- Phoenix's built-in form-builder functions make building a form easy—especially when fed a changeset.
- You can render a template inside another template. This can be helpful when more than one template needs to share the same HTML.

10 Plugs, assigns, and dealing with session data

This chapter covers

- Creating modules that implement the `Plug` behavior
- Passing information through your application in assigns
- Handling user authentication

In the past couple of chapters, you've created routes and controllers needed for creating, viewing, and editing items for your auction web application. That's been great, but there's a glaring hole: bids. How can you have an auction without bids? Furthermore, how can you track who a bid is from if you don't have users?

Before you expand the number of structs in your application by adding bids (which you'll do in the next chapter), we'll discuss creating users in your application. The main focus of this chapter is using session data in your application. Session data will allow you to know when a user is logged in and what pages they're visiting.

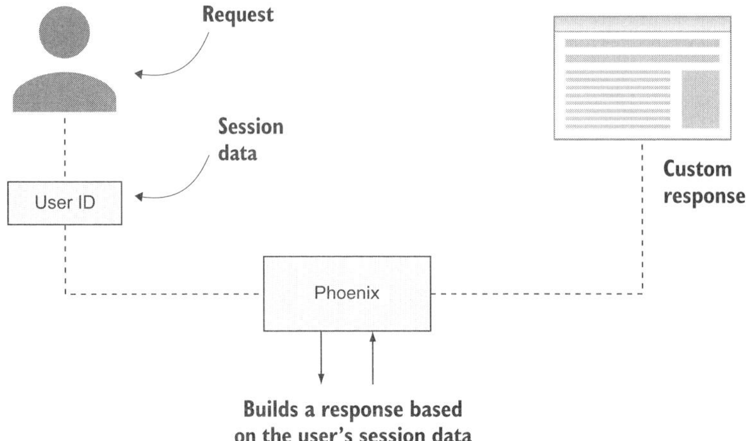

Figure 10.1 A user's session data will help Phoenix build a web page specific to them.

Figure 10.1 illustrates this concept. Each user of your auction site carries session data in their browser that lets you know who they are. Phoenix will use that session data to build a custom response for them as they navigate the site.

These custom responses could be as simple as displaying their name in a welcome message, or as complex as restricting access to certain parts of the auction site based on their permission level.

10.1 Preparing your application for user registration

The first step you need to take in this chapter is to define what a user is. Will they have usernames or just an email address? What information will you collect about them? These are decisions that you need to make before you allow user registration. And for the most part, these choices will be implemented on the `Auction` side of your umbrella application (as opposed to the Phoenix-focused `AuctionWeb` side).

There are three things you need to do in `Auction` before you move back over to Phoenix:

1 Define a schema to describe the data of a user.
2 Create a database migration to create a place to hold that user data.
3 Define a changeset for the user.
4 Define some API endpoints to interact with the user data in the database.

You'll take them in order.

10.1.1 Defining the Auction.User schema

Your auction site is going to be pretty bare-bone. You don't need a whole lot of information about your users—just enough to ensure they're unique and identifiable. A username, email address, and password will be plenty in your case.

All three will be string data types, which you've seen before. But you'll introduce a new schema field type: the `virtual` type, which won't actually enter the database. You don't want to store your users' passwords in a string column unencrypted, so you'll encrypt them before they enter the database. You'll store the encrypted password in a column named `hashed_password`, but you'll still accept the user's password input in a `password` attribute. Accepting an attribute but not having a spot in the database for it is what makes this a `virtual` type. This may sound a bit confusing now, but it will make sense when you see the code.

In chapter 7, you covered Ecto migrations and schemas, and you'll use them again in this section. If you need a reminder on the details of those topics, take a look back at that chapter before moving on here.

You've decided on your requirements, so let's create an Auction.User module. This file will exist at auction_umbrella/apps/auction/lib/auction/user.ex, and the following listing shows the contents of that file with the schema defined.

Listing 10.1 Defining the `Auction.User` module

```
defmodule Auction.User do
  use Ecto.Schema

  schema "users" do
    field :username, :string
    field :email_address, :string
    field :password, :string, virtual: true
    field :hashed_password, :string
    timestamps()
  end
end
```

virtual: true means that this field won't be persisted in the database.

You can use this schema to help you determine what your migration will look like. Each of these fields (with the exception of `password`) will be a column in the users table of your database. That table doesn't yet exist, so you need to create it first.

10.1.2 Creating a migration to create the users table

You *could* create the migration from scratch, but it's much nicer to use Ecto's Mix tasks for the heavy lifting—specifically, `mix ecto.gen.migration`. You only need to pass it the name of the migration you want to create.

Be sure to run the task from the auction_umbrella/apps/auction/ directory. Here's what it looked like when I ran the task:

```
> mix ecto.gen.migration create_users
Compiling 1 file (.ex)
Generated auction app
* creating priv/repo/migrations/20181213015711_create_users.exs
```

create_users is the name of the migration.

The file this task creates is a template for an Ecto migration—you just need to fill in the details. You already know which fields you want and what data types they are, so populating the migration is pretty easy.

We've already discussed most of the functions used in the migration in the following listing, but one hasn't been mentioned. `unique_index/2` is a database constraint that ensures, at a database level, that no two entries will have the same `username`.

Listing 10.2 The migration to create the users table

```
defmodule Auction.Repo.Migrations.CreateUsers do
  use Ecto.Migration

  def change do
    create table(:users) do
      add :username, :string
      add :email_address, :string
      add :hashed_password, :string
      timestamps()
    end

    create unique_index(:users, [:username])
  end
end
```

Creates a database constraint ensuring that username is universally unique

Once the migration has been created and saved, you can migrate the database by running `mix ecto.migrate`:

```
> mix ecto.migrate
17:58:19.828 [info]  == Running 20181213015711
     Auction.Repo.Migrations.CreateUsers.change/0 forward
17:58:19.829 [info]  create table users
17:58:19.887 [info]  create index users_username_index
17:58:19.893 [info]  == Migrated 20181213015711 in 0.0s
```

Ecto knows that you're migrating your database in the forward direction.

With that, you have a users table in your database!

10.1.3 Defining changesets for Auction.User

You know you want validations for your user data, so you're going to want a changeset. In fact, you'll likely want more than one changeset. We covered changesets in previous chapters, but I didn't mention that you're not limited to one changeset per module.

Why would you want multiple changesets? Well, each changeset could correspond to different actions the user takes. Suppose there are two different forms that a user of your website will be interacting with:

- A user registration form in which they enter a password
- A user profile form, where they can update profile information apart from a password

You definitely need the password when you create the user, or if the user is changing the password, but otherwise, you won't want password information to get through to the database. For other edit/update situations, you can restrict the password from reaching the database by using two different changesets: a registration one, and a profile update one. If the password is included in the profile update changeset, you can filter it out so it never gets past the changeset function.

If `password` is in the list of changes, you hash it using the `comeonin` hex package, which provides multiple ways to encrypt data. You can read about the different algorithms and how to choose one, but I've chosen the `Pbkdf2` implementation for the application because it requires no other dependencies on your local machine. `comeonin` and `Pbkdf2` are external dependencies, so you need to add them to the mix.exs file for the `auction` application. The following listing shows what the `auction` deps function looks like now.

Listing 10.3 Including `comeonin` and `pbkdf2_elixir` as deps

```
defmodule Auction.MixProject do
  # ...
  defp deps do
    [
      {:ecto_sql, "3.0.3"},
      {:postgrex, "0.14.1"},
      {:comeonin, "~> 4.1"},
      {:pbkdf2_elixir, "~> 0.12"}
    ]
  end
end
```

Add these lines.

After you add those dependencies, make sure you run `mix deps.get` in your terminal to fetch those new packages.

For the changeset with the password, you'll want to validate the presence of `password`, a minimum length (I chose 5 characters), and you'll want to hash the password if it's in the list of changes. If it's not being changed, you won't worry about hashing it. Keep in mind, `password` isn't a field that's persisted in the database—`hashed_password` is.

You can make your own changes in a changeset by using the `Ecto.Changeset.put_change/3` function. It requires the changeset, the key the change is associated with, and the value of the change. You'll use that function in your password-hashing function, which will store the hashed version of the password in the `hashed_password` attribute.

Your normal changeset will also do a few important things:

- Require the `username` and `email_address` to be present
- Validate that the `username` is at least three characters long
- Ensure that the `username` is unique in the database

NOTE The `unique_index` in the migration will ensure that the `username` is unique in the database, and `unique_constraint` in the changeset will convert the database error into a changeset error if it's not unique.

The following listing puts this all together.

Listing 10.4 Defining the `Auction.User` changesets

```
defmodule Auction.User do
  import Ecto.Changeset                    <-- Imports Ecto.Changeset

  # ...

  def changeset(user, params \\ %{}) do
    user
    |> cast(params, [:username, :email_address])
    |> validate_required([:username, :email_address, :hashed_password])    <-- Ensures a password exists for the user
    |> validate_length(:username, min: 3)
    |> unique_constraint(:username)
  end

  def changeset_with_password(user, params \\ %{}) do
    user
    |> cast(params, [:password])
    |> validate_required(:password)
    |> validate_length(:password, min: 5)
    |> validate_confirmation(:password, required: true)
    |> hash_password()
    |> changeset(params)                   <-- Uses the regular changeset inside the one for passwords
  end

  defp hash_password(%Ecto.Changeset{changes: %{password: password}} =
  ➥ changeset) do
    changeset
    |> put_change(:hashed_password, Auction.Password.hash(password))
  end
  defp hash_password(changeset), do: changeset
end
```

Uses pattern matching in the function definitions to determine if password is in the list of changes

You probably noticed that the preceding code calls a function in a module that doesn't yet exist. You need to implement `Auction.Password.hash/1` next. Why make it its own module? The main reason is that it's a great place to put all the password-management functions you'll create. The `Auction.User` module, itself, shouldn't be concerned with how you implement password encryption.

Your password module will be small at first, only containing `hash/1`. In the following listing, you simply hand off the work of hashing the password string to the `Pbkdf2` module you included in your list of dependencies. I created this file at auction_umbrella/auction/lib/auction/password.ex.

Listing 10.5 Implementing the beginnings of the `Auction.Password` module

```
defmodule Auction.Password do
  import Pbkdf2, only: [hash_pwd_salt: 1]    <-- You're only using the hash_pwd_salt/l function, so you can limit it to being the only one imported.
```

```
  def hash(password), do:
    hash_pwd_salt(password)     <-- This function comes from Pbkdf2.
end
```

The best way to demonstrate how this new function is used is to try it out in an IEx session. Load one up (`iex -S mix`) and try it out as follows. Put a set of attributes through the general `changeset`, and then through `changeset_with_password`.

Listing 10.6 Trying out the changesets in IEx

```
iex(1)> alias Auction.User
iex(2)> User.changeset(
iex...> %User{},
iex...> %{username: "geo", email_address: "geo@phoenixinaction.com",
     password: "security"})
#Ecto.Changeset<
  action: nil,
  changes: %{email_address: "geo@phoenixinaction.com", username: "geo"},  <--
  errors: [hashed_password: {"can't be blank", [validation: :required]}],
  data: #Auction.User<>,
  valid?: false
>
    Notice that the password didn't make it through the filter on your
    regular changeset because it wasn't included in your cast call.

iex(2)> User.changeset_with_password(
iex...> %User{},
iex...> %{username: "geo", email_address: "geo@phoenixinaction.com",
iex...> password: "security", password_confirmation: "security"})
#Ecto.Changeset<
  action: nil,
  changes: %{
    email_address: "geo@phoenixinaction.com",
    hashed_password:
     "$2b$12$hvLAzfjp4WQRPC2aTK7YFuOpKBnbWmGkM6wPWRxXyijjW.XsjpzCm",  <--
    password: "security",
    username: "geo"
  },
  errors: [],
  data: #Auction.User<>,
  valid?: true
>
    Check out this password hash. This string is what will be
    persisted to the database.
```

The `hashed_password` attribute only shows up in your list of changes when you use the `changeset_with_password` version of the changeset. Otherwise, no password changes are sent to the database. You can use different changesets, depending on what should (or shouldn't) make it to your database.

10.1.4 Creating API functions in Auction

You don't want the Phoenix side of your application to directly access database-related functions—you want to keep a strong boundary between those domains. Just as with `Auction.Item`, you'll want some functions in `Auction` that allow you to look up an

Auction.User by ID and by username/password combo, that set up a new user changeset for user registration, and that insert new users into the database. (We won't be covering editing and updating users in this book, but you'll learn enough by the end of the chapter to implement those yourself.) Each of these functions will look very similar to the Auction.Item functions.

The following listing shows the functions you need to add to your Auction module.

Listing 10.7 Implementing the new Auction functions

```
defmodule Auction do
  alias Auction.{Repo, Item, User}     <-- Adds Auction.User to the list of aliases
  # ...

  def get_user(id), do: @repo.get!(User, id)

  def new_user, do: User.changeset_with_password(%User{})

  def insert_user(params) do
    %User{}
    |> User.changeset_with_password(params)
    |> @repo.insert
  end
end
```

These functions will set you up to deal with users on the Phoenix side of your application umbrella.

10.1.5 User registration web flow

You've taken care of the database and business logic for registering users. Now you need a way to allow users to register for an account. That means that you'll create a new RESTful route, including a new controller, view, and some templates. In chapter 9, we discussed how to create these things, so we'll move through those steps more quickly in this chapter. If you need a refresher, take a look back at chapter 9.

Let's start with the router. For now, you'll only implement the new, create, and show routes for users. You aren't going to allow the listing of registered users (which would be index), nor are you going to implement an update or change function for user information (which would be a good idea in a real-world application, but space is limited in this book).

Route the requests to the AuctionWeb.UserController, as shown in the following listing.

Listing 10.8 Creating RESTful routes for your User resource

```
defmodule AuctionWeb.Router do
  # ...
  scope "/", AuctionWeb do
```

```
    pipe_through :browser
    # ...
    resources "/users", UserController, only: [:show, :new, :create]
  end
end
```

Limits your routes to the show, new, and create actions

Once the routes are defined, you need to implement the controller module and create corresponding `AuctionWeb.UserController.show/2`, `new/2`, and `create/2` functions. As a reminder, each function takes two arguments: a `Plug.Conn` struct and the request parameters from the user. Just like with `AuctionWeb.ItemController`, you'll care about the user parameters for `show` (the ID of the user) and `create` (the attributes for the user to create):

- `show/2` needs to know the ID of the user to look up and needs to pass the template the `user` to display.
- `new/2` doesn't need any request parameters but needs to pass an `Auction.User` changeset to the template for the new user form.
- `create/2` needs the attributes the user submitted from the new user form. If the new user is valid, `create/2` will redirect the user to the `show/2` route. If the user is invalid, it will rerender the form.

Create a new file at auction_umbrella/apps/auction_web/lib/auction_web/controllers/user_controller.ex and implement `AuctionWeb.UserController`, as in the following listing.

Listing 10.9 The `AuctionWeb.UserController` controller

```
defmodule AuctionWeb.UserController do
  use AuctionWeb, :controller

  def show(conn, %{"id" => id}) do
    user = Auction.get_user(id)
    render conn, "show.html", user: user
  end

  def new(conn, _params) do
    user = Auction.new_user()
    render conn, "new.html", user: user
  end

  def create(conn, %{"user" => user_params}) do
    case Auction.insert_user(user_params) do
      {:ok, user} -> redirect conn, to: Routes.user_path(conn, :show, user)
      {:error, user} -> render conn, "new.html", user: user
    end
  end
end
```

Uses case to pattern-match the result of inserting the new user into the database

Now that the controller is implemented, the next steps the request data takes is through the view and finally the template. Just as in chapter 9, you'll create a very minimal `AuctionWeb.UserView` and then move on to creating your templates. The following listing shows the full implementation of `AuctionWeb.UserView`. Save it to .../auction_web/views/user_view.ex.

Listing 10.10 `AuctionWeb.UserView` implementation

```
defmodule AuctionWeb.UserView do
  use AuctionWeb, :view        <- Brings in all you need for now
end
```

You can now create the template and the user form. You aren't collecting a whole lot of information from your users—the following listing shows all you need in the .../auction_web/templates/user/new.html.eex file.

Listing 10.11 Creating new.html.eex

```
<h1>User Registration</h1>

<%= form_for @user, Routes.user_path(@conn, :create), fn f -> %>
  <%= if @user.action do %>        <- If there's an action key on @user, the changeset had an error, so you render this error message.
    <div class="alert alert-danger">
      Unfortunately, there are errors in your submission.
      ➥ Please correct them below.
    </div>
  <% end %>

  <%= label f, :username %>
  <%= error_tag f, :username %>
  <%= text_input f, :username %>

  <%= label f, :email_address %>
  <%= error_tag f, :email_address %>
  <%= text_input f, :email_address %>

  <%= label f, :password %>
  <%= error_tag f, :password %>
  <%= password_input f, :password %>

  <%= label f, :password_confirmation %>
  <%= error_tag f, :password_confirmation %>
  <%= password_input f, :password_confirmation %>

  <div>
    <%= submit "Submit" %>
  </div>
<% end %>
```

With this, you have something you can see in your browser. Make sure the Phoenix server is running and visit http://localhost:4000/users/new. You should see something like figure 10.2.

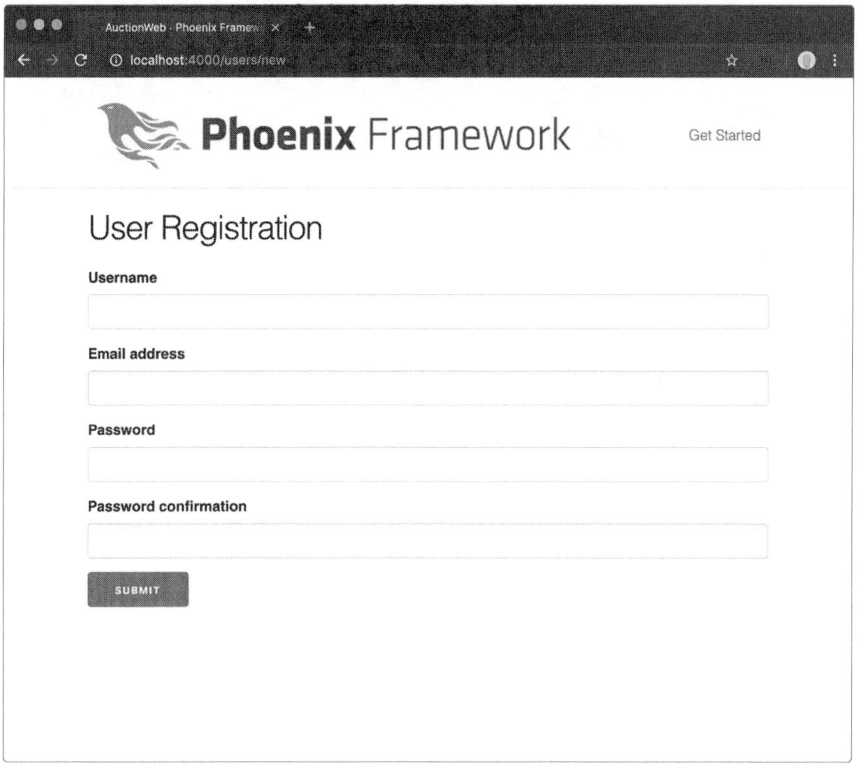

Figure 10.2 The user registration form

If you fill out the form, you'll get an error because you haven't yet created the show.html.eex template—but if you get that error, it means the form submission successfully created the user and redirected correctly. If there are any validation errors, the form will be rerendered with error messages accompanying the fields that have errors.

You don't need a really fancy page for `AuctionWeb.UserController.show/2`. Just like the item's show page, you only need a listing of the attributes and their values, as in figure 10.3. The following listing shows how I implemented this (in .../auction_web/templates/user/show.html.eex).

Listing 10.12 The user details page

```
<h1>User details</h1>

<dl>
  <dt>Username</dt>
  <dd><%= @user.username %></dd>
  <br />
  <dt>Email address</dt>
  <dd><%= @user.email_address %></dd>
</dl>
```

You don't need to show any further detail at this point in your app's life.

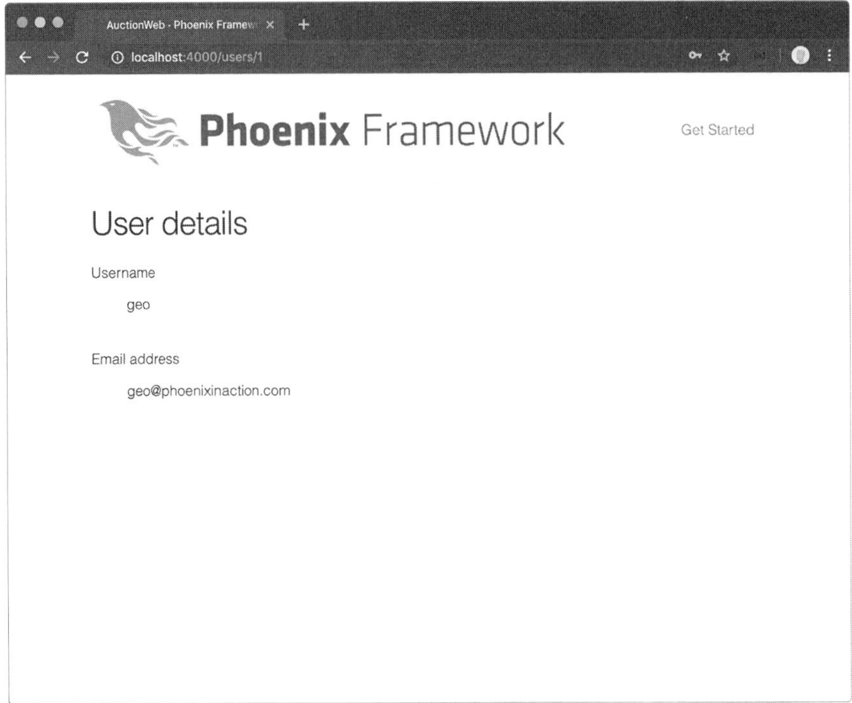

Figure 10.3 Viewing the details of the new user

Once you save that file and reload the page, you'll see something like figure 10.3 (only with your information and not mine).

10.2 Handling user login and sessions

What you've created so far in this chapter is pretty cool, but there's a small problem: any user can see the details of any other user if they know the other user's ID number. Nothing protects a user's information because no permissions are checked before loading the information. In the real world, you want to limit who can view a user's information to that user.

How can you know who's viewing the page? Right now, you can't. You need to ask a user to log in and then track them as they navigate the site. Once you know who's viewing a page, you can limit which pages they can see and what's displayed on those pages.

To track a user from request to request, you need to create a `Plug.Session` for the user when they log in. In that session, you store their `user_id`. On each web page load, you look up the user based on that `user_id` and verify that they're on an allowed page and possibly modify the page to show them only what they're allowed to see.

The good news is that Phoenix has session support built-in—you don't have to do anything. Beyond that, the data in the session can be encrypted if you want to keep your users' prying eyes out of the data you store in there. If you open .../

auction_web/endpoint.ex, you'll see all the plugs that the connection is fed through before it hits the router. One of those is `Plug.Session`, shown in the following listing, and it's generated by default.

Listing 10.13 The section of endpoint.ex that sets up your session

```
defmodule AuctionWeb.Endpoint do
  # ...

  # The session will be stored in the cookie and signed,
  # this means its contents can be read but not tampered with.
  # Set :encryption_salt if you would also like to encrypt it.
  plug Plug.Session,
    store: :cookie,
    key: "_auction_web_key",
    signing_salt: "T/6rc89M"

  # ...
end
```

You can encrypt your session by setting :encryption_salt here.

Your signing_salt will be different than mine. Security!

You can also see, in your router module (at .../auction_web/router.ex), that the default `browser` pipeline runs through a plug named `:fetch_session`. That plug sets up the session so it can be read from and written to within the `Plug.Conn` struct that passes from point to point during a request.

You'll do a couple of things in this section to support user logins:

- Create a new route and accompanying controller, functions, view, and templates for `/login` and `/logout`.
- Insert the user `user_id` into the session cookie if the login was successful.

10.2.1 Creating the route, controller, view, and templates for logging in and out

You should be pretty familiar with the flow at this point, so I'll quickly outline how I implemented each of these. We'll come back to anything that you haven't covered previously. The goal here is to get a lot of the boilerplate out of the way before diving into the meat of this section.

I named the controller `SessionController` and used the routes `login` and `logout`.

Listing 10.14 Adding new routes in .../auction_web/router.ex

```
defmodule AuctionWeb.Router do
  # ...

  scope "/", AuctionWeb do
    # ... user and item resources
    get "/login", SessionController, :new
    post "/login", SessionController, :create
    delete "/logout", SessionController, :delete
  end
end
```

I used three of the RESTful resource routes, but split them out into individual definitions (instead of using resources/4) in order to use specific routes for them.

Instead of using `resources "/sessions"`, you want custom names for the login and logout routes. In such cases, it can be easier to specify them individually, as in the preceding listing.

The only function you need to implement at the moment is `new`, shown in the following listing.

Listing 10.15 Creating .../auction_web/controllers/session_controller.ex

```
defmodule AuctionWeb.SessionController do
  use AuctionWeb, :controller

  def new(conn, _params) do
    render conn, "new.html"
  end

  def create(conn, %{"user" => user}) do
    # you'll implement this later in the chapter
  end

  def delete(conn, _params) do
    # you'll implement this later in the chapter
  end
end
```

You'll implement these functions later in the chapter.

The `new` function will render the new.html.eex template through `SessionView`, created in the following listing.

Listing 10.16 Creating .../auction_web/views/session_view.ex

```
defmodule AuctionWeb.SessionView do
  use AuctionWeb, :view
end
```

Brings in everything you need for your view

Finally, you need to build the actual login form in apps/auction_web/templates/session/new.html.eex.

Listing 10.17 Creating .../auction_web/templates/session/new.html.eex

```
<h1>Log In</h1>

<%= form_for @conn, Routes.session_path(@conn, :create), [as: :user],
➥ fn f -> %>
  <%= label f, :username %>
  <%= text_input f, :username %>

  <%= label f, :password %>
  <%= password_input f, :password %>
```

This version of form_for accepts a connection instead of a changeset. as: :user will namespace the fields under "user" when it's POSTed to the server.

```
  <div>
    <%= submit "Submit" %>
  </div>
<% end %>
```

These additions give you a solid groundwork upon which you can build the session-handling capabilities of your application. You should be familiar enough with Phoenix at this point to understand what's happening in each of the preceding listings. Now that those are out of the way, let's dive into something new.

10.2.2 Implementing the dirty details of sessions and authentication

You've implemented the things you need to bring up the login form, but we haven't yet discussed how to check whether the username and password supplied by the user matches an existing user. Beyond that, if it *does* relate to an actual user, how do you log them in? You'll implement those things in this section.

If you load http://localhost:4000/login (after ensuring that your Phoenix server is running), you'll see the page in figure 10.4.

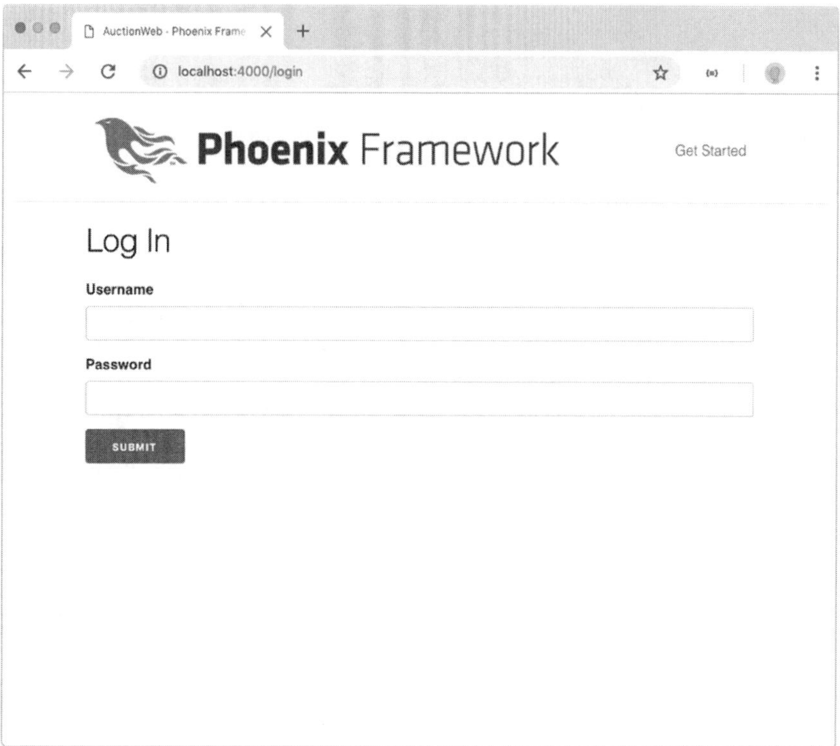

Figure 10.4 The user login page

If you submit that form, however, you'll get an error, because you have yet to implement the `AuctionWeb.SessionController.create/2` function. Here's how this function should work:

- If a user can be found with the username/password combination that was submitted, you store the `user_id` in the session.
- If a user can't be found, you set a generic error message in the `flash` and render the login form again. The `flash` is a great place to store temporary messages for the user.

To look up a user based on the submitted username and password, you also need to implement a new function in the `Auction` API module. This function should return the `Auction.User` if one is found, or return `false` (or, really, anything else) if one isn't found.

First, let's write the controller to match how this API should work. The following listing implements the previous points.

Listing 10.18 Implementing `AuctionWeb.SessionController.create/2`

```
defmodule AuctionWeb.SessionController do
  def create(conn, %{"user" => %{"username" => username, "password" =>
  ➥ password}}) do
    case Auction.get_user_by_username_and_password(username, password) do
      %Auction.User{} = user ->
        conn
        |> put_session(:user_id, user.id)
        |> put_flash(:info, "Successfully logged in")
        |> redirect(to: Routes.user_path(conn, :show, user))
      _ ->
        conn
        |> put_flash(:error, "That username and
        ➥ password combination cannot be found")
        |> render("new.html")
    end
  end
end
```

You'll implement this function next. (annotates the `case Auction.get_user_by_username_and_password` line)

Pattern-matches against %Auction.User{} struct and binds that to user for use in the function that follows (annotates the `%Auction.User{} = user ->` line)

Plug.Conn.put_session/3 stores a value for a key in a conn. (annotates the `put_session` line)

This pattern (_) matches anything else. (annotates the `_ ->` line)

Now you need to think about how `Auction.get_user_by_username_and_password/2` should work:

1. Attempt to retrieve an `Auction.User` from the database with the supplied `username`.
2. If one exists, verify that the password matches the hashed password stored in the database.
   - If it matches, return the `Auction.User` record.
   - If it doesn't match, return `false`.

3 If one doesn't exist, pretend you're doing the work of hashing a password to check for its existence, and return `false`.

Figure 10.5 offers a visual representation of the decision tree your code will run through.

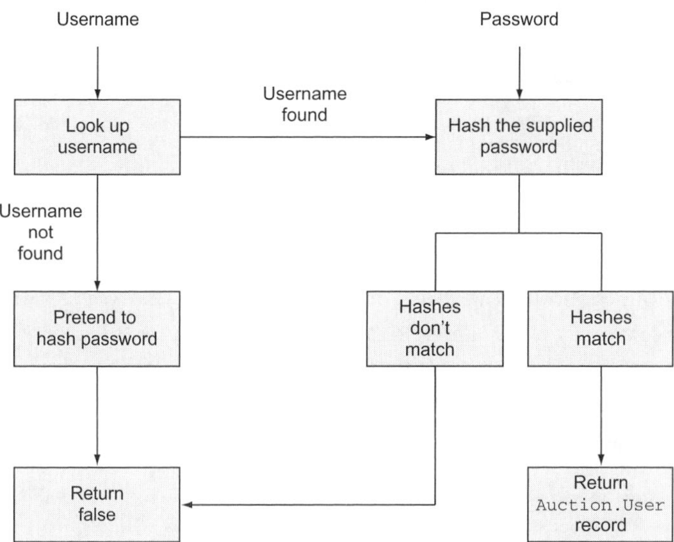

Figure 10.5 The decision tree for the authentication module

You may be wondering about the third step: why pretend to hash a password if a user doesn't even exist in the database? The answer is to hamper would-be attackers on your site. Some web-attack software is so precise it can detect minute differences in the speed of responses from the server. If you didn't make the server do the work of hashing a password when you couldn't find a user, some software could detect the shorter request/response cycle (resulting from not checking a password hash) and would know that the user wasn't found for the supplied `username`.

This is also why you display only a *generic* error message to the user. You don't want the requester to know that the `username` was found and the `password` was wrong. That would lead to an attacker knowing one of the two things that keep unauthorized people out of an account. This is a common-enough practice (or should be) that the `pbkdf2_elixir` package you're using for hashing includes a dummy hashing function. You'll utilize it in your function.

In keeping with the spirit of having your modules worry about as few things as possible, you'll offload the password-hashing activities to the `Auction.Password` module. You'll implement those functions momentarily. For now, let's write the other functionality in the `Auction.get_user_by_username_and_password/2` function.

Listing 10.19 Implementing `Auction.get_user_by_username_and_password/2`

```
defmodule Auction do
  alias Auction.{Repo, Item, User, Password}    <-- Adds Auction.Password to the list of aliases
  @repo Repo
  # ...

  def get_user_by_username_and_password(username, password) do
    with user when not is_nil(user) <- @repo.get_by(User, %{username:
    ➥ username}),
         true <- Password.verify_with_hash(password, user.hashed_password) do
      user
    else
      _ -> Password.dummy_verify
    end
  end
end
```

You now know enough about how your functions will work that you can implement `Auction.Password.verify_with_hash/2` and `Auction.Password.dummy_verify/0`. Just like `Auction.Password.hash/1`, your functions will be simple wrappers around functions provided by your hashing package of choice, `pbkdf2_elixir`. The following listing shows the full module.

Listing 10.20 Implementing more of `Auction.Password`

```
defmodule Auction.Password do
  import Pbkdf2                <-- You're now using most of the functions in the Pbkdf2 module, so you can remove the only limitation.

  def hash(password), do:
    hash_pwd_salt(password)                          <-- These functions come from Pbkdf2.

  def verify_with_hash(password, hash), do:
    verify_pass(password, hash)                      <--

  def dummy_verify, do: no_user_verify()             <--
end
```

You've implemented enough now that you can try submitting the login form at http://localhost:4000/login. I suggest submitting the form with invalid information first, to check out the error message you receive. Figure 10.6 shows what I received.

If you submit the form with the username and password you created earlier, your controller should successfully redirect you to your user details page and inform you of your successful login (see figure 10.7).

You may be wondering where those flash messages are being rendered—you didn't implement them. One piece of the HTML that's rendered as a response is the *layout*. By default, that layout is located at .../auction_web/templates/layout/app.html.eex, and in that file the `:error` and `:info` flashes are generated for you. The layout wraps

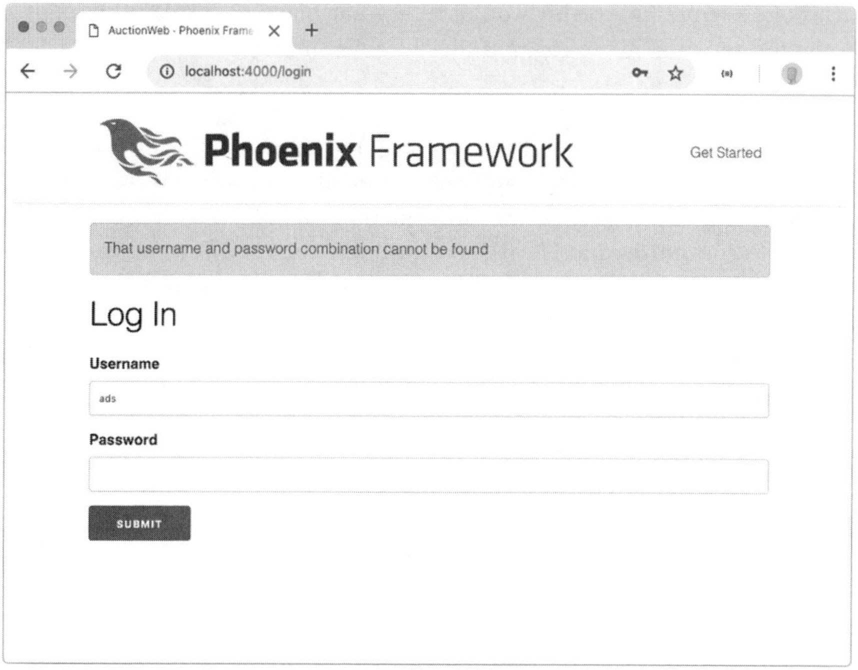

Figure 10.6 Submitting invalid information to the login form

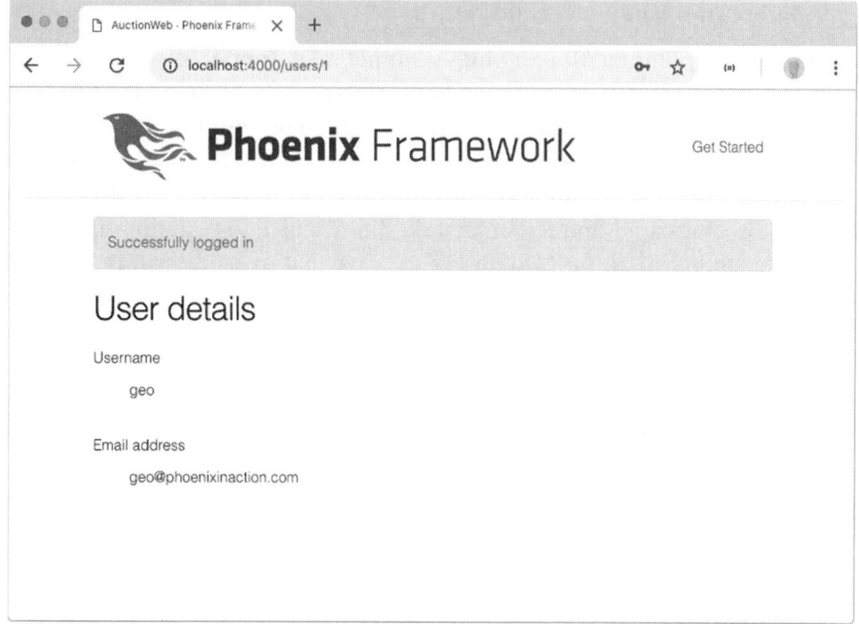

Figure 10.7 Redirected to the user details page

each page's template, so this would be a great place to display the login info for a logged-in user, or a link to log in if they haven't already.

10.3 Plugs

I'm excited. I'm excited *for you* because you get to learn about plugs—potentially for the first time. Plugs are crazy simple and very powerful, so—for safety—strap in and read on.

You need a way to get the user information on each page request for authentication and to customize what HTML is returned to the user. You've saved the `user_id` in the session cookie, which is stored in the user's browser memory, so ideally you can use that to look up the user and provide the user information for every request.

This focus on things that happen on every request (or nearly every request) brings us to plugs. You've undoubtedly noticed that the `AuctionWeb.Endpoint` and `AuctionWeb.Router` modules are littered with calls to `plug :this_function` and `plug ThatModule`. A `Plug` is simply a behavior that accepts a connection request (the `Plug.Conn` struct that's passed into every controller function), transforms it in some way, and then passes it on. There are two types of plugs: functions and modules.

For a *function* to be considered a `Plug`, it has to do two things:

- Accept two parameters: a `Plug.Conn` struct and options
- Return a `Plug.Conn` struct

For a *module* to be considered a `Plug`, it also needs to do two things:

- Define an `init/1` function that initializes any arguments or options for the plug
- Define a `call/2` function that does what the function version of a `Plug` does: accepts two parameters and returns a `Plug.Conn` struct

The idea and implementation of plugs is simple yet extremely powerful. How powerful, you may wonder? Almost the entire journey a request/response cycle takes throughout the Phoenix framework is handled by plugs. You could build your own web framework by implementing a series of plugs if you're so inclined. There's nothing stopping you from plugging your own plug into the cycle to set up whatever needs setting up.

Function plugs are good for small tasks, but it's nice to contain implementations of ideas, like plugs, in their own modules. For that reason, you'll implement your authentication plug in its own module. This plug should check for the existence of a `user_id` in the session, and if it's there, put that user record into the `conn` as an `assign` (which you can then access in a template).

Given this data flow, you can implement a module plug as follows. I created this module at .../lib/auction_web/authenticator.ex.

Listing 10.21 Creating an authentication module plug

```
defmodule AuctionWeb.Authenticator do
  import Plug.Conn

  def init(opts), do: opts

  def call(conn, _opts) do
```

A Plug module must define the init/1 and call/2 functions.

```
    user =
      conn
      |> get_session(:user_id)
      |> case do
        nil -> nil
        id -> Auction.get_user(id)
      end
    assign(conn, :current_user, user)
  end
end
```

`Plug.Conn.get_session(conn, :user)` returns either an `Auction.User` record or `nil`. If it's not `nil`, you retrieve the user by their `id`. Either way, you store that as the `current_user` in the connection `conn`. Any function that handles the connection `conn` after this plug will have the `current_user` information available.

The next question is, "Where do you plug this thing in?" You want this plug to run on every connection request that's made from a browser, so the perfect place would be in the `browser` pipeline in the router. The current `browser` pipeline is shown in the following listing.

Listing 10.22 The current `browser` pipeline

```
defmodule AuctionWeb.Router do
  use AuctionWeb, :router

  pipeline :browser do
    plug :accepts, ["html"]
    plug :fetch_session
    plug :fetch_flash
    plug :protect_from_forgery
    plug :put_secure_browser_headers
  end
  # ...
  scope "/", AuctionWeb do
    pipe_through :browser        <- You currently route all your requests
    # ...                           through the browser pipeline.
  end
end
```

Every request that goes through the / top-level route is piped through this browser pipeline. You need to fetch the session before you try to access it in your plug (with `Plug.Conn.get_session/2`), so perhaps the best place to put the authenticator is at the end of that `browser` pipeline.

The following listing shows the authenticator plug in the pipeline.

Listing 10.23 Adding the authenticator plug to the `browser` pipeline

```
defmodule AuctionWeb.Router do
  use AuctionWeb, :router

  pipeline :browser do
    plug :accepts, ["html"]
```

```
    plug :fetch_session
    plug :fetch_flash
    plug :protect_from_forgery
    plug :put_secure_browser_headers
    plug AuctionWeb.Authenticator        <-- Add the plug here.
  end
  # ...
end
```

When the connection finally hits the `plug AuctionWeb.Authenticator` line, it knows to call `init/1` and then `call/2` from that module. As long as you stick to the `Plug` contract, your module can be plugged in to the application.

Now you can do things like check to see if the user is logged in before displaying a login link. Or you could welcome them by name. Or you could limit their viewing of user profiles.

Let's implement the first item in that list: if a user isn't logged in, display a login link in the header area (and some other navigation).

10.4 Adding site navigation

Right now, a user would have to be pretty familiar with the structure of your site to know how to navigate it. The only links you've provided users with so far are links to item details. Clearly, users will need to do more than that. What you need is to display a simple navigation header on each page of the site as a user navigates.

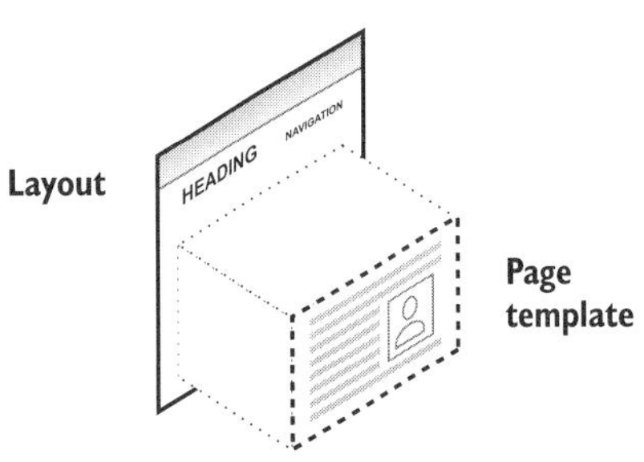

Figure 10.8 The layout template wraps every page template of your site.

You could add the same code to each view template or even render a shared partial template on each of those pages, but a better idea is to edit the *layout template*. The layout template is like the outer peel of your templates. It renders first and then renders your view template inside it (see figure 10.8). The layout template is where the Phoenix Framework logo and the Get Started link, which are currently rendered on every page of your site, come from.

By default, the template that's rendered on each request is the app.html.eex template, found at .../auction_web/templates/layout/app.html.eex. I say *by default* because you can configure your controller or controller functions to render themselves inside a different template if you like, though we won't cover that in this book.

When you open that file for editing, you'll see all the HTML boilerplate, including the `html`, `head`, and `body` tags that make up the shell of your site. For now, you'll add some links to the main areas of the site (`/items` and `/login` if users aren't logged in; `/items`, `/users/:id`, and `/logout` if they are logged in). You're likely a better designer than I am, so feel free to put your links in a different spot—I'm putting mine just after the closing header tag (`</header>`).

You can check to see if the user is logged in by looking at the value of `@current_user` in the layout template. If it's not `nil`, it's a user (because the connection has gone through the authenticator plug). The following listing shows a snippet of my implementation (the part just after the `</header>` tag).

Listing 10.24 Rendering site navigation

```
<div class="container" style="border-bottom: 1px solid #777777;
     margin-bottom: 2rem; padding-bottom: 1rem;">
  <%= link "Items", to: Routes.item_path(@conn, :index) %>
  |
  <%= if @current_user do %>
    Logged in as <%= link @current_user.username,
     to: Routes.user_path(@conn, :show, @current_user) %>
    |
    <%= link "Log out", to: Routes.session_path(@conn, :delete), method:
     :delete %>
  <% else %>
    <%= link "login", to: Routes.session_path(@conn, :new) %>
  <% end %>
</div>
```

Specifies the :delete method for the link because you defined the route to listen for :delete.

Figure 10.9 shows what my browser renders before I'm logged in, and figure 10.10 shows what it renders after I'm logged in.

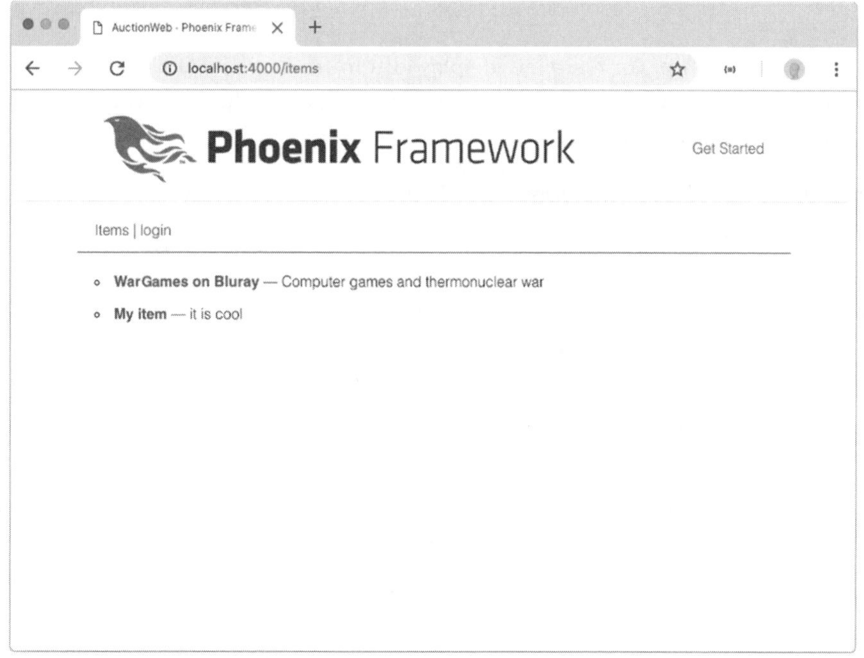

Figure 10.9 Navigation when logged out

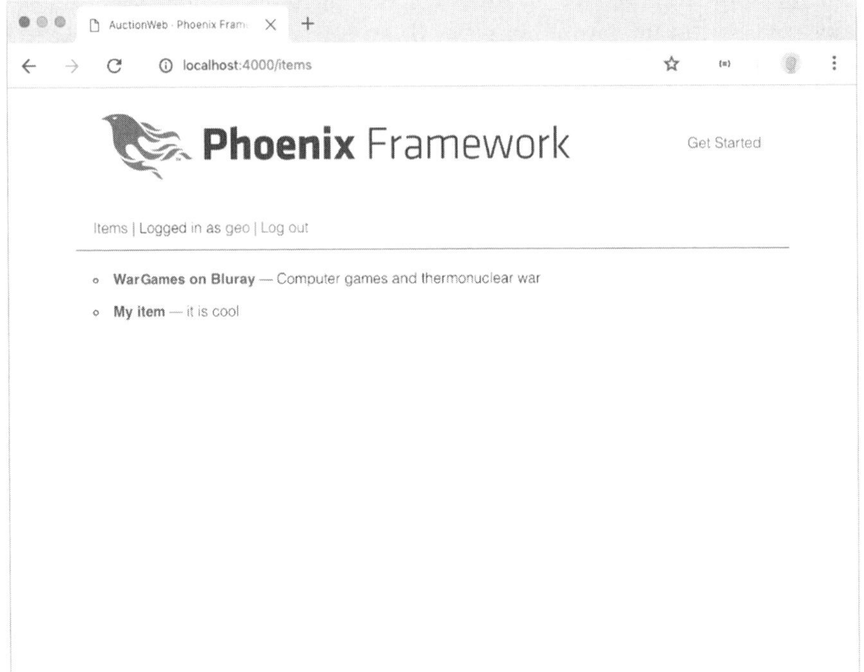

Figure 10.10 Navigation when logged in

You've now set up your site to display different navigational links depending on whether a user is logged in or not. You can use similar logic in your views to display navigation paths based on any number of conditions.

10.4.1 Implementing the log out function

You have a link to log out, but if you click on that link, you'll get an error. `AuctionWeb.SessionController.delete/2` is the last session controller function you need to implement. You'll use a number of functions from `Plug.Conn` to log out your user. You'll do the following things:

1. Clear the session.
2. Drop it from the response.
3. Redirect the user to the list of items.

The following listing shows how.

Listing 10.25 Logging the user out by dropping their session

```
defmodule AuctionWeb.SessionController do
  use AuctionWeb, :controller
  # ...
```

```
  def delete(conn, _params) do
    conn
    |> clear_session()
    |> configure_session(drop: true)
    |> redirect(to: Routes.item_path(conn, :index))
  end
end
```

Dropping the session means it's not included in your response to the user.

This will clear any cookies in the user's browser of data that would indicate that they're logged in to the site. You'll then treat them as a visitor.

10.5 Restricting users from certain pages

We've covered a lot in this chapter and gone a long way toward locking your system down, but we need to cover one final thing: if a user tries to view the details of another user, you want to do the following:

1. Disallow it.
2. Redirect the user to the items page.
3. Show the user a message in the error flash.

Figure 10.11 shows what my implementation generates in that situation.

One way to do that is to check the `current_user` in the `assign`. If it's `nil`, the user shouldn't be on *any* user page. If it's an `Auction.User`, then you compare its `id` with the `id` of the requested user. If they're equal, you let the user in because they're viewing their own profile. If they're not equal, you send the user packing.

You'll split out the authorization check into a separate function so you can use it later in some other spot if you want. Plus, that allows you to implement a plug as a function. Open your `AuctionWeb.UserController` and modify it with the following code.

Listing 10.26 Restricting a user from accessing another user's profile

```
defmodule AuctionWeb.UserController do
  use AuctionWeb, :controller
  plug :prevent_unauthorized_access when action in [:show]

  def show(conn, %{"id" => id}) do
    user = Auction.get_user(id)
    render(conn, "show.html", user: user)
  end

  # ...

  defp prevent_unauthorized_access(conn, _opts) do
    current_user = Map.get(conn.assigns, :current_user)

    requested_user_id =
      conn.params
      |> Map.get("id")
      |> String.to_integer()

    if current_user == nil || current_user.id != requested_user_id do
```

Limits the plug to only run when you're handling the :show action

Checks to see if no user is logged in or if the logged-in user's ID isn't the same as the requested ID

```
      conn
      |> put_flash(:error, "Nice try, friend. That's not a page for you.")
      |> redirect(to: Routes.item_path(conn, :index))
      |> halt()
    else
      conn
    end
  end
end
```

Tells the plugs to stop processing the request

If access is allowed, you return the original conn untouched (a Plug has to return a Plug.Conn).

Whenever a user tries to load someone else's profile, or when a logged out user tries to access any user profile, they'll be redirected to the list of items with an error message. When I attempt to do either one of those things, I get the page in figure 10.11. Use a pattern like this whenever you need to restrict access to certain areas of your site.

One of the benefits of implementing these checks in a plug is that you can put them in their own module or use them in other areas of your site. The function in listing 10.26 is specific to looking at user profiles, so it probably won't be useful in other areas as it is, but you can use similar ideas all over your site.

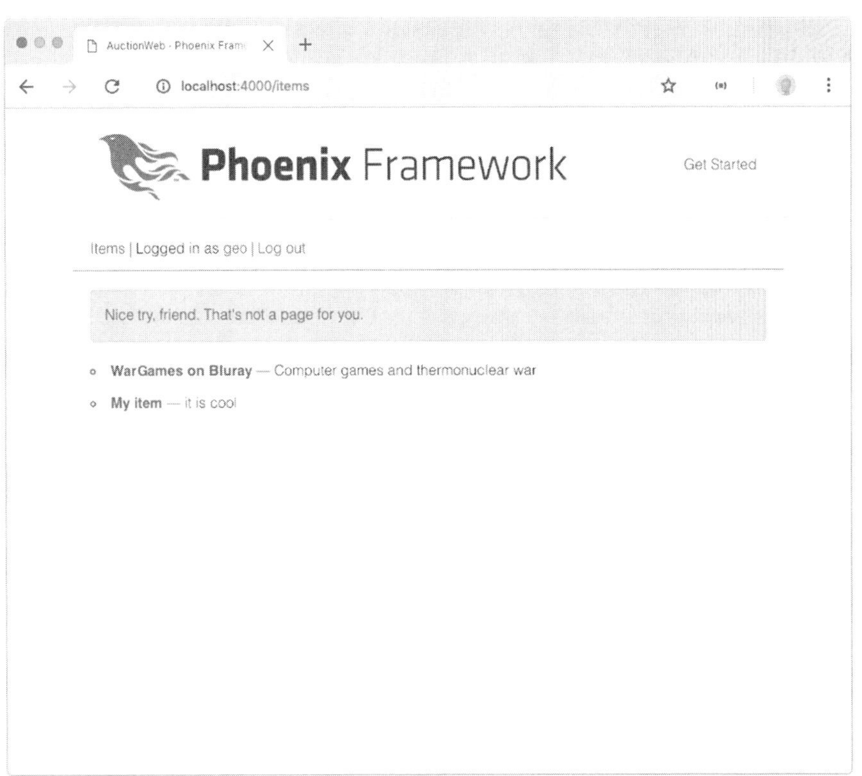

Figure 10.11 Protecting user profiles

For now, we'll leave this topic and move on. But the next chapter will again use the idea of tracking users as they navigate your site—we'll discuss allowing users to create and bid on items.

Summary

- Use virtual columns in a schema to keep data from being persisted in a database.
- Never store user passwords in your database without first encrypting them. When displaying error messages after a login attempt, provide as few identifying details as possible.
- You can create multiple changesets for a single module and focus those changesets to only allow certain attributes through, based on the situation.
- You can track a user with a session cookie as they navigate your site. By default, it's signed but not encrypted, meaning the contents can be viewed but not tampered with.
- Plugs are extremely powerful even though their behavior "contract" is very simple. Almost the entire request/response cycle in Phoenix is processed with plugs.

11 Associating records and accepting bids

This chapter covers

- Allowing users to bid on items
- Defining Ecto associations between items, bids, and users
- Using Ecto to load associated schemas
- Preloading associations to avoid N+1 queries

In the past few chapters, we've discussed using Ecto to define schemas for users and items. You can create new auction items, register a user, and log in and out as a user. There are a couple of things missing, though:

- There's no way for a user to bid on an item.
- Items aren't owned by anyone. In fact, a random stranger could create new auction items on your site right now.

Both of these points are similar in that they rely on associating one record or schema with another. Bids (which don't yet exist) should belong to a user and an item. When you create new items, you want an item to be owned by a user, and a user can own many items. Both a user and an item can have many bids.

This chapter covers Ecto associations. You'll explore them in this chapter by creating bids and allowing a user to bid on an item, creating associations between the three. Figure 11.1 illustrates these associations. Each dotted arrow indicates that one type has many of the other it's pointing to. Likewise, each solid arrow represents a type that belongs to the type it's pointing to.

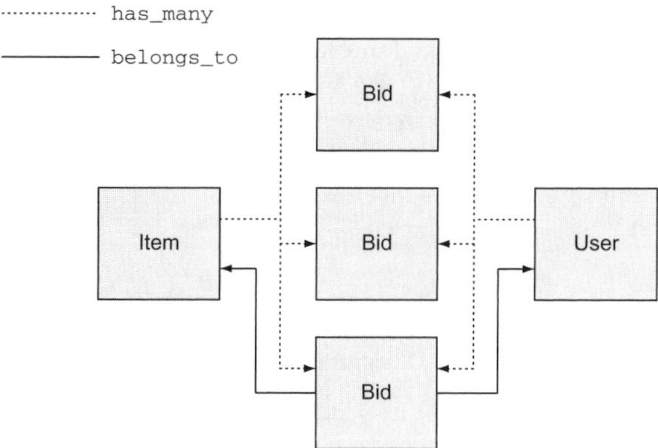

Figure 11.1 Each bid will belong to an item and a user.

This is the last chapter that deals with the user-facing side of your application—once you've grasped the concepts in this chapter, you should be able to create your own Elixir and Phoenix applications (or enhance this auction application).

11.1 Creating bids

First things first: you need to create a schema for bids to get the concept into your application. You've created schemas a few times already, so you'll move quickly through this section. You'll eventually need to associate bids, items, and users, but you'll leave that until after you create the initial schema.

Bids need to have two things (apart from the associations):

- A bid creation timestamp
- A bid amount

With that in mind, you can create the following schema.

Listing 11.1 Creating the bid schema at apps/auction/lib/auction/bid.ex

```
defmodule Auction.Bid do
  use Ecto.Schema

  schema "bids" do
    field :amount, :integer
```

We briefly covered the idea of storing price information in an integer field rather than a float in chapter 7.

```
    timestamps()
  end
end
```

Once the schema is created, you can create the migration.

```
> mix ecto.gen.migration create_bids
* creating priv/repo/migrations
* creating priv/repo/migrations/20181213025720_create_bids.exs
```

The migration is named create_bids.

Now that the migration has been created, you can edit it.

Listing 11.2 Editing the autogenerated migration

```
defmodule Auction.Repo.Migrations.CreateBids do
  use Ecto.Migration

  def change do
    create table(:bids) do
      add :amount, :integer
      timestamps()
    end
  end
end
```

Normally, the name of the table will be the plural noun of the thing you're storing in that table—bids, in this case.

Finally, you can run the migration on your repo to create the bids table.

```
> mix ecto.migrate
18:58:32.607 [info]  == Running 20181213025720
     Auction.Repo.Migrations.CreateBids.change/0 forward
18:58:32.607 [info]  create table bids
18:58:32.617 [info]  == Migrated 20181213025720 in 0.0s
```

This will migrate your database forward.

Those steps should be familiar from previous chapters. Now we can move on to things we haven't discussed before, like associations.

11.2 Adding associations to the Auction.Bid schema

So far in this book, you've only dealt with migrations that *create* tables. But Ecto is much more powerful than that—it can edit tables as well. You created the bids table without the associations you'll eventually need, so you can create a new migration that edits the bids database table to add the associations.

Before you do so, let's talk a little bit about associations.

11.2.1 A little detour into associations

A database like MySQL or PostgreSQL is called a *relational database*. Relational databases have been around for decades and can vary in their implementation, but they all have a few things in common.

- *Tables*—Data is stored in tables. Typically, each "thing" in your database (item, user, and bid) has its own table.

- *Columns*—Each table has a series of columns that store the thing's attributes (for example, the username, first name, and user password).
- *Records*—Each record in a table has a key that uniquely identifies each row or record in the table. Typically, this is an integer ID, but it can be a number of other things (like a UUID).
- *Associations*—Tables can reference other tables to identify *associations* between the things in your database. For example, an item can have an identifying column that ties it to a specific user. There are typically three types of associations that tables (things) can have with other tables (things). The following terminology has sprung up to define these associations (using *A* and *B* to describe the different sides):
  - *One-to-one*—Each *A* has *one and only ever one* link to *B*, and each *B* has *one and only ever one* link to *A*. For example, an acorn can only produce one oak tree, and an oak tree can only come from one acorn. You can say that an oak tree `belongs_to` an acorn, and the acorn `has_one` oak tree. Figure 11.2 illustrates this concept.[1]

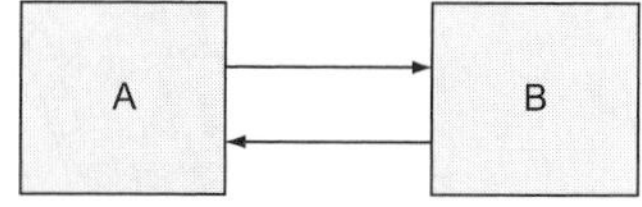

Figure 11.2 One-to-one association

  - *One-to-many*—Each *A* can have multiple *B*s, but each *B* can have only one *A*. For example, the (very small) garden in your backyard can have multiple vegetables (a radish, a head of lettuce, and a carrot), but that specific carrot can only ever be in your garden. You can say your garden *has many* vegetables, but a vegetable only *belongs to* your garden. Figure 11.3 illustrates one-to-many associations.

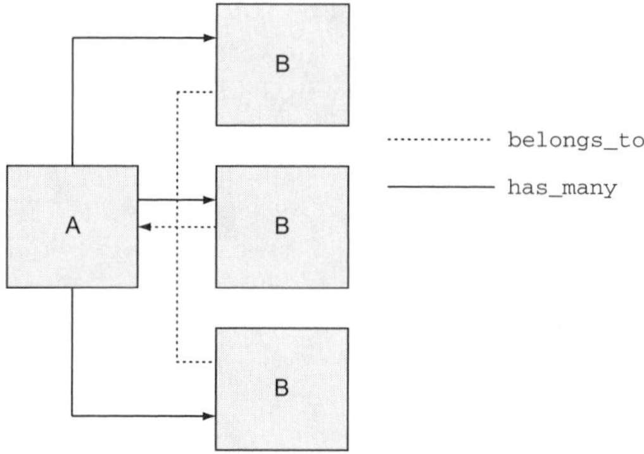

Figure 11.3 One-to-many association

[1] Because this is a one-to-one association, either side could have the `belongs_to` or the `has_one`. Technically speaking, the only difference is which database table the primary key of the other side lives in. If the acorns table has a `tree_id` column, the acorn `belongs_to` the tree and the tree `has_one` acorn. If the trees table has an `acorn_id` column, the acorn `has_one` tree and the tree `belongs_to` the acorn.

- *Many-to-many*—Each *A* can have multiple *B*s, and each *B* can have multiple *A*s. To keep the agricultural theme going, a farmer can sell their goods at multiple different farmers' markets, and each farmers' market can have multiple different farmers selling at the market. You can say a farmer *has many* farmers' markets, and a farmers' market *has many* farmers. Figure 11.4 illustrates many-to-many associations.

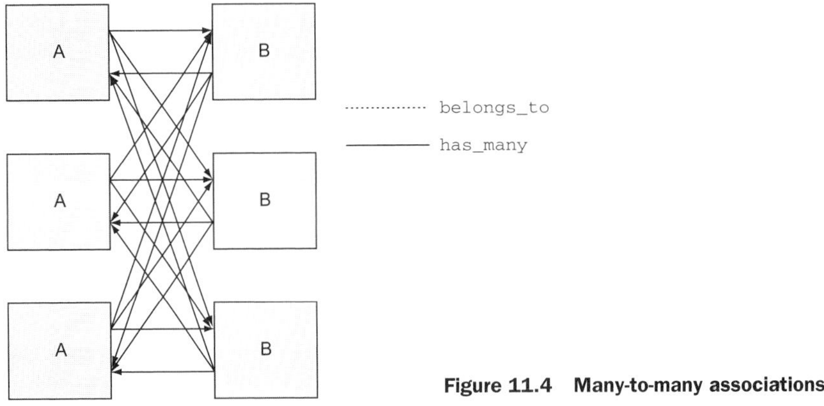

Figure 11.4 Many-to-many associations

Now that you've looked briefly at each of these types of associations, you can move on to using them in your application.

11.2.2 Creating a migration that describes the associations

As you might imagine, Ecto—the database library you're using in your application—has the idea of associations built in, and it uses the terminology I've used (`belongs_to`, `has_one`, `has_many`). In plain English, you say that a bid (and its amount) belongs to a user, and it also belongs to an item (as illustrated in figure 11.5).

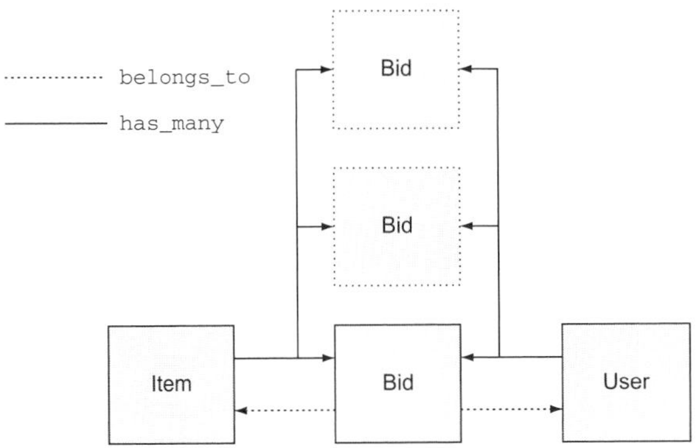

Figure 11.5 A bid belongs to an item and a user; items and users have many bids.

You created the bids table with a bid `amount` column in listing 11.2, and now you need to add the associations. You can do that the same way you create tables—through a migration. Here's the command I used to create the migration:

```
> mix ecto.gen.migration addAssociationsToBids
* creating priv/repo/migrations/20181213025907_add_associations_to_bids.exs
```

Notice that Ecto automatically takes the InitCase text and underscores it for the migration filename. You can use either format.

In previous migrations, you used the `create table(:table_name) do` syntax to create a table. Ecto also has an `alter` macro with similar syntax. Inside an `alter table(:table_name) do` block, you can `add` columns, `modify` columns, and `remove` columns. You'll want to `add` two columns to track your associations: an `item_id` and a `user_id`. When the bids table has those columns, you then can say that a bid *belongs to* an item and *belongs to* a user, storing the unique item and user IDs in those columns.

Beyond that, you can ask Ecto to ensure that a provided `item_id` has a corresponding `item` with that ID. For example, if I had two items in my database with IDs of `1` and `2` but then created a bid that referenced `item_id 3`, that would be a problem, because there is no item `3`. Fortunately Ecto provides a `references` function that sets up that association for you. You'll use it along with `add` to add your columns in the migration (see listing 11.3).

You'll also notice in the following listing that there are three additional lines that create indexes for the table. In most cases, it's good to create a table index on columns that you'll be searching on (though there are exceptions and trade-offs). In your application, it's unlikely you'll search for bids with a specific bid amount, but it's probable that you'll search for bids on a specific item (using `item_id`), bids from a specific user (using `user_id`), or bids on specific items from specific users (using `item_id` and `user_id`). Because of this, I've created indexes for each of those situations.

Listing 11.3 Editing the migration to add columns, references, and indexes

```
defmodule Auction.Repo.Migrations.AddAssociationsToBids do
  use Ecto.Migration

  def change do
    alter table(:bids) do
      add :item_id, references(:items)
      add :user_id, references(:users)
    end

    create index(:bids, [:item_id])
    create index(:bids, [:user_id])
    create index(:bids, [:item_id, :user_id])
  end
end
```

You can use references to indicate a belongs_to association in the database.

NOTE Very briefly, a table index can speed up queries on those columns, but it takes up more disk space on your server. There are trade-offs, and a discussion of these trade-offs could span multiple chapters. You can feel free to leave the indexes out of your migration.

I ran that migration as follows:

```
> mix ecto.migrate
18:59:56.981 [info]  == Running 20181213025907
    Auction.Repo.Migrations.AddAssociationsToBids.change/0 forward
18:59:56.981 [info]  alter table bids
18:59:56.998 [info]  create index bids_item_id_index
18:59:57.005 [info]  create index bids_user_id_index
18:59:57.010 [info]  create index bids_item_id_user_id_index
18:59:57.018 [info]  == Migrated 20181213025907 in 0.0s
```

This is the compound index of [:item_id, :user_id].

That's all you need to do on the database side to tell Ecto about the associations. A bid can now belong_to a user and an item.

INFORMING YOUR SCHEMA MODULES ABOUT THE ASSOCIATIONS

You've finished with the database side, but you also want your Ecto schemas to know about the associations in your application. For that, you need to edit the corresponding modules. First, you'll work on Auction.Bid, and then Auction.Item and Auction.User.

Just as you used the references function to tell the database all it needs to know about the migration, you can use the belongs_to macro in your schema definitions. Ecto.Schema.belongs_to/3 expects the name of the association (in English, "bid belongs to item"), the module in which the referenced name has its schema defined, and an optional list of options. With that in mind, you can edit apps/auction/lib/auction/bid.ex as follows.

Listing 11.4 The modified Auction.Bid module

```
defmodule Auction.Bid do
  use Ecto.Schema

  schema "bids" do
    field :amount, :integer
    belongs_to :item, Auction.Item
    belongs_to :user, Auction.User
    timestamps()
  end
end
```

Defines the belongs_to associations

Putting this in the schema for Bid will allow you to write code that gets directly to the item or user that the bid belongs to. For example, after you preload the association (we'll cover preloading later in this chapter), you can write code like bid.item or bid.user and be able to operate on those associations.

You have some associations in this schema that you'd like to verify on every insert and update, so you can create a changeset to help you out. As you may have guessed, Ecto.Changeset has functions that deal directly with associations. The new Changeset function you'll use is Ecto.Changeset.assoc_constraint/2. The assoc_constraint/2 function will keep your database clear of associations that can't exist. It does that by looking for the associated records in the database, and if they don't exist, it won't let the main query succeed.

Let's say you have a user that submits a bid for an item with an ID of 123. For some strange reason, a developer on your team manually deletes item 123 from the database the second before the user submits a bid on that item. If that bid submission were to go through successfully, there would be an invalid entry in your database, because that bid `belongs_to` item 123, which no longer exists. If `assoc_constraint` is used during the bid creation, an error will bubble up through your system, and that bad data would never be saved.

I expect you can see the value of including `assoc_constraint` calls in your changesets when dealing with data associations. You just need to add a single line in your schema to take advantage of this protection (along with the `references` you used in the database migration). The `assoc_constraint` function takes three arguments: a changeset, the association name you'd like to constrain, and a list of optional options. The rest of your changeset is pretty straightforward: you validate that `amount`, `item_id`, and `user_id` are all present. The following listing shows the implementation.

Listing 11.5 Implementing `Auction.Bid.changeset/2`

```
defmodule Auction.Bid do
  use Ecto.Schema
  import Ecto.Changeset

  schema "bids" do
    field :amount, :integer
    belongs_to :item, Auction.Item
    belongs_to :user, Auction.User
    timestamps()
  end

  def changeset(bid, params \\ %{}) do
    bid
    |> cast(params, [:amount, :user_id, :item_id])
    |> validate_required([:amount, :user_id, :item_id])
    |> assoc_constraint(:item)
    |> assoc_constraint(:user)
  end
end
```

Imports Ecto.Changeset

assoc_constraint infers the association name from the atom you pass in, such as an association named item and one named user.

The Bid module with its schema and changeset are now ready for you to try out. There are a few things you can verify: that it requires all three attributes, that it won't allow a bad `item_id` to be saved, and that it won't allow a bad `user_id` to be saved.

You can fire up an IEx session and follow along as I demonstrate each of those.

Listing 11.6 Trying the validations and constraints in IEx

```
iex(1)> alias Auction.Bid
Auction.Bid
iex(2)> Bid.changeset(%Bid{}, %{})
```

```
#Ecto.Changeset<
  action: nil,
  changes: %{},
  errors: [
    amount: {"can't be blank", [validation: :required]},
    user_id: {"can't be blank", [validation: :required]},
    item_id: {"can't be blank", [validation: :required]}
  ],
  data: #Auction.Bid<>,
  valid?: false
>

iex(3)> Bid.changeset(%Bid{}, %{amount: 100, user_id: -1000, item_id: -1000})
#Ecto.Changeset<
  action: nil,
  changes: %{amount: 100, item_id: -1000, user_id: -1000},
  errors: [],
  data: #Auction.Bid<>,
  valid?: true
>
```

Ecto reports this as a valid changeset because the assoc_constraint is at the database level, which hasn't been touched yet.

```
iex(4)> Bid.changeset(%Bid{}, %{amount: 100, user_id: 1, item_id: -1000})
➥ |> Auction.Repo.insert()
19:05:43.610 [debug] QUERY ERROR db=15.1ms queue=1.9ms
INSERT INTO "bids" ("amount","item_id","user_id","inserted_at","updated_at")
➥ VALUES ($1,$2,$3,$4,$5) RE
TURNING "id" [100, -1000, -1000, ~N[2018-12-13 03:05:43],
➥ ~N[2018-12-13 03:05:43]]
{:error,
 #Ecto.Changeset<
   action: :insert,
   changes: %{amount: 100, item_id: -1000, user_id: -1000},
   errors: [
     item: {"does not exist",
      [constraint: :assoc, constraint_name: "bids_item_id_fkey"]}
   ],
   data: #Auction.Bid<>,
   valid?: false
 >}
```

Try to execute the query here.

The query fails because there's no item with ID -1000 in the database.

Hopefully, you've started to wonder why you're using the changeset and `Auction.Repo.insert` directly, instead of writing a function that decouples the process. And you're right: you need to add another public interface function that allows you to easily create and insert new bids without having to know about the details of the database. In the `Auction` module, you add an `insert_bid/1` function that takes some params, creates the changeset, and inserts it into the database for you.

Listing 11.7 Adding `insert_bid/1` to the `Auction` module

```
defmodule Auction do
  alias Auction.{Bid, Item, Repo, User, Password}

  # ...
```

You need to add Bid to the list of aliased modules or call Auction.Bid fully.

```
  def insert_bid(params) do
    %Bid{}
    |> Bid.changeset(params)
    |> @repo.insert()
  end
end
```

11.2.3 Creating a form to accept bids

You now need a way to accept a bid for an item on behalf of a user. Just like in the past few chapters, when you've added new abilities to your site, you need to touch more than one file to make it work:

- apps/auction/lib/auction.ex
- apps/auction_web/lib/auction_web/router.ex
- apps/auction_web/lib/auction_web/controllers/item_controller.ex
- apps/auction_web/lib_auction_web/templates/items/show.html.eex

Once this section is finished, you should be able to submit a bid like in figure 11.6.

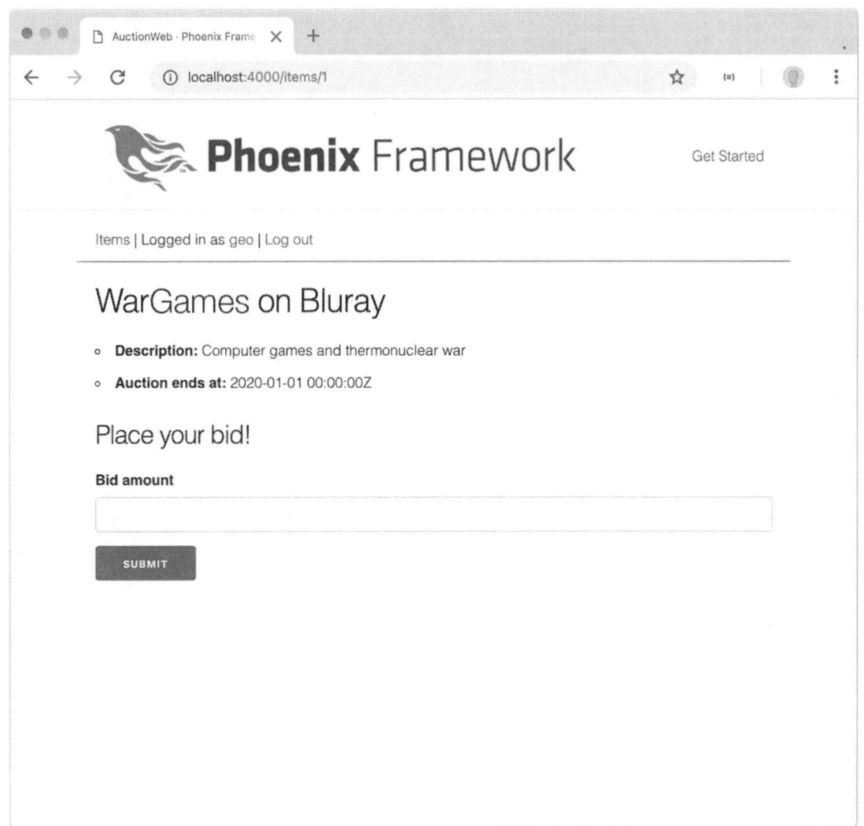

Figure 11.6 Accepting item bids

CREATING A FUNCTION FOR A NEW BID

To render your bid form the way you'd like, you need a way to create a new, fresh `Bid` struct and pass that into the form. This is very easy to do in the `Auction` module in apps/auction/lib/auction.ex: add a blank `Bid` that goes through a blank changeset as in the following listing. This will return all the information the bid form will need to know in order to render the form and any errors correctly. You did something similar for `Auction.new_item/0` and `Auction.new_user/0`.

Listing 11.8 Adding `Auction.new_bid/0`

```
defmodule Auction do
  # ...
  def new_bid, do: Bid.changeset(%Bid{})
  # ...
end
```

This is a simple function: it returns a blank changeset.

Now you can use that function in the `AuctionWeb.ItemController` to pass on the new `Bid` changeset to the template.

Listing 11.9 Using the new `Auction.new_bid/0` function

```
defmodule AuctionWeb.ItemController do
  # ...
  def show(conn, %{"id" => id}) do
    item = Auction.get_item(id)
    bid = Auction.new_bid()
    render(conn, "show.html", item: item, bid: bid)
  end
  # ...
end
```

Creates the new Bid changeset and passes it to the view template

This will make a new `Bid` changeset available in the view template. The `Bid` changeset allows your form to track changes, errors, and validations.

ADDING ROUTES TO THE ROUTER TO ACCEPT A BID

So far, your routes have been straightforward: each resource has had its own top-level entry. But in the case of bids, because a bid `belongs_to` an item, you should accept bids in a URL that contains a reference to the item being bid on. Ideally, your URL would look something like this: http://localhost:4000/items/1/bids. To make this happen, your bids resource needs to be nested inside your items resource.

This is your first nested resource, and as you might guess, Phoenix's router has a very easy and succinct way to handle these situations. The `resources` function you've used so far can also accept a block in which other resources and routes can be defined. The resources defined inside another resource's block will be nested inside the outer resource. That means you can use code like the following to get exactly what you want. Note that you only allow the `:create` action for the new bids resource.

Listing 11.10 Adding the nested `bids` route

```
defmodule AuctionWeb.Router do
  # ...
  scope "/", AuctionWeb do
    pipe_through :browser # Use the default browser stack

    resources "/items", ItemController, only: [
      :index,
      :show,
      :new,
      :create,
      :edit,
      :update
    ] do                                              <-- Start of the block
      resources "/bids", BidController, only: [:create]    <-- Nested bids resource
    end                                               <-- End of the block
    # ...
  end
end
```

Now you can verify that you have a nested resource by running `mix phx.routes` inside the apps/auction_web directory of your application. I get the following output when I run it locally.

Listing 11.11 Displaying all your routes

```
> mix phx.routes
    item_path  GET    /items                AuctionWeb.ItemController :index
    item_path  GET    /items/:id/edit       AuctionWeb.ItemController :edit
    item_path  GET    /items/new            AuctionWeb.ItemController :new
    item_path  GET    /items/:id            AuctionWeb.ItemController :show
    item_path  POST   /items                AuctionWeb.ItemController :create
    item_path  PATCH  /items/:id            AuctionWeb.ItemController :update
               PUT    /items/:id            AuctionWeb.ItemController :update
item_bid_path  POST   /items/:item_id/bids  AuctionWeb.BidController :create
    user_path  GET    /users/new            AuctionWeb.UserController :new
    user_path  GET    /users/:id            AuctionWeb.UserController :show
    user_path  POST   /users                AuctionWeb.UserController :create
 session_path  GET    /login                AuctionWeb.SessionController :new
 session_path  POST   /login                AuctionWeb.SessionController
     :create
 session_path  DELETE /logout               AuctionWeb.SessionController
     :delete
```

Output from adding the nested route (item_bid_path)

You can see the `item_bid_path` entry in the output. Perfect! You can now use that nested route to create bids related to an item.

CREATING THE AUCTIONWEB.BIDCONTROLLER

In the last section, you told the router in the nested route that you wanted to direct the traffic to `AuctionWeb.BidController`. You still need to create that controller, but it will be a pretty minimal one. This is all you need to do in it:

- Send the `amount`, `item_id` and `user_id` to `Auction.insert_bid/1`.
- Redirect the user to the item's page on success.
- Rerender the form with errors on error.

When you make the new bid form in the next section, you'll have an `amount` field inside a `bid` key in the params. You can get the `item_id` directly from the URL path (see the `:item_id` section in the `mix phx.routes` output in listing 11.11). Finally, you can get the user ID because you'll require them to be logged in, and that information will be in the session.

Before attempting to create a bid, you'll also run the connection through a functional plug to ensure that the user is logged in. This is very similar to what you did in the `AuctionWeb.UserController`, but instead of checking that they're allowed to view the requested user ID, you ensure that there's a logged-in user. The following listing shows the implementation. The file is located at auction_umbrella/apps/auction_web/lib/auction_web/controllers/bid_controller.ex.

Listing 11.12 The `AuctionWeb.BidController`

```
defmodule AuctionWeb.BidController do
  use AuctionWeb, :controller
  plug :require_logged_in_user

  def create(conn, %{"bid" => %{"amount" => amount}, "item_id" => item_id}) do
    user_id = conn.assigns.current_user.id
    case Auction.insert_bid(%{amount: amount, item_id: item_id, user_id:
     user_id}) do
      {:ok, bid} -> redirect(conn, to: Routes.item_path(conn, :show,
     bid.item_id))
      {:error, bid} ->
        item = Auction.get_item(item_id)
        render(conn, AuctionWeb.ItemView, "show.html", item: item, bid: bid)
    end
  end

  defp require_logged_in_user(%{assigns: %{current_user: nil}} = conn, _opts) do
    conn
    |> put_flash(:error, "Nice try, friend. You must be logged in to bid.")
    |> redirect(to: Routes.item_path(conn, :index))
    |> halt()
  end
  defp require_logged_in_user(conn, _opts), do: conn
end
```

Uses pattern matching to determine there's no current user

Passes on the connection because there is a current user

The preceding listing uses pattern matching in the function definitions: one for when there's no current user, and one for when there is a current user. In the former case, you redirect them back to the list of items and show them an error message. In the latter case, you let them continue with their request.

ADDING A FORM TO THE ITEM-SHOW TEMPLATE

The final piece of the puzzle is to actually add the form to accept bids. Once this step is complete, the entire bidding process should work as planned, and a bid will be created (it will look like figure 11.6). You'll create a very simple form for the time being—you can pretty it up with more styles and formatting if you'd like to later.

You'll render a form that uses a bid changeset, point it to the `item_bid_path` route that you created a few sections ago, and render an amount field with the `Phoenix.HTML.Form.number_input/3` function. The `number_input/3` function is a helper that adds an input field with type `number`. I put the input field below the item details with a header.

One more thing you'll do is *not* show the bid form if there's no logged-in user. To do that, you can check for the presence of `@current_user` in the template, just as you did when you created the navigation.

The following listing shows the implementation of the template.

Listing 11.13 The modified item-show template

```
<h1><%= @item.title %></h1>

<ul>
  <li><strong>Description:</strong> <%= @item.description %></li>
  <li><strong>Auction ends at:</strong> <%= @item.ends_at %></li>
</ul>

<%= if @current_user do %>                    <- The new code starts here.
  <h2>Place your bid!</h2>

  <%= form_for @bid, Routes.item_bid_path(@conn, :create, @item), fn f -> %>
    <%= if @bid.action do %>
      <div class="alert alert-danger">
        Unfortunately, there are errors in your
        submission. Please correct them below.
      </div>
    <% end %>

    <div class="form-group">
      <%= label f, :amount, "Bid amount", class: "control-label" %>
      <%= error_tag f, :amount %>
      <%= number_input f, :amount, class: "form-control" %>
    </div>

    <%= submit "Submit", class: "btn btn-primary"%>
  <% end %>
<% end %>
```

With that code added, you should be able to log in, go to an item's page, and submit a bid for the item. But the bid won't be displayed on the page quite yet.

11.3 Using has_many with items and users

There's another side to these `belongs_to` associations that you can set up and use—an item `has_many` bids, and a user `has_many` bids. In this section, you'll get your template set up so that it shows the bids that have been submitted, as in figure 11.7.

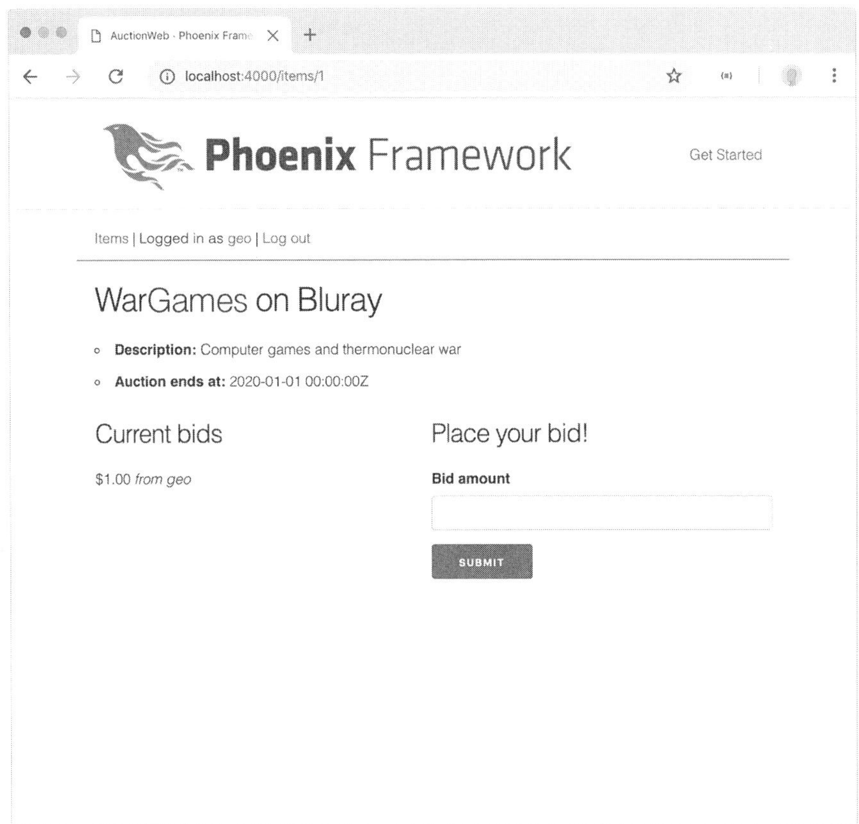

Figure 11.7 A bid listing

The first step is setting up the associations on the bid side. To do that, you'll use `Ecto.Schema.has_many/3`. The `has_many/3` function expects the same arguments as `belongs_to/3`: the name of the association, the module the association references, and an optional list of options. You can open apps/auction/lib/auction/item.ex and add the `has_many` call to Auction.Item.

Listing 11.14 Adding `has_many :bids` to Auction.Item

```
defmodule Auction.Item do
  use Ecto.Schema
```

```
  # ...

  schema "items" do
    field :title, :string
    field :description, :string
    field :ends_at, :utc_datetime
    has_many :bids, Auction.Bid             <-- Add has_many here.
    timestamps()
  end

  # ...
end
```

You can name the association in `has_many` anything you want (`:bids`, `:offer`, `:tender`, `:wet_dog`, and so on); it will look for the association information in `Auction.Bid`. With that addition, you can now access the bids associated with an item.

Now, do the same thing with `Auction.User` at apps/auction/lib/auction/user.ex.

Listing 11.15 Adding `has_many :bids` to `Auction.User`

```
defmodule Auction.User do
  use Ecto.Schema

  # ...

  schema "users" do
    field :username, :string
    field :email_address, :string
    field :password, :string, virtual: true
    field :password_confirmation, :string, virtual: true
    field :hashed_password, :string
    has_many :bids, Auction.Bid             <-- Add has_many :bids here.
    timestamps()
  end

  # ...
end
```

With these additions, bids can now be associated with both items and users. You'll use these associations in the following sections.

11.3.1 Preloading and avoiding N+1 queries

A number of other database wrappers in other languages do something called *lazy loading*. This means that they don't load the associated information from the database until your application asks for it. Although that sounds great on the surface, it does come with a caveat: you can easily get into a situation in which you're doing N+1 queries.

An N+1 query can occur (among other places) where you have data associations. Let's say you wanted to list all the users in your database and the amounts of the bids they've made. In many other database wrappers, you could do something like the following.

Listing 11.16 An example of an N+1 query in Ruby with ActiveRecord

```
# Ruby
Users.all.each do |user|                    <-- Gets all the users in the database
  print "#{user.name}: "                    <-- For each user, prints their name
  user.bids.each do |bid|                   <-- For each user, fetches their bids from the database
    print "#{bid.amount}, "                 <-- For each bid, prints the amount of the bid
  end
  print "\n"
end
# => geo: 300, 375, 400
# => kelly: 1000, 225
```

The problem with this solution is the number of database calls required to produce the output. For each user in the database, a separate database call is made to retrieve their bids. If you had 100 users, that would be 101 database calls (one to get all the users, and 100 to get each of their bids). That's an example of an N+1 query.

To be fair, Ruby's ActiveRecord library (like other language libraries) does give you tools to avoid N+1 queries, but a lot of beginner programmers don't know how to use them (or don't understand the importance of doing so). The nice thing about Ecto is that you have to be explicit about what data you want to load.

Let's look at an example using your new `has_many` association. You first create a bid for a user and then view the bids associated with that user.

Listing 11.17 Trying out the `has_many` association

```
iex(1)> Auction.insert_bid(%{user_id: 1, item_id: 1, amount: 100})
{:ok, %Auction.Bid{...}}

iex(2)> user = Auction.get_user(1)
%Auction.User{
  __meta__: #Ecto.Schema.Metadata<:loaded, "users">,
  bids: #Ecto.Association.NotLoaded<association :bids is not loaded>,    <-- A bids attribute for your user
  email_address: "geo@phoenixinaction.com",
  hashed_password: "$pbkdf2-
    sha512$160000$L9Uz9m3UeU2ADPuqHaX2Lw$pnzBLf5R6mOrCyUIo7p1EcWP5KkSA336Jfq
    U8vdhKuEJiYsr6U69uSZpxwYsGjF2Yd5cBPJBdr7mPZSk8AEx/A",
  id: 1,
  inserted_at: ~N[2018-12-13 02:14:38],
  password: nil,
  updated_at: ~N[2018-12-13 02:51:35],
  username: "geo"
}

iex(3)> user.bids                                                  <-- Trying to access the bids attribute
#Ecto.Association.NotLoaded<association :bids is not loaded>       <-- Responds that it's not loaded
```

Ecto retrieved exactly what you requested of it: just the user. You didn't ask it for the bids, so it didn't give them to you. And to avoid an N+1 query, it won't lazily give them to you. Ecto uses a pattern known as *eager loading* to force you to think through what data you actually need from the database and explicitly grab that (nothing more or less) in an optimized query.

What would it look like to eagerly load your bids in the association? Ecto has a function named `Ecto.Repo.preload/3` that you can use to let it know what associations (if any) you want preloaded. It then will hit the database in a highly optimized way to get the data you requested.

To use this function, you can provide it the structs you have and the associations you'd like preloaded. The third parameter is an optional list of options. The following listing demonstrates how you'd use it with your users and bids.

Listing 11.18 Using `preload` to eagerly fetch the data you need

```
iex(4)> user = Auction.Repo.preload(user, :bids)    <-- Uses Ecto.Repo.preload/3 to eagerly preload the data
20:05:04.007 [debug] QUERY OK source="bids" db=2.8ms
SELECT b0."id", b0."amount", b0."item_id", b0."user_id", b0."inserted_at",
     b0."updated_at", b0."user_id" FROM "bids" AS b0 WHERE (b0."user_id" =
     $1) ORDER BY b0."user_id" [1]
%Auction.User{
  __meta__: #Ecto.Schema.Metadata<:loaded, "users">,
  bids: [                                    <-- You can already see that the response differs from listing 11.17.
    %Auction.Bid{
      __meta__: #Ecto.Schema.Metadata<:loaded, "bids">,
      amount: 326,
      id: 2,
      inserted_at: ~N[2018-12-13 03:17:55],
      item: #Ecto.Association.NotLoaded<association :item is not loaded>,
      item_id: 4,
      updated_at: ~N[2018-12-13 03:17:55],
      user: #Ecto.Association.NotLoaded<association :user is not loaded>,
      user_id: 1
    }
  ],
  email_address: "geo@phoenixinaction.com",
  hashed_password: "$pbkdf2-
     sha512$160000$L9Uz9m3UeU2ADPuqHaX2Lw$pnzBLf5R6mOrCyUIo7p1EcWP5KkSA336Jfq
     U8vdhKuEJiYsr6U69uSZpxwYsGjF2Yd5cBPJBdr7mPZSk8AEx/A",
  id: 1,
  inserted_at: ~N[2018-12-13 02:14:38],
  password: nil,
  updated_at: ~N[2018-12-13 02:51:35],
  username: "geo"
}

iex(5)> user.bids                  <-- Attempting to access user.bids
[                                   <-- Getting the list of bids in the database
  %Auction.Bid{
    __meta__: #Ecto.Schema.Metadata<:loaded, "bids">,
    amount: 326,
    id: 2,
    inserted_at: ~N[2018-12-13 03:17:55],
```

```
    item: #Ecto.Association.NotLoaded<association :item is not loaded>,
    item_id: 4,
    updated_at: ~N[2018-12-13 03:17:55],
    user: #Ecto.Association.NotLoaded<association :user is not loaded>,
    user_id: 1
  }
]
```

The bid itself also has some unloaded associations.

You can, in fact, also preload the nested associations inside of the bids (you'll do that later in the chapter).

11.3.2 Preloading associations in the public interface module and controller

You want the item-show page to present all of an item's bids along with the bidders' usernames, so you need to preload the bids and their nested users when you fetch the item. You can create a new public interface function that returns what you need. `Auction.get_item/1` won't cut it anymore, because it does no preloading.

For your new function—`Auction.get_item_with_bids/1`—you use your old `get_item/1` function as the first step, and then pass it through the `preload/3` function. The following listing shows that code.

Listing 11.19 Preloading the bids and the nested users

```
defmodule Auction do
  # ...
  def get_item_with_bids(id) do
    id
    |> get_item()
    |> @repo.preload(bids: [:user])
  end
  # ...
end
```

- Uses the get_item/I function already defined in this module
- Preloads the item's bids and the users for those bids

You can use this function in the `AuctionWeb.ItemController` in place of `Auction.get_item`. It simply requires a change to the function name.

Listing 11.20 Using `Auction.get_item_with_bids/1`

```
defmodule AuctionWeb.ItemController do
  # ...
  def show(conn, %{"id" => id}) do
    item = Auction.get_item_with_bids(id)
    bid = Auction.new_bid()
    render(conn, "show.html", item: item, bid: bid)
  end
  # ...
end
```

- This is the only change needed.

With this change, you can now access a user's associated bids in the view template—and that's exactly what you'll do next.

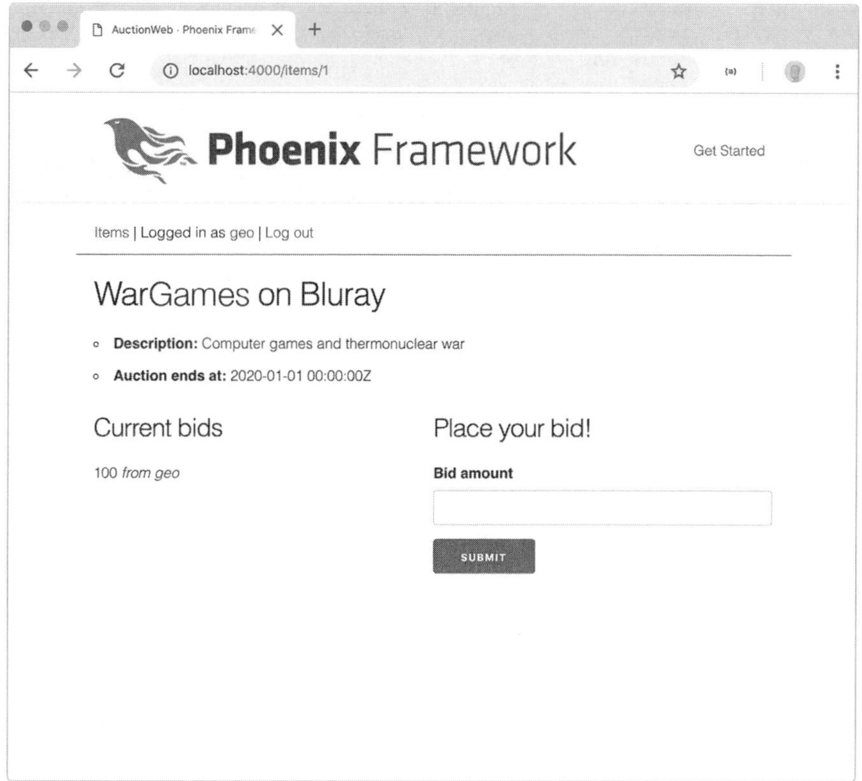

Figure 11.8 After the output is added

11.3.3 Adding the list of bids to the view template

Your most recent change preloads the associations for an item so they're ready to be used in the view template. All you need to do now is iterate through the bids and output the information you'd like to see. Along with displaying the list of bids, you'll add a bit of extra formatting to keep the page from getting too busy (see figure 11.8).

You can see the important additions: you're iterating through the bids with a `for` comprehension and displaying the information you'd like to see. The following listing shows the updated version of apps/auction_web/lib/auction_web/templates/items/show.html.eex.

Listing 11.21 Displaying the bids for an item

```
<h1><%= @item.title %></h1>

<ul>
  <li><strong>Description:</strong> <%= @item.description %></li>
  <li><strong>Auction ends at:</strong> <%= @item.ends_at %></li>
</ul>
```

```
<div style="display: flex; flex-direction: row;">
  <div style="flex: 1;">
    <h2>Current bids</h2>
    <%= for bid <- @item.bids do %>
      <p><%= bid.amount %> <em>from <%= bid.user.username %></em></p>
    <% end %>
  </div>

  <div style="flex: 1;">
    <%= if @current_user do %>
      <h2>Place your bid!</h2>

      <%= form_for @bid, item_bid_path(@conn, :create, @item), fn f -> %>
        <%= if @bid.action do %>
          <div class="alert alert-danger">
            Unfortunately, there are errors in your
            submission. Please correct them below.
          </div>
        <% end %>

        <div class="form-group">
          <%= label f, :amount, "Bid amount", class: "control-label" %>
          <%= error_tag f, :amount %>
          <%= number_input f, :amount, class: "form-control" %>
        </div>

        <%= submit "Submit", class: "btn btn-primary"%>
      <% end %>
    <% end %>
  </div>
</div>
```

The for comprehension iterates through the bids.

As you may have noticed in figure 11.8 (or your own screen), you output the full integer value of the bid, in cents, to the page. In order to display it correctly, you need to convert it from cents to dollars and cents. You can use a view helper function for that very purpose.

View helper functions are defined in the corresponding view file (`AuctionWeb.ItemView`, in this case) and are available for use in your view templates. You need to write a new function that takes the integer cents amount of a bid and converts it into a `Decimal` type, rounding to the precision you'd like to display (`2`, for two places after the decimal point). Finally, you return the string you'd like to display back to the template. The `integer_to_currency/1` function is shown in the following listing.

Listing 11.22 Creating `AuctionWeb.ItemView.integer_to_currency/1`

```
defmodule AuctionWeb.ItemView do
  use AuctionWeb, :view

  def integer_to_currency(cents) do
    dollars_and_cents =
      cents
```

```
      |> Decimal.div(100)
      |> Decimal.round(2)
    "$#{dollars_and_cents}"
  end
end
```

You could also write this as "$" <> dollars_and_cents.

This will take the total cents, divide by 100 (which will give you dollars and cents), and round it to two digits, representing cents.

All that's left is to use that new function in the item-show template for items. You can replace this line,

```
<p><%= bid.amount %> <em>from <%= bid.user.username %></em></p>
```

with this one:

```
<p><%= integer_to_currency(bid.amount) %> <em>from <%= bid.user.username %></
    em></p>
```

With that change, your view should look very similar to figure 11.9.

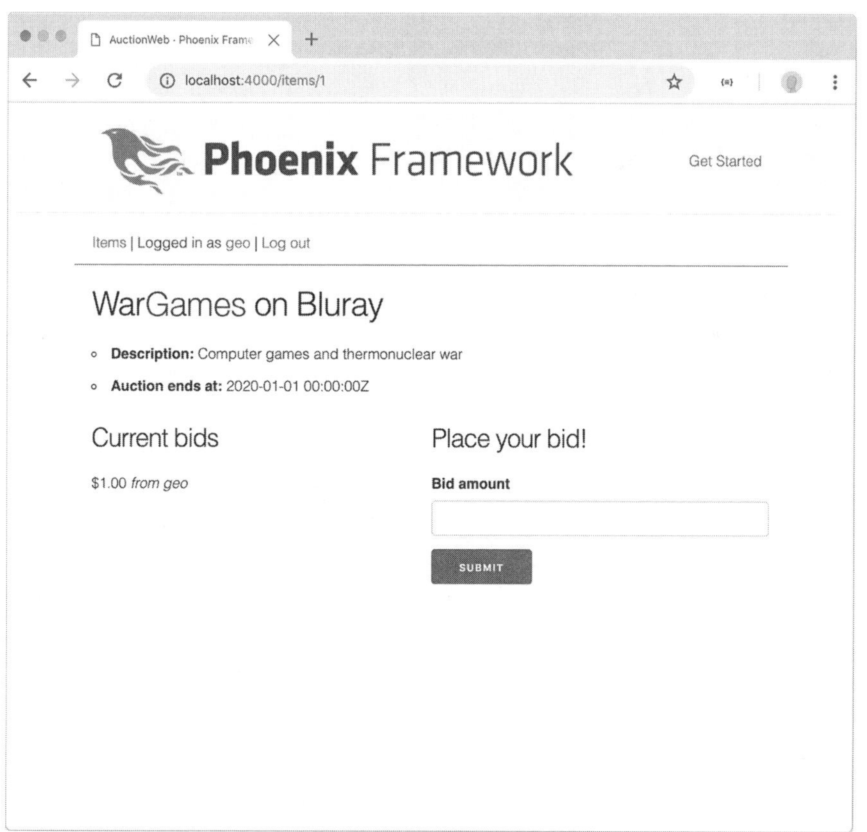

Figure 11.9 The final view template rendered correctly

You've taken the gross cents and converted them to dollars and cents. That amount is displayed next to the username of the user who made the bid.

11.4 Listing a user's bids on their profile page

Before we move on from the topic of associations and wrap up the chapter, let's add one more feature to the application: showing a user's bid activity on their profile page. Doing this will demonstrate a few more things:

- Using Ecto's `Ecto.Query` library for constructing complex (or simple) database queries
- Moving the `integer_to_currency/1` function into its own module and making it available to every page in the application
- Formatting a date and time with the `Timex` library

Let's tackle each of these things in order. Once you're done with this section, your page should look like figure 11.10.

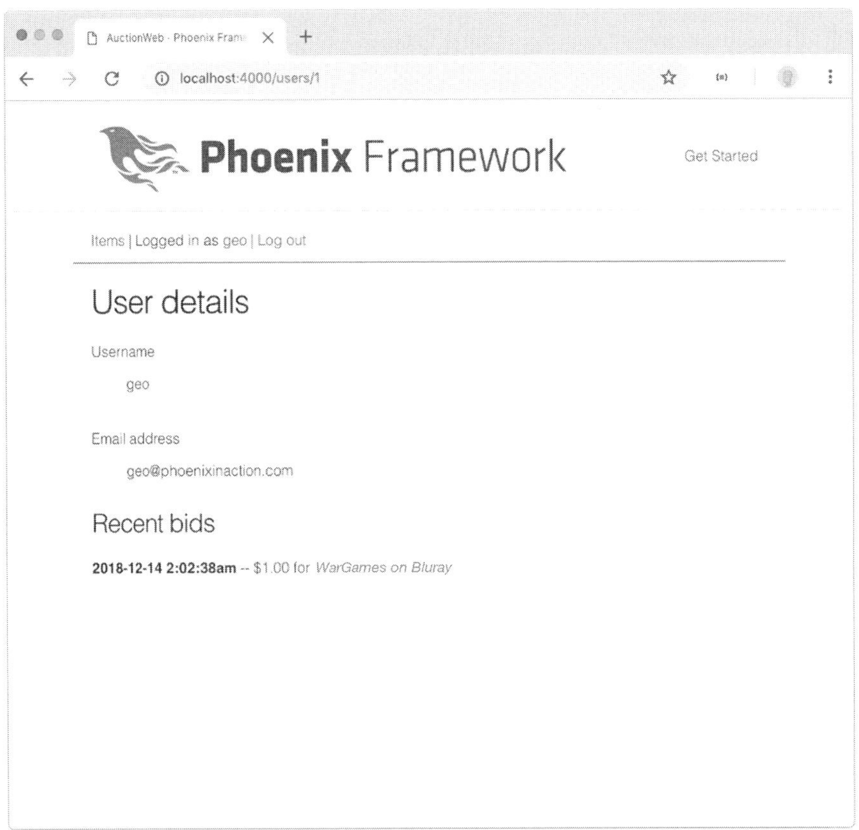

Figure 11.10 The finished page listing a user's bids

11.4.1 Using Ecto.Query to construct database queries

Ecto has a useful module that allows you to construct complex or simple database queries. So far, you've either been fetching a record based on its `id` or fetching all the records for a particular schema. But sometimes you'll want more control over what's retrieved from the database.

For example, you could add a search bar on the site that allows a user to search for items based on name or description. You could filter the list of items to display auctions that end within a few hours or sort them by the highest bid amounts.

For the page that displays a user's bids, you won't go too crazy. You just want to limit the results you get from the database to bids that were created by a specific `user_id` and order them from the most recent to the oldest. You'll also limit the results to the first 10, so your page doesn't become too long.

The first thing you'll do is add a function to `Auction` that allows you to get exactly what you want. You'll call it `get_bids_for_user/1`, and you'll pass in the `Auction.User` struct of the user that you'll limit the bids to. Before you write the function, you'll `import Ecto.Query` into the Auction module. This isn't necessary, but it will prevent you from having to type out the full `Ecto.Query.function_name` every time.

You'll use five macros from `Ecto.Query` to construct your search:

- `from/1`—This is the start of every query for `Ecto.Query`. It says you'd like to bind the specific database schema to a variable name that you can use throughout the rest of the query. For example, you could say `from u in User`. The `u` can then be used in the rest of your query to refer to the table that the `Auction.User` schema references. In your case, you use a variable in the `where` statement to limit the search to a specific `user_id`.
- `where/2`—This is used to filter the returned records to a specific set. You provide `where/2` with an expression that returns `true` or `false`, and in this expression you can use the variable assigned in the `from` portion of the query. In your case, you filter the records such that the bid's `user_id` column value equals the user ID that you receive in the function arguments.
- `order_by/2`—You use this to order the results that the database gives you. You can order on any field that the schema has in the database. `order_by` expects the names of the fields to order on and (optionally) the direction of that ordering in atom form (`:asc` or `:desc` for ascending and descending order, respectively). You order your results by the bid-creation time (`inserted_at`) with the most recent bid first (`desc` order).
- `preload/2`—You've used a different version of `preload` previously (`Ecto.Repo.preload/3`) to preload associations. The difference here is that the function is in the query itself. There isn't necessarily a best way to do the preloading, but this is a good place to introduce this function.
- `limit/2`—This function limits the number of results. You'll limit yours to 10.

Finally, you can feed that query into the repo to retrieve the records that match your query (well, the first 10 anyway).

Listing 11.23 The `Auction.get_bids_for_user/1` function

```
defmodule Auction do
  import Ecto.Query
  # ...
  def get_bids_for_user(user) do
    query =
      from b in Bid,
      where: b.user_id == ^user.id,
      order_by: [desc: :inserted_at],
      preload: :item,
      limit: 10
    @repo.all(query)
  end
end
```

Imports Ecto.Query so you can use its functions without specifying the module name in every call

Remember, the pin operator (^) makes it so that the previously bound value is used.

You can use this new function in the `AuctionWeb.UserController` and provide it as an assign to the view template.

Listing 11.24 Adding bid retrieval to the controller

```
defmodule AuctionWeb.UserController do
  # ...
  def show(conn, %{"id" => id}) do
    user = Auction.get_user(id)
    bids = Auction.get_bids_for_user(user)
    render conn, "show.html", user: user, bids: bids
  end
  # ...
end
```

Retrieves bids for the user

Makes bids available in the view template

11.4.2 *Making a view helper function global and using the bids assign*

The bids associated with a user have been retrieved from the database, and now you need only to use them. As you've done in the past, you'll iterate through the retrieved bids in a `for` comprehension and output a descriptive line of text for each. You're aiming for a page that looks like figure 11.11.

The following listing shows the implementation.

Listing 11.25 Displaying a user's recent bid activity

```
# apps/auction_web/lib/auction_web/templates/user/show.html.eex
<h1>User details</h1>

<dl>
  <dt>Username</dt>
  <dd><%= @user.username %></dd>
  <br />
  <dt>Email address</dt>
```

```
  <dd><%= @user.email_address %></dd>
</dl>

<h2>Recent bids</h2>

<%= for bid <- @bids do %>
  <p>
    <strong><%= bid.inserted_at %></strong>
    --
    <%= bid.amount %>
    for
    <em><%= link bid.item.title, to: Routes.item_path(@conn, :show, bid.item)
     %></em>                                          <-- Allows easy navigation
  </p>                                                    to the items bid on
<% end %>
```

This gives you the information, but there a couple things that you could improve:

- Format the bid amount as you did in the item details page
- Format the date/time so it's more readable (do you really need to display microseconds?)

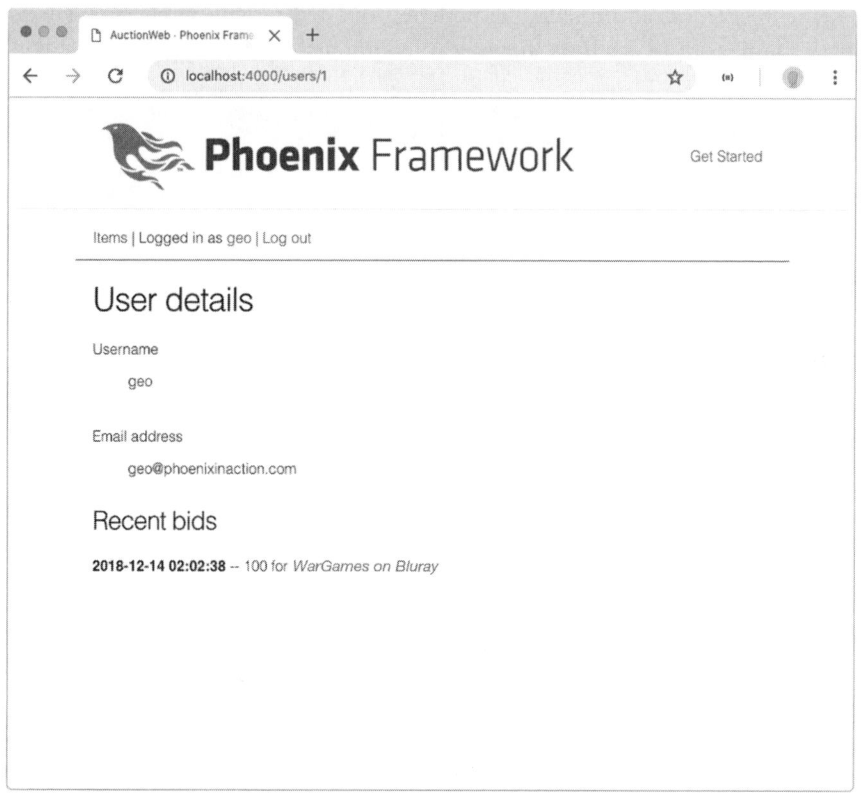

Figure 11.11 Showing a user's bid activity without data formatting

You already have an `integer_to_currency/1` function defined in the `AuctionWeb.ItemView` module, but because you're in this template through the `AuctionWeb.UserView` module, you don't have access to that function. You could copy and paste the function into the `UserView` module, but then you'd be repeating yourself. If you ever needed to make a change to that function, you'd have to do it twice. This seems like a good opportunity to make this function available everywhere on the site, as it's likely you'll be doing similar formatting on a large number of pages.

When you ran the `mix phx.new` mix task back in chapter 6, it generated the files necessary for Phoenix to operate. One of those files is located in apps/auction_web/lib/auction_web.ex; it's the main `AuctionWeb` module. In most of the files Phoenix needs (like controllers and views), there's a call to `use AuctionWeb, :controller` (or `:view`, as necessary). This brings in modules that you'd like to have available in all controllers or views.

If you open that file, you'll see sections of `use` and `import` for controllers, views, routers, and channels. This is where different modules are made available. In your case, you'd like to have a global helper module that can be made available in all views. The perfect way to do this is to `import` it in the `view` section of this file.

You can call your global helper module `AuctionWeb.GlobalHelpers` to correspond to some of the other similarly named helpers in that file. The `view` section of the `AuctionWeb` module will look like the following listing.

Listing 11.26 The modified `view` section of `AuctionWeb`

```
defmodule AuctionWeb do
  # ...
  def view do
    quote do
      use Phoenix.View,
        root: "lib/auction_web/templates",
        namespace: AuctionWeb

      # Import convenience functions from controllers
      import Phoenix.Controller, only: [get_flash: 1, get_flash: 2,
     view_module: 1]

      # Use all HTML functionality (forms, tags, etc)
      use Phoenix.HTML

      import AuctionWeb.ErrorHelpers
      import AuctionWeb.Gettext
      alias AuctionWeb.Router.Helpers, as: Routes
      import AuctionWeb.GlobalHelpers          <-- This is the new import.
    end
  end
  # ...
end
```

You still have to define the `AuctionWeb.GlobalHelpers` module itself, but this makes it so that every module that calls `use AuctionWeb, :view` imports functions from

AuctionWeb.GlobalHelpers. All that's left is to create that file (at apps/auction_web/lib/auction_web/views/global_helpers.ex) and move the definition of integer_to_currency/1 into that module.

NOTE If you only *copy* the function definition and don't *move* it, it will cause an error because it will be defined twice.

The following listing shows the AuctionWeb.GlobalHelpers module.

Listing 11.27 The new AuctionWeb.GlobalHelpers module

```
defmodule AuctionWeb.GlobalHelpers do
  def integer_to_currency(amount) do
    dollars_and_cents =
      amount
      |> Decimal.div(100)
      |> Decimal.round(2)
    "$#{dollars_and_cents}"
  end
end
```

This is the same function that used to be in ItemView.

You'd like to use this function in your view to show a user's bids (figure 11.12).

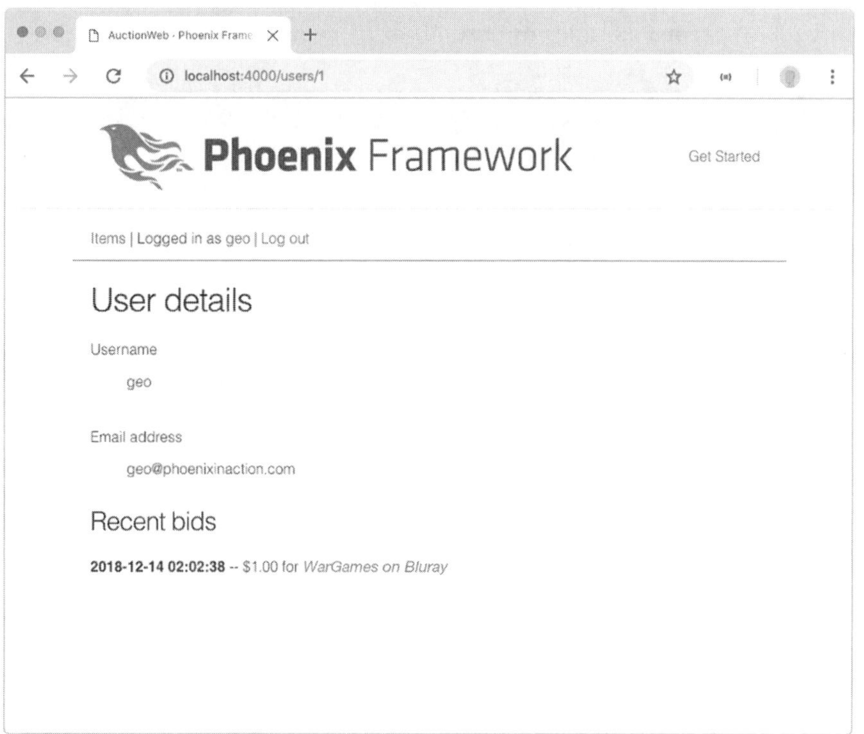

Figure 11.12 Formatting the bid amount

To do so, just replace this line,

```
<%= bid.amount %>
```

with this one:

```
<%= integer_to_currency(bid.amount) %>
```

You can now use `integer_to_currency/1` in all view templates, and it's now on the user's show page.

11.4.3 Using Timex to format dates and times

Finally, you'll format the date/time display so it's a little more friendly, such as a `year-month-day hour:minute:second am/pm` format. Unfortunately, as of Elixir version 1.7, there aren't any easy, built-in ways to format these kinds of strings. There is a fantastic library for doing this, though, named Timex.

You'll use Timex in your application. Add `timex` as a dependency for `auction_web` (if you've forgotten how, check out chapter 5; you can specify `{:timex, "> 0.0.0"}` to grab the most recent version). Then, run `mix deps.get`, and restart your application. It will now be available to use.

I won't go too much into using the module—you can read the documentation if you'd like deeper insight into the workings of Timex. You'll use it in the `AuctionWeb.GlobalHelpers` module, and use `Timex.format!/2` in a function there.

Listing 11.28 Creating `formatted_datetime` as a global helper

```
defmodule AuctionWeb.GlobalHelpers do
  use Timex

  def integer_to_currency(amount) do
    dollars_and_cents =
      amount
      |> Decimal.div(100)
      |> Decimal.round(2)
    "$#{dollars_and_cents}"
  end

  def formatted_datetime(datetime) do
    datetime
    |> Timex.format!("{YYYY}-{0M}-{0D} {h12}:{m}:{s}{am}")
  end
end
```

This will format my DateTime like 2019-01-09 1:38:08pm.

Because you imported the `GlobalHelpers` module in listing 11.27, you can use the `formatted_datetime/1` function in various places around the site. Simply replace this line,

```
<strong><%= bid.inserted_at %></strong>
```

with this one:

```
<strong><%= formatted_datetime(bid.inserted_at) %></strong>
```

Once you've done that, you'll be able to log in and navigate to the user profile page and see something similar to figure 11.12. All the user's recent bids will be displayed using your new formatting.

11.5 Some ideas for further improvement

With the knowledge and techniques presented in this and previous chapters, you can add many small details to make your site more useful and user-friendly. Here are some ways you could use what you've learned to make the site better:

- Only allow bids that have a higher amount than the current high bid.
- Don't allow bids on items after the item's `ends_at` date and time have passed.
- Only allow the creation of an item if a user is logged in.
- Associate newly created items with the logged-in user.
- Try making more complex database queries using the Ecto.Query module.
- Display the bid datetime in the user's time zone (it's currently in UTC)

Apart from adding real-time interactions with Phoenix channels in chapter 12, the main functionality of the site—as far as this book is concerned—is complete. There are obviously many things that could be added before you launch your next startup around it, but you know enough to either do it now, or to follow the documentation within Elixir, Phoenix, or Ecto and make it happen on your own.

The next part of the book covers some of Phoenix's nice-to-have elements, including real-time interaction with channels (a killer feature of Phoenix), creating a public API so others can build their own applications around your application, and testing and documentation.

Summary

- Ecto provides functions to handle database associations.
- You can use `belongs_to`, `has_many`, and `has_one` to let Ecto know about the associations between your schemas.
- Ecto ensures you avoid N+1 queries by requiring you to eagerly load associations from the database if you need them.
- Complex database queries can be programmatically constructed using `Ecto.Query`.
- If you have functions inside a module that you'd like to make globally available in Phoenix, you can import them in the `AuctionWeb` module.

Part 3

Those important extras

In part 2, you learned the basics of getting a website up and running in Phoenix and Elixir. You could create some great web applications using only what you've learned so far, but there are a few extras that could make your sites that much better.

Specifically, part 3 covers

- Using Phoenix channels to provide real-time communication and push updates to users on the site
- Building a simple API to allow third parties (or yourself) to build applications with data from your application
- Documenting and testing your Elixir and Phoenix code

It's the extra little things like these that can take your web applications to the next levels of interactivity and utility. Ready? Let's do this!

12 Using Phoenix channels for real-time communication

This chapter covers

- Making use of Phoenix's real-time channels
- Using channels to update an item's bids in real time
- Using Phoenix's JavaScript helpers in association with channels

Believe it or not, this may be the most surprising chapter in the book. Not necessarily because of the content, but because of the disconnect between the perceived difficulty of real-time communication and updates and how easy Phoenix makes this with channels. I think it's fair to say that in most books about web development, apart from Phoenix, covering a topic like this would take up multiple chapters and certainly would require more code than you'll see here.

You'll be using some JavaScript in this chapter, but only minimal knowledge will be required to follow along. Ready to get started? Let's do it.

12.1 What are Phoenix channels?

You'll use channels to update an item's page with the current bid information. If another user enters a bid, the item's page will be updated without your intervention to show that new bid. If you enter a new bid, that other user's browser will reflect that bid without them (or the client) refreshing the web page.

You'll use JavaScript to update the HTML, and Phoenix has an official JavaScript library that's already part of the Auction application (it's included in every generated app). One of the neat things about Phoenix and the channels idea is that it's not limited to JavaScript. There are clients for Swift (iOS), Java (Android), C#, and other languages.

Behind the scenes, Phoenix channels make use of Elixir processes. We discussed Elixir processes in chapter 1, but the main thing you need to know is that they're very lightweight—they take up minimal server resources, and they allow Elixir modules to pass messages back and forth and maintain state. Without getting too much into the technical details, Phoenix uses those Elixir processes and a *pubsub* (publish-subscribe) mechanism to allow different clients to subscribe to different "topics" and "subtopics." One of the great consequences of Elixir processes being so lightweight (and channels being implemented on top of them) is that a huge number of simultaneous connections can be handled—it's been tested with millions of clients being connected to moderate server hardware.

For your Auction application, when a user visits an auction item's page, the user will be subscribed to a topic of "item" and a subtopic of the item's ID (for example, `"item:123"`). You can then broadcast messages on that topic/subtopic combo, and the user's client will receive that message. You can then write some simple JavaScript to respond to that message. For this implementation, the response will be to update the list of bids in the user's browser with the information passed along in the broadcasted message. On the other side of the channel, whenever a user submits a new bid for an item, you'll accept that bid and broadcast it to all the clients connected to that item's topic/subtopic.

If this process sounds complicated, that's because it is. The good news for you is that nearly all of the internal complications are handled by Phoenix and Elixir. In fact, the best way to describe how uncomplicated it can be is to just dive in.

12.2 Connecting a user to a channel and a topic

When you generated the Phoenix app with `mix phx.new`, one of the files that was generated was lib/auction_web/channels/user_socket.ex. Most of that file is comments, letting you know how to get started with channels. This is where you do the initial setup and enabling of channels.

If you look near the top of that file, you'll find a heading comment of `Channels`, as shown in the following listing. By default, channels aren't enabled, which is why you'll find this section commented-out.

Listing 12.1 The initial state of user_socket.ex

```
defmodule AuctionWeb.UserSocket do
  use Phoenix.Socket

  ## Channels
  # channel "room:*", AuctionWeb.RoomChannel     <-- room:* is the channel name pattern.

  # ...
end
```

To enable channels, you need to add a call to `channel` in this file. There are two arguments to this function: the topic name you're listening for, and the module that handles those broadcasts.

Topics are formatted as `topic:subtopic`. The commented-out example has `room:*` as the topic—this specifies any broadcast that goes to the `room` topic with any subtopic. If a broadcast that matches this pattern is sent, it will be forwarded to `AuctionWeb.RoomChannel` (if this line were uncommented).

As we discussed in the last section, you'd like each item to have its own topic so that you can broadcast item-specific updates. With that in mind, your pattern might look like `item:*`, and you'll pass the item's `id` as the wildcard. For example, item 123 would have a topic named `item:123`.

As for the name of the module that will handle those messages, you'll use `AuctionWeb.ItemChannel`. The following listing shows the updated `AuctionWeb.UserSocket` module.

Listing 12.2 The updated `AuctionWeb.UserSocket`

```
defmodule AuctionWeb.UserSocket do
  use Phoenix.Socket

  ## Channels
  channel "item:*", AuctionWeb.ItemChannel     <-- Sends all channel requests that begin with item: to AuctionWeb.ItemChannel

  # ...
end
```

When a channel request is received with the topic of `item:*`, it's forwarded to `AuctionWeb.ItemChannel` to be handled.

12.2.1 Handling topic join requests

Now whenever a client requests to join the topic `item:*`, the request will be handled by `AuctionWeb.ItemChannel`. The signature of that request is `join/3`, so you need to implement `AuctionWeb.ItemChannel.join/3`. The arguments to `join/3` are

- The topic name
- Any parameters passed along with the request
- The socket that the request is communicating on

You can use Elixir's pattern-matching feature on function definitions to match topic names exactly, or to match any subset of parameters passed along. That means you can pattern-match the topic and grab the `id` out of the string for use later. As a response, it's expected that your implementation will return `{:ok, socket}` or `{:ok, reply, socket}` on success, or `{:error, reply}` if there's an error.

You can do any number of things in a function to determine whether a user should be able to join a specific topic. In your application, though, the topics will be wide open to allow any user, logged-in or not, to receive updates on item pages. For that reason, you'll allow all connections and always return a successful response.

The implementation of this join handler is very simple (apps/auction_web/lib/auction_web/channels/item_channel.ex).

Listing 12.3 Setting up the join handler

```
defmodule AuctionWeb.ItemChannel do
  use Phoenix.Channel

  def join("item:" <> _item_id, _params, socket) do
    {:ok, socket}
  end
end
```

Pattern-matches the topic string when a join request is received (the pattern is "item:" and an id)

By pattern matching the topic string, you can pull out the `id` of the item whose topic you're subscribing to. In this case, you don't need the `id`, so it's denoted with an underscore (_) before the variable name.

12.2.2 Getting the user's browser to join a topic

Whenever a user visits the page for an item, you'd like their browser to join a topic for that item. That way, you can broadcast a message to every client currently on that channel when an item has a new bid (or send any other message you need to send). For web clients, the best way to join a topic is via JavaScript. Thankfully for you, Phoenix already has set up a good JavaScript client for interacting with these channels: socket.js.

> **Assets in Phoenix**
>
> By default, Phoenix uses Webpack to compile JavaScript and CSS into compact files that the browser can understand. That means you can use multiple sources or styles of JavaScript and combine them in the final app. You can split out implementation details for JavaScript or have a different stylesheet for each area of your site. When it comes time to render your site in your browser, Webpack will have already compiled those assets into a small number of files (one JavaScript and one stylesheet, by default). Webpack is very powerful but also very flexible.

Where do all these assets live? If you look in the apps/auction_web directory, you'll notice that there's an assets directory within it.

That directory contains the files that are considered assets for your application (JavaScript, stylesheets, images, fonts, and so on). JavaScript that needs to be compiled goes in the js directory, CSS goes in the css directory, and anything that needs to be copied directly to the served site goes in the static directory (images, fonts, and the like).

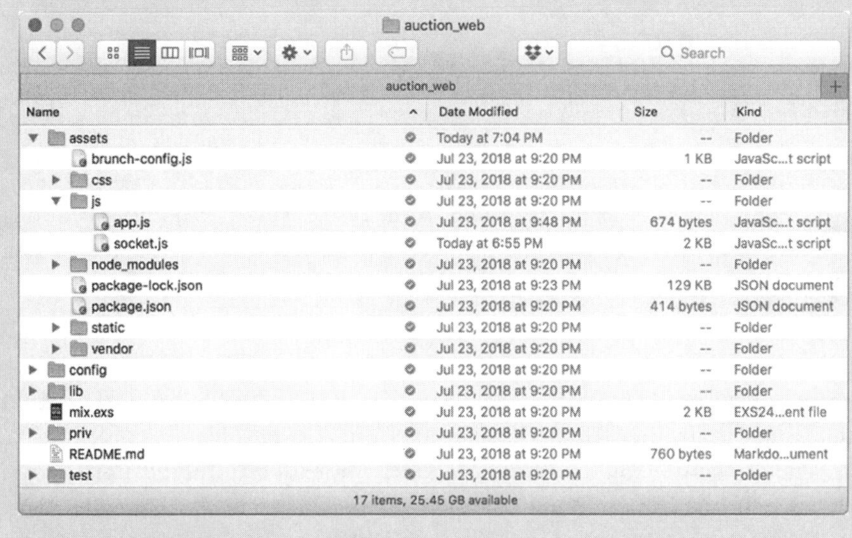

The assets directory

The socket.js file can be found in apps/auction_web/assets/js. If you take a moment to open that file, you'll see that the vast majority of the file is comments letting you know how to correctly set up the socket connection on the client side (browser).[1] The following listing shows the contents of this file with the comments removed. You'll see that most of the work you need to do has already been done for you.

Listing 12.4 The socket.js file with comments removed

```
import {Socket} from "phoenix"

let socket = new Socket("/socket", {params: {token: window.userToken}})

socket.connect()
```

[1] It's stuff like this that makes Elixir and Phoenix such a joy to develop with. It makes your life as a developer so much easier.

```
let channel = socket.channel("topic:subtopic", {})
channel.join()
  .receive("ok", resp => { console.log("Joined successfully", resp) })
  .receive("error", resp => { console.log("Unable to join", resp) })

export default socket
```

This example code joins a topic and subtopic of "topic" and "subtopic," respectively.

If you aren't familiar with JavaScript, the syntax can be a little bit intimidating. Let's break this file down bit by bit.

IMPORTING THE SOCKET LIBRARY

The first line in listing 12.4 simply extracts the `Socket` class from the `phoenix` JavaScript library.

```
import {Socket} from "phoenix"
```

Where did the `phoenix` library come from? It's provided with Phoenix and is indicated as a JavaScript package your application requires in auction_web/assets/package.json.

CREATING A NEW SOCKET INSTANCE

Now that you've imported the `Socket` class, you need to instantiate a new instance of the class with the parameters you require. By default, channels communicate over the /socket path of your app (you can customize this in `AuctionWeb.Endpoint`), so you'll tell it that that's the path you'd like to connect over. Furthermore, you pass a `userToken` as a param. You could use that param for user authentication if you needed or wanted authentication. This is all code that's generated by Phoenix's Mix task; you won't need a `userToken` in your implementation.

```
let socket = new Socket("/socket", {params: {token: window.userToken}})
```

This new `Socket` instance is referenced via the newly created `socket` variable.

CONNECTING TO THE CHANNEL

Now that you've set up the properties of the connection, you can connect:

```
socket.connect()
```

SETTING UP THE CORRECT CHANNEL

The connection to the socket has been initiated, but the connection hasn't requested any particular topic for the connection yet. No messages will be sent or received by this connection until a particular topic is set up. The following line sets up the channel to listen to a specific topic and subtopic (passing in an empty object as the params):

```
let channel = socket.channel("topic:subtopic", {})
```

Note that this is just Phoenix's example code. You'll soon change this to request the correct topic for your Auction application.

JOINING THE CHANNEL AND SETTING UP MESSAGE LISTENERS

Once the topic has been specified, you can join the topic and start responding to messages sent on that topic. One of the cool things that the `phoenix` JavaScript library provides is a form of function pattern matching in `receive`.

The example code has two different `receive` function calls looking for different messages. The matched message is the first argument to `receive`, and the second argument is the function to call once the message is matched.

```
channel.join()
  .receive("ok", resp => { console.log("Joined successfully", resp) })
  .receive("error", resp => { console.log("Unable to join", resp) })
```

In this example, `resp` is the response from the server. In case of `ok` or `error`, the example simply logs a message to the console.

MAKING THE SOCKET AVAILABLE TO IMPORT ELSEWHERE

The final line of the example exports the `socket` variable you set up so that it can be imported in other JavaScript files.

```
export default socket
```

MAKING CHANGES TO THE JAVASCRIPT

Now that you've looked at what each line of the example JavaScript does, you can make the changes you need. You don't need to make many changes in this file. The major thing that needs to change is the name of the topic to join (instead of the default `topic:subtopic`). You also don't want to try to connect on every page.

You want the topic to be `item:${item_id}`, and because you only want updates on item pages, you only need to connect on item pages. This book isn't about JavaScript itself, so I'll try to stay as elementary as possible when making these changes. Here's the plan:

1. Check to see if the browser's location is an item page (`/items/:id`).
2. If it is an item page, grab the item ID from the location and connect to the ID's topic.
3. If it's not an item page, don't try to connect to a topic.

For the first step, you'll use a regex pattern to see if the page contains `/items/:id`. The good thing about doing it this way is that you can use regex capture groups to capture the ID for use later in the script. The following regex will look for the pattern and capture any digits at the end:

```
let match = document.location.pathname.match(/\/items\/(\d+)$/)
```

> **Regular expressions**
>
> A *regular expression* (regex) is a search pattern that allows you to search text for a sequence of characters. The pattern you're searching for here is
>
> ```
> /\/items\/(\d+)$/
> ```

(continued)

Briefly, this pattern starts by searching for the literal characters `/items/` (the slashes / need to be escaped by backslashes \). Next, it searches for any digit (`\d`) one or more times (+). That digit search is surrounded with parentheses in order to "capture" them for use later. Next, you make sure that those digits are the last thing in the string by using the `$`metacharacter, which matches the end of a string. Finally, you surround the whole expression with slashes (/), which is the customary way to indicate a regex.

You can then use this `match` variable to enter an `if` block. If there is a match, the `if` statement will evaluate to truthy. If there's no match, it's falsy.

```
if (match) {
  // ...
}
```

If you do have a match, you enter that block and evaluate the code there. The first thing you do is grab the item ID from the capture group you originally set up in the regex. The way JavaScript's `match` function works with capture groups is that the first item in the matched array is the entire matched string. The subsequent indexes in the array are the capture groups in order. As a reminder, JavaScript indexes start with 0.

Because you had only one capture group, your item ID is captured in the array index of `1`.

```
let itemId = match[1]
```

The last change you need to make to the original example script is to use that item ID to join the correct topic. In JavaScript, you can interpolate strings by surrounding the string with backticks (`` ` ``). Inside the backticks, you can interpolate JavaScript variables inside a `${…}` call.

With that in mind, you can join the correct item topic/subtopic with this line:

```
let channel = socket.channel(`item:${itemId}`, {})
```

The rest of the example channel-joining code inside the `if` block will suffice.

Once you've made these changes, the final socket.js file will look like the following listing.

Listing 12.5 The edited socket.js file

```
// NOTE: The contents of this file will only be executed if
// you uncomment its entry in "assets/js/app.js".

import { Socket } from "phoenix"

let socket = new Socket("/socket", { params: { token: window.userToken } })
socket.connect()
```

```
let match = document.location.pathname.match(/\/items\/(\d+)$/)
if (match) {
  let itemId = match[1]
  let channel = socket.channel(`item:${itemId}`, {})
  channel
    .join()
    .receive("ok", resp => {
      console.log("Joined successfully", resp)
    })
    .receive("error", resp => {
      console.log("Unable to join", resp)
    })
}

export default socket
```

If the channel receives "ok", you respond by logging "Joined successfully" to the console.

If there was an error joining the channel, you respond by logging "Unable to join" to the console.

You've created this JavaScript, but it won't run unless it's imported into the main app.js file. The first comment in socket.js tells you exactly what you need to do:

```
// NOTE: The contents of this file will only be executed if
// you uncomment its entry in "assets/js/app.js".
```

If you open assets/js/app.js, you'll see more comments. Those comments say that even though Webpack compiles all the JavaScript files in the assets/js directory, none of them will be run unless they're explicitly imported.

The final line of app.js has such an import for `socket`. Remember that on the last line of socket.js you called `export default socket`? Well, you can `import` it into app.js to execute it.

After uncommenting the appropriate line, app.js will look like the following listing.

Listing 12.6 The app.js file after uncommenting the appropriate line

```
// you need to import the CSS so that webpack will load it.
// The MiniCssExtractPlugin is used to separate it out into
// its own CSS file.
import css from "../css/app.css"

// webpack automatically bundles all modules in your
// entry points. Those entry points can be configured
// in "webpack.config.js".
//
// Import dependencies
//
import "phoenix_html"

// Import local files
//
// Local files can be imported directly using relative paths, for example:
import socket from "./socket"
```

Uncomment this line.

With those changes made, you have a system set up to connect a user's client to an item-specific channel on page load. On my system, this only took changing or adding 30 lines of code. Even though you haven't quite finished the real-time connection

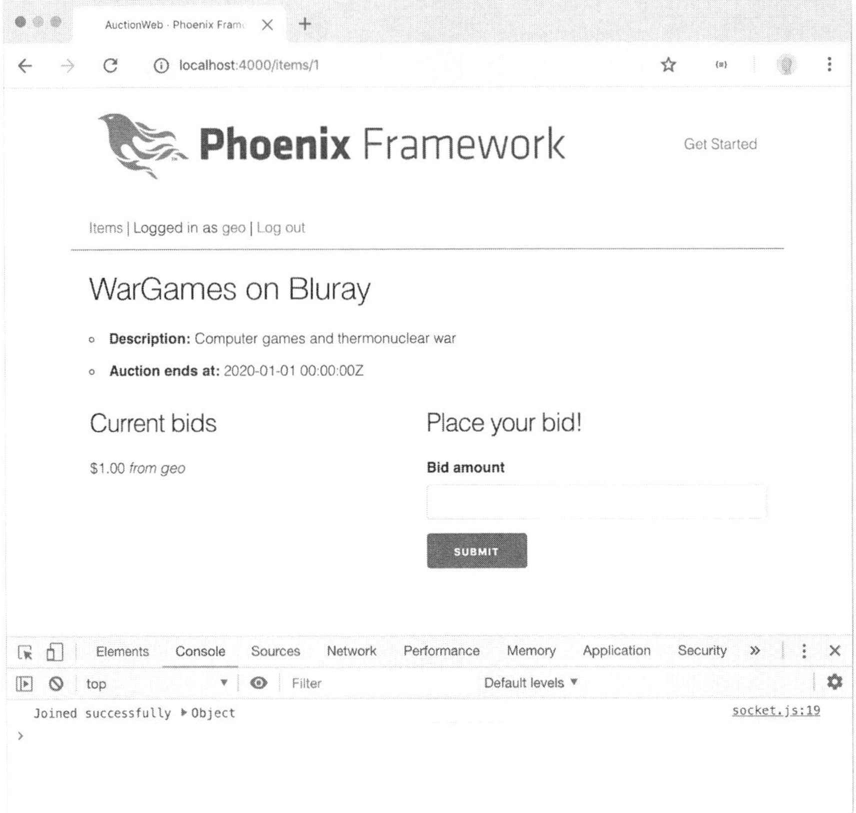

Figure 12.1 The JavaScript console reports a successful channel join on loading.

(you haven't set up the JavaScript client to respond to messages), it's amazing how little it takes to get this set up.

If you fire up the Phoenix server, visit the item's page (such as http://localhost:4000/items/1), and open the browser's JavaScript console, you'll see a message: "Joined successfully." That's exactly what you told the JavaScript client to log on a successful channel join (see figure 12.1).

Beyond that, if you look at the logged output of the Phoenix server itself (my output is shown in the following listing), you'll see some debug strings letting you know that a user (you) successfully connected to a channel.

Listing 12.7 The debug output of the Phoenix server

```
17:46:18.171 [info]  GET /items/1
# ...
17:46:18.182 [info]  Sent 200 in 11ms
```

```
17:46:18.261 [info]  CONNECT AuctionWeb.UserSocket
  Transport: :websocket
  Connect Info: %{}
  Parameters: %{"token" => "undefined", "vsn" => "2.0.0"}

17:46:18.261 [info]  Replied AuctionWeb.UserSocket :ok

17:46:18.266 [info]  JOIN "item:1" to AuctionWeb.ItemChannel
  Transport:  :websocket
  Serializer: Phoenix.Socket.V2.JSONSerializer
  Parameters: %{}

17:46:18.266 [info]  Replied item:1 :ok
```

The server sent :ok to the topic of item:l.

This debug output shows that `:ok` was sent to the channel topic of `item:1`. This corresponds to the request from the user's browser to join `item:1`.

12.3 Sending real-time messages to a user

To this point, you've automatically had a user join a channel in a topic that depends on the viewed item's ID. That's half of what's required to get real-time communication going with the server. What you need now is for the client to receive messages on a channel and have the server send messages over a channel.

Enabling the client to receive messages will require changes in the socket.js JavaScript file you were editing in the last section. Sending messages to the client will require some changes on the Elixir/Phoenix side of the application. We'll look at those in order.

12.3.1 Receiving messages in the user's browser

You'll first change the auction_web/assets/js/socket.js file to allow a user's browser to receive messages over the connected channel. To do so, you need to add a listener to the channel.

When a message is sent over a channel, it will contain two things:

- A string corresponding to the message type sent
- The body of the message sent from the server

For the first point, you can pattern-match the message from the server with the provided JavaScript library. For the second point, you can provide a callback function that's called with the body of the message from the server.

You'll have your client listen for a `new_bid` message type and log the body of the message in the browser's JavaScript console, and have the JavaScript set this listener up before it joins the specific channel topic.

Listing 12.8 Setting up the message listener

```
// ...
if (match) {
  let itemId = match[1]
  let channel = socket.channel(`item:${itemId}`, {})
```

```
  channel.on("new_bid", data => {
    console.log("new_bid message received", data)
  })

  channel
    .join()
    .receive("ok", resp => {
      console.log("Joined successfully", resp)
    })
    .receive("error", resp => {
      console.log("Unable to join", resp)
    })
}
// ...
```

The channel you've joined, with the message "new_bid"

Takes the message from the server (data) and logs it to the console

Save the socket.js file. If you're still running the Phoenix server and you check the page for an item, you'll notice that the browser has automatically reloaded the page. That's thanks to Webpack and the automatic code watcher/reloader.

You'll also notice that the console has the same output as it did before you added the changes in listing 12.8. You haven't sent it any messages, so you see the `Joined successfully` message.

12.3.2 Configuring the channel to handle messages

Before you can send a message over a channel, you need to set up `AuctionWeb.ItemChannel` to handle those messages. Whenever the channel is sent a message, the module set up to handle it looks for a matching `handle_in/3` function, so it's up to you to implement that function to handle the messages.

Because you're expecting a `new_bid` message in the JavaScript you added in listing 12.8, you need a matching `handle_in/3` function to handle `new_bid` messages. Part of the `handle_in/3` function implementation broadcasts a message to the channel's connected sockets, so although you could receive one message type and send another, it's helpful to match the handled messages with the corresponding broadcasted messages.

The `handle_in/3` function expects three arguments:

- The message type string
- A params object
- The socket of the connection

For the `item:${item_id}` topic, you pass the message that `AuctionWeb.ItemChannel` received to the socket. Any client that's connected on that socket will receive the message and can decide what to do with it. Because you set up your JavaScript to log the message body to the console, your application isn't doing much at the moment. Finally, the `handle_in/3` function must return one of the following:

- `{:noreply, socket}`
- `{:reply, message, socket}`
- `{:stop, reason, socket}`
- `{:stop, reason, message, socket}`

Most of the time, the message sender doesn't require a reply. For your purposes, you just respond with `{:noreply, socket}`.

With these things in mind, write the `handle_in/3` function.

Listing 12.9 Writing the `handle_in/3` implementation

```
defmodule AuctionWeb.ItemChannel do
  use Phoenix.Channel
  # ...
  def handle_in("new_bid", params, socket) do
    broadcast!(socket, "new_bid", params)
    {:noreply, socket}
  end
end
```

Pattern-matches on the new_bid message

The `broadcast!` function broadcasts (using `Phoenix.Channel.broadcast!/3`) the message you received (`params`) with the type of `new_bid` to all connections on `socket`.

12.3.3 Sending your browser a message from IEx

If you didn't start your server via an IEx session (with `iex -S mix phx.server`), use Ctrl-C to exit the server and restart it using that command. This allows you to interact with the application from an IEx session while also running the Phoenix server. In this section, you'll send the browser a message from IEx through the channel the browser has connected over.

As configured in `AuctionWeb.Endpoint`, channel communication happens over the path of `/socket`. But you can also send messages to channels outside of a Phoenix request (that is, not hitting `/socket` with an HTTP request). You can do so using `AuctionWeb.Endpoint.broadcast/3`.

`AuctionWeb.Endpoint.broadcast/3` expects three parameters:

- The `topic:subtopic` to broadcast the message to
- The message type as a string
- The message to send, which must be an Elixir map

Navigate to an item's page in your browser (noting the `id` of the item), and open the JavaScript console. If everything has been hooked up correctly, you'll see a notice in the console that a message has been received, along with the message itself. Then, in your IEx session, send all the connected clients a message with `AuctionWeb.Endpoint.broadcast/3`, making sure you use the `id` of the item you're looking at (I'm using an `id` of `1`).

```
iex(1)> AuctionWeb.Endpoint.broadcast("item:1", "new_bid", %{body: "Hello
     from IEx!"})
:ok
```

Notifies you that your message has been successfully queued. Make sure you replace 1 with the ID of the item you're currently viewing.

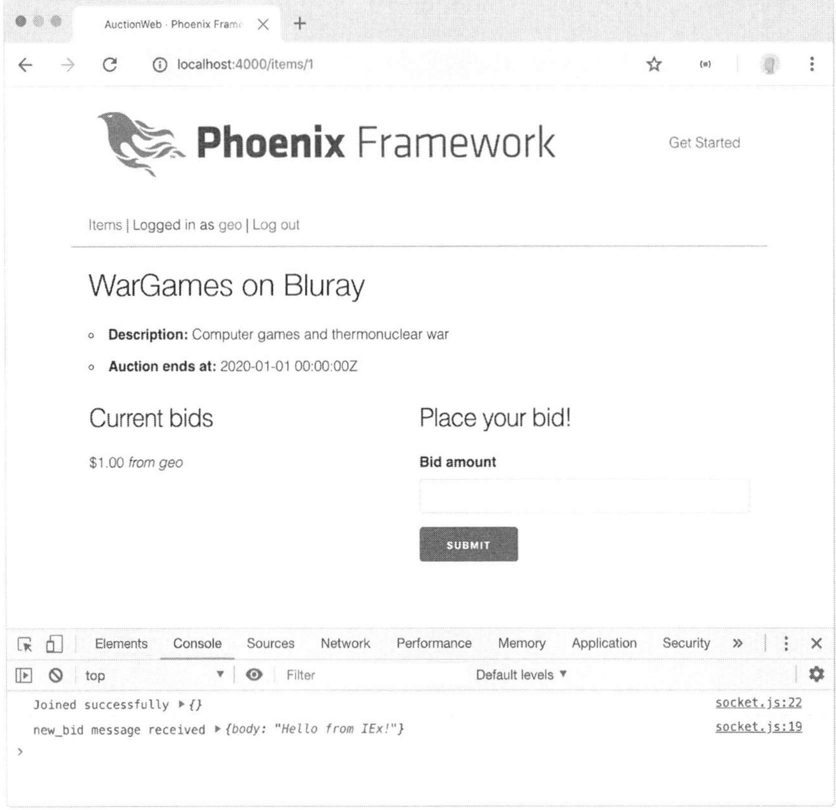

Figure 12.2 The message has been received!

If you now look in your browser, you'll see that the message has been received, as in figure 12.2.

12.4 Updating all users when a new bid is made

Before we get into how you can update all the listeners on the `item:item_id` topic, let's take a quick detour into rendering collections of items. On your show item page, you have a section named Current Bids. In the code for this section, you iterate through `@item.bids` and display a bit of HTML for each bid.

At this point, it would be a good idea to extract that bit of HTML into its own template and render that small template for each bid. Phoenix provides a `Phoenix.View.render_many/4` function that will render a collection of things based on a single template—just like your bids.

The following listing shows the specific portion of HTML in auction_web/lib/auction_web/templates/item/show.html.eex that you'll extract. All this code is from before the refactoring and should be the same as when you last left it.

Listing 12.10 The code you'll refactor

```
# ...
<h2>Current bids</h2>
<%= for bid <- @item.bids do %>
  <p>
    <%= integer_to_currency(bid.amount) %>
    <em>from <%= bid.user.username %></em>
  </p>
<% end %>
# ...
```

Once you're done refactoring this code, you'll render a collection of bids based on this HTML.

12.4.1 Refactoring the rendering of an item's bids

The `render_many/4` function requires three arguments in order to work correctly:

- The collection of things to render
- The view the template belongs to (such as `AuctionWeb.ItemView`)
- The template name
- Optionally, a map of assigns to pass into the template

You could put this code in `AuctionWeb.ItemView`, but it isn't really displaying anything about the item. Instead, it's displaying something about the bid. For that reason, this template would belong more in a new view named `AuctionWeb.BidView`.

In previous instances where you've created a view, you also created a controller (such as `AuctionWeb.BidController`). In this situation, though, you don't need a controller for handling interactions with bids—you just need to display bids. You can thus create a `BidView` without a corresponding controller.

Listing 12.11 Creating auction_web/lib/auction_web/views/bid_view.ex

```
defmodule AuctionWeb.BidView do
  use AuctionWeb, :view
end
```

You can now extract the code from listing 12.10 into its own template file. Because you're creating the HTML for displaying a single bid, you'll name this template file bid.html.eex (in auction_web/lib/auction_web/templates/bid/).

You'll mostly copy and paste the code from item.html.eex, but there's one important change: this time you'll use `Map.get/3` to get the username. You'll have preloaded the `user` association when loading an item's page, but when you create an item, you won't have the user preloaded. Instead, you'll pass in a new `@username` assign. `Map.get/3` looks for the `username` key in `@bid.user`, and if it's not found there, falls back to `@username`. The following listing shows that template code.

Listing 12.12 HTML template for a single bid

```
<p>
  <%= integer_to_currency(@bid.amount) %>
  <em>from <%= Map.get(@bid.user, :username) || @username %></em>
</p>
```

You changed from bid to @bid because you're in a new template with no knowledge of the bid variable.

How do you know that the assign in the template will be named `@bid`? Phoenix automatically names the assign after the view name. In this case, you have `BidView`, so it named the assign `@bid`. If you had a `GlobeView`, the assign name would be `@globe`. If desired, that can overridden with the `as` option. For example, if you wanted to render something in `GlobeView` but name the assign `@sphere`, you could call `render_many @globes, GlobeView, "globe.html.eex", as: :sphere`.

Now you can replace the code in the view itself with the call to `render_many/4`.

Listing 12.13 The modified code in item/show.html.eex

```
<h2>Current bids</h2>
<div id="bids">
  <%= render_many @item.bids, AuctionWeb.BidView, "bid.html" %>
</div>
```

Adds an ID on the div so you can reference it later in JavaScript

If you reload the show item page, you should notice no difference in how the Current Bids section looks. If that's the case, good job: successful refactoring!

12.4.2 Modifying the controller to broadcast a message

You're now able to receive messages in the browser, but to make this real-time bid update feature work, you need to respond to new bids and broadcast that bid information to the item's topic. You already have a controller and action that accepts bids (`AuctionWeb.BidController.create/2`), and this is probably the best place to broadcast the bid information.

Figure 12.3 illustrates what you're trying to achieve. The browser on the left submits a new bid and the browser refreshes after the form is submitted. It now shows three bids. However, the browser on the right has received a message from Phoenix letting it know that the left browser submitted a new bid. You won't make any UI changes in this section, so the right browser just logs the message in the console.

Once a bid is placed and recorded, you broadcast that bid information to all browsers currently connected to that item's topic. To do so, you use the `AuctionWeb.Endpoint.broadcast/3` function you used previously in IEx.

The `AuctionWeb.BidController.create/2` function has two paths via the `case` statement:

- A successful bid (`{:ok, bid}`)
- An unsuccessful bid (`{:error, bid}`)

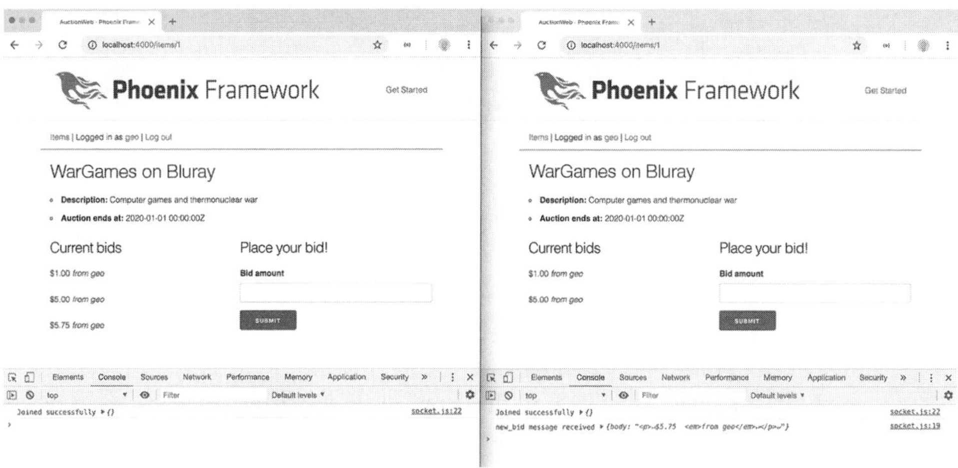

Figure 12.3 The browser on the right receives a `new_bid` message when the browser on the left submits a bid.

You don't want the bid information to be broadcast on an unsuccessful bid, so you only broadcast in the `{:ok, item}`path of the `case` statement. All you need to know is the item ID (which you can get from `item_id` in the params), the message type to send (`new_bid`), and the message payload.

For the message payload, you use the new `BidView` template you extracted in the last section to send the HTML you'd like displayed in the Current Bids section of the show item page. Phoenix has a nice function named `Phoenix.View.render_to_string/3` that you can use to get the HTML of the template and send it to the topic via the broadcast. `render_to_string/3`, like `Phoenix.View.render`, requires as arguments the view module, the template name, and a map of assigns to pass on. In this case, you use the `AuctionWeb.BidView` module and the bid.html template, and you need to send in a `bid` and a `username` assign (because the bid's `user` association won't be preloaded). For clarity, I've broken this out into an `html` variable before sending it in the payload to the `broadcast/3`function.

Listing 12.14 Modifying the controller to broadcast a successful bid

```
defmodule AuctionWeb.BidController do
  # ...
  def create(conn, %{"bid" => %{"amount" => amount}, "item_id" => item_id}) do
    case Auction.insert_bid(%{amount: amount, item_id: item_id, user_id:
     conn.assigns.current_user.id}) do
      {:ok, bid} ->
        html = Phoenix.View.render_to_string(AuctionWeb.BidView,
                                             "bid.html",
                                              bid: bid,
                                            username:
```

```
                                       conn.assigns.current_user.username)
          AuctionWeb.Endpoint.broadcast("item:#{item_id}",
          ➥ "new_bid", %{body: html})
          redirect conn, to: item_path(conn, :show, bid.item_id)
        {:error, bid} ->
          item = Auction.get_item(item_id)
          render conn, AuctionWeb.ItemView, "show.html", [item: item, bid: bid]
      end
    end
    # ...
  end
```

Before this change, redirect was the only call on the successful path.

In order to see this work, you need to have two browser windows open to the same item page. Once you submit a bid in one browser, that browser is redirected, which refreshes the page. The second browser gets the broadcast, as shown in figure 12.3.

12.4.3 Handling the broadcasted HTML in the browser

Your browser now gets sent the HTML payload when another user (or you in another browser window) submits a bid. In order to get other browsers listening on the topic's channel to update their HTML with that template fragment, you need to dive back into JavaScript and edit auction_web/assets/js/socket.js. You'll *prepend* the new bids to the list of current bids so the newest one is on top.

With that in mind, it would make more sense for the most recent bid to be on top when the page loads as well. You can easily change the ordering of the Ecto query that fetches an item's bids in auction_umbrella/apps/auction/lib/auction.ex using the Ecto `from` syntax you used in `get_bids_for_user/1`. `Ecto.Repo.preload/3` can accept an Ecto query, and you'll use this to order the preloaded bids by their `inserted_at` attribute, with the most recent bid first (see figure 12.4).

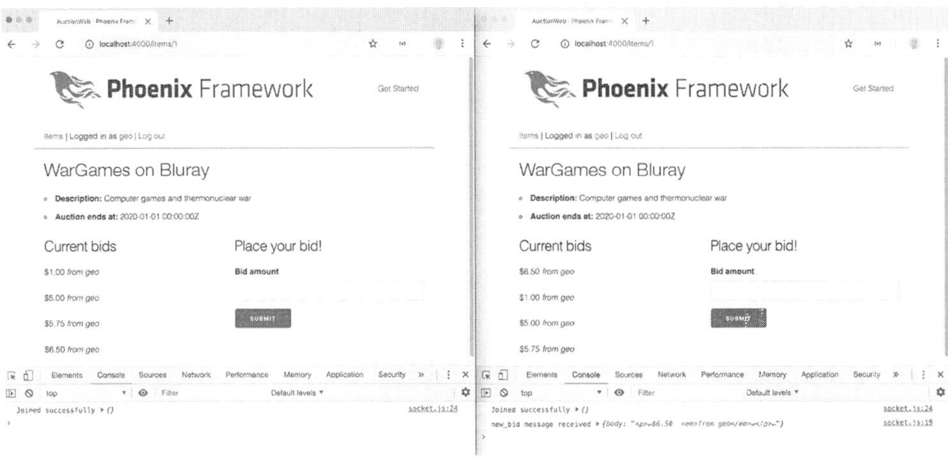

Figure 12.4 On the left: submitting bids; on the right: receiving broadcasts and updating the page

Listing 12.15 Ordering the preloaded bids

```
defmodule Auction do
  # ...
  def get_item_with_bids(id) do
    id
    |> get_item()
    |> @repo.preload(bids: from(b in Bid, order_by: [desc: b.inserted_at]))
    |> @repo.preload(bids: [:user])
  end
  # ...
end
```

This is the line you're adding.

You keep the nested user preload as well.

If you open auction_web/assets/js/socket.js, you'll be reminded of the code you added earlier in this chapter to listen for the `new_bid` message on your channel. Previously, whenever you received that event, you logged the payload to the console. You now want to modify that behavior to also prepend the HTML in the payload to the Current Bid list. In order to do so, do two things:

1. Find the `div` with the `id` of `bids` (which you added in the show.html.eex HTML template)
2. Prepend the new HTML you received in the event listener to that `div` with `insertAdjacentHTML`.

The following listing shows that implementation.

Listing 12.16 Prepending the HTML

```
// ...
let match = document.location.pathname.match(/\/items\/(\d+)$/)
if (match) {
  let itemId = match[1]
  let channel = socket.channel(`item:${itemId}`, {})

  channel.on("new_bid", data => {
    console.log("new_bid message received", data)
    const elem = document.getElementById("bids")
    elem.insertAdjacentHTML("afterbegin", data.body)
  })
  // ...
}
// ...
```

Finds the element with the ID of bids and assigns it to elem

In the elem HTML node, inserts HTML. The first argument ("afterbegin") tells JavaScript that you want to insert this HTML before the first child of the element; data.body is the HTML received from the broadcast.

Voila! You now have real-time updates in your browser. Any time a user submits a bid for an item, anyone else looking at that page in their own browser will see the new bid pop up in the list of Current Bids without refreshing the page!

Summary

- Phoenix channels are powerful tools that can have many client-side implementations—JavaScript in the browser is just one.

- Sockets are split into `topic:subtopic` channels to limit who can receive messages.
- Phoenix comes with a powerful JavaScript library for handling real-time communication.
- When a user's browser connects to a channel, you can set up listeners for specific messages and react accordingly when those messages are received.
- Use `Phoenix.View.render_many/4` when rendering a collection of things.
- Use `Phoenix.View.render_to_string/3` to render a template to a string in order to send it in a broadcasted payload.

13 Building an API

This chapter covers

- Scoping different types of requests via the router
- Responding to JSON requests with JSON
- Using `render_many/4` and `render_one/4` to render collections of resources

So far, you've dealt with handling HTML requests that presumably come through a web browser. A request comes in for a web page, and your Phoenix application handles the request and returns valid HTML markup for the user's browser to render. But Phoenix is also excellent at returning other kinds of responses. In this chapter, we'll look at handling requests for JSON by responding with JSON.

This kind of request/response cycle is something you'll often see in an API application. These could be mobile applications or even third-party integrations. In both cases, they consume the data that your application controls and then do whatever they need with that data, whether that's populating mobile application fields or using it for deep learning. It's up to the end user how they use the data—the API application just makes it available.

For your Auction application, you'll make data regarding auction items available. Each item will also return the collection of bids made on that item. Going even deeper into the associations, each bid will return minimal information about the user that made the bid. All this will be returned in JSON format for end users to consume however they wish.

13.1 Scoping API requests to a new controller

Before you can get into returning responses from an API request, you need to set up your router to handle those requests. So far, your router is only set up to handle requests for HTML versions of your site. If you look in the auction_umbrella/apps/auction_web/lib/auction_web/router.ex file, you'll see that there's a `:browser` pipeline set up near the top of the file. Currently, all requests are taken through that pipeline. The first thing the pipeline sets itself up for is accepting a specific request: `html`.

Listing 13.1 The `:browser` pipeline only accepts HTML requests

```
defmodule AuctionWeb.Router do
  use AuctionWeb, :router

  pipeline :browser do
    plug :accepts, ["html"]
    plug :fetch_session
    plug :fetch_flash
    plug :protect_from_forgery
    plug :put_secure_browser_headers
    plug AuctionWeb.Authenticator
  end
  # ...
end
```

The pipeline is only set up to handle HTML requests. (annotation on `plug :accepts, ["html"]`)

Most APIs are expected to return something other than HTML—typically XML or JSON (though many other formats are also used). In the router.ex file, you'll likely notice that another pipeline is already set up for JSON. This pipeline is a great starting point for an API—all it does is set itself up for accepting `json` requests. The pipeline already has the name of `:api`.

Listing 13.2 The `api` pipeline

```
defmodule AuctionWeb.Router do
  use AuctionWeb, :router
  # ...
  pipeline :api do
    plug :accepts, ["json"]
  end
  # ...
end
```

This pipeline is set up to only accept JSON requests. (annotation on `plug :accepts, ["json"]`)

If you compare the pipelines for `:api` and `:browser`, you'll notice that `:browser` does a lot of stuff that `:api` doesn't. `fetch_session`, `fetch_flash`, `protect_from_forgery`, and `put_secure_browser_headers` are all browser-specific plugs that you won't need when forming a JSON response. The final plug (`AuctionWeb.Authenticator`) is one you created yourself. The API won't be returning any private information and will be read-only, so you don't need to do any authentication on the request.

You may also notice in the `AuctionWeb.Router` module that there's some commented-out code that uses the `:api` pipeline.

Listing 13.3 Phoenix generator guessing that you want an API

```
defmodule AuctionWeb.Router do
  use AuctionWeb, :router
  # ...

  pipeline :api do
    plug :accepts, ["json"]
  end

  # ...
  # Other scopes may use custom stacks.
  # scope "/api", AuctionWeb do
  #   pipe_through :api
  # end
end
```

The commented-out use of the :api pipeline starts here.

To get your application ready to accept API requests, you don't need to modify this router very much at all, beyond uncommenting the commented-out code. As we discussed in chapter 9, the `scope` macro allows you to define routes for requests that match a specific scope. In the case of `scope "/api"`, it will match any previously unmatched requests whose URL paths begin with `/api`. If a request's URL path begins with `/api`, it will be piped through the `:api` pipeline and then be handed off to the specified controller. You'll set up your application to handle `/api/items` and `/api/items/:id` requests, which the `resources/2` macro can handle for you.

An idiomatic thing to do is handle API requests in their own module namespace. If you just uncommented the code that was generated, it would look for an `AuctionWeb.*` controller module. Instead, you'll namespace all API requests under `AuctionWeb.Api.*`. Notice that change in the following listing, which also uncomments the code and handles item requests.

Listing 13.4 Adding routes to handle item API requests

```
defmodule AuctionWeb.Router do
  use AuctionWeb, :router
  # ...
  scope "/api", AuctionWeb.Api do
    pipe_through :api

    resources "/items", ItemController, only: [:index, :show]
  end
end
```

AuctionWeb.Api along with ItemController tell the router to expect the AuctionWeb.Api.ItemController module to handle the requests.

You already have an AuctionWeb.ItemController that handles HTML requests, but now you'll introduce a AuctionWeb.Api.ItemController to handle JSON requests. The namespacing keeps them separate and communicates their purpose.

13.2 Creating the AuctionWeb.Api.ItemController controller and view

Creating a controller to handle the API requests is dead simple. You only need to handle two different actions: index and show. In index, you get the list of items and render a view to display them. In show, you get the specific item by id, preload the bids for that item, and pass that item along to the view.

You already have functions set up to do those things (you used them in AuctionWeb.ItemController), and you can reuse them here. The only significant change you need to make, compared to AuctionWeb.ItemController, is that you render the index.json or show.json views instead of index.html or show.html views. The following listing shows the implementation. Create this file at auction_web/lib/auction_web/controllers/api/item_controller.ex.

Listing 13.5 The AuctionWeb.Api.ItemController implementation

```
defmodule AuctionWeb.Api.ItemController do
  use AuctionWeb, :controller

  def index(conn, _params) do
    items = Auction.list_items()                    <-- Bids aren't included in
    render conn, "index.json", items: items             your listing of items.
  end

  def show(conn, %{"id" => id}) do
    item = Auction.get_item_with_bids(id)           <-- But bids are included for an
    render conn, "show.json", item: item                individual bid's JSON payload.
  end
end
```

As in previous chapters when you added a new controller, you also need to create a corresponding view. Unlike in previous chapters, though, you'll create a couple of your own functions in this view.

In a view, when use AuctionWeb, :view is called near the top of the module definition, it automatically defines a few render functions. In most cases, especially when dealing with renders that eventually end up in html.eex templates, you don't have to define any functions of your own for rendering. In this case, though, for JSON responses, you want to override the render function that's already been defined because you won't have a template file. Instead, you'll directly return the JSON information you'd like the requestor to receive.

As in all function definitions, you can use pattern matching to define render functions that specifically apply to the situations your controller is in. For example, you can define a render("show.json", %{item: item}) function that handles the render conn, "show.json", item: item call from the AuctionWeb.Api.ItemController. You'll implement the show.json render function first.

The return value of the render function you'll define will be the JSON data structure you return to the user. You can use an Elixir map to define the structure that's converted to JSON by Phoenix. In that map, you can list the different attributes you'd like the requestor to know about the item: its type, id, title, description, and ends_at timestamp. To return organized JSON, you make that information a child of a top-level data key. This is shown in the following listing (auction_web/lib/auction_web/views/api/item_view.ex).

Listing 13.6 Returning a map containing item attributes

```
defmodule AuctionWeb.Api.ItemView do
  use AuctionWeb, :view

  def render("show.json", %{item: item}) do
    %{
      data: %{
        type: "item",
        id: item.id,
        title: item.title,
        description: item.description,
        ends_at: item.ends_at
      }
    }
  end
end
```

This map data structure will automatically be converted into valid JSON by Phoenix.

Once you've created that file, you'll have enough implemented to make your first API call. I made my call inside a browser and used a browser extension that displays the JSON in a more friendly format. The response I got when I requested http://localhost:4000/api/items/1 in my browser is shown in figure 13.1, as expected.

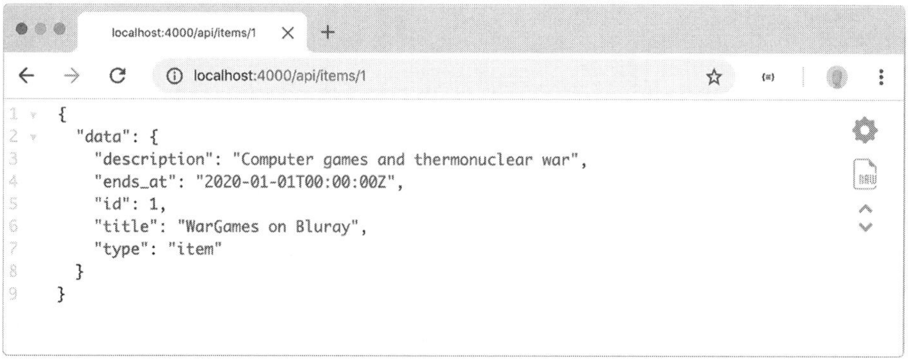

localhost:4000/api/items/1

localhost:4000/api/items/1

```
{
  "data": {
    "description": "Computer games and thermonuclear war",
    "ends_at": "2020-01-01T00:00:00Z",
    "id": 1,
    "title": "WarGames on Bluray",
    "type": "item"
  }
}
```

Figure 13.1 The JSON returned from my request

Note that you typically don't consume the data returned from the API in this manner. Viewing the data in a browser is simply a good way to determine whether you receive what you expect.

Often, in programming, you'll encounter a natural spot to refactor your current code so it can be more widely useful or even just easier to read. This is one of those natural spots. Let's refactor your view code a bit. You've defined the data structure for one item in your API, but you've defined it in a specific `render` function. It would be better if that data structure were more widely available to other functions in your application.

Instead of returning the full data structure for the item directly, you can use the `Phoenix.View.render_one/4` function. `render_one/4` expects the resource to be rendered (an item, in your case), the view module that will handle rendering (AuctionWeb.Api.ItemView), and the template to use (as well as optional options). You can use pattern matching again to render the correct template. I'll use the string `item.json` for the template string and use pattern matching in a new function definition that looks for `item.json`.

The modified view is shown in the following listing.

Listing 13.7 Using `render_one/4` in the `show.json` template

```
defmodule AuctionWeb.Api.ItemView do
  use AuctionWeb, :view

  def render("show.json", %{item: item}) do
    %{data: render_one(item, __MODULE__, "item.json")}
  end

  def render("item.json", %{item: item}) do
    %{
      type: "item",
      id: item.id,
      title: item.title,
      description: item.description,
      ends_at: item.ends_at
    }
  end
end
```

The __MODULE__ special form macro returns the current module name. It's replaced by AuctionWeb.Api.ItemView here (which you could type out).

The name of the map's item key is inferred from the view name (ItemView). If the view had been named something different, the variable name would change as well.

If you reload your browser, you should see the same result as before. That means your refactoring went perfectly.

If the returned information is the same as before, why go through the trouble of refactoring at all? I'm glad you asked. Would the refactoring make more sense if I mentioned that along with `Phoenix.View.render_one/4`, there's also a `Phoenix.View.render_many/4` function? Let's explore that while implementing the `index.json` render method, and you'll see the benefit of refactoring.

The `index` method will list all the items up for auction, and each one should have the same JSON data structure (figure 13.2). The `render_many/4` function makes it easy to render a collection of similar data.

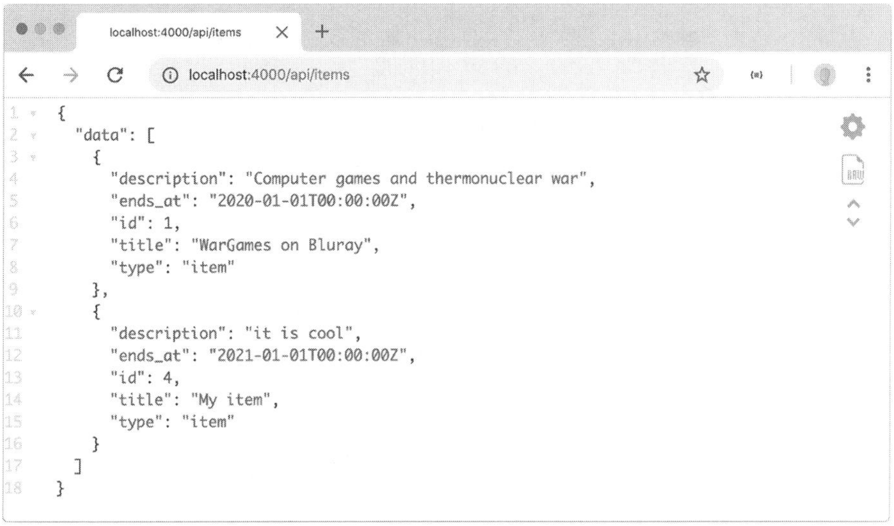
localhost:4000/api/items
localhost:4000/api/items
{
"data": [
{
"description": "Computer games and thermonuclear war",
"ends_at": "2020-01-01T00:00:00Z",
"id": 1,
"title": "WarGames on Bluray",
"type": "item"
},
{
"description": "it is cool",
"ends_at": "2021-01-01T00:00:00Z",
"id": 4,
"title": "My item",
"type": "item"
}
]
}

Figure 13.2 Many items with the same data structure

The `render_many/4` function is much like `render_one/4` in that it expects the collection of resources to render, the view module to render from, and the template to render (along with optional options). This makes the definition of `render("index.json", %{items: items})` simple and a lot like `render("show.json", %{item: item})`.

Listing 13.8 Implementing `render("index.json", %{items: items})`

```
defmodule AuctionWeb.Api.ItemView do
  use AuctionWeb, :view

  def render("index.json", %{items: items}) do
    %{data: render_many(items, __MODULE__, "item.json")}
  end
  # ...
end
```

Instead of render_one/4, use render_many/4 here.

As a reminder, you can view the output of this function by visiting http://localhost:4000/api/items.

Phoenix will take the data structure of one item and render a collection of items with the same data structure. This is a powerful and helpful addition.

13.3 Including related bid and user data

You now have either a single item or a collection of items being returned as JSON successfully from Phoenix, but you'd also like to get associated data—particularly about the bids an item has received. Adding that related data is as easy as rendering the main data.

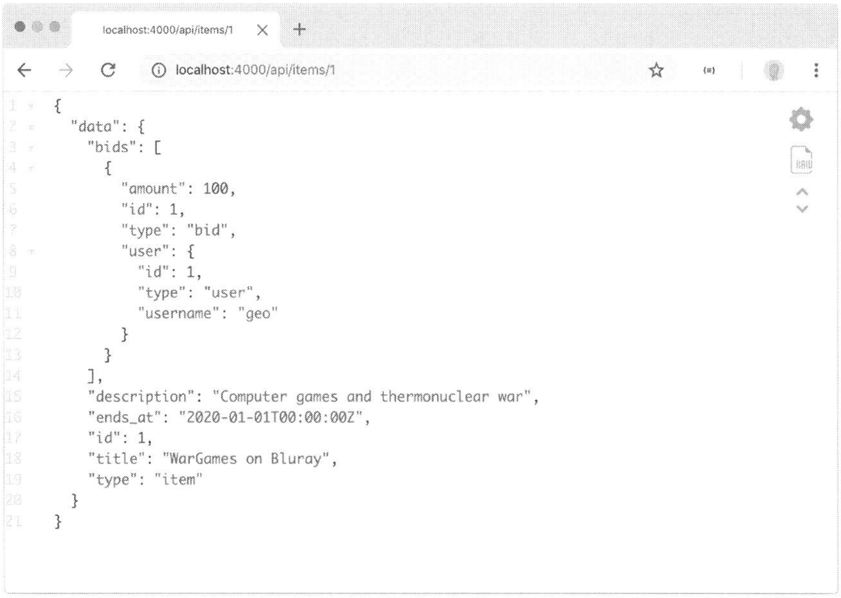

localhost:4000/api/items/1


```
{
  "data": {
    "bids": [
      {
        "amount": 100,
        "id": 1,
        "type": "bid",
        "user": {
          "id": 1,
          "type": "user",
          "username": "geo"
        }
      }
    ],
    "description": "Computer games and thermonuclear war",
    "ends_at": "2020-01-01T00:00:00Z",
    "id": 1,
    "title": "WarGames on Bluray",
    "type": "item"
  }
}
```


Figure 13.3 An item with bid and user information

The main thing you need to do is add a new key to the structure being returned and render the collection of related data. Once you complete this section, the JSON for a single item should look like figure 13.3.

The first thing you need to decide is what data to return regarding a bid. For this example, you'll return the type (which is `bid`), `id`, and bid `amount` (see figure 13.4).

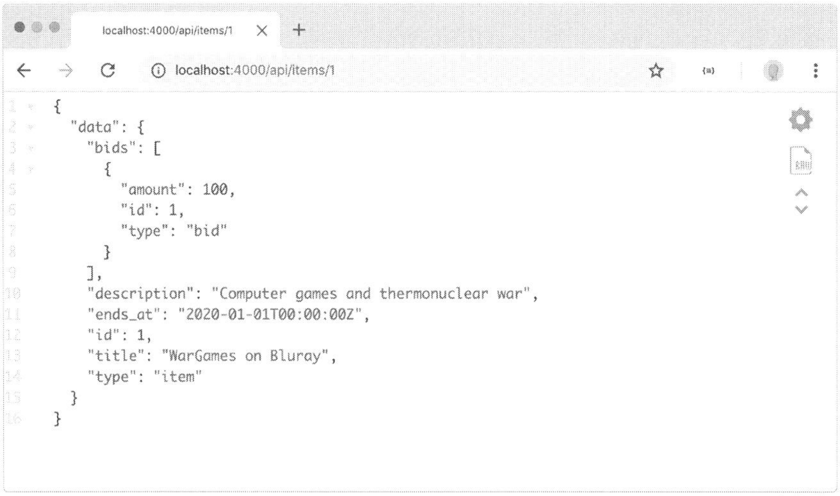

localhost:4000/api/items/1


```
{
  "data": {
    "bids": [
      {
        "amount": 100,
        "id": 1,
        "type": "bid"
      }
    ],
    "description": "Computer games and thermonuclear war",
    "ends_at": "2020-01-01T00:00:00Z",
    "id": 1,
    "title": "WarGames on Bluray",
    "type": "item"
  }
}
```


Figure 13.4 The JSON returned after adding bid information

You'll also eventually add information about the user who submitted each bid. You could implement this data structure inside the `AuctionWeb.Api.ItemView` view, but I think it clearly belongs in its own view (`AuctionWeb.Api.BidView`), because it describes its own data. Add the following code to a file at auction_web/lib/auction_web/views/api/bid_view.ex.

Listing 13.9 The implementation of `AuctionWeb.Api.BidView`

```
defmodule AuctionWeb.Api.BidView do
  use AuctionWeb, :view

  def render("bid.json", %{bid: bid}) do
    %{
      type: "bid",
      id: bid.id,
      amount: bid.amount
    }
  end
end
```

The data structure for a bid is simple and includes the type, id, and amount.

You can now create a new render function to use the new data structure and call `render_many/4` on the item's bids.

Listing 13.10 Calling `render_many/4` from the item_with_bids.json structure

```
defmodule AuctionWeb.Api.ItemView do
  # ...
  def render("show.json", %{item: item}) do
    %{data: render_one(item, __MODULE__, "item_with_bids.json")}
  end

  def render("item_with_bids.json", %{item: item}) do
    %{
      type: "item",
      id: item.id,
      title: item.title,
      description: item.description,
      ends_at: item.ends_at,
      bids: render_many(item.bids, AuctionWeb.Api.BidView, "bid.json")
    }
  end
end
```

Change the call from item.json to item_with_bids.json to use the new render function.

Add this to render the collection of bids for an item.

Note that you don't have any sort of controller or route to get this data. It can only be retrieved by calling directly from inside the `AuctionWeb.Api.ItemView` module.

The last thing you need to do is add the bid's user information to the bid data structure. You'll only expose the `username` and the user `id` (as well as the `type`). Any further identifying information is unnecessary and could potentially be private.

You could define this structure in any view module, but let's put it in its own: AuctionWeb.Api.UserView. The following listing shows the full implementation.

Listing 13.11 Implementing AuctionWeb.Api.UserView

```
defmodule AuctionWeb.Api.UserView do
  use AuctionWeb, :view

  def render("user.json", %{user: user}) do
    %{
      type: "user",
      id: user.id,
      username: user.username
    }
  end
end
```

Just like with a bid, the data structure required for a user is pretty minimal.

Finally, you need to go back to the structure of AuctionWeb.Api.BidView and render the user key with render_one.

Listing 13.12 Adding the user information to AuctionWeb.Api.BidView

```
defmodule AuctionWeb.Api.BidView do
  use AuctionWeb, :view

  def render("item_bid.json", %{bid: bid}) do
    %{
      type: "bid",
      id: bid.id,
      amount: bid.amount,
      user: render_one(bid.user, AuctionWeb.Api.UserView, "user.json")
    }
  end
end
```

Add this to render the user information for each bid.

This is one of the shortest chapters in the book, but I hope it clearly demonstrates what you can do when you break out data structures and use Phoenix.View.render_one/4 and Phoenix.View.render_many/4. You can use the information from this API to build a mobile app or other external application that only needs the information that you decide to make public.

Summary

- Use a new scope in the router module to separate different styles of requests. In this chapter's example, you used the api scope and :api pipeline.
- When rendering structured data, break out a single structure into its own render template.
- Use render_one/4 to render a single resource of the data structure.
- Use render_many/4 to render a collection of resources.

14 Testing in Elixir and Phoenix

This chapter covers

- Writing tests for simple Elixir functions
- Writing tests for Phoenix interactions
- Using doctests to simultaneously document and test your functions

Some developers love them and write them before writing anything else, and some developers can only barely stomach them. But even developers who'd rather not write a single one can agree that they're helpful and can be critical to a healthy application. What can cause such extremes of emotion? Tests!

Tested code can help a developer sleep better at night. Tested code allows a developer to refactor code while being confident that no regressions occur. But testing can also be tedious and time-consuming. If you've had bad experiences with tests in the past, I have good news for you: testing Elixir code is a first-class concern, and the Elixir standard library contains a number of helpful utilities to help make sure your code isn't only well tested, but also well documented.

For starters, a fantastic testing library called ExUnit is included with Elixir's standard library.

14.1 An introduction to ExUnit

I have a surprise for you: your application already has tests! Don't believe me? Try running `mix test` from the top of your application (auction_umbrella/). You'll likely see some compilation notices and then, at the bottom, something like this:

```
Finished in 0.08 seconds
3 tests, 1 failure
```

Depending on the version of Elixir and Phoenix you had when you first ran the `mix new --umbrella` or `mix phx.new.web` generators, the number of tests you have and even the number of failures may be different. One thing is for certain, though: your application already has at least one test. Doesn't that already make you sleep better at night?[1]

The tests that ran were automatically generated for you when you first ran the `mix new --umbrella` or `mix phx.new.web` generators. Let's take a look inside one of the tests—the one located at auction_umbrella/apps/auction/test/auction_test.exs. Mine is shown in the following listing.

Listing 14.1 The contents of my auction_test.exs file

```
defmodule AuctionTest do
  use ExUnit.Case
  doctest Auction

  test "greets the world" do
    assert Auction.hello() == :world
  end
end
```

This test was automatically generated when I created the app.

This happens to be the test that's currently failing for me. I no longer have an `Auction.hello/0` function defined, because I replaced the contents of the module when I first started work on the application. Nevertheless, let's go through this file line by line and see what you can learn:

- `defmodule AuctionTest do … end`—A test module is defined like any other module is. It's idiomatic to name the module after the module being tested, with `Test` appended to the module name. For example, if you were testing a module named `Phoenix.Action`, you'd name your module `Phoenix.ActionTest`.
- `use ExUnit.Case`—This sets up the test module so it can run tests with the functions that `ExUnit.Case` provides. You'll see those functions shortly.
- `doctest Auction`—Any module can include documentation. Not only is it helpful for you as you look at your source code, it's used by documentation generators and is output into a nice format, like the documentation at https://hexdocs.pm. Beyond that, your documentation can include usage examples of the function being documented. In the past, that practice was frowned on, because it can be easy to let your documentation examples grow stale when

[1] Of course not. A test suite is only as good as the things it actually tests.

your function is refactored and rewritten over the years. The beautiful thing about `doctest Auction` is that it actually *runs the examples in your documentation* as a test to verify that the results are as expected. We'll dive into this in a later section in this chapter.

- `test "greets the world" do … end`—A test is actually a macro (`ExUnit.Case.test/3`) that accepts a string as a description, some optional variables, and a code block that contains the test.
- `assert Auction.hello() == :world`—The actual testing is done with the `ExUnit.Assertions.assert/1` macro (and its friends). All `assert/1` does is verify that its argument (the return value of `Auction.hello() == :world`, here) is truthy.

You'll soon use these functions in tests to make sure your code is actually doing what you think it's doing.

Assertions provided by ExUnit.Assertions

`ExUnit.Assertions` provides a number of assertion macros that you can use in your tests. For the majority of the tests you'll write, you'll find that `assert` is exactly what you need. But there are other macros you can use if the situation calls for them, a few of which are listed in the following table.

A selection of other assertions

Function or macro	Description	Example
`assert`	Asserts that the given value is true	`assert true`
`refute`	Asserts that the given value is false	`refute false`
`assert_in_delta`	Asserts that the difference between two values is within the delta	`assert_in_delta 1.0, 1.5, 0.6`
`assert_raise`	Asserts that a specific exception is raised	`assert_raise ArgumentError, fn -> Integer.to_string(3.5) end`

14.1.1 Writing a first test

The test in listing 14.1 fails for me because I have no `Auction.hello()` function defined. Let's delete that test and write one that passes.

You can write a simple test to verify that the test suite works. You'll test "the truth."

Listing 14.2 The new `AuctionTest` module

```
defmodule AuctionTest do
  use ExUnit.Case
  doctest Auction
```

```
  test "the truth" do
    assert true
  end
end
```

assert ensures that the resulting code returns a truthy value.

I could run `mix test` again, but I'd like to be more specific and see more information about the tests that are running. `mix test` alone will search for every test file in the project (determined by a filename of *_test.exs).

`mix test` also accepts a filename, or a list of filenames if you want to be specific about which files to test. But the way it works in an umbrella application like yours is a little strange. When you run `mix test` in the top level of your umbrella application, you can think of it then `cd` ing into each app and running `mix test` in its directory. This means that your file, even from the root of your umbrella application, is referenced only as test/auction_test.exs and not apps/auction/test/auction_test.exs.

You can also pass `mix test` the `--trace` flag to get more verbose output from the tests being run. Otherwise, a test will only output a period (`.`) when run.

The following listing shows the result of running `mix test test/auction_test.exs --trace`.

Listing 14.3 The output of my test run

```
> mix test test/auction_test.exs --trace
==> auction

AuctionTest
  * test the truth (0.00ms)


Finished in 0.03 seconds
1 test, 0 failures

Randomized with seed 418767
```

The output matches the test name from listing 14.2.

You can see that the truth is `true` (that's a relief)! But what happens if a test fails? You can modify your test to easily fail by asserting `false`.

```
test "the truth" do
  assert false
end
```

If you run the tests again, you see the output of the failing test.

Listing 14.4 A failing test

```
> mix test test/auction_test.exs
==> auction

  1) test the truth (AuctionTest)
     test/auction_test.exs:5
     Expected truthy, got false
```

What it expected vs. what it got

```
    code: assert false
    stacktrace:
      test/auction_test.exs:6: (test)

Finished in 0.05 seconds
1 test, 1 failure

Randomized with seed 348538
```

The code that failed the assertion test (code: assert false)

File and line number of the failing code (test/auction_test.exs:6)

The information that Elixir gives you about a failing test is great. As your test suite grows, you'll undoubtedly run into some failing tests, and the output will typically point out where they fail and how. That kind of information is invaluable during development.

14.2 Setting up tests for Ecto

Now that we've briefly explored a passing and a failing test, let's modify the test so it's a little more helpful in your application. Your `Auction` module deals extensively with your database queries, so it will use Ecto and hit the database that you configure for it. Ecto has a nice guide for setting up your Ecto-using application for testing (https://hexdocs.pm/ecto/testing-with-ecto.html), but we'll go over it briefly here.

There are a few things you need to do:

1. Configure a new database.
2. Configure a sandbox pool for tests, and tell Ecto about the sandbox.
3. Set up the database before the tests run.
4. Create a Mix alias to make test setup easier.

Let's look at each of those in turn.

14.2.1 Configuring a new database

At the beginning of the book, you set up a new database for the Auction application. If you followed along with the text, that database is likely named `auction`, and it's using a Postgres adapter. You'll now create a new, separate database that you can safely add rows to and delete rows from during tests, without affecting any existing development data.

The first step is to create a new database (I named mine `auction_test`). You need to reference your preferred database documentation for how to do that.

After you've created the database, you need to configure your application to communicate with it. As you'll recall, you put a lot of configuration information in the config directories of your applications. This will be no different.

In the auction_umbrella/apps/auction/config directory, you already have a config.exs file. This is where you initially configured your application's database while you developed it. There are some comments in this file, and the one to pay attention to is echoed in the following listing. It tells you that you can use multiple configuration files based on the environment you run your application in.

Listing 14.5 Important comments from config.exs

```
# It is also possible to import configuration files, relative to this
# directory. For example, you can emulate configuration per environment
# by uncommenting the line below and defining dev.exs, test.exs and such.
# Configuration from the imported file will override the ones defined
# here (which is why it is important to import them last).
#
# import_config "#{Mix.env}.exs"
```

Uncomment this line to take advantage of environment-specific configs.

If you uncomment that last line (go ahead and do so, and save the file), Mix will automatically look for additional config files based on the name of the environment you're in (typically `dev`, `test`, or `prod`). In these environment-specific files, you can override any configuration done in the main config.exs file, or you can provide additional configuration as needed.

In your case, you need to configure the test environment to use the test database and repo. To do so, you create an auction_umbrella/apps/auction/config/test.exs file and override the database configuration.

Listing 14.6 The new test.exs config file

```
use Mix.Config

config :auction, Auction.Repo,
  username: "postgres",
  password: "postgres",
  database: "auction_test",
  hostname: "localhost",
  port: "5432",
  pool: Ecto.Adapters.SQL.Sandbox
```

Every Mix config file needs this as the first line, even environment-specific files like this.

Update this line with your database name.

Ecto provides this adapter to help pool database connections.

The test environment won't be the only environment you run your application in. If you simply ran `mix phx.server` or `iex -S mix phx.server`, the environment would be `dev`, and Mix would complain that it couldn't find config/dev.exs. Although you don't have any `dev`-specific configuration to do at the moment, you still need to create the config/dev.exs file and put `use Mix.Config` in it.

Create auction_umbrella/apps/auction/config/dev.exs with the following line in it:

```
use Mix.Config
```

That's all you need in the file to get things started.

14.2.2 Creating a sandbox and configuring Ecto to use it in tests

Ecto provides something called a *sandbox* that's useful when running tests. It's a pool of connections to your database. The sandbox can share these connections with any tests that request access.

You need to configure Ecto to use a sandbox and start it up when you run your tests. Elixir creates a file named test_helper.exs; and you can put whatever setup you need in that file, and it will be run before your tests. In this case, Ecto requires a special function before you can use the test database. In short, it tells Ecto that you'd like to use the sandbox mode for a particular repo (`Auction.Repo`, in your case).

The command is a one-liner: `Ecto.Adapters.SQL.Sandbox.mode(Auction.Repo, :manual)`. Adding that line to auction_umbrella/apps/auction/test/test_helper.exs gives you the following.

Listing 14.7 The test helper file contents

```
ExUnit.start()
Ecto.Adapters.SQL.Sandbox.mode(Auction.Repo, :manual)
```

This function call was already here and is what starts ExUnit. (annotates `ExUnit.start()`)

This helper will be executed before every test run. You can put any setup code you need to run before your tests in this file.

14.2.3 Setting up the database before tests run

So far, you've configured the database and let Ecto know about the sandbox in the test helper. Before you actually start testing with information from the test database, you need to start the database connection in the tests that require them. Your entire `Auction` module needs a connection to the database, so you can use a `setup` block in your test file to start that connection.

`ExUnit.Callbacks.setup/1` takes a block as its argument and runs that block of code before each and every associated test. This is the perfect place to call `Ecto.Adapters.SQL.checkout/1`. `checkout/1` will "check out" a connection from the `Sandbox` pool of connections, and that connection is usable during the rest of that test run (or until `checkin/1` is called). `checkout/1` expects the repo name as the one and only argument.

You can then modify your `AuctionTest` module to use that `setup` block. `setup` expects `:ok`, a keyword list, or a map as its return value. Fortunately, `checkout/1` returns `:ok` on success, which makes it easy to pattern-match.

Listing 14.8 Modifying the `AuctionTest` module

```
defmodule AuctionTest do
  use ExUnit.Case
  alias Auction.{Repo}
  doctest Auction

  setup do
    :ok = Ecto.Adapters.SQL.Sandbox.checkout(Repo)
  end

  test "the truth" do
```

Aliases Auction.Repo so you can simply type "Repo" in this file

```
    assert true
  end
end
```

After making that edit, you should be able to successfully run your test again from the command line.

If you get an error about the database not existing, run the following command from the command line to set up the test database. Note that you can force the environment you want Mix to run in by setting `MIX_ENV` in the command. (Here, you'll run it in the `test` environment.)

```
> MIX_ENV=test mix do ecto.create, mix ecto.migrate
```

As you can see, this command uses `mix do` to run multiple tasks in one command. It creates the test database and makes sure it's migrated up to the latest version.

14.2.4 Creating a Mix alias for use during test runs

Mix allows you to create "aliases" to use during Mix tasks. You can use these to run multiple functions with one command or do regular setup tasks. You'll use one in this section to make sure your test database is created and migrated every time you run your tests.

You can set up aliases in the mix.exs file for an application. In this case, you need to edit auction_umbrella/apps/auction/mix.exs.

The `project` function defined in each mix.exs file specifies a list of options used for setting up the application. One option you can set is `aliases`. When setting up aliases, the first element is what you type after `mix` (for example, `mix my_alias`), and the second element is a list of commands to run in order. You set your alias to first run `ecto.create`, then `ecto.migrate`, and finally the original `test` task. You can specify that as follows.

Listing 14.9 Setting up aliases for the `auction` application

```
defmodule Auction.MixProject do
  use Mix.Project

  def project do
    [
      app: :auction,
      version: "0.1.0",
      build_path: "../../_build",
      config_path: "../../config/config.exs",
      deps_path: "../../deps",
      lockfile: "../../mix.lock",
      elixir: "~> 1.7",
      start_permanent: Mix.env() == :prod,
      deps: deps(),                          <-- Don't forget the new trailing comma on this line.
      aliases: aliases()                     <-- Aliases will be defined by the aliases/1 function.
    ]
```

```
  end

  # ...                                   Defines the
                                          aliases/1 function
  def aliases do                    <-
    [test: ["ecto.create --quiet", "ecto.migrate", "test"]]   <- The --quiet flag for
  end                                                           ecto.create silences
end                                                             the output.
```

Now if you run `mix test` from within the auction_umbrella/apps/auction application, it will ensure that the database is created and migrated to the latest version, and the tests for the application are run.

14.3 Testing Ecto queries in Auction

Now you can finally get to the fun part: testing your application code! For the sake of space in this book, we'll walk through setting up just three tests for the `Auction` module in `AuctionTest`, but you should be able to apply what you learn and test the entire module.

The three functions you'll test are `Auction.list_items/0`, `Auction.get_item/1`, and `Auction.insert_item/1`.

14.3.1 Testing Auction.list_items/0

`ExUnit` provides the `describe/2` macro, which is a convenient way to group together tests that belong together. The first argument is the string description of the group, and the second is a block of tests. You'll use this `describe` macro for each of the functions you test. It will look something like this:

```
describe "list_items/0" do
  # ... tests
end
```

The first function you test is `Auction.list_items/0`. This function is supposed to return all the items in the database as a list. To test this, you first need some items in your database.

You can use another `setup` block to create items before your tests run. Plus, you can provide those created items to every test in the current `describe` block. Do you remember me saying that `setup/1` expects a return value of `:ok`, a keyword list, or a map? Anything you return from the setup block is provided to the `test` macro as its second argument, and you can then make use of that data in your tests. This data is called a *context*.

Finally, you need to actually make an assertion in a test. For this function, you test that the return value of `list_items/0` is a list of all the items you'll insert into the database during setup. You can use the data in the context from the setup block to make that assertion.

This is one of those times when showing is clearer than explaining. Take a look at the test in the following listing. Pay special attention to the setup block and its return value (the last line), the nesting of the test within the `describe` block, and the use of the context (which is passed as the second argument to the `test/3` macro).

Listing 14.10 Testing `list_items/0`

```
defmodule AuctionTest do
  use ExUnit.Case
  alias Auction.{Item, Repo}       <-- Adds Item to the list of aliases
  doctest Auction

  setup do
    :ok = Ecto.Adapters.SQL.Sandbox.checkout(Repo)
  end

  describe "list_items/0" do
    setup do                       <-- You can have an additional setup block inside a describe block. This will run for each test in the describe block.
      {:ok, item1} = Repo.insert(%Item{title: "Item 1"})
      {:ok, item2} = Repo.insert(%Item{title: "Item 2"})
      {:ok, item3} = Repo.insert(%Item{title: "Item 3"})
      %{items: [item1, item2, item3]}    <-- This map will be passed in as an argument to the tests in this block.
    end

    test "returns all Items in the database", %{items: items} do    <-- Pattern-matches the passed map and assigns it to an items variable for use in the test
      assert items == Auction.list_items
    end
  end
end
```

If you run the tests with the `--trace` flag, as before, the test descriptions have a nice flow.

Listing 14.11 Output from testing `/0`

```
> mix test --trace test/auction_test.exs
21:31:26.341 [info] Already up

AuctionTest
  * test list_items/0 returns all Items in the database
21:31:26.460 [debug] QUERY OK db=1.8ms
begin []
21:31:26.478 [debug] QUERY OK db=3.1ms

[ REMOVED: LOTS OF DATABASE DEBUG NOISE ]    <-- This noise isn't very helpful, is it?

  * test list_items/0 returns all Items in the database (45.4ms)


Finished in 0.08 seconds
1 test, 0 failures

Randomized with seed 385816
```

You may have noticed that *a lot* of database `debug` output was present in your test run. For your purposes, that's just noise that gets in the way of the test results. How can you turn that off? Earlier I mentioned that you can use environment-specific config files to override configuration settings. In this case, you can set the logger level to `:info` for the `test` environment so that all these debug-level statements aren't output to the screen.

Modify your auction_umbrella/apps/auction/config/test.exs file and add the final config line in the following listing.

Listing 14.12 Changing the logging level in test.exs

```
use Mix.Config

config :auction, Auction.Repo,
  username: "postgres",
  password: "postgres",
  database: "auction_test",
  hostname: "localhost",
  port: "5432",
  pool: Ecto.Adapters.SQL.Sandbox

config :logger, level: :info
```

Add this line to silence debug-level logs.

If you save that file and run the tests again, you see a nicely output list of tests that were run and their results (see the following listing). You may see other debug information, like the compilation of files or compilation warnings for those files. Unless there are errors, you can ignore the warnings.

Listing 14.13 The nicely cleaned-up run of tests

```
> mix test --trace test/auction_test.exs

AuctionTest
  * test list_items/0 returns all Items in the database (22.0ms)


Finished in 0.05 seconds
1 test, 0 failures

Randomized with seed 34812
```

No more debug output

Your one test passes, and all the noisy debug output has been removed. You can now move on to testing `Auction.get_item/1`.

14.3.2 Testing Auction.get_item/1

The next function you'll test is `Auction.get_item/1`. The purpose of this function is to retrieve a specific item by `id`, which is the parameter you pass in. In order to test this function, you need to have an item in the database already, and then you need to verify that the item you get back from the function is the item you requested.

Because you create the items during the test run, you won't know for certain what the id of the item is beforehand. Instead of passing an integer directly, you just pass in the id attribute of one of the items you create.

You create two items in this setup block. Why? Because you want to make sure that you only get one item back, and not two as you would in Auction.list_items/0. Finally, you pass the result of inserting the items into the database in the setup block as context for the test. The following listing puts it all together.

Listing 14.14 Testing Auction.get_item/1

```
defmodule AuctionTest do
  # ...

  describe "get_item/1" do
    setup do
      {:ok, item1} = Repo.insert(%Item{title: "Item 1"})
      {:ok, item2} = Repo.insert(%Item{title: "Item 2"})
      %{items: [item1, item2]}
    end

    test "returns a single Item based on id", %{items: items} do
      item = Enum.at(items, 1)
      assert item == Auction.get_item(item.id)
    end
  end
```

Makes sure that the item you get is the one you requested

In the test, you pass the first item's id into Auction.get_item/1 and make sure you get the correct item back.

14.3.3 Testing Auction.insert_item/1

The last Auction function you'll test in this chapter is Auction.insert_item/1. This function takes the attributes of the item to insert into the database, and it returns {:ok, item} on success or {:error, changeset} on error. The following listing tests each of those paths.

Listing 14.15 Testing Auction.insert_item/1

```
defmodule AuctionTest do
  import Ecto.Query

  # ...

  describe "insert_item/1" do
    test "adds an Item to the database" do
      count_query = from i in Item, select: count(i.id)
      before_count = Repo.one(count_query)
      {:ok, _item} = Auction.insert_item(%{title: "test item"})
      assert Repo.one(count_query) == before_count + 1
    end
```

Imports Ecto.Query so you can use from and select later in your tests

Queries can be assigned to a variable. You do that here because you use the same query twice in this test.

Reuses the query to make sure there's an additional item in the database after the insert_item call

```
    test "the Item in the database has the attributes provided" do
      attrs = %{title: "test item", description: "test description"}
      {:ok, item} = Auction.insert_item(attrs)
      assert item.title == attrs.title
      assert item.description == attrs.description
    end

    test "it returns an error on error" do
      assert {:error, _changeset} = Auction.insert_item(%{foo: :bar})
    end
  end
end
```

You can have as many assertions as you like in a test.

The tests you've written here obviously only cover a small portion of the functions in the `Auction` module. I'll leave the testing of the rest as an exercise for you to tackle.

14.4 Simultaneously writing documentation and tests with doctests

Well-documented code is typically easier to use (especially for developers who *aren't* the author). But documentation can easily get out of sync with what the functions actually do, particularly as refactorings take place and project requirements change. Elixir provides doctests: documentation and tests wrapped up together. Although this feature doesn't automatically create top-notch documentation, it does provide a guard against documentation examples getting out of sync with what the functions actually do.

14.4.1 Writing function-level documentation

Let's first focus on how to write regular documentation and then later add tests. For the purposes of this section, you'll document `Auction.get_user_by_username_and_password/2`. This function requires a username and password to be passed as arguments, and it returns a user if the username and password match ones in the database or `false` if one can't be found.

The following listing should remind you of the function's implementation—it's the same as in previous chapters.

Listing 14.16 The `Auction.get_user_by_username_and_password` function

```
def get_user_by_username_and_password(username, password) do
  with user when not is_nil(user) <- @repo.get_by(User, %{username:
     username}),
       true <- Password.verify_with_hash(password, user.hashed_password) do
    user
  else
    _ -> Password.dummy_verify
  end
end
```

Function documentation starts with a `@doc` module attribute just above the function declaration. If the documentation is multiple lines long (and it usually is), it also starts a HEREDOC string (a multiline string prepended and appended by three double quotes: `"""`); for example, `@doc """`.

The line after `@doc` is the first line of the documentation. It's normally good practice to keep this line short and sweet, as it shows up in multiple places as a summary of the function's functionality.

So far, your documentation might look like the following.

Listing 14.17 Beginning documentation for `get_user_by_username_and_password/2`

```
@doc """
Retrieves a User from the database matching the provided username and
    password
"""
def get_user_by_username_and_password(username, password) do
  # ...
end
```

The documentation starts with @doc.

After the summary line, an empty line and then more descriptive text follows. This descriptive text can be as long as you want, and it should provide enough information to let future developers know how to use the function. For your example function, you describe the different return values that can occur (a user or `false`) and what they mean.

Oh, and did I mention that documentation supports Markdown?[2] Woohoo!

The following listing shows how I documented the function.

Listing 14.18 Further documenting `get_user_by_username_and_password/2`

ExDoc uses Markdown for formatting, which allows you to use things like ## for a second-level heading and * for bullet points. Not only does it look nice in plain text, it transforms into nice HTML as well.

```
@doc """
Retrieves a User from the database matching the provided username and password

## Return values

Depending on what is found in the database, two different values could be
returned:

  * an `Auction.User` struct: An `Auction.User` record was found that matched
    the `username` and `password` that was provided.
  * `false`: No `Auction.User` could be found with the provided `username`
    and `password`.

You can then use the returned value to determine whether or not the User is
authorized in your application. If an `Auction.User` is _not_ found based on
```

[2] Not familiar with Markdown? It's a tool that allows you to provide text formatting inside plain text. See Daring Fireball's Markdown page for more information: https://daringfireball.net/projects/markdown/.

```
`username`, the computational work of hashing a password is still done.
"""
def get_user_by_username_and_password(username, password) do
  # ...
end
```

That should provide *almost* enough information for future me or any other developer who needs to use the function.[3]

The text above the function definition is nice in and of itself, but your written documentation really comes to life when used inside an IEx session and with the ExDoc package.

14.4.2 Viewing documentation in IEx

In chapter 2, I showed how you can use the `IEx.Helpers.h/1` macro to print out documentation for a function or module in an IEx session. You used it to learn about the `Enum` module and the `Enum.map/2` and `Enum.reverse/1` functions. Because I'm reminding you about those here, you may be able to guess where that documentation came from. If you guessed from their in-module function documentation, you're correct! That also means that your own function documentation can be seen in IEx the same way.

For example, you can ask IEx about the `Auction.get_user_by_username_and_password/2` function. (Make sure you start the IEx session while including your application with `iex -S mix`.)

Listing 14.19 Displaying your documentation in IEx

```
iex(2)> h Auction.get_user_by_username_and_password/2

           def get_user_by_username_and_password(username, password)

Retrieves a User from the database matching the provided username and
     password

## Return values

Depending on what is found in the database, two different values could be
returned:

  • an Auction.User struct: An Auction.User record was found that matched
    the username and password that was provided.
  • false: No Auction.User could be found with the provided username and
    password.

You can then use the returned value to determine whether or not the User is
authorized in your application. If an Auction.User is not found based on
username, the computational work of hashing a password is still done.
```

Use h to show the documentation for a module or function.

This text listing doesn't quite do it justice because the real IEx output has color and Markdown markup (like an underline under not in the last sentence). Neat, huh?

[3] Spoiler: you need examples! You'll add them in the next section.

14.4.3 Viewing documentation with ExDoc

Another no-less-awesome way to view your application documentation is through the ExDoc module. If you've ever viewed the online documentation for a package at hexdocs.pm, you'll be pretty familiar with the look of ExDoc's output. ExDoc will take in your application documentation and output very nice HTML that you can read in your web browser.

Although ExDoc is provided by the Elixir team, it's not included in the standard library. That means you need to explicitly require it in your mix.exs config. You only need this package during development, so you can use the `dev: true` option to make sure it isn't included when you build your application for production.

Edit auction_umbrella/mix.exs so that your `deps` function looks like the following listing. You add ExDoc as an umbrella-level dependency so that you can use it in all the apps inside the umbrella.

Listing 14.20 Including `ex_doc` during development

```
defp deps do
  [
    {:ex_doc, "~> 0.19", dev: true, runtime: false}
  ]
end
```

dev: true specifies that this dependency isn't included in your production builds.

Once that change has been made, run `mix deps.get`, and then `mix compile`. Those two commands ensure that ExDoc's Mix tasks are installed and ready to go.

Once the compilation is complete, you can run `mix docs` to generate your documentation. All that's left to do after that is to marvel at the beauty of your documentation in your browser, as in figure 14.1.

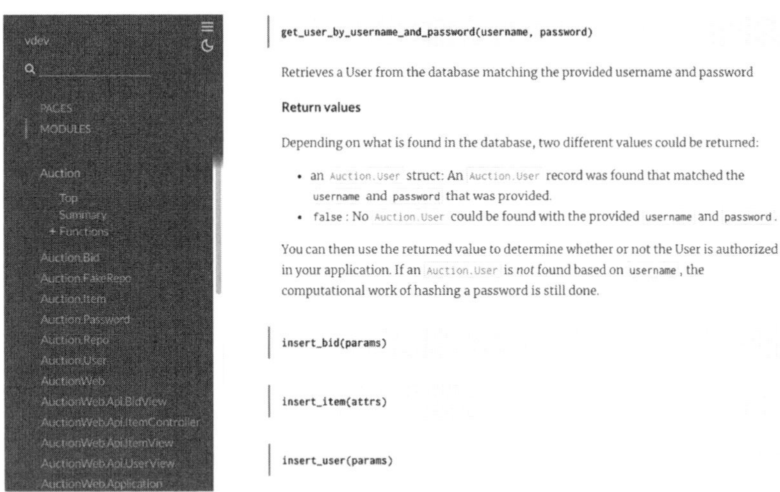

Figure 14.1 Your documentation in a browser

14.4.4 Adding examples and doctests

I mentioned earlier in this section that you *almost* have enough information in your documentation. One thing that would make it a lot better is usage examples. There's a specific format you can use for examples, and a side benefit of this format is that it's testable as doctests!

As you'll recall, your generated test file has `doctest Auction` in it. This is what tells ExUnit to test your documentation. For the sake of brevity in your tests, you can also pass in an `import` option:

```
doctest Auction, import: true
```

With this done, you won't have to prepend your function names with the module name in your doctests. For example, you only have to write `list_items` instead of `Auction.list_items`.

A doctest line starts with `iex>` and a call to your function. If you require multiple lines, you can start subsequent lines with `...>`. After you're finished with the example call of your function, the expected return value is provided on the next line.

This is easiest to understand by looking at an example. You'll add a usage example to your current `get_user_by_username_and_password/2` documentation.

Listing 14.21 Adding examples and doctests

```
@doc """
Retrieves a User from the database matching the provided username and password

# current documentation ...

## Examples

    iex> get_user_by_username_and_password("no_user", "bad_password")
    false
"""
def get_user_by_username_and_password(username, password) do
  # ...
end
```

The documentation you've already written for this function

Creates a Markdown subsection in the documentation for examples

Calls your function

Shows what you expect to get back in return

Markdown uses four spaces of indentation to indicate a code block

It would be nice to also include an example of the "happy path"—when a user *is* found with the provided username and password combination. To include multiple examples, you separate them by an empty line. In this case, you need to have a user in the database before looking it up, so you first create the user and then use `get_user_by_username_and_password/2` to retrieve it.

A limitation of doctest is that you can't pattern-match the return value inside a test. Because of that, you have to go through an extra step or two to make sure you get back something comparable to what you expect (in this case, a user with the username of "geo").

The following listing shows the updated examples.

Listing 14.22 Adding happy-path documentation

```
@doc """
Retrieves a User from the database matching the provided username and
     password

# current documentation ...

## Examples

    iex> insert_user(%{username: "geo", password: "example",
     password_confirmation: "example", email_address: "test@example.com"})
    ...> result = get_user_by_username_and_password("geo", "example")
    ...> match?(%Auction.User{username: "geo"}, result)
    true

    iex> get_user_by_username_and_password("no_user", "bad_password")
    false
"""
def get_user_by_username_and_password(username, password) do
  # ...
end
```

- Inserts the new user into the database
- Stores the result from your function
- Uses Kernel.match?/2 to ensure that the User struct you get back has the username of "geo"

Note that you haven't only added examples to your documentation—they're also doctests. This means that as long as you have `doctest Auction` in your auction _test.exs module (which you do), `ExUnit.Case` will go through your documentation looking for these `iex>` examples. When it finds one, it runs the code provided in the documentation and compares the result it gets with what you document that it should get. This is a doctest!

You can verify that these doctests are being tested by running `mix test` in the application root.

Listing 14.23 Running your doctests with your test suite

```
> mix test
.......

Finished in 1.1 seconds
2 doctests, 5 tests, 0 failures
```

- Declares that it tested two doctests, both of which you added for Auction.get_user_by_username_and_password/2

You can also see the code examples nicely formatted in the ExDoc output in figure 14.2. You can refresh your browser to see those changes after you generate your documentation again with `mix docs`.

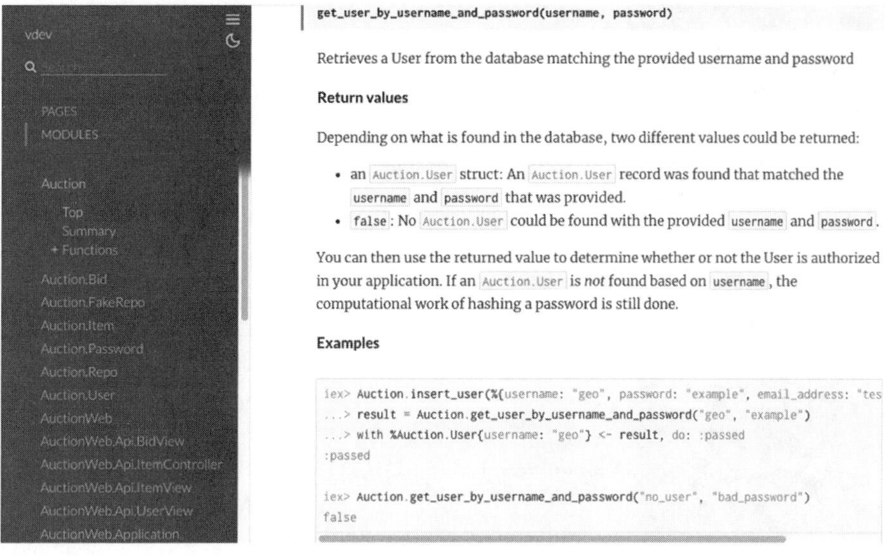

Figure 14.2 Updated documentation with examples

14.4.5 Module-level documentation

Most of what we've focused on in this chapter is documenting and testing specific functions, but you can also write module-level documentation. To do so, you declare a `@moduledoc` module attribute inside the module definition.

We won't spend a lot of time on module documentation, because it's so similar to function documentation. And like function documentation, you can view it in IEx (figure 14.3).

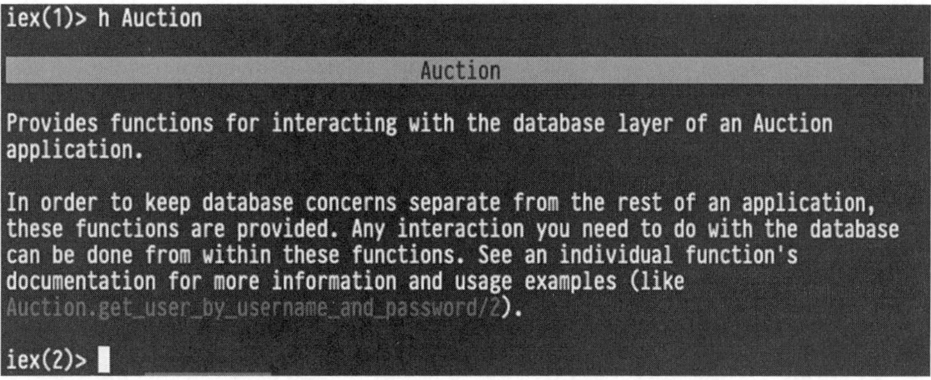

Figure 14.3 IEx module-level documentation

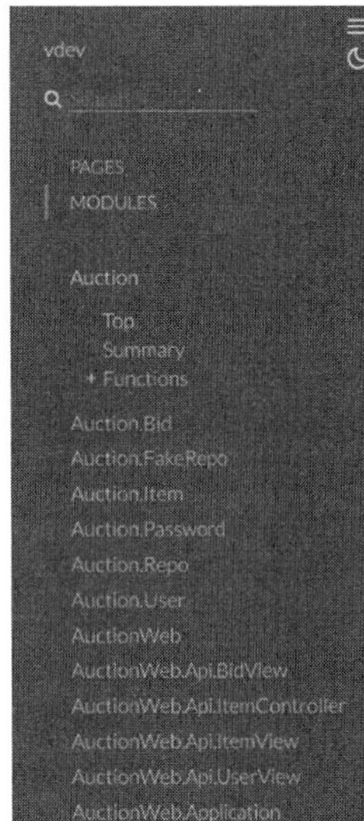

Figure 14.4 ExDoc module-level documentation

You can also view the documentation in the browser with ExDoc (figure 14.4).

The following listing shows my minimal initial documentation for the `Auction` module.

Listing 14.24 Minimal documentation for the `Auction` module

```
defmodule Auction do
  @moduledoc """
  Provides functions for interacting with the database layer of an Auction
     application.

  In order to keep database concerns separate from the rest of an
     application, these
  functions are provided. Any interaction you need to do with the database
     can be done
  from within these functions. See an individual function's documentation for
     more
  information and usage examples (like
     `Auction.get_user_by_username_and_password/2`).
  """

  # ...
end
```

Always refer to functions with their full names, including modules. This allows ExDoc to automatically add hyperlinks to function documentation.

Module documentation is written with the same standards and best practices as function documentation. In other words, keep the first line short and sweet, and expand your description in the following paragraphs. Feel free to provide examples (and doctests).

14.5 Writing tests For Phoenix

So far, you've only tested the non-Phoenix parts of your application. We started there because it made for an easier introduction to the basics of testing, but testing Phoenix doesn't involve much more than what we've already covered. The main difference is that Phoenix also provides some extra helpers you can use to verify that you get back what you expected.

The Phoenix `mix phx.new` generators provide some example tests, and I have one that's failing.

Listing 14.25 I get an error when running the Phoenix tests

```
1) test GET / (AuctionWeb.PageControllerTest)          <-- This test sends a GET request to /.
   test/auction_web/controllers/page_controller_test.exs:4
   Assertion with =~ failed                                   <-- This is the code that failed the test.
   code:  assert html_response(conn, 200) =~ "Welcome to Phoenix!"
   left:  "<!DOCTYPE html>"          <-- I've removed the actual HTML here for space reasons.
   right: "Welcome to Phoenix!"
```

You can open that test (auction_umbrella/apps/auction_web/test/auction_web/controllers/page_controller_test.exs) and see what it's attempting to test. Based on listing 14.25, it's attempting to send a `GET` request to / and assert that not only did it receive a `200` response, but that the body of the response contained the phrase "Welcome to Phoenix!" As you'll recall, you changed the `PageController` to display a list of items instead.

Ideally, you'd like any request for / to be handled by the `ItemController index` function, so users can see the items up for auction. You can make that happen with the `Phoenix.Router.get/4` function. The following listing details the changes to the router.ex file.

Listing 14.26 Adding a default route to your application

```
defmodule AuctionWeb.Router do
  # ...
  scope "/", AuctionWeb do
    pipe_through :browser # Use the default browser stack

    get "/", ItemController, :index        <-- If no path is entered into the browser, this is how the request is routed.
    # ...
  end
end
```

Now you no longer even need a `PageController`. You can safely delete that file, along with its test, and create one for `ItemController` instead. That test should be located in auction_umbrella/apps/auction_web/tests/auction_web/controllers/item _controller_test.exs, and you can copy what was in PageControllerTest, taking care to rename PageControllerTest to ItemControllerTest.

Listing 14.27 The initial ItemControllerTest

```
defmodule AuctionWeb.ItemControllerTest do
  use AuctionWeb.ConnCase

  test "GET /", %{conn: conn} do
    conn = get conn, "/"
    assert html_response(conn, 200) =~ "Welcome to Phoenix!"    <-- The test expects the page to contain the string "Welcome to Phoenix!"
  end
end
```

Now that that's taken care of, you can run the tests again. This time you get the same error saying that it expected the words "Welcome to Phoenix!"

You need to fix the test. You no longer display the "Welcome to Phoenix!" phrase and instead display the list of items. You can insert an item and test that the result body has the title of the item in the generated HTML.

Listing 14.28 The new test for your index page

```
defmodule AuctionWeb.ItemControllerTest do
  use AuctionWeb.ConnCase

  test "GET /", %{conn: conn} do
    {:ok, _item} = Auction.insert_item(%{title: "test item"})    <-- Makes sure there's an item in the database
    conn = get conn, "/"
    assert html_response(conn, 200) =~ "test item"    <-- Tests that the title of the item is on the web page
  end
end
```

If you now run the test, you should see a successful run. We won't take the time to test every endpoint in this chapter, but let's test one more. This time, let's try testing the submission of a form to create a new item. This would be handled in ItemController.create/2.

Let's test four things for this action:

- On success, an item should be added to the database.
- On success, you should be redirected to the item's show page.
- On error, no item should be added to the database.
- On error, you should be shown the form again.

You'll use a describe block to group all the tests for this section together.

14.5.1 Testing that an item is added to the database on success

The first thing you test here is that an item is successfully added to the database, based on your params. To do so, you first count all the items currently in the database and assign that count to the before_count variable. Then you make the request. Finally, you count all the items in the database again and assert that the new count is one more than `before_count`.

The following listing shows the code I ended up with.

Listing 14.29 Testing that an item is added to the database

```
defmodule AuctionWeb.ItemControllerTest do
  # ...
  describe "POST /items" do            <-- Uses a describe block to group similar tests together
    test "with valid params, creates a new Item", %{conn: conn} do
      before_count = Enum.count(Auction.list_items())
      post conn, "/items", %{"item" => %{"title" => "Item 1"}}
      assert Enum.count(Auction.list_items()) == before_count + 1
    end
  end
end
```

If you're coming from another language with a very expressive testing suite syntax, it may take a while to get used to the simplicity that Elixir provides. I'll admit that at first I didn't particularly take to it and wished for something more like Ruby's RSpec.[4] But as I've used it more and more, I've come to enjoy that almost everything I need to know about the test and setup is very visible, and that there's not much "magic" happening out of view. Even though I may type more for a test, when I go back to view it later, I don't have to dig around as much to find out what's happening.

Feel free to run that test in your environment. I got a notification that all the tests are still passing.

14.5.2 Testing that you're redirected to the new item on success

You've successfully tested the first part of the success path (the "green" path). Now, let's ensure that the user is redirected to the page you expect. `Phoenix.ConnTest` has more helpers than just `html_response/2`. One of them is `redirected_to/2`, which tests that a `conn` is redirected to a particular URL or path. You can pattern-match against the path to ensure that you're sent to `/items/:id`.

Listing 14.30 Code to test redirection

```
defmodule AuctionWeb.ItemControllerTest do
  # ...
  describe "POST /items" do
    test "with valid params, redirects to the new Item", %{conn: conn} do
      conn = post conn, "/items", %{"item" => %{"title" => "Item 1"}}
      assert redirected_to(conn) =~ ~r|/items/\d+|   <-- Asserts that you're redirected and that the URL matches the regex pattern you expect
    end
    # ...
  end
end
```

[4] If you *still* wish you had something like Ruby's RSpec (or some other language's test suite), you can likely find a similar implementation on hex.pm.

This test makes sure that after a new item is created, the user's connection is redirected to the item's show page. You don't know the ID of the item that was just inserted, but you can match against the path, expecting one or more integers to be in a particular position, with a regular expression. `~r|…|` defines a regular expression, and `/items/\d+` matches that the characters of "/items/" are followed by one or more "digits" (integers)—the item ID.

14.5.3 Testing that no item is created on error

Now you can test the red path—the path of errors. First, you'd like to ensure that no item will be created if the controller is passed bad params.

The `ExUnit.Assertions` module provides the `assert` macro, and it also provides the `refute` macro, which is the opposite of `assert`—it tests the falsity of the statement. One way you could go about testing this is by copying and pasting the green path test, in which you store the `before_count` and assert that the new count is one more than that. But that could leave some edge cases open. If all you do is refute that the counts differ by one, the test would pass if your controller ended up deleting an item. Or it could add two items.

The point is that it's nice to be as specific as possible in your tests. For that reason, you'll explicitly test that `before_count` and the after count are exactly the same.

Listing 14.31 Testing that no item is created on error

```
defmodule AuctionWeb.ItemControllerTest do
  # ...
  describe "POST /items" do
    test "with invalid params, does not create a new Item", %{conn: conn} do
      before_count = Enum.count(Auction.list_items())
      post conn, "/items", %{"item" => %{"bad_param" => "Item 1"}}
      assert Enum.count(Auction.list_items()) == before_count
    end
    # ...
  end
end
```

Sends bad params in to the controller

Asserts that the item count hasn't changed

You may have a lot of database debug noise in your test run. If so, you can configure logger to ignore `:info` messages and below, just as you did in listing 14.12.

Listing 14.32 Ignoring database noise in auction_web/config/test.exs

```
use Mix.Config

# ...

config :logger, level: :warn
```

Ignores any logs that are of a lower priority than :warn

Configuring this logger level in both applications in the umbrella application will keep the noise down while you're testing.

14.5.4 Testing that the new item form is rendered on error

Finally, you'll test that the user is shown the new item form after an error, so that they can correct any mistakes and retry their submission. You know that the new item form has an `<h1>` tag that says "New Item," so you assert that the page that's rendered has that in its HTML response. You could also test that a `<form>` tag is rendered.

Listing 14.33 Testing that the new item form is rendered

```
defmodule AuctionWeb.ItemControllerTest do
  # ...
  describe "POST /items" do
    test "with invalid params, shows the new Item form", %{conn: conn} do
      conn = post conn, "/items", %{"item" => %{"bad_param" => "Item 1"}}
      assert html_response(conn, 200) =~ "<h1>New Item</h1>"      # Ensures that the new item form is rendered
    end
    # ...
  end
end
```

When running this test, you should get a green passing message. You've completed testing the four points you wanted to test in the `ItemController`.

14.5.5 The entire ItemControllerTest module

You've worked on this module small piece by small piece in the previous sections. It's helpful to see the full test suite in one listing, so that's how you'll finish up this chapter.

Listing 14.34 The full `ItemControllerTest`

```
defmodule AuctionWeb.ItemControllerTest do
  use AuctionWeb.ConnCase

  test "GET /", %{conn: conn} do
    {:ok, _item} = Auction.insert_item(%{title: "test item"})
    conn = get conn, "/"
    assert html_response(conn, 200) =~ "test item"
  end

  describe "POST /items" do
    test "with valid params, redirects to the new Item", %{conn: conn} do
      conn = post conn, "/items", %{"item" => %{"title" => "Item 1"}}
      assert redirected_to(conn) =~ ~r|/items/\d+|
    end

    test "with valid params, creates a new Item", %{conn: conn} do
      before_count = Enum.count(Auction.list_items())
      post conn, "/items", %{"item" => %{"title" => "Item 1"}}
      assert Enum.count(Auction.list_items()) == before_count + 1
    end

    test "with invalid params, does not create a new Item", %{conn: conn} do
      before_count = Enum.count(Auction.list_items())
```

```
    post conn, "/items", %{"item" => %{"bad_param" => "Item 1"}}
    assert Enum.count(Auction.list_items()) == before_count
  end

  test "with invalid params, shows the new Item form", %{conn: conn} do
    conn = post conn, "/items", %{"item" => %{"bad_param" => "Item 1"}}
    assert html_response(conn, 200) =~ "<h1>New Item</h1>"
  end
 end
end
```

You've only tested a couple of the endpoints for the `ItemController`—there are more to be tested. With what we've covered here, you should be able to add your own tests to verify that your controllers are working as they should.

14.6 What next?

Testing is as much an art as it is a science. You may not agree with what someone else tests against, or you and a colleague may test for exactly the same thing in two different ways. In this chapter, I've given you an overview of how testing works in Elixir, but my approach is not necessarily the best way for *you* to write tests. That's something you'll have to discover on your own as you hone your toolset and develop your own style. As an exercise, consider going back through previous chapters and experiment with turning the examples you've run in IEx sessions into tests or doctests.

If you'd like more information on testing in Elixir, a good place to start would be the ExUnit documentation at https://hexdocs.pm/ex_unit/ExUnit.html.

For more information on testing in Phoenix, the Phoenix guides are a great resource. They can be found at https://hexdocs.pm/phoenix/testing.html.

With that in mind, go write more tests!

Summary

- Use Elixir's built-in test framework named ExUnit, which provides everything you need to start testing your Elixir code.
- Configure Ecto to use its sandbox repo, which allows you to test against a database without messing up your development database.
- Write documentation (which Elixir treats like a first-class concept) in Elixir with the inclusion of `@moduledoc` and `@doc` module attributes.
- Write documentation examples and tests simultaneously with doctests.
- Use Phoenix's test helper macros to make testing your Phoenix applications more straightforward.

appendix A Installing Elixir and Phoenix

Before you get started, you need to have Elixir and Phoenix installed in your local environment. There are many precompiled distributions available for many platforms including macOS, Unix and Linux variants, Windows, Docker, and even Raspberry Pi. Furthermore, because Elixir is open source, you can download the source code and compile it yourself if you feel so inclined.

The first thing to do is install Elixir.

A.1 Installing Elixir

There's only one prerequisite for Elixir itself: Erlang. But most of the install procedures that follow will also ensure that Erlang is installed.

You can either install Elixir with your OS's package manager or build it yourself from source.

A.1.1 macOS and Unix/Linux variants

Simply use your package manager to install Elixir—almost all the standard repositories have Elixir in them. For example, if you're running Homebrew on macOS, run `brew update && brew install elixir`. `pacman`, `yum`, `pkg`, `apt-get`, and others have their own install commands.

If your package manager doesn't install Elixir in the traditional manner, visit http://elixir-lang.org/install.html for more detailed instructions.

A.1.2 Windows

Elixir provides an installer you can use to install Elixir and its prerequisites. Just run the installer and it will put everything where it needs to be. The installer can be downloaded from https://repo.hex.pm/elixir-websetup.exe.

A.1.3 From source

If you'd like to build and install Elixir from source, you can always download the latest code from its master branch.

```
> git clone https://github.com/elixir-lang/elixir.git
> cd elixir
> make clean test
```

Unless you get errors from running those commands, you're ready to go!

A.1.4 Installing Erlang

If your preferred way of installing Elixir doesn't automatically install Erlang for you, you'll need to install it manually. The best way to do so is through the precompiled packages for your system, found at https://www.erlang-solutions.com/resources/download.html.

A.2 Installing Phoenix

Hex is the package manager for Elixir, and because Phoenix is a package, you need to ensure that Hex is installed. After you successfully install Elixir, run the following command:

```
> mix local.hex
```

Phoenix itself uses Mix to run commands related to working with Phoenix applications. Because of that, a special archive file needs to be downloaded by Hex:

```
> mix archive.install hex phx_new 1.4.0
```

This file, once installed by Mix, is used along with Mix to create new Phoenix applications.

Note that this archive is tied to a specific version of Phoenix (1.4.0, in this case). When Phoenix updates its generators, you need to rerun this command with the new version number.

A.2.1 PostgreSQL

This isn't technically a prerequisite, but if you follow along directly with this book, you need PostgreSQL installed. We'll be working with a database in many of the chapters, and the default database preference for Phoenix is PostgreSQL. That's what I've used. If you prefer to use MySQL or some other database that Ecto supports (see https://github.com/elixir-ecto/ecto#usage for support details), you need to modify the code listings in the book to match.

If you'd like to install PostgreSQL, check out the PostgreSQL wiki at https://wiki.postgresql.org/wiki/Detailed_installation_guides for detailed instructions for your system.

A.2.2 Node.js

To compile assets like CSS files and JavaScript, Phoenix uses Webpack, and Webpack requires Node.js to be installed. Webpack will be installed by Mix when needed, but Node.js should be installed to make sure Mix can install Webpack and other dependencies.

You can install Node.js with your preferred package manager (such as Homebrew) or via Node's download page at https://nodejs.org/en/download/. Note that Phoenix requires a Node.js version of 5.0.0 or greater.

appendix B *More Elixir resources*

Chapter 2 covers just enough Elixir to get you started with this wonderful, powerful, deep, fun language. As this is ultimately a book about Phoenix and not Elixir, I ended our discussion there. But if you'd like to dig deeper, there are some great resources out there for you.

On the web

- Elixir's own Getting Started guide: https://elixir-lang.org/getting-started/introduction.html
- Elixir's online documentation: https://hexdocs.pm/elixir/
- Elixir School: https://elixirschool.com/en/

Books

- *Elixir in Action*, 2nd ed., by Saša Juric (Manning, 2019)
- *The Little Elixir & OTP Guidebook* by Benjamin Tan Wei Hao (Manning, 2016)
- *Programming Elixir* by Dave Thomas (Pragmatic Bookshelf, 2018)
- *Adopting Elixir* by Ben Marx, José Valim, and Bruce Tate (Pragmatic Bookshelf, 2018)

Community

- Elixir Forum: https://elixirforum.com/
- #elixir-lang IRC channel on Freenode
- Elixir Slack community: https://elixir-slackin.herokuapp.com/

There are many other resources available for the budding Elixir developer. Check out the preceding resources and do some searches to find your favorites.

index

Symbols

A

B

L

M

N